Interpreting
John Calvin

Ford Lewis Battles

Interpreting John Calvin

Ford Lewis Battles

Edited by Robert Benedetto
With Introductory Essays by
I. John Hesselink *and*
Donald K. McKim

The H. Henry Meeter Center For Calvin Studies

Baker Books

A Division of Baker Book House Co
Grand Rapids, Michigan 49516

Published by Baker Books
a division of Baker Book House Company
P.O. Box 6287, Grand Rapids, Michigan 49516-6287

Printed in the United States of America

Library of Congress Cataloging-in-Publication Data

Battles, Ford Lewis.
    Interpreting John Calvin / Ford Lewis Battles ; edited by Robert Benedetto ; with introductory essays by I. John Hesselink and Donald K. McKim.
      p. cm.
    "The H. Henry Meeter Center for Calvin Studies."
    Includes bibliographical references.
    ISBN 0-8010-2097-2
    1. Calvin, Jean, 1509–1564. I. Benedetto, Robert. II. H. H. Meeter Center for Calvin Studies. III. Title.
BX9418.B19   1996
230′.42′092—dc20
                                                96-33394

For information about academic books, resources for Christian leaders, and all new releases available from Baker Book House, visit our web site:
                    http://www.bakerbooks.com/

In Memoriam
MARION DAVIS BATTLES (1921–94)

Contents

List of Tables   *9*
Foreword, by Richard C. Gamble   *13*
Editor's Preface   *15*
Acknowledgments   *17*
Introductory Essays by I. John Hesselink
    and Donald K. McKim   *19*
Abbreviations   *43*

PART 1 **The Origin and Structure of Calvin's Theology**
   1 Calvin's Humanistic Education   *47*
   2 The Sources of Calvin's Seneca Commentary   *65*
   3 The First Edition of the *Institutes of the Christian
      Religion* (1536)   *91*
   4 God Was Accommodating Himself to Human Capacity   *117*
   5 *Calculus Fidei:* Some Ruminations on the Structure
      of the Theology of John Calvin   *139*

PART 2 **Calvin's Poetry, Piety, and Morality**
   6 The Theologian as Poet: Some Remarks about the "Found"
      Poetry of John Calvin   *249*
   7 True Piety According to Calvin   *289*
   8 Notes on John Calvin, *Justitia,* and the Old Testament
      Law   *307*
   9 Against Luxury and License in Geneva: A Forgotten
      Fragment of Calvin [1546–47]   *319*

   Appendixes
   1 The Chief Lineaments of Calvin's Religious Experience   *343*
   2 The Antithetical Structure of Calvin's *Institutes*   *347*
   3 Chief Motifs in Calvin's *Institutes*   *351*
   4 Tabulation of Biblical Citations in the *Institutes*   *359*

Ford Lewis Battles Bibliography   *361*
Contributors   *371*
Index   *373*

Tables

The Sources of Calvin's Seneca Commentary

  A. The sources of Calvin's *Commentary on Seneca's De Clementia*   86

  B. The classical tradition in John Calvin's *Commentary on Seneca's De Clementia*   89

Calculus Fidei

  C. The true gospel of the Reformers distinguished from the false gospel of the papal church   *154*

  D. The party of reform distinguished from the radicals   *154*

  E. Virtues in relation to vices   *155*

  F. Shifts and additions of material in the five chief Latin editions of the *Institutio*   *156*

  G. Spiritualist/papist spectrum in the *Institutio*   *160*

  H. The reality of angels   *164*

  I. Should the Scriptures be given to the people?   *164*

  J. Spiritualism and Romanism   *166*

  K. Calvin's scriptural exegesis   *166*

  L. The nature of prayer   *167*

  M. The true/false principle   *167*

  N. The working of the Holy Spirit in Providence: represented by concentric circles   *168*

  O. The working of God's Spirit in the cosmos   *171*

  P. *Bonitas dei*   *172*

  Q. Providence of God expressed in a dichotomy   *172*

  R. The human quest expressed in terms of limits   *175*

  S. True and false religion   *176*

  1. *Institutes*, Books 1–2: knowledge of God and humanity   *182*

  2. The knowledge of God as Creator (*Inst.* 1.1–14)   *183*

2a. Humanity as created (*Inst.* 1.15)   *184*

3. Humanity after the Fall (*Inst.* 2.1–5; with generalized linkage to Book 3)   *185*

4. The knowledge of God as Redeemer (*Inst.* 2.6–7)   *186*

5. Abrogation of the law (*Inst.* 2.8–9; ch. 8 generalized)   *187*

6. Relation of law and gospel (*Inst.* 2.10–14)   *188*

7. Why was Christ sent? (*Inst.* 2.15–16)   *189*

8. Christ's merit (*Inst.* 2.17)   *190*

9. *Institutes,* Book 3: Christ, Holy Spirit, and faith   *190*

10. Gift of faith (*Inst.* 3.2–10 generalized)   *191*

11. Gift of faith (2) (*Inst.* 3.11–13)   *192*

12. Gift of faith (3) (*Inst.* 3.14)   *193*

13. Gift of faith (4) (*Inst.* 3.15–18)   *194*

14. Gift of faith (5) (*Inst.* 3.19)   *195*

15. Exercise of faith and nature of prayer (*Inst.* 3.20.1–27 generalized)   *196*

16. Exercise of faith (prayer) (2) (*Inst.* 3.20.28–33 generalized)   *197*

17. Limitation of gift of faith (*Inst.* 3.21–24 generalized)   *198*

18. Final resurrection (*Inst.* 3.25)   *199*

19. *Institutes,* Book 4: Ecclesiastical and civil power   *199*

20. Marks of the church (*Inst.* 4.1–2)   *200*

21. Government of the church (*Inst.* 4.3–7)   *200*

22. Power of the church in doctrine (*Inst.* 4.8–9)   *201*

23. Power of the church in legislation (*Inst.* 4.10)   *201*

24. Power of the church in jurisdiction (*Inst.* 4.11)   *202*

25. Discipline of the church in censures and excommunication (*Inst.* 4.12)   *203*

26. Discipline of the church in vows (*Inst.* 4.13)   *204*

27. Sacraments of the church (*Inst.* 4.14–19 generalized)   *205*

28. Sacraments of the church: baptism (2) (*Inst.* 4.15.1–13)   *206*

29. Baptism (*Inst.* 4.15.14–22)   *207*

30. Paedobaptism (*Inst.* 4.16)   *207*

31. Lord's Supper (*Inst.* 4.17 generalized)   *208*

32. Lord's Supper (2) (*Inst.* 4.17 in detail)   *209*

33. The sacraments and the papal Mass (*Inst.* 4.18)   *210*

34. Sacraments (2) (*Inst.* 4.19)   *211*

35. Ecclesiastical and civil power (*Inst.* 4.20.1–13)   *212*

36. Civil government (*Inst.* 4.20.14–21)   *213*

37. Civil government (2) (*Inst.* 4.20.22–32) *214*
38. The "hub": *religio/pietas* *220*
39. The definition of *fides* and its detailed exposition *220*
40. *Legitimus cultus dei* *221*
41. *Theatrum mundi* *229*
42. The *virtutes dei* as to be perceived by humanity in the *theatrum duplex* *234*
43. The *virtutes dei* in and after the creation *235*
44. The placing of providence and predestination in the successive editions of the *Institutio* *236*

The Theologian as Poet

45. Poetic structure of Romans 11:33–36 *251*
46. Poetic structure of Tertullian's *Adversus Praxean* 2.4 *255*
47. Poetic structure of Augustine's *De Doctrina Christiana* 1.5.5 *257*
48. Poetic structure of Cyprian's *De Unitate Ecclesiae* *259*
49. Poetic structure of Calvin's preface to Pierre Robert's French New Testament *265*
50. Poetic structure of Calvin's *Institutio* 3.7.1, "on the Christian life" (1539) *271*
51. Poetic structure of Calvin's *Institutio* 4.17.7, "on the Lord's Supper" (1539) *275*
52. Poetic structure of Calvin's *Form of Prayer and Songs of the Church*, "prayer of confession" (1543) *276*
53. Calvin's metrical paraphrase of Psalm 113 (1539) *279*
54. Poetic structure of Calvin's *Commentary on I Corinthians* 15:24 (1546) *283*
55. Poetic structure of Calvin's *Commentary on I Corinthians* 15:24 (1546) (2) *285*

True Piety According to Calvin

56. Interrelationships of piety and religion *290*

Notes on John Calvin, *Justitia*, and the Old Testament Law

57. Uses of punishment, law, and church discipline *316*
58. Outline of Calvin's *Commentary on a Harmony of the Last Four Books of Moses* *317*

Against Luxury and License in Geneva

59. Uses of punishment, law, and church discipline (2) *325*

Foreword

Ford Lewis Battles was a man of tremendous ability and learning and it is a great pleasure to see this volume published. Ably edited by Robert Benedetto, who was instrumental in preparing Battles' festschrift, *Reformatio Perennis* (Pickwick, 1981), this volume contains previously unpublished material and makes available extremely valuable interpretative articles and diagrams.

The introductory essays by I. John Hesselink and Donald K. McKim are very insightful. They not only summarize Battles' work but importantly place that work, completed over fifteen years ago, in the context of modern Calvin scholarship. Hesselink delivered Battles' address, *Calculus Fidei*, at the 1979 Calvin Congress in Amsterdam when the author was too ill to attend. His intimate knowledge of the work of Ford Battles is demonstrated in his essay. I share with Benedetto and McKim a continuing enthusiasm for these materials and also a common bond since the 1970s when we were students of Professor Battles at Pittsburgh Theological Seminary.

Had the Lord given him more years of life, Professor Battles would have been the first director of the H. Henry Meeter Center for Calvin Studies. This was not to be, but the Center was competently administered by his spouse, Marion Davis Battles, until her retirement. Mrs. Battles supported this project and gave the editor her assistance as advisor and proofreader. Unfortunately, she was not able to see the fruit of her labor. The Meeter Center is honored to demonstrate its high regard for Marion and Ford Lewis Battles by sponsoring this publication.

Richard C. Gamble
Director, H. Henry Meeter Center for Calvin Studies
Calvin College and Calvin Theological Seminary

Editor's Preface

This collection contains the primary writings of Calvin scholar Ford Lewis Battles. Two unpublished works are featured: *Calvin's Humanistic Education* and Battles' penetrating, but less understood work, *Calculus Fidei*. The latter work, published posthumously in an extremely abbreviated form in 1980, is presented here for the first time in its entirety. Added to these unpublished works are several articles from journals and festschriften. While a few of these articles have been reprinted in various collections of Calviniana, others have not been widely accessible. Collecting these essays in a single volume enables readers to ponder the interrelationships among the various pieces and to approach Battles' work in a holistic manner. The result is a presentation of the theology of John Calvin as interpreted by Ford Lewis Battles.

To provide a context for the essays, the editor invited I. John Hesselink and Donald K. McKim to introduce Ford Battles and to briefly interpret his work. In addition, a complete bibliography of the works of Ford Battles is also provided.

The passage of time made some revision of the essays imperative. Accordingly, the text and notes of the various essays have been harmonized, as far as possible, with the *Chicago Manual of Style*. Original endnotes have been changed throughout to footnotes. The publication data in the footnotes have been brought up-to-date and new footnotes have been added to the text where warranted by Battles' presentation. No attempt has been made to preserve the format or footnote numbering of the original essays. The editor has also supplied English translations to accompany longer passages of Latin text.

As a skilled teacher, Ford Battles was cognizant of the different ways that students learn. He found some students to be visual, rather than textual learners. He also found that textual learners could often gain new perspective by visual presentations. Thus, Battles frequently accompanied his lectures and essays with diagrams. For Battles, a diagram was often worth a thousand words. There are many diagrams in this book. The titles and page numbers of these diagrams are given in

the List of Tables. In order to preserve the original numbering of the ex-
planatory diagrams on Calvin's *Institutes* that appear in *Calculus Fidei*,
the tables that proceed this exposition have been given letter designa-
tions, from "A" to "S"; tables that follow simply continue the numbering sequence. Study of the diagrams, particularly those prepared in
connection with *Calculus Fidei*, will help readers appreciate the sweep
of Calvin's theological method throughout the *Institutes* and better understand the structure of his theology.

Acknowledgments

I would like to acknowledge the H. Henry Meeter Center for Calvin Studies and its director, Richard C. Gamble, for encouraging the preparation of this book, for providing research materials, and for issuing the volume in the Meeter Center publication series. I am also grateful to Calvin College and Seminary for providing funds from the "Ford Lewis Battles Publication Fund" to help defray production costs, and to seminary librarian, Paul Fields, who rendered cheerful and prompt assistance on several occasions.

I am indebted to Union Theological Seminary in Virginia for providing funds for travel, and to the seminary's Office of Communications, particularly director Alice E. Addleton and production manager William G. Trout, for their counsel and assistance in preparing the volume's many tables.

I. John Hesselink and Donald K. McKim graciously accepted the editor's invitation to prepare the introductory essays. I am very grateful for their perceptive analysis, which provides an important context for the works collected in this volume and helps introduce the author to a new generation of students, pastors, and scholars. Of the many other individuals who also gave unselfishly of their time and expertise, I would like to acknowledge the work of my student assistant, Amy L. Busse, who typed the greater part of the manuscript, a complex and tedious job; and the competent labors of retired Union Seminary librarian, Martha Aycock Sugg, who assisted with proofreading.

Pickwick Press, Baker Book House, William B. Eerdmans, and *Interpretation: A Journal of Bible and Theology* kindly gave permission to reproduce various essays.

It would have been impossible to produce this work without the quiet labors of Marion Battles, a Calvin scholar in her own right, who gladly checked references, proofread the text, and gave sound advice. The preparation of this volume brought her great joy and she would have rejoiced to see its publication. This work is respectfully and lovingly dedicated to her.

Introduction

I. Ford Lewis Battles: The Catholic Calvinian
I. John Hesselink

Relationships

Long before I met Ford Lewis Battles, I was greatly indebted to him. In the midst of my graduate student days at the University of Basel in Switzerland the Library of Christian Classics edition of Calvin's *Institutes*, translated by Battles and edited by John T. McNeill, was published. It appeared just in the nick of time for me (1960), as I was in the midst of writing my doctoral dissertation on "Calvin's Concept and Use of the Law."[1] Prior to that I had been relying primarily on my copy of the Allen translation of the *Institutes*, purchased while I was in seminary. As I checked out key passages with the Latin original, I became more and more disenchanted with it. I had also used the Beveridge translation, which was an improvement stylistically but also lacked the precision I needed for my research.

What a boon, then, to have this new translation, with its wonderful indexes, notes, and cross-references, which made my work immeasurably easier. If Ford Battles had produced nothing else, the scholarly world would be profoundly indebted to him. Now, over forty years later, countless students, lay people, pastors, and scholars are similarly indebted to Ford Battles for this marvelous accomplishment. This edition of the *Institutes* has worn well and is unlikely to be superseded for many years.

---

1. This was eventually published as *Calvin's Concept of the Law* (Allison Park, Pa.: Pickwick, 1992). The linkage with Pickwick Press was no accident, for Battles had encouraged the owner and editor of the press, Dikran Hadidian (his former colleague at Pittsburgh Seminary), to publish it many years before. Hadidian agreed to publish it simply on the basis of the recommendation and urging of his friend Ford Battles.

I returned to Japan in 1961, where my wife and I had served as missionaries for five years prior to my study in Basel. I was not to meet Ford Battles personally until ten years later. In the meantime, I had been teaching historical theology, particularly courses on Calvin, at Tokyo Union Seminary. I also taught ecclesiastical Latin where we read portions of the *Institutes* in Latin the second year. That gave me further appreciation for Battles' accomplishment.

The only other publication of Battles of which I was aware was another volume in the Library of Christian Classics, *Advocates of Reform: From Wyclif to Erasmus* (1953), edited by Battles' colleague at that time at Hartford Seminary, Matthew Spinka. Battles translated several essays for this volume, two by Wyclif and one by Erasmus.[2]

Nevertheless, on the basis of the impact of his translation of the *Institutes* and what I had heard about the man from some mutual acquaintances, I was determined to make a pilgrimage to Pittsburgh during the furlough year of 1971–72. This was possible in the spring of 1972 when my wife and our two youngest children and I drove back from our General Synod which met in New Jersey that year. The visit was enhanced by the gracious hospitality of the Battles family, who welcomed us into their home as if we were old friends.

During this first encounter two winsome characteristics of Ford Battles quickly became apparent: his encouragement of others in their personal and scholarly pursuits and his willingness and joy in working with others in joint ventures. Both qualities have been noted by others, but I can reaffirm and illustrate them from my own personal experience.

We had just met, but almost immediately he asked me if I would be willing to consider joining him in a project that might involve several volumes, a study of the sources and influences that shaped the young Calvin's theology, to be entitled *Calvinus Juvenalis*. He would do the

---

2. Battles had published numerous works prior to our first encounter in 1971. Almost all of his study outlines of the Church Fathers and medieval theologians were published privately during his tenure at Pittsburgh Seminary. Four of his larger works were also published privately while he was at Pittsburgh: a Latin grammar, *Magna Charta Latina*, done in cooperation with Eugen Rosenstock-Huessy, with the delightful subtitle: *"The privilege of singing, articulating and reading a language and of keeping it alive"*; *Analysis of the Institutes of the Christian Religion of John Calvin*, originally published while he was at Hartford Seminary, but revised with the assistance of John Walchenbach and published at Pittsburgh in 1970 (a later revised edition was published by Baker in 1980); *A First Course in Church History and the History of Doctrine: The Patristic Era and the Middle Ages* (1967–68), with a seventh revised edition entitled *Itinerarium Fidei* published later at Calvin Seminary in 1977; and *The Piety of John Calvin: An Anthology Illustrative of the Reformer of Geneva* (1969), also revised several times and published eventually by Baker in 1978.

One major work done in cooperation with André M. Hugo was also published commercially during this period, *Calvin's Commentary on Seneca's De Clementia* (Brill, 1969). For a complete listing of all of Battles' publications, see the bibliography appended to this volume.

technical historical research and make the necessary translations. I was to read the secondary literature and deal more with the theological aspects of the study. The following two paragraphs from a letter to me following our visit in June 1972 are probably indicative of his approach to other scholars (and often graduate students) to collaborate with him in similar ventures.

> I see this project as one with a perfectly natural division of labor. I do not wish to be unduly influenced by secondary literature, at least in the early stages of formulating my problem from the sources. On the other hand, there must be an exhaustive and creative search of that literature, if the project is to have any value. I view us as two researchers working along parallel lines, converging at the end in a grand synthesis.
>
> If this is a valid modus operandi, I know that your strengths will be a necessary part of a true partnership. Most of my projects have been done in partnership with other scholars, a way I find exciting and far more absorbing than a mere solo performance.

This venture never came to fruition, partially because of his health problems, which began soon thereafter, and partially because of my inability to follow through with my end of the agreement due to my becoming president of Western Seminary the next year. However, Battles did pursue on his own a subject he had proposed as a logical starting point, Calvin's so-called *conversio subita* (sudden conversion). He continued to deal with this subject in various contexts throughout his career.

Fortunately, a much more modest collaborative venture on our part will finally be realized next year (1997), when my *Introduction to Calvin's Theology*, based on the Ford Lewis Battles translation of Calvin's first *Catechism* of 1538 is published by Westminster/John Knox.[3] In Japan in my introductory Calvin courses I had used Nobuo Watanabe's Japanese translation of the French edition of Calvin's first *Catechism, Instruction de Foy* (1537), and had begun to develop a commentary based on it. One of my first gifts from Ford Battles was his translation of the 1538 Latin edition of this *Catechism*.[4] Upon my return to the United States in 1973 I decided to use his translation as the basis for my Calvin course (supplemented by passages from the *Institutes* and commentaries) and proposed to him that this be published together with my commentary. He readily agreed and approved the commentary, which was still incomplete at that time. After Battles' death, his wife Marion also gave her ap-

---

3. To be published by Westminster/John Knox Press in the Columbia Series in Reformed Theology. The eventual title may differ.

4. An English translation was made by Paul Fuhrman and published by Westminster Press in 1954. For several years it was out of print but the work has been recently reprinted by Westminster/John Knox.

proval to this proposal. She felt that in this way his translation of the *Catechism*, previously only distributed privately, would have a much greater readership.

It was this willingness to collaborate with others—often students and people far less gifted and knowledgeable than himself—which was one of the many admirable qualities of Ford Battles.[5] Unlike some scholars, who use much of their students' research and then give them little or no credit, Battles generously acknowledged any assistance he had received.[6] A perusal of the bibliography of Battles' publications, which appears at the end of this volume, reveals that many of his major publications were done in collaboration.[7]

It would be a grievous omission, however, not to mention his greatest and most valued collaborator, his wife Marion. Some scholars and professionals have sacrificed their families for the sake of their careers. Not so Ford Battles. He not only deeply loved his wife and two daughters, Nancy and Emily, but was also very supportive of their development and careers. His wife, Marion, was a gifted musician and scholar in her own right.[8] Unlike many wives she did not type her husband's manuscripts; he preferred to do that himself. But she counseled, proofread, and did editorial and other tasks that provided invaluable assistance to her husband. More than that, she was a real partner in all his efforts, always showing interest and providing encouragement.

5. This quality is also noted by Jim O'Brien, a graduate student at Calvin Seminary at the time of Battles' death. See O'Brien's fine tribute "Ford Lewis Battles: 1915–1979. Calvin Scholar and Church Historian Extraordinary," *Calvin Theological Journal* 15, no. 2 (November 1980): 183–84.

6. Cf., for example, his *Analysis of the Institutes* which has on the cover "Ford Lewis Battles, assisted by John Walchenbach." Walchenbach did his master's and doctor's theses under the supervision of Battles. Similarly, although the contribution is a minor one, in Battles' *The Piety of John Calvin: An Anthology Illustrative of the Spirituality of the Reformer*, he gives credit to the musician who harmonized his translation of some of Calvin's metrical psalms. Such credit might well have been given in the preface but instead in bold print on the cover underneath the title is: "Translated and edited by Ford Lewis Battles. Music edited by Stanley Tagg."

7. In the case of a few study outlines the principal work is done by someone else and Battles is the assistant, e.g., the one on John of Damascus. This volume was prepared by "Daniel Sahas, with the editorial assistance of Ford Lewis Battles." Cf. the study outlines on Henry and Hildebrand, Athanasius, and Caspar Schwenckfeld.

8. Marion Davis Battles graduated from Tufts University *magna cum laude* and *Phi Beta Kappa* and received her master's degree from the Fletcher School of Law and Diplomacy in Massachusetts. She worked for the government in Washington, D.C., during the war and then served as an interpreter in the charter meetings of the United Nations in San Francisco and also specialized in human rights for prisoners of war at those meetings. She translated from German and edited Rosenstock-Huessy's *The Fruit of Lips: or Why Four Gospels* (Allison Park, Pa.: Pickwick, 1978). She was also an accomplished pianist and studied advanced piano performance at Yale University. After her husband's death she worked for several years at the H. Henry Meeter Center for Calvin Studies in Grand Rapids. She was also an active church worker and served as deacon at the Calvin Christian Reformed Church prior to her death in 1994.

Another gift of Ford Battles was his support and encouragement of others. Donald G. Miller, former president of Pittsburgh Seminary, who was instrumental in hiring Battles and became a close friend, testifies to this quality in his essay in *Reformatio Perennis*, "Ford Lewis Battles—An Appreciation."[9]

> He was not only gifted in enabling graduate students to learn how to do research, but had that rare quality of inspiring them with enthusiasm for their task. His rigorous demands for scholarship were matched with a personal interest both in the student and his subject which fostered diligence on the part of the candidate and brought encouragement when his spirit flagged.[10]

As many former students and friends can testify, this kind of encouragement and support continued long after a thesis or project was completed. Like his own mentor, John Calvin, Ford Battles not only had many friends; he sustained and deepened those friendships long after direct personal contact was generally not possible.

Historical Theology as Autobiography

Many novels are thinly veiled autobiographies of the author. Others, though entirely fictional, utilize historical events and the locale of the author. To some extent the same is often true of theological works, albeit more indirectly. Augustine's *Confessions* and Pasal's *Pensees* are the most obvious illustrations of this approach, but there is also a certain carryover with theologians or Christian writers as diverse as Karl Barth or C. S. Lewis. Their writings reflect their times, their environments, and their personal histories. Or, in the words of José Ortega y Gassett, "Tell me the landscape in which you live, and I will tell you who you are."

The same can be said of Ford Lewis Battles, although in this case it is not so much his personal background as his admiration for Calvin that shines through much of his approach to historical theology. Just as Calvin saw himself mirrored in many of the Psalms of David, so Ford Battles consciously and unconsciously reflected the theology and piety of his chief mentor, John Calvin. Evidence of this can be seen in at least eight facets of Battles' work.

9. This essay, which provides a wonderful insight into the personality of Battles, is divided into four parts: Scholar, Teacher, Churchman, and Human Being. See *Reformatio Perennis: Essays on Calvin and the Reformation in Honor of Ford Lewis Battles,* ed. by B. A. Gerrish in collaboration with Robert Benedetto (Allison Park, Pa.: Pickwick, 1981). Battles knew that a festschrift was being prepared in his honor, and even had a hand in formulating its title, but unfortunately he died before the book was published.
10. Ibid., 6.

Interest in the Sources

The young Calvin was noted for his love of the original languages: first Latin, then Greek, and later Hebrew. He is well known for his facility in both Latin and French and his ability to discern the meaning of scriptural passages based on his independent reading of the original Hebrew and Greek texts. This was further enhanced by his knowledge of the Church Fathers and medieval theologians, which enabled him to debate effectively with his Roman Catholic opponents.

Ford Battles had a similar passion for working with the original sources in their original languages. Also, Calvin's humanistic education finds a parallel in Battles' classical background. There are, of course, obvious differences. Calvin became a minister, an expositor of Scripture, and a theologian. Battles had studied the biblical languages and had worked in the Old Testament en route to a Ph.D. in church history at Hartford Theological Seminary, but he was never ordained and was quite content to exercise his calling in theological schools as a lay person and historian. He often pointed out that the major English translators of Calvin's *Institutes* were, like himself, lay persons.

While there are obvious dissimilarities between the two, the Renaissance slogan, *ad fontes* (to the sources), applies equally well to Calvin and Battles. Although the latter preferred to work directly with Calvin and the sources which influenced him, his knowledge of German and French enabled him to keep abreast of the secondary Calvin literature. However, he used secondary literature sparingly; the focus was always on Calvin's own writings—or those of Chrysostom, Lombard, and others whose works influenced Calvin.[11]

Whether at work on Calvin's *Commentary on Seneca's De Clementia*, his *Catechism* of 1538, or the *Institutes*, Battles was always in relentless pursuit of the sources that provided the background or dialogue partners for Calvin's works.[12]

11. This was the impetus for Battles' many study outlines. Since translations of key works were not always available, he made his own. The range is impressive; his study outlines include early Church Fathers such as Irenaeus and Hilary but also medievals such as Abelard and Bernard of Clairvaux.

12. For an illustration of Battles' careful research into the sources of the Seneca Commentary, see table A (pp. 86–88.). In the case of Calvin's first catechism (the Latin edition of 1538), the numerous notes that accompany the Latin text are mainly references to parallels or variations in the 1536 *Institutes*. Unfortunately, the Latin text and these notes are not being published in my forthcoming *Introduction to Calvin's Theology* that includes Battles' English translation of the 1538 Catechism. However, the LCC edition of the 1559 *Institutes* contains not only Battles' translation but also a marvelous critical apparatus, much of which was also a product of Battles' research. Although he was assisted by the editor, John T. McNeill, and an able team of scholars who checked the text, the majority of the numerous footnotes—especially the references to ancient sources—are also the fruit of Battles' prodigious knowledge of the Church Fathers and medieval theologians.

Concern for Lucidity and Precision

Calvin's goal in writing was *brevitas et facilitas,* or "lucid brevity."[13] One might add, also Calvin's concern for precision. No one has ever accused Calvin of being a sloppy thinker, although there are times when there are twists and turns in his theological writings that still leave Calvin scholars perplexed. Ford Battles shared the same concerns. He was not given to jargon and, like his mentor, was always trying to improve on previous efforts. Calvin's many editions of the *Institutes* find something of a parallel in Battles' various editions of the 1538 *Catechism.* The first edition was published in 1972. There were revisions in 1974, 1975, 1976, and at least one more in 1979—a never-ending project that he kept working on until his death.[14]

He was also not completely satisfied with his more literal and prosaic translations of the 1536 and 1539 *Institutes.* Consequently, he expended considerable energy in retranslating key portions of the *Institutes* and other writings in a freer, more poetic fashion. Moreover, Battles saw a poetic tendency in Calvin himself and felt that this should be reflected in translation. An illustration of this is found in part 2 of this volume: "The Theologian as Poet: Some Remarks about the 'Found' Poetry of John Calvin."

There is, as Battles pointed out, only one extant poem of Calvin's in classical form, but he "practiced this gift throughout his life, but in implicit rather than explicit forms." Battles, accordingly, finds many poetic passages in the *Institutes* and elsewhere, passages that "take on the character of hymns sung by one who was on fire with the love of Christ" (260).[15]

Here, too, there is a parallel between Calvin and Battles. The latter also had a poetic strain, which found expression most often in lyrics for hymns. This love of hymnody took two forms: (1) articles about hymnody and the composition of lyrics for new hymns; (2) hymn texts drawn from the Old and New Testaments and the translation of some of Calvin's metrical psalms with harmonization by Stanley Tagg.[16]

13. Cf. Richard Gamble, *"Brevitas et facilitas:* Toward an Understanding of Calvin's Hermeneutic," *Westminster Theological Journal* 47 (1985): 1–17.

14. I visited Battles in the Butterworth Hospital just three days before his death. He was still alert and remarkably vigorous, considering his condition. Just before I left he proudly gave me a special cloth-bound copy of his latest edition of the 1538 *Catechism!* This penchant for constantly editing and improving earlier publications can be seen in comparing his earlier editions of his *Analysis of the Institutes* (1970–76) that were privately published while he was in Pittsburgh with the final commercially published version by Baker in 1980.

15. Numbers in parentheses following a quotation refer to pages in this volume. For an illustration of Calvin's poetic style, see table 54: "Poetic Structure of *Calvin's Commentary on I Corinthians* 15:24."

16. Several of these metrical psalm arrangements are found in the book, *The Piety of John Calvin,* chapter 6. They are not included in the selection that appears in this book.

Calvin's Conversion

One cannot understand Calvin's sense of calling and personal faith apart from his conversion experience. Given the nature of Calvin's personality, it is not surprising that the account of his conversion is so brief. In fact, it is fortunate that we have any information at all of this significant turn in his life. All we have is a brief paragraph in the preface to his commentary on the Psalms and perhaps allusions to this experience in his famous letter to Cardinal Sadolet.[17]

We know little of Battles' own conversion experience, if there was such in the narrow sense of the word, nor of his youthful progress in faith. Reading medieval literature with C. S. Lewis while a Rhodes Scholar at Oxford undoubtedly made an impact, as did his studies at Hartford Theological Seminary. Battles' fascination with Calvin's conversion may indicate a spiritual empathy with this aspect of the Reformer's life. This interest first comes to light in one of Battles' lectures given at Union Theological Seminary in Virginia in July 1973; at a special lecture at Western Seminary in Holland, Michigan, in 1974; in the introduction to his translation of the 1536 *Institutes* in 1975; and briefly in his book *The Piety of John Calvin* (see pp. 293–94 in this volume).

Although Calvin describes his conversion as sudden (*subita*), Battles sees it as a process that came to a climax in 1534. More particularly, he sees five stages or "moments" in this process:[18] (1) the preparation; (2) the travail of conscience; (3) the call of the gospel; (4) the conversion; (5) first steps in the Christian life.[19] Battles concludes that this conversion "cannot be confined to a merely personal, inward change" but also

---

For Battles' involvement in contemporary hymn writing and hymnal committees, see the bibliography, the years 1967, 1970, 1971, 1973, 1977.

17. Calvin scholars are not agreed on the nature of the latter. Battles was convinced that in the letter to Cardinal Sadolet we have an "oblique" reference to his conversion in his account of the evangelical layman before the judgment seat of God. Battles' originality in the quest for sources that may clarify the nature of Calvin's conversion is found in his addition of what he calls "the kernel of Calvin's faith" contained in the first pages of Chapter I of the 1536 *Institutes* and possibly the preface to Pierre Robert's New Testament. See the Introduction to his translation of the 1536 edition of the *Institutes of the Christian Religion* (Atlanta: John Knox, 1975), xxvi.

18. Something similar to this approach had been taken earlier by Paul Sprenger, *Das Rätsel um die Bekhrung Calvins* (Neukirchen: Neukirchener Verlag, 1960). Battles does not refer to this study, but he does acknowledge the research of Alexandre Ganoczy, *La Jeune Calvin* (1966), concerning Calvin's conversion, in his own discussion of Calvin's conversion in the Introduction to the 1536 *Institutes*, xxvi.

19. These "moments" are filled out in outline form in appendix 1, "The Chief Lineaments of Calvin's Religious Experience" (343–45). Battles' strophic translation of Calvin's own words as found in his preface to his Psalms commentary and the letter to Sadolet of 1539 is found in the Introduction to the 1536 *Institutes*, xxviii–xxxiv.

"involves a total reorientation to history and the institutions—political, social, and ecclesiastical—of Calvin's own time."[20]

Then he adds a comment that provides one of several clues to Battles' own understanding of the distinctive nature of Calvin's theology: "This is one reason why his theology defies ultimate systematization; it is salvation-history faith. It must be told as the story of Israel, narrowly begun in the Old Testament, but in Christ embracing all nations."[21]

Balanced Piety

Earlier Calvin scholarship paid little attention to a key word and major motif in Calvin's theology, *pietas*, which can be translated as either piety or godliness.[22] There is no ready explanation for this serious omission. It may be due to an aversion to some of the vagaries of pietism. Whatever the reasons, Battles was one of the first to focus on this important theme in Calvin's theology.[23] Happily, a selection from his beautifully produced book, *The Piety of John Calvin*, is included in this volume (289). Battles points out that piety, for Calvin, is not some inward self-centered spirituality divorced from daily life but the root of love that expresses itself in the love of God and neighbor. It includes prayer and devotion, on the one hand, and obedience and service, on the other (290–91). As Battles shows in a diagram (table 56), several other ideas are interlaced with piety: faith, fear, reverence, love, knowledge—and also religion. However, as Battles perceptively notes, the best way to get at Calvin's understanding of piety is to read his classic brief discussion of the Christian life in Book III of the *Institutes*, chapters 6–10.

Thus, in Calvin we have a well-rounded, balanced piety, a this-worldly asceticism, not unlike that of his student, Ford Lewis Battles. Like Calvin, Battles has probably rarely been described as a "pious" person. Neither one would talk about his piety or spirituality, but each in his own distinctive way was a profoundly devout person. Even Battles' friends knew little about his private devotional life; he did not talk about things like that. But he was a profoundly religious man in a quiet, modest way, one who loved to worship and praise God while at the same time exerting all his efforts toward serving his colleagues, students, the church, and the world at large with his many gifts.

20. Ibid., xxxiv. Battles, following Louis Goumaz, also emphasizes "the crucial place of the Scriptures in Calvin's Conversion" (xxvii).

21. Ibid.

22. Battles translates "the untranslatable word *pietas*" both ways but generally as piety. The French is *piété*.

23. The first, and only other significant treatment of this subject is by the Roman Catholic theologian, Lucien Joseph Richard, *The Spirituality of John Calvin* (Atlanta: John Knox, 1974). Battles' book, *The Piety of John Calvin: An Anthology Illustrative of the Spirituality of the Reformer*, appeared four years later.

Commitment to the Gospel

Calvin was capable of discussing fine points of theology at a very sophisticated level with the greatest theologians of his time, both Catholic and Protestant. Melanchthon was not off the mark when he dubbed Calvin "the theologian." Yet at heart Calvin was a simple believer whose aim in life was to preach and teach the gospel as simply and relevantly as possible. One of the reasons his theology has stood the test of time is its evangelical warmth and simplicity. His first catechism (1537–38) is a good illustration of this characteristic.

The same was true of Ford Battles. Although he had many and diverse scholarly interests and was a scholar's scholar, his ultimate goal was simply that of sharing the gospel and building up the church. Few people have had a greater admiration for Calvin than he, but this fondness for Calvin did not become idolatrous. Nor, technically speaking, could Battles be described as a Calvinist. He did not disparage seventeenth-century theological developments (the heyday of orthodoxy), nor the developments of neo-Calvinism in the nineteenth and twentieth centuries, but he did not care to get involved in debates over questions such as limited atonement or common grace.

However, he was a feisty defender of the faith. He could brook no nonsense, whether from the fundamentalist Right or the liberal Left. Unfortunately, we have no polemical tracts from his hand, but those who knew him well know how upset and impatient he could get with church leaders, administrators, or colleagues whom he felt had compromised the faith. Yet his witness was basically a positive one. In many ways he was a simple man whose ultimate goal was to live out faithfully his calling as a servant of Jesus Christ.

Catholic Calvinian

Ford Battles, like John Calvin, was not sectarian. He was a loyal and active member of the church, most of his life as a Congregationalist, later as a member of the United Church of Christ, and in his final years as a member of the Christian Reformed Church. But his denominational membership was incidental to his love for the church catholic. He had little interest in conciliar ecumenism (the NCC, WCC, etc.), but he was ecumenical or catholic in the best sense of the word. Just as one could speak of *Calvinus Oecumenicus*,[24] so one could speak of the ecumenical Battles. He did not get as actively involved in unity conversations as did Calvin, but he supported the formation of the United Church of Christ in 1957 and practiced a grassroots ecumenism throughout his life. For several years he taught a course, "Seminar on the Unity of the Church,"

---

24. The title of "the" book on the subject by Wilhelm Nijenhuis (1959). Cf. my more recent essay bearing this same title in the *Reformed Review* 44, no. 2 (Winter 1990).

at Pittsburgh Theological Seminary and published a 119-page guide that drew from the New Testament and patristic writers. He particularly delighted in teaching courses on Calvin to Roman Catholic students when he was in Pittsburgh. He also assembled a large study guide, *The Documents of Vatican II in Historical Perspective* (1970). One of his favorite hymns was one he adapted from Cyprian, "The Church of Christ is One," published in *The Hymnal of the United Church of Christ* (1974). All of Battles' writings are suffused with this spirit.[25] Moreover, his study guides in particular show the catholicity of his thinking, for he wanted his students to know firsthand some of the key writings of ancient and medieval theologians as well as Renaissance thinkers.

Calvin's Theology and the Theology of Ford Lewis Battles

Ford Battles was a historian, not a theologian; or, to be more precise, his field was historical theology, not systematic theology. Hence, even if he had lived longer, he probably would never have attempted a book on Calvin's theology, as such. The closest we come to that is his *Calculus Fidei*, his most definitive and comprehensive approach to Calvin's theology, published in its entirety for the first time in this volume. But note the subtitle, not an introduction to Calvin's theology, but a more modest "Some Ruminations on the Structure of the Theology of John Calvin."

Calvin, though a theologian par excellence (as well as a preacher, pastor, biblical expositor, and administrator), was always revising the ordering of topics in his *Institutes*. Only in the final edition did he feel he had come close to the ideal for which he was always striving in the various revisions of the *Institutes*. It was precisely this interest in structure that fascinated Battles. One reason might be called congenital. He had a mathematical mind and often thought in terms of mathematical-like outlines and designs.[26] This is amply illustrated in this volume. He

25. One might misinterpret the approach taken in *"Calculus Fidei:* Some Ruminations on the Structure of the Theology of John Calvin" as being a polemic against the Anabaptists, on the one hand, and the Roman Catholics on the other. However, Battles would respond that he was merely trying to interpret Calvin's theological approach in the light of the concrete historical-theological situation in which he found himself.

26. Battles' elder daughter, Nancy, recently came across an old volume in her father's library which she thinks may provide a clue for the title and nature of *Calculus Fidei*. This book, *Number: The Language of Science* (1930) by Tobias Dantzig, contains diagrams and ideas that may well have inspired Battles, e.g., the comments on pp. 128–29. Following Archimedes, the author states: "Modern analysis is but the theory of infinite processes, and infinite processes have for foundation the idea of *limit.* . . . The concept *limit* derives from the notion that two variable magnitudes will approach a state of equalization if their difference can become deliberately small, and this idea is the very basis of the method of exhaustion." It was an adaptation of this notion of limit that was employed in *"Calculus Fidei."*Concerning this approach, see McKim's introductory essay in this volume.

On Battles' fondness and rationale for using so many diagrams, see the editor's preface to this volume.

was also intrigued by "the many interconnections or symmetries of the various parts of the *Institutio*" (179).

Closely related to the notions of limits and polarities is Battles' analysis of the *Institutes* in terms of the true/false principle (179).[27] He sees this principle at work already in the first edition, where Calvin's future theological course is set by a "determination to hold a middle course between the right [institutionalized Roman Catholicism] and left [revolutionary, disruptive spiritualism]" (100). Constantly he strove to find a middle, scripturally informed ground between extremes: "here [in the *Institutes*] it lies between Roman Catholic and Anabaptist" (299).

Battles also reflected the mind and spirit of his mentor in his interest in the practical or ethical aspect of theology. In the midst of his relatively small number of essays about Calvin's theology, it is significant that several of them deal with ethical themes. Two of them are included in part 2 of this volume. For Battles, as well as for John Calvin, theology was never an abstract, ivory tower exercise. Its goal was always "usefulness" (*utilitas*).

Finally, what are some of the key elements in Calvin's theology that Battles perceived as foundational? At first glance one might expect to find the answer in appendix 3: "Chief Motifs in Calvin's Institutes" (351ff.), which is an expansion of a study by a Dutch historian, Antoon Veerman. However, these "motifs" turn out to be a listing of the various figures and images which Calvin frequently uses in his theology. They are helpful in understanding how Calvin thought and illustrated his theological ideas, but they do not provide us with the distinctive characteristics of Calvin's theology. For this we need to turn elsewhere in Battles' various studies of Calvin. Some of these characteristics, as understood by Battles, are the following:[28]

Revelation. The Scriptures, of course, are foundational for Calvin, and his concept of the internal or secret witness of the Spirit is crucial (see *Inst.* 1.7.1.4–5). This has been dealt with at length by several Calvin scholars. Battles, however, goes one step further and focuses on the accommodated nature of God's revelation. Thus, one of the key essays in this volume is "God Was Accommodating Himself to Human Capacity." Here Battles shows how this hermeneutical principle enabled Calvin to deal with seeming inconsistencies in Scripture (124f.), our understanding of God (126ff.), how God bridges the gap between the Creator and

27. Cf. "The Antithetical Structure of the *Institutes*," 347–50. This approach to Calvin's theology was already being developed in Battles' lectures given at Union Seminary in the summer of 1973. He sent me his outline for those lectures and the title for Lecture V reads: "Antithesis: Key to the Theology of Calvin." He concluded the lecture with some observations about "the relevance of Calvin's antithetical method for the present theological task."

28. One of the sources for determining these characteristics is the Introduction to the 1536 edition of Calvin's *Institutes*, the section prior to the portion included here (91ff.).

the creature (131ff.), moral pedagogy (133f.), and ultimately in the greatest act of condescension and accommodation, the incarnation of the eternal Son of God.

Knowledge of God. Edward Dowey and T. H. L. Parker had earlier published books on the question of the knowledge of God in Calvin's theology,[29] but Battles develops this theme of the two knowledges, that of God and of self, in his own way. In conjunction with what he sees as the overarching scheme of Calvin's theology he points to two key phrases in the *Institutes,*

> As often as I descended into myself
> Or raised my mind to thee . . .

and then concludes: "These two movements of the human mind lead to the knowledge of God and the knowledge of ourselves, set in antithesis to one another; the gulf between the all-holy God and the fallen sinner which only the incarnate Son of God can bridge" (149–50).[30]

The Center: Jesus Christ. Other key motifs in Calvin's theology have been discussed above, such as the importance of *pietas* for understanding the Christian life. But no motif is more fundamental to Calvin's theology than the centrality of Jesus Christ.[31] Battles refers to this in various contexts (see above and p. 148), but includes it in a wider context in a lovely summary statement toward the end of his essay on Calvin as poet. For Calvin's Christ-centeredness is no narrow Christocentrism but must be seen in the larger context of creation and redemption.

> When Calvin is driving home those themes closest to his heart—the clear evidence of God in the theater of the universe and in the theater of human history and society and church, the consequent inexcusability of human blindness, the mystery of God's merciful condescension summed up in the incarnation of Christ, the great ring of the going forth from God and return to him of the physical creation, the ineffable mysteries of God before which we must stand in mute adoration: these themes demand a higher and deeper speech than mere prose can give (286).

Thus, Battles concludes this essay on Calvin as poet with an acknowledgment of the mystery of salvation centered in Jesus Christ.

---

29. Cf. Dowey, *The Knowledge of God in Calvin's Theology* (New York: Columbia University Press, 1952); and Parker, *Calvin's Doctrine of the Knowledge of God* (Edinburgh: Oliver and Boyd, 1952).

30. Cf. pp. 149–50, where Battles spells out the implications of this twofold knowledge.

31. A case could also be made for the special place Calvin assigns to the Holy Spirit in his theology. Accordingly one can also refer to Calvin as "the theologian of the Holy Spirit," as was done in a previous generation by B. B. Warfield and in our time by Werner Krusche in his magisterial study, *Das Wirken des Heiligen Geistes nach Calvin* (Göttingen: Vandenhoeck and Ruprecht, 1957).

This mystery is described by Battles as the "Calvinian poetry of the faith." This approach to Christian faith is pastoral and poetic, rather than doctrinaire. While Battles, like his mentor John Calvin, was very much concerned with theology, both recognized the mystery of faith that lay behind all church dogmas and theological formulations.

II. The Calvinian Works of Ford Lewis Battles
Donald K. McKim

The motto of Renaissance humanism was *"Ad fontes!"*—"To the sources!" This same motto summarizes the work of Ford Lewis Battles, a scholar who was always mining the sources. Behind all of his work on John Calvin stand years of diligent labor in the primary materials. Battles' breathtaking knowledge of patristic writers, medieval theologians, and the milieu of Renaissance humanism—in which Calvin was trained—gave him unparalleled insight into the context and the fertile soil from which Calvin's own theology grew. One could not be in his presence without sensing the tremendous expanse and profundity of his reservoirs.[32] His careful attention to the smallest detail coupled with his gift of discerning broad, overarching structures meant that Battles plumbed his subjects with a grasp of both the "forest" and the "trees." His capacity to bring all his great learning to bear on a specific point made him an imposing scholar indeed. Yet he wore his learning with an honest humility.

Apart from Battles' considerable translation work, including Calvin's Seneca commentary of 1532, Calvin's 1536, 1539 (incomplete), and 1559 editions of the *Institutes*, and the *Catechism* of 1538, the essays that comprise this book are the Calvinian legacy of Ford Lewis Battles. The essays are divided into two major sections. The first five are concerned with "The Origin and Structure of Calvin's Theology," while the remaining four focus on "Calvin's Poetry, Piety, and Morality." These two groupings suggest Battles' dual focus on both the way Calvin ordered his work and the ethical and other implications of his theology. Thus, the focus of the book is on the interpretation of John Calvin, whose *Institutes of the Christian Religion* Battles had "come to cherish . . . next only to the Scripture."[33] May the essays that follow introduce

32. See the same sentiments expressed in Donald G. Miller, "Ford Lewis Battles: An Appreciation," in *Reformatio Perennis: Essays on Calvin and the Reformation in Honor of Ford Lewis Battles*, ed. by B. A. Gerrish in collaboration with Robert Benedetto (Pittsburgh: Pickwick, 1981), 1–8.

33. Foreword, in Jack B. Rogers and Donald K. McKim, *The Authority and Interpretation of the Bible* (San Francisco: Harper & Row, 1979), xv.

a new generation of students and scholars to both the Genevan Reformer and one of John Calvin's most remarkable interpreters.

The Origin and Structure of Calvin's Theology

"Calvin's Humanistic Education" (1975) is an examination of Calvin's academic training under six prominent teachers in three universities. This study clearly indicates the path Calvin traveled in his training in the arts and law, and the influence of particular teachers who helped shape the contours of his mind. Calvin's professors introduced him to Renaissance humanism, providing him with an educational philosophy, a concern for how ancient texts are studied, and fluency in languages, in law, and in much else.[34] These formative influences also gave direction to Calvin's educational plan for Geneva,[35] a plan that had a profound influence on the history of the Protestant churches and the development of Reformed theology. Calvin's academic pilgrimage, as traced in this brief essay, is of primary importance in understanding the future course of his life and work.

"The Sources of Calvin's Seneca Commentary" (1966) is another essay that explores the background and training of the young Calvin. This essay is derived from Battles' work on Calvin's Seneca commentary, the first book Calvin wrote as a humanist scholar. Battles' seven-year translation and annotation project, carried out with André M. Hugo, resulted in the publication of *Calvin's Commentary on Seneca's De Clementia* (1969) in English. The essay we have before us not only identifies the ancient writers that Calvin used in his commentary, but also tells us how he utilized his sources. Battles reveals the process by which Calvin worked, thereby giving us insight into his later, Christian writings.

The essay identifies two "modern pillars" or authorities for Calvin: Gulielmus Budaeus (1467–1540) and Desiderius Erasmus (1469–1536). These authorities are used extensively by Calvin in his study of legal terms, Roman institutions, political philosophy, philosophy, and literature. A third "modern" authority is Philippus Beroaldus the Elder (1453–1505). Two "ancient pillars" are identified as Seneca and Cicero, the latter being "the first pillar of Roman philosophy and literature." Battles then identifies the three layers of tradition through which Calvin's contacts with the ancient writers passed, as well as a host of other classical authors to whom Calvin made allusions in the com-

---

34. Some implications of Calvin's humanist training for his view of the nature and function of Scripture are suggested in Rogers and McKim, *The Authority and Interpretation of the Bible*, 89ff.; see also the preface written by Ford Lewis Battles, xv–xvi.

35. See "Calvin's Humanistic Education," 47–64. Cf. Gillian Lewis, "The Geneva Academy," in *Calvinism in Europe: 1540–1620*, ed. by Andrew Pettegree, Alastair Duke, and Gillian Lewis (Cambridge: Cambridge University Press, 1994), 35–63.

mentary.[36] Classical intermediaries and humanist compilers also played a role.

Battles finds in Calvin's Seneca commentary "the beginnings of Calvin the exegete." For "the same attention to the close study of the text will later mark Calvin's Christian writings."[37] The message of the commentary is also significant: "that the mighty should rule with mercy, accountable to God." This message is recast by Calvin in his "passionate essays in Christian political teaching that introduce and conclude the *Institutio Christianae Religionis.*" This tells us something about "the high seriousness of the Stoic ethic, also transformed by Christian faith, [which] prevailed at least for a time in Geneva and in her spiritual daughters."[38] These elements are the enduring legacies of Calvin's classical studies.

"The First Edition of the *Institutes of the Christian Religion*" (1975) is from Battles' introduction to his English translation of Calvin's 1536 *Institutes.*[39] This essay demonstrates that Calvin intended the *Institutes* to be a Protestant catechism issued in response to "the demands of his acquaintances." First and foremost, Calvin wanted to convey the "sound doctrine" of the French evangelicals.

However, the *Institutes* also evolved into an apologetic work in light of Roman Catholic attacks and the precarious political situation of the French Protestants.[40] King Francis I of France, in a royal memorandum dated 1 February 1535, characterized the emerging evangelicals, with whom Calvin was associated, as seditious persons no different than the Anabaptists of Germany. The evangelicals deserved to be put to death. To counter this charge and the threat of persecution, Calvin responded with a theological essay, *The Psychopannychia* (1534/35?; pub. 1542), which considers the question of what happens to the soul and body at the time of death. Calvin writes against Anabaptist views of "soul sleep," and supports the immortality of the soul, so that evangelicals could not be accused of holding a "fanatical" view. It was Calvin's way of distinguishing the views of the evangelicals from other groups of religious dissidents.

In the *Institutes,* as revealed in the dedicatory letter[41] to Francis I, Calvin continues his defense by asserting that the evangelicals do not hold heretical views nor do they threaten the state. Calvin hoped that his presentation would clarify evangelical beliefs and thereby bring an

36. See "The Sources of Calvin's Commentary on Seneca's *De Clementia,*" table A below.
37. "The Sources of Calvin's Seneca Commentary," 86.
38. This theme is exemplified in Battles' translation of "Against Luxury and License in Geneva: A Forgotten Fragment of Calvin," below.
39. See *1536a* and *1536b.*
40. "The First Edition of the *Institutes of the Christian Religion,*" 93–100.
41. Ibid., 116.

end to persecution. In stating his case, Calvin positions himself in a "middle direction between the right and left," that is, between institutionalized Roman Catholicism and the radicals.[42]

"God Was Accommodating Himself to Human Capacity" (1977) is a summary of the principle of "accommodation" as Calvin used it.[43] The verb *accommodare* or *attemperare* refers to the adjustment made by speakers to the capacities and understandings of the listeners they wish to persuade. Just as rhetoricians adjust their use of language and presentation to the level of their hearers, so God "accommodates" the divine Self to human capacities. In effect, God speaks "baby talk" so that limited and sinful humans may hear the divine Word and receive knowledge of God. Battles traces the use of accommodation in classical rhetoric, in the writings of the Church Fathers (Clement of Alexandria, Origen, Chrysostom, Augustine, etc.), and in Calvin's work.

The principle of accommodation is not only used by Calvin as a way to resolve scriptural inconsistencies;[44] it is also understood as God's method of self-disclosure. Scripture portrays God as father, teacher, and physician in order to communicate the divine Self to sinful humans, who have only a limited capacity (Lat. *captus*) to receive the knowledge of God. God uses several avenues of accommodation, including the law, the language of the Lord's Prayer, and the sacraments. We find in the incarnation of Jesus Christ God's supreme act of divine accommodation: God actually *becomes* a human being. Calvin made substantial use of the principle of accommodation. He particularly depends on it as a context for understanding the nature and function of Scripture.[45]

The publication of the complete text of Battles' "*Calculus Fidei: Some Ruminations on the Structure of the Theology of John Calvin*" is a significant event. The work was prepared for the International Congress on Calvin Research held in Amsterdam on 28 September 1978. In

42. Ibid., 100. Battles considered Calvin's emphasis on the *via media* between extremes to be an important hermeneutical key for understanding all of his theological work. See especially "*Calculus Fidei*" below.

43. In 1952 Edward A. Dowey, Jr., recognized "accommodation" as characteristic of Calvin's view of the knowledge of God. He defined accommodation as "the process by which God reduces or adjusts to human capacities what he wills to reveal of the infinite mysteries of his being, which by their very nature are beyond the powers of the mind of man to grasp." See Edward A. Dowey, Jr., *The Knowledge of God in Calvin's Theology*, expanded edition (Grand Rapids: Eerdmans, 1994), 3. Cf. *passim*.

44. David F. Wright has recently questioned whether the tracing of accommodation to the categories of classical Roman rhetoric is valid. See "Calvin's Accommodating God," *Papers of The Sixth International Congress on Calvin Research*, Edinburgh, Scotland, 16 September 1995, at note 34.

45. See Rogers and McKim, *The Authority and Interpretation of the Bible*, 98–100. In a personal interview on 10 May 1976, Battles commented that "God chose men to be writers of Scripture while he could have had gold plates."

"Calculus Fidei" we find Battles' detailed analysis of the structure of Calvin's *Institutes*. Battles claims that a "true/false" or antithetical structure not only underlies the *Institutes*, but is the structural basis of all Calvin's theological work.

According to Battles, Calvin's theology, as embodied in the *Institutes*, is written in constant dialogue with his opponents and with the whole of the Christian tradition. Calvin's understanding of the Christian gospel led to a *"via media* between the Scylla of aberrant Romanism and the Charybdis of the radical tendencies of his time, whatever name he might give to them."[46] Calvin's "middle way" emerged in relation to the extreme views with which he was in dialogue. Thus, Battles writes, "There is in Calvin a single principle, but it is expressed in many ways: every fundamental notion of his thought is defined in a field of tension—a true middle between false extremes."[47] What distinguishes Calvin's approach from the "true/false" principle as expressed in Erasmus, Luther, and Zwingli is that Calvin realized that "the expression of truth never exhausts the possibility of falsehood" and that "unfaith is always present in faith." This means that truth emerges in the midst of conflicting alternatives that range on a continuum from what may be called "defect" to "excess."[48]

Calvin's theological method is rooted in the Pauline contrast between truth and falsehood, as found in the first chapter of Romans.[49] Romans 1, in turn, is rooted in the Hebrew polemic against idolatry, dramatically expressed in the prophetic antithesis between "idols" (Heb. אֱלִיל; *oelîl*; "things of weakness, nought") and "the God of might and power" (Heb. אֵל; *'ēl*; Ger. *Goetze* and *Gott*). Thus "idolatry" for Calvin had profound implications, extending far beyond the making and worship of idols, to the constructs of the human mind. This form of falsehood either reduces God's majesty and revelation to a mere mental shadow, or constructs a physical representation of the divine image as an object of worship. For Calvin, "one is a defect of the truth; the other, an exaggerated imitation of it. Both are false; truth lies in between."[50]

Battles finds in Isaac Newton's mathematical theory of limits a modern, secularized rubric for understanding Calvin's theological views.[51]

---

46. *"Calculus Fidei,"* 138. Cf. Battles' comment that Calvin's theology "steering a middle course of truth between the Scylla of the falsity of defect and the Charybdis of the falsity of excess, was not the faith of a Christian philosopher with reason virtually intact, but the faith of a scriptural exegete, resting his ever-growing rational insight into divine truth upon the grace of God in Christ, given by the Holy Spirit." In Rogers and McKim, *The Authority and Interpretation of the Bible,* xv.

47. *"Calculus Fidei,"* 140.

48. Ibid.

49. Ibid., 142ff.

50. Ibid., 163.

51. See ibid., 140, 172ff.

Newton taught that one can never arrive at a literal, absolute value or truth, but only finite approximations of what is infinite. In Newton's theory Battles sees "a secularized form of the scriptural view of reality." For "mathematics and Scripture both view the human grasp of reality as increasingly approximated to, but never identified with, the human symbols we use to represent reality." Theologically, "our grasp of all Christian truth has this dynamic bipolarity—between absence and presence, between nothing and infinity, between Creator and created—growing toward perfect comprehension but in this life not reaching it."

The limits in which human rationality operates (Lat. *captus*; inherent limits and fallenness) "can be breached only in the act of adoration, of giving honor and gratitude to the majesty of God, and this act itself is God's gift through Christ, in the Spirit. The two extremes of ignorance and speculation are, conversely, the dishonoring of God." God's salvation history, with the incarnation as the "midpoint," is seen as "a pathway toward truth which, throughout its length, is fraught with turnings to either side, which to take is disaster. Faithful listening to Scripture prevents us from turning to either side. Truth, then, is an approaching, by human creatures, under divine guidance, to the goal of God their Creator, Redeemer, and Judge."[52]

It is important to note that the interpretative principles of "accommodation" and "approximation" are not original to either Calvin or Newton; both draw heavily on the Christian tradition which, even in Thomas Aquinas, recognizes the importance of analogous language. Use of such language has long been a staple of commentators who have tried to harmonize Moses' Genesis with the created order. This tradition is even more powerful in the Eastern Church, which emphasizes the "Negative Way," that language is so limited that one can say only what God is not. For Battles, Newton's mathematical theory is a modern use of this idea of approximation and limits. While one can say that both Calvin and Newton gave renewed emphasis to these principles, neither is original, since they are both mining out of the same Judeo-Christian tradition that recognizes the importance of avoiding literalism when speaking about God, when interpreting the Bible, and when describing the created order.

Battles develops his argument by setting out four basic "assumptions" concerning the nature of Calvin's conversion and his theological reflection on it, and five "theses" on the structure and organizing principles of Calvin's thought. His six appendixes further amplify key Calvinian concepts. The extensive tables in this work illustrate the ways this structure is worked out by Calvin throughout the *Institutes*, and its successive editorial embodiments, as he "sorted and resorted the dialogues

52. Ibid., 173.

with his opponents, and in so doing came to an ever more satisfying (to him) formulation of his reading of the Christian gospel."[53] In this respect, Calvin is supremely a biblical and "contextual" theologian.[54]

The question of what organizing principle or structure might best summarize Calvin's theology has long engaged scholars. Differing views continue to emerge.[55] Battles' detailed proposal found in "*Calculus Fidei*" is part of this ongoing dialogue but has not yet received sustained analytical study or discussion.[56] It is hoped that the publication of this work will stimulate further exposition and comment.[57]

Calvin's Poetry, Piety, and Morality

"The Theologian as Poet: Some Remarks about the 'Found' Poetry of John Calvin" (1978) is a fascinating look at the poetic structures in Calvin's writings. Calvin certainly did not intend to write poetry, and at first glance his work may not appear to be "poetic." However, Battles

---

53. Ibid., 140.

54. Battles' reading of Calvin does not turn him into a Ramist or a "Protestant Scholastic"—two groups concerned in their own ways with the "logical" explication of theology. The Calvinian method as portrayed by Battles is neither Ramist nor philosophical, but rather thoroughly theological and historical in orientation. See appendix A, "*Speculum Institutionis* Prolegomena," 179, note 1; and Donald K. McKim, *Ramism in William Perkins' Theology* (New York: Peter Lang, 1987).

55. See Brian G. Armstrong, "*Duplex cognitio Dei*, Or? The Problem and Relation of Structure, Form, and Purpose in Calvin's Theology," in *Probing the Reformed Tradition: Historical Studies in Honor of Edward A. Dowey, Jr.*, ed. by Elsie Anne McKee and Brian G. Armstrong (Louisville: Westminster/John Knox, 1989), 135–53; and Philip Walker Butin, *Revelation, Redemption, and Response: Calvin's Trinitarian Understanding of the Divine–Human Relationship* (New York: Oxford University Press, 1995), 15–19.

56. Armstrong writes of Battles' *Calculus Fidei* that it "has not received the attention it may merit. He fastens on the antithetical structure of Calvin's logic and shows convincingly that in developing his material Calvin always moves between two poles in a series of near-infinite regressions. Battles tries to relate this to the theory of limits of the mathematical sciences. The result, he avers, is that Calvin is always seeking the *via media*" (152, note 3). He continues: "I am unsure about the use of the mathematical model, but readily agree that Calvin's formulations always must be seen as the result of a dynamic interplay of dialectical pairs. 'Knowledge of God' and 'knowledge of self,' e.g., is a pairing which is constantly applied in every single formulation of this thought in the *Institutio*." Armstrong goes on to express his reservation: "The main problem with Battles' proposal, as I see it, is that it comprehends *only* structure and does not lead beyond that to *what it means* for Calvin's theology." Butin's criticism of "dialectical interpretations" is that they "tend to underestimate the significance of Calvin's own explicit and persistent use of the trinitarian structure of the Apostles' Creed as the organizing paradigm for successive editions of the *Institutes*" (19). David L. Puckett supports Battles' views of Calvin's "middle way" principle for Calvin's Old Testament exegesis. See David L. Puckett, *John Calvin's Exegesis of the Old Testament* (Louisville: Westminster/John Knox, 1995), 139.

57. I have sought to do this in a limited way in my "John Calvin: A Theologian for an Age of Limits," in *Readings in Calvin's Theology*, ed. by Donald K. McKim (Grand Rapids: Baker, 1984), 291–310.

maintains that poetry is "found" in the writings of many great theologians as they reach for words to express the inexpressible. Calvin's poetic structures are found in three broad categories: doxological, christological, and soteriological. Battles writes:

> The greatest theologians soberly confess that there are limits beyond which human language as the instrument of rational analysis and explication cannot pass when it has to do with God and man. Then do those high theological flights, at this barrier, end not in frustration but in doxology. At that juncture mind and heart break forth into a hymn, a paean of praise to God. There theologizing, prayer, song, converge and become one. . . . This doxological response, then, recognizes the utter ineffability of God's ways.[58]

Battles illustrates his point by exploring some of the "found" poetry in the works of several early Christian theologians, emphasizing doxological utterances invoked in praise of the Trinity.

In his discussion of "John Calvin as Poet," Battles illustrates the ways in which Calvin turned his expressive talents—honed as a humanist scholar—into labors for the Christian gospel: "After his conversion Calvin was to press his rhetorical skill unreservedly into God's service."[59] Passages from Calvin's early preface to the French translation of the New Testament and his *Psychopannychia* are cited to illustrate poetic structures such as chiasmus, anaphora, and parallelism. Other examples are drawn from the *Form of Prayer and Songs of the Church* (1543), Calvin's metrical paraphrase of Psalm 113, the *Institutes*, and his *Commentary on 1 Corinthians* 15:24. Poetic devices such as homeoteuleton and assonance (rhyme and near-rhyme of verbs at ends of lines), repetition, antitheses, chiasmus, and various types of parallelism are employed. These poetic forms, Battles maintains, are employed by Calvin when he is "driving home those themes closest to his heart"; he breaks forth into poetics since "these themes demand a higher and deeper speech than mere prose can give."[60]

"True Piety According to Calvin" is from Battles' introduction to *The Piety of John Calvin* (1978). This essay explores the meaning of Calvin's faith through a careful study of the term *pietas*. Piety is "that reverence joined with love of God which the knowledge of his benefits induces."[61] It is filial devotion to God. Battles also examines the concept of piety as mirrored in Calvin's life—called the "kernel" of Calvin's faith—particularly as it relates to his conversion. Battles sets the term "piety" in the context of Calvin's view of the Christian life as set forth in the *Institutes*

58. "The Theologian as Poet," 250.
59. Ibid., 261.
60. Ibid., 286.
61. *Inst.* 1.2.1.

(3.6–10). His concluding section examines the obstacles to piety according to Calvin's polemical tracts.

"Notes on John Calvin, *Justitia*, and the Old Testament Law" (1981) is a continuation of Battles' careful linguistic work. This essay examines the Greek term *epieikeia* (Lat. *aequitas*) or "equity" as a clue to understanding Calvin's concept of justice. This discussion is prefaced by a discussion of Calvin's study of Roman law and its relation to Jewish law, his analysis of the law in the fourfold grouping of Mosaic codes, the uses of the law, and the common ends of Hebrew and Gentile law.

For Calvin, equity is the attempt to "penetrate beneath the surface, the literal language of the law, the time-bound form in which the law was originally cast, to the spirit and intent of the original."[62] It is this principle that serves Calvin exegetically and theologically as a way of understanding how Jesus interiorized the Decalogue in the Sermon on the Mount. The principle of equity gives flexibility to the interpreter or to the judge who applies the law. For "the most just way to administer the law is not to be governed by its letter, but to show compassion in pronouncing sentences."[63] This is what Calvin learned from his study of Seneca's *De Clementia*.

After his conversion, Calvin carried over the principle of equity to his Christian understanding of law so that it became a primary tool for the exegesis of Scripture. Equity is a key principle for understanding true justice. True justice emerges not when the letter of the law is carried out, but when the intent of just laws is honored. Compassion is not antithetical to justice, but integral to it. According to Battles, the "most sublime task" to which this principle is put is Jesus' interiorizing of the Decalogue in the Sermon on the Mount. Here "murder is more than a physical act: murder is committed in the heart before the hand does the deed, or even when the outward deed is never done." Here Jesus transforms the Second Table of the Decalogue from "a moral code to an ethic of intention." Thus "through the classical principle of *epieikeia*, Calvin has plumbed the depths of the Decalogue and delineated at the same time the true Christian concept of *justitia*."[64]

"Against Luxury and License in Geneva: A Forgotten Fragment of Calvin" (1965) is an introduction, translation, and annotation of Calvin's *De Luxu*. This fragment, considered by the editors of the *Corpus Reformatorum* to have been an "unfinished study of the young Calvin," was judged by Battles to reflect the aftermath of Calvin's efforts to reform Genevan morality following his return from Strasbourg (1541) and perhaps dating from 1546–47.[65]

---

62. "Notes on John Calvin, *Justitia*, and the Old Testament Law," 313.
63. Ibid.
64. Ibid., 315. Cf. I. John Hesselink, *Calvin's Concept of the Law* (Allison Park, Pa.: Pickwick, 1992).
65. Ibid., 319–21.

The document reveals Calvin's thinking about the opposition to his moral reforms in Geneva and particularly his disgust with the various forms of "luxury" he finds there. Calvin finds excessive extravagance in "dancing, eating, drinking, dressing lavishly, using the mirror, [and] hating offspring. Actors flourish while the poor starve." For Calvin, "luxury of the rich is a sin against the poor" while "public and private vices breed each other."[66] Here, too, the influence of Calvin's study of Seneca is pervasive. As a Christian, however, Calvin was concerned that the "covetous rich" and "ambitious" have their consciences "called back to a specific awareness of their own evil."[67] Calvin's moral reforms and his view of the relation of church and state in Geneva is another significant study in itself.[68]

---

66. "Against Luxury and License in Geneva," 322. Cf. the translation of this piece and others on "Ecclesiastical Discipline" in *Calvin's Ecclesiastical Advice*, trans. by Mary Beaty and Benjamin W. Farley (Louisville: Westminster/John Knox, 1991), 83ff.

67. See "Against Luxury and License in Geneva," 327, citing from the 1543 *Inst.* 4.13.13. On matters of morals and the regulation of Genevan life, see William G. Naphy, *Calvin and the Consolidation of the Genevan Reformation* (Manchester: Manchester University Press, 1994); *Sin and the Calvinists: Moral Control and the Consistory in the Reformed Tradition*, ed. by Raymond A. Mentzer (Kirksville, Mo.: Sixteenth Century Journal Publishers, 1994); and Robert M. Kingdom, *Adultery and Divorce in Calvin's Geneva* (Cambridge, Mass.: Harvard University Press, 1995).

68. Among much other literature, see Harro Höpfl, *The Christian Polity of John Calvin* (Cambridge: Cambridge University Press, 1982).

Abbreviations

The Works of John Calvin

CR	*Corpus Reformatorum.* 1834–.
OC	*Opera Calvini.* 1869–. *Opera Quae Supersunt Omnia.* Ed. by Guilielmus Baum, Eduardus Cunitz, and Eduardus Reuss. 59 vols. *Corpus Reformatorum,* vols. 29–87. Brunsvigae: Schwetschke, 1863–1900.
OO	*Ioannis Calvini Noviodvnensis Opera Omina: In novem tomos digesta.* Ed. by Schipper. 9 vols. Amsterdam: Schipperi, 1667–1671.
OS	*Opera Selecta.* Ed. by Petrus Barth and Guilielmus Niesel. 5 vols. Monachii: Kaiser, 1926–1952.
SC	*Supplementa Calviniana: Sermons inedits, iussu corporis presbyterianorum universalis.* Neukirchen Kreis Moers: Neukirchener, 1936–.

The Works of Ford Lewis Battles

Comm. Sen. De Clem.	*Calvin's Commentary on Seneca's De Clementia.* With intro., trans., and notes by Ford Lewis Battles and André Malan Hugo. Leiden: E. J. Brill, 1969.
Inst. 1536a	*Institution of the Christian Religion . . . M.D. XXXVI.* Trans. and annotated by Ford Lewis Battles. Atlanta: John Knox, 1975.
Inst. 1536b	*Institutes of the Christian Religion . . . M.D. XXXVI.* Rev. ed. Trans. and annotated by Ford Lewis Battles. Grand Rapids: H. H. Meeter Center for Calvin Studies/Eerdmans, 1986.
Inst.	*Calvin: Institutes of the Christian Religion.* Ed. by John T. McNeill; trans. by Ford Lewis Battles. 2 vols. Philadelphia: Westminster, 1960.
Concord. 1559	*A Computerized Concordance to Institutio Christianae Religionis 1559 of John Calvin.* With the assistance of Charles Miller. Pittsburgh: Pittsburgh Theological Seminary, 1972. Guidebook and seven reels microfilm. See also Richard Wevers, *A Concordance to Calvin's Institutio 1559.* 6 vols. Grand Rapids: Digamma, 1992.

Analysis 1980   *Analysis of the Institutes of the Christian Religion of John Calvin.* Ford Lewis Battles; assisted by John Walchenbach. Grand Rapids: Baker, 1980.

Catechism 1538 *John Calvin: Catechism 1538.* Trans. by Ford Lewis Battles. Rev. ed. with corrections. Pittsburgh: Pittsburgh Theological Seminary, 1972, 1976. See also I. John Hesselink, *Introduction to Calvin's Theology Based Primarily on Ford Lewis Battles' Translation of Calvin's First Catechism (1538)* (Louisville: Westminster/John Knox, 1997), which incorporates the Battles text.

Piety 1978   *The Piety of John Calvin: An Anthology Illustrative of the Spirituality of the Reformer.* Trans. and ed. by Ford Lewis Battles; music ed. by Stanley Tagg. Grand Rapids: Baker, 1978.

PART 1

The Origin and Structure of Calvin's Theology

1   Calvin's Humanistic Education[1]

Let us look at the changing idea of the university as seen in the educational experience of the Protestant Reformer of Geneva, John Calvin, during his university decade (1523–33), a time of great political, cultural, and religious change in western Europe. In the education of the young Calvin we see what hundreds of other men of that day also went through in a time when the new humanism was transforming the medieval university.

Calvin's formative years have been a battleground of scholars for more than a century, and the debate does not seem to be slackening. In my own effort to adduce some new evidence, I devoted seven years to the close study of Calvin's first published book, his *Commentary on the De Clementia of Seneca*,[2] completed in his twenty-second year (1532). From the evidence of the authors used in that work, I was able to indicate with some certainty what Calvin had read up to that time. In three published studies, I did not, however, attempt to correlate my findings based on such internal evidence with the known external evidence or informed scholarly conjecture.

The present essay is a preliminary attempt to bring together the details of Calvin's life, information on the three universities he attended, and accounts of his chief teachers, in conjunction with my own findings, to characterize more fully his humanistic education. Another task of this essay will be to examine Calvin's 1559 educational plan for what was to become to Académie de Genève, as the mature pedagogical reflection on and corollary to his own education and intellectual growth. No attempt will be made here to deal specifically with the paramount question: his conversion and religious formation, which presumably occurred in the year following the close of his formal education.

1. This previously unpublished essay was originally presented at the Ph.D. colloquium held at Pittsburgh Theological Seminary on 19 September 1975.
2. See the introduction in *Comm. Sen. De Clem.*, 72*–140*.

Three Universities

Paris (1523–27). Our attention will be directed to the resident colleges of the University of Paris, where by the sixteenth century the teaching of the arts course was centered, with especial attention to the Collège de la Marche and the Collège de Montaigu.

At the end of the summer of 1523, Calvin, aged fourteen years (the normal age for a Parisian freshman during this period), journeyed more than sixty miles from Noyon in Picardy to enroll at the university in order to fulfill his father's wish that he study for the priesthood. Already in minor orders and supported by a benefice in the gift of the diocese of Noyon, he spent about three months (it is estimated) at the Collège de la Marche, which had been founded in 1363 by Maître Jean de la Marche on the ruins of the ancient Collège de Constantinople. His chief teacher during this brief time was Mathurin Cordier, an excellent Latinist, of whom more will be said later.

At the end of 1523 he transferred to the famous Collège de Montaigu, where he spent the next four years pursuing the licentiate in arts. This basic degree was the normal preparation for more advanced work in such university faculties as that of law or theology. Montaigu (blessed to the memory of Erasmus!) was an ancient foundation, illustrative of the continuity of death and life through which so many medieval educational foundations went in the course of their checkered history. It had been founded originally in 1314 as the Collège des Aicelins by Giles Aicelin, archbishop of Rouen, renamed Collège de Montaigu upon its restoration in 1388 by Pierre Aicelin de Montaigu, bishop of Nevers and Laôn and Cardinal, and when it again fell into disrepair, revived by John Standonck of Malines at the end of the fifteenth century. Standonck, himself educated by the Brethren of the Common Life at Gouda in the Low Countries, had also studied at Paris and founded a hospice there for the education of poor boys. He incorporated this house in the rebuilt college (beginning in 1483), for which he provided a stern set of statutes in 1503. Alexandre Ganoczy in his work *Le Jeune Calvin*[3] relates how the flourishing college dwindled both in numbers and in fervor under the equally stern but successively less inspired leadership of Noël Béda (to 1513) and Pierre de la Tempête (to 1528). Their theological conservatism was of the sort so frequently deplored by Calvin in his later writings as "Sorbonnist," or to use his nickname, "Sophist."

The Collège de Montaigu included two kinds of students, those who could pay and those who could not. Both, however, though separately domiciled, led a rigorous and self-denying life. Possibly Calvin's (as well as Erasmus') digestion was victim of Montaigu's frugal and sometimes

---

3. See Alexandre Ganoczy, *The Young Calvin*, trans. by David Foxgrover and Wade Provo (Philadelphia: Westminster, 1987).

careless kitchen. It is interesting to note that the rigor of the *devotio moderna* without its spirit was made known not only to Calvin but also to Ignatius of Loyola, who followed him as a student there. The strenuous faith and practice of both men doubtless owed something to the rigorous regimen of Montaigu.

While at the Collège de Montaigu, Beza in his *Life of Calvin* tells us, Calvin studied philosophy, that is, logic, under a "certain Spaniard." At the end of 1527 or the beginning of 1528, Calvin completed the licentiate in arts, in preparation for the study of theology. However, this was not to be, for John Calvin's father, Gérard Calvin, autocratically decided that his promising son should not waste his efforts on theology, but should undertake the study of law.

Orléans (1528–29; 1532–33?). Where was the best place in France to study law? Unquestionably, the greatest French law university of the Middle Ages was that of Orléans, an ancient city situated at the northernmost point of the Loire River and commanding access from Paris to the Loire basin. It is less than eighty miles south-southwest of Paris.

The University of Orléans holds the key to French legal education in the Middle Ages; let us then summarize, chiefly from Rashdall, in the 1936 revision of Powicke and Emden,[4] the development of this university.

As early as the ninth century Orléans is reported as offering the study of law (then as a branch of the "liberal arts"); the eminence, however, of that university as a school of civil and canon law is usually associated with the Bull of Honorius III, which in 1219 prohibited the study of civil law at the University of Paris, and with the "great dispersion" of 1229, which began in an incident arising out of a tavern brawl and eventuated in the killing of several students by the police and in the withdrawal of the masters from Paris with the closing of the university. A number of the Paris masters settled in Orléans. The bishop of Orléans asked Pope Gregory IX in 1235 whether the prohibition of civil law of his predecessor applied also to Orléans: he was advised that, on the bishop's permission, the study of civil law was open freely except to certain beneficed.

From this point on, Orléans became the outstanding medieval university for the study of law in the Kingdom of France. The shape of the university emerged slowly, in the familiar pattern of town-gown rivalry, episcopal pressure, royal initiative, and papal privilege. Orléans' development was complicated by the feud between Philip IV and the papacy that marked the end of the Roman and the beginning of the Avignonese papacy. Hence it was not until the early fourteenth century that favor-

---

4. Hastings Rashdall, *The Universities of Europe in the Middle Ages*, 3 vols., new edition, ed. by F. M. Powicke and A. B. Emden (London: Oxford University Press, 1936).

able conditions for a university constitution—a compromise between the Paris and Bologna types—emerged.

The former head, the *scholasticus*, was supplanted by a rector (usually a doctor elected by the student nations) as head of the university. A college consisting of the doctors ordinary and the ten proctors (licentiates or at least bachelors) of the student nations (France, Germany, Lorraine, Burgundy, Champagne, Picardy, Normandy, Touraine, Aquitaine, and Scotland) administered the ordinary affairs of the university. Extraordinary matters were decided in a general congregation; gradually student power increased.

Orléans in the fourteenth and fifteenth centuries consisted solely of a faculty of law, in which it was preeminent among the universities of France. Evidence of the comparative wealth of its students and the lucrative character of the legal profession is to be seen in the fact that the university had no endowed college for poor students; students generally lived in *hospicia* presided over by doctors, bachelors, or students.

It was to this university, still preeminent in the study of law, that Calvin repaired in 1528, after completing the licentiate in arts at Paris. There, as will subsequently be discussed, he sat under the renowned jurisconsult Pierre de l'Estoile (Petrus Stella).

Bourges (1529–31). The third university John Calvin attended was the University of Bourges, founded in the duchy of Berry by the Bull of Paul II in 1464. Louis XI (a native of Bourges) and his brother Charles, duke of Berry, had petitioned the pope and received his permission. Bourges, in the Middle Ages the capital of the duchy of Berry, is situated about 150 miles south of Paris and 75 miles southeast of Orléans. Presumably the university, which concentrated on the study of law, was a modified student university. By Calvin's day the original four nations had increased to five, namely, France, Berry, Touraine, Aquitaine, and Germany. Bourges came to the forefront of the French provincial law universities with the call of Andrea Alciati, the famous Italian jurisconsult, to its faculty by Marguérite d'Angoulême, duchess of Berry, in 1529. She had become queen of Navarre and duchess of Berry, and thus protectress of the University of Bourges, in 1527. It was the fame Alciati had previously won at the University of Avignon that gained him the call to Bourges, where he taught for five years. The reputation of Bourges was further buttressed by the presence there, with interruptions, of Jacques Cujas between the years 1555 and 1590. Cujas, whose career extended beyond Calvin's lifetime into the period of the Wars of Religion, dealt with the Roman law within the broadest understanding of Latin and Greek classical authors and institutions, laying aside the amassed glosses of the ignorant commentators of the past. In this he was perfecting the method already initiated by his predecessor, Alciati.

Paris again (1531–32). Calvin spent nearly a year in his second sojourn in Paris. Later in this essay we examine the details of this period of his life. Here it will suffice to mention a new educational force that came on the scene at the University of Paris in 1529. The dominant and very reactionary force at Paris was the Sorbonne—the faculty of theology—whose power was increased in 1525–26 by the tragic absence of King Francis I, prisoner at Madrid after the defeat at Pavia. The Paris theological faculty mounted an all-out campaign to extirpate all reform tendencies. At the prompting of Guillaume Budé, whose career will be examined shortly, the king appointed five royal lecturers, the nucleus of what was to become eventually the Collège de France. This was in 1530. As Professor Hugo states in our study of Calvin's Seneca commentary:

> these men commenced their classes in various buildings of the University of Paris, but the University had no authority over them. They were appointed by the King and paid by the King. They taught under the direct personal protection of the sovereign. The avowed purpose of their appointment was to counteract the bigoted spirit which then dominated the Faculty of Theology . . . and through that strong faculty, all the rest of the University. The five men embodied the spirit of independent academic teaching and free scientific research, unfettered by the arbitrary decrees of an all-powerful Theological Faculty. The lectures were free, the choice of courses was free, the whole spirit of the enterprise was a spirit of freedom. The very subjects, Greek and Hebrew, were revolutionary for those days (although cities like Alcalà, Oxford and Louvain had already taken the lead in this), and were regarded by the Paris theologians as dangerous in the extreme. The theologians smelt Lutheranism, and they did not hesitate to say so; but neither the King nor his chosen band of professors heeded such talk, and the institution grew apace, attracting students from far and wide.[5]

It was to the lectures of Pierre Danès, eminent Hellenist, that Calvin confessed he was attracted. During the plague months of September–October 1531 Calvin took refuge in suburban Chaillot, later returning to lodgings in the Collège Fortet (until the spring of 1532?).

Six Teachers

Having looked briefly at the educational institutions at which John Calvin took his university training, let us look at some of the teachers who, either by Calvin's later admission or by later evidence, had a share in his intellectual formation. There is an element of the arbitrary in the list of six about to be proposed, for Calvin was, if anything, more

5. *Comm. Sen. De Clem.,* 3*–4*.

formed by his reading than by direct teaching. In terms of influences on his first important literary effort, the Seneca commentary, I have elsewhere discussed the two modern "pillars"—Erasmus and Budé. Only one of them, Budé, will be included among Calvin's "teachers," although Budé's instruction of the young Calvin was more that of a friend and an author than of a pedagogue. The others—Mathurin Cordier, Pierre de l'Estoile, Melchior Wolmar, Andrea Alciati, and Pierre Danès—actually taught Calvin in an academic setting, although in some cases for a very brief time. When we come to the two teachers of law, de l'Estoile and Alciati, the history of medieval legal instruction will be briefly surveyed to illuminate the marked contrast between the two men.

Mathurin Cordier (middle to end of 1523). In his *Commentary on First Thessalonians* (1550), Calvin has left the memorial of a grateful pupil at the beginning of his university studies for a beloved teacher:

> It is fitting that you also should have a part in my labors, for it was under your guidance that I entered on a course of studies, and made progress at least to the extent of being of some benefit to the Church of God. When my father sent me as a boy to Paris, I had done only the rudiments of Latin. For a short time, however, you were an instructor sent to me by God to teach me the true method of learning, so that I might afterwards be a little more proficient. You presided over the first class in the most estimable way. You saw, however, that pupils who had been trained ambitiously by other teachers produced mere show and nothing of worth, which meant that you had to train them all over again. In that year, therefore, you came down to the fourth class, since you were tired of having this trouble. This, at any rate, was your intention, but for me it was a singular kindness of God that I happened to have a propitious beginning to my studies. Although I was permitted to enjoy this for only a brief period, because we were soon advanced in our studies by an unenlightened individual, who regulated our course as his own choice or rather fancy led him, yet I received such help afterwards from your instruction that it is with good reason that I acknowledge such progress as I have made to be due to you. It was my desire to testify to posterity that, if they derive any profit from my writings, they should know that to some extent you are responsible for them.[6]

No better teacher could have been found for the young Calvin who, at the time he was sent to Paris by his father to do the arts course in preparation for theology, "had done only the rudiments of Latin." For Cordier had one passion: the proper preparation of youth in the Latin language. Almost all the books he published were written to this end:

6. John Calvin, *The Epistles of Paul the Apostle to the Romans and to the Thessalonians*, trans. by Ross MacKenzie, ed. by David W. Torrance and Thomas F. Torrance (Grand Rapids: Eerdmans, 1961), 331.

for well over a hundred years his *Grammatica Latina* went through successive editions. He knew that all subsequent education must rest on the foundation laid in the early years.

Born in 1479, he began his teaching career in Paris (1513) at the Collège de la Marche where, as we have seen, Calvin aged fourteen years presented himself in the fall of 1523; thereafter Cordier transferred to the Collège de Navarre. Brief as Calvin's period of study under Cordier was—no more than four months at the most—it was decisive, for the groundwork for Calvin's consummate Latin style was then laid. Cordier was subsequently converted to Protestantism by his close friend the printer Robert Estienne. He served as regent at Nevers (1534–36) and at Bordeaux, coming thereafter to Geneva in 1536 (1537?) to work with Antoine Saunier in the school (reconstituted when the Reform was accepted at Geneva in May 1536). Both men were exiled in 1538, a fact we discuss later in this essay. After 1545 Cordier taught in Lausanne, returning thence to Geneva at age eighty, after two previous unsuccessful attempts by Calvin to call him back in 1541 and 1545. Subsequently we note how some of Mathurin Cordier's pedagogical views clearly found their way into Calvin's plan for the Geneva schools (1559).

Calvin's transfer from the Collège de la Marche to the Collège de Montaigu brought him under teachers who, with one exception, go unmentioned. Attempts to prove his instruction at the hands of such theological luminaries as the nominalist Scot John Major have been inconclusive. On this period of Calvin's life, the Roman Catholic Alexandre Ganoczy discounts any extensive scholastic theological education. Certainly, the first edition of the *Institutes* written in 1535 reveals no sign of the impact of such teachers. Calvin was, after all, an arts student at this time.

It was in 1528 that Calvin's future plans were altered, as we have already noted, by Gérard Calvin's decision. To quote Calvin's clearest testimony from the preface to his *Commentary on the Psalms* (1555):

> From my early childhood
> My father had destined me
> For theology:
> But after a time,
> Having considered that the knowledge of the law
> Commonly enriches those who follow it,
> This hope suddenly made him change his mind.
> That was the reason
> I was withdrawn
> From the study of philosophy
> And was put into the study of law,
> To which, although in obedience to my father,

> I tried to apply myself faithfully,
> God nevertheless by his secret providence
> Finally made me turn
> In another direction.[7]

Excursus on the teaching of law in the Middle Ages. Before, however, we attempt to follow the fortunes of John Calvin as he transferred, in 1528, from Paris to the University of Orléans, after receiving the licentiate in arts, we review briefly the evolution of legal education in the previous five hundred years, for the upheaval in legal instruction that occurred in the midst of Calvin's course of studies was as fateful for the shaping of his theology as any single aspect of his education.[8]

Before the great Irnerius made his impact on the University of Bologna in the early twelfth century, law had been taught within the framework of the Seven Liberal Arts by dividing rhetoric into three branches (demonstrative, deliberative, and judicial). Law was taught under judicial rhetoric, and thus was closely allied to the study of literature, including *dictamen* or the art of composition, especially letter writing. Thus early medieval law teaching was primarily literary or philosophical.

Bologna, especially under Irnerius, effected a revolution in legal education. Heretofore, of the three divisions of Justinian's *Corpus Juris Civilis,* only the *Institutes* and the *Codex* were studied. The *Digest* now came to the forefront, comprising the responses of the great classical jurists who alone revealed fairly the spirit of Roman law. Thus for the first time in the medieval epoch the whole of Roman law was studied in a closer, more critical way with particular attention to the text. The result was the development of legal studies as a separate and highly technical department of medieval university education, to which was attracted a class of more mature and prosperous students bent on the pursuit of knowledge of direct benefit in political and commercial circles.

For the next century and a half, Irnerius' successors—the glossators Rogerius, Placentius, Azo, and Hugolinus—carried on the tradition, working at the improvement of the basic text of the *Corpus* and expounding the meaning of Roman law. With the Guelf revolutions in the mid-thirteenth century in the Lombard cities of northern Italy, including Bologna, the fortunes of the doctors of law declined. The Irnerian school had flourished in an aristocratic setting. The importance of the learned jurisconsults was now in eclipse, and their place was taken by a scholastic glossator tradition. Accursius, the initiator of these glossators, treated the text and its accumulated glosses as of equal authority. His epigonoi, to use Rashdall's phrase, busied "themselves more with

---

7. Cf. *Piety 1978,* 30–31.
8. Our summary is based on Rashdall, *The Universities of Europe in the Middle Ages.*

this gloss than with the text. Instead of trying really to develop the meaning of the text, they aimed at a tediously exhaustive recapitulation and criticism of all the glosses and comments they could collect. . . . They lost sight of the end and aim of their work, which consequently became more and more stagnant and pedantic" [1.256].

Thus in the latter Middle Ages Accursius' successors, glossators like Bartolus of Sassoferrato, were highly regarded. They were practical scholars who "adapted Roman law to the needs and practice of their own time" [1.258]. It was at this low point in the scientific study of Roman law that the young Calvin came to the University of Orléans to sit under the renowned but conservative teacher, Pierre de l'Estoile. New life had already begun to stir in Italy under Politian in the fifteenth century, who considered Roman law a branch of Roman literature and connected it with the ancient institutions and history. However, this new trend had not reached Orléans.

Pierre de l'Estoile (1528–29; 1532–33?). In his preface to the *Antapologia* of Nicolas du Chemin (Calvin's first published piece), John Calvin shows his high regard for his professor of law at the University of Orléans: he is a man "endowed with such sharpness of wit, such industry and finally also with such skill in the law, that he has without question won preeminence over all his contemporaries."[9] Calvin also pays tribute to his moral qualities: "de l'Estoile is a man occupied with serious business, who is in this case upheld by his confidence in the truth, and is unwilling to waste effort on utterly insignificant matters."[10] We return later to the quarrel that brought forth the *Antapologia*.

Pierre de l'Estoile was a native of Orléans, born around 1480. He undertook the teaching of law at the university in 1512 and was considered by many the foremost jurisconsult in France in his day.[11] He was a conservative in both his teaching of law and his religious views. On the death of his wife, he was ordained to the priesthood and became vicar general to the diocese of Orléans. It was in this capacity that he represented his bishop at the Provincial Council of Sens, which met in 1528 at the Paris Church of Grands-Augustins. This council under the presidency of Cardinal Antoine du Prat, the king's chancellor, took draconian measures against the Lutheran "heresy" as well as against the

9. Nicolas Duchemin, *Antapologia adversus Aurelii Albucii defensionem pro And. Alciatio contra Petrum Stellum* . . . (Parisiis: Ex Officiana G. Morrhii, 1531). The quotation is actually from a letter Calvin sent to François de Connan telling him about the preface. See Aimé-Louis Herminjard, ed., *Correspondance des Réformateurs dans les pays de langue française*, 9 vols. (Genève: H. Georg, 1866–97), tome 2, p. 316, lines 7–10. For an accessible outline of the text, see Quirinus Breen, *John Calvin: A Study in French Humanism*, 2nd ed. (New York: Archon Books, 1968), 54.

10. See Breen, *John Calvin*, 53–54.

11. François Wendel, *Calvin, Sources et évolution de sa pensée religieuse*, 2d ed. (Genève: Labor et Rides, 1985), 8, note 17.

means by which it was being spread in France, the circulation of the
French Bible. Translators, printers, publishers, and readers of the
French Bible were proscribed. Yet, on the other hand, the council endeavored to further the needed reform of the church: nonresident cu-
rates, clerical concubinage, the abuse of excommunication, disruptive
popular piety, and the needed purification of preaching all came under
their scrutiny.

We obviously cannot attribute to de l'Estoile's influence (Calvin sat
under him for at least a year and a half and possibly longer) any of
Calvin's later zeal for the evangelical party, but he doubtless by character and precept contributed to the more conservative side of Calvin's
view of law and institutions. His close and careful attention to detail
and his intelligence must have left its mark on the young law student.

Andrea Alciati (autumn 1529–end of 1530). After John Calvin had
been studying Roman law for about a year and a half under Pierre de
l'Estoile at Orléans, reports came of a brilliant lecturer at the neighbor-
ing University of Bourges, the famous Milanese jurisconsult Andrea Alciati. A migration of some law students from Orléans to Bourges occurred in the fall of 1529, including Calvin and a number of his close
friends. Beginning with his sojourn at the University of Avignon, Alciati
made a meteoric rise into the legal heavens; his five subsequent years
at Bourges were followed by professorships at Milan, Bologna, and Ferrara, until his death in 1550. Alciati dealt a deathblow to the traditional
school of the glossators who, as we have seen, had determined the character of legal education for a long time. By viewing Roman law within
the larger context of Latin language, literature, and history, Alciati
brought a new humanistic method to the obscure passages of the *Corpus*. In this he was but carrying on a movement that had, as we have
seen, begun in the previous century with Politian. And his method was
not uniquely practiced by him, for the great Guillaume Budé, as we
shall subsequently see, had for some time been studying classical institutions and annotating the *Pandects* on the broadest cultural base.

Nevertheless, this vain and pompous Italian made a mark on Calvin,
who, though he detested the Milanese's bombast and aspersions
against the beloved de l'Estoile, respected his scholarship. In this positive judgment of Alciati, he was in agreement with his friend Pierre
Daniel and with the great Erasmus himself.

These legal mentors of Calvin were tied together by what may be
called a negative bond: Alciati had been caught in the act of plagiariz-
ing from Budé's writings, by none other than Pierre de l'Estoile himself.
In a difficult position, Alciati tried "to defend himself by publishing an
Apologia in the name of one of his students, Albuzio." This interchange
aroused not only the offended loyalties of former students but also na-
tionalist honor. A friend and fellow student of Calvin, Nicolas du

Chemin, wrote a defense of his old teacher, de l'Estoile, against Alciati in 1529. This *Antapologia* (as it was titled) was not published until 1531, with a preface by Calvin and the latter's help in seeing the book through the press. It is in this prefatory letter that both his appreciation of de l'Estoile (already quoted) and his judgment of Alciati are printed. Of Alciati, his young pupil wrote that in the *Antapologia* the Italian "has been attacked with justice in the first place, and further also with modesty and truthfulness, and not without the deference he deserves." Scattered throughout the *Commentary on Seneca's De Clementia*, published in the spring of 1532 but obviously begun during the sojourn at Bourges (1530?), are evidences of Alciati's influence on the young Calvin. Most striking perhaps is the general impact of Alciati's search for principles in Roman history, his linking of legislation, customs, and institutions of the ancient classical world. Yet we cannot lay this influence fully at Alciati's door, for Calvin drew much more substance from Budé, as will be shown. One passage of the commentary in particular shows Calvin's pique at Alciati's opposition to Pierre de l'Estoile. Yet the idea of a commentary that drew broadly on classical antiquity to adumbrate an ancient text still influential in the sixteenth century may have come from listening to Alciati's lectures.

Melchior Wolmar (end of 1530–end of February 1531). The internal evidence of the Seneca commentary discloses that Calvin's humanistic education was in 1532 deficient in the study of Greek; the few direct quotations in Greek are imperfect, and the young author leans heavily on known Latin translations of such Greek authors as he was citing in the commentary. This conclusion is borne out by such external evidence as has come down to us. In this early period Calvin twice undertook a brief effort to learn Greek. His first attempt took place probably in the short period (three months or less?) at the beginning of 1531, under the tutelage of Melchior Wolmar. Let us look first at Calvin's own estimate of this man's influence on him, expressed in the dedication of his *Commentary on Second Corinthians*. After apologizing for his long silence Calvin offers this commentary "as fair compensation" for his "past neglect"; he remembers in moving language the long friendship and its beginning sixteen years before at Bourges.

> First, I remember how faithfully you have cultivated and strengthened the friendship between us which had its first beginnings so long ago, how generous you have been in putting yourself and your services at my disposal, whenever you found an opportunity of giving proof of your friendship, how assiduously you offered your help in promoting my advancement, although my calling at the time prevented me from accepting it. But the main reason has been my recollection how, the first time my father sent me to study civil law, it was at your instigation and under your tuition that I also took up the study of Greek, of which you were at that

time a most distinguished teacher. It was not your fault that I did not make greater progress. In your kindness you would have been ready to lend me a helping hand till I had completed the course, had not my father's death called me away when I was just starting. Nevertheless my indebtedness to you for this is still great for you gave me a good grounding in the rudiments of the language and that was of great help to me later on. And so I could not rest content without leaving to posterity some token of my gratitude to you, and at the same time showing you yourself that your labors with me have borne some fruit.[12]

Melchior Wolmar was born in Rothweil in 1496; he succeeded his uncle Michael Röttli as principal of a Latin school at Berne in 1515. After serving as a schoolmaster in Fribourg (Switzerland, 1519), in 1521 he went to Paris, where he studied Greek under Glareanus and Nicolas Bérauld. In 1523 he published his annotations on two books of Homer's *Iliad*. Of one hundred candidates for the licentiate in arts at Paris he ranked number one. According to Bulaeus (6.963), one historian of the University of Paris, despite this brilliant beginning, his freely expressed religious opinions forced him to leave Paris. About 1527 he realized "his supreme happiness in the education of the young" by founding a pensionnat in the city of Orléans. A letter of Calvin to his friend Francis Daniel dated 6 September 1530 indicates that Wolmar was at that time visiting Daniel at Bourges. On the basis of other evidence, Herminjard, the editor of the correspondence of the Reformers of French-language countries, thinks Wolmar did not actually settle in Bourges until the end of 1530. We can surmise from this that Calvin may have been introduced to him earlier in Orléans, but serious study under Wolmar must have been confined to a brief interval between December 1530 and the end of February 1531. Theodore Beza also studied Greek under him.

After his stay at Bourges, Wolmar continued his education at Tübingen, where he was awarded the degree of Doctor of Law, immediately thereafter being named to the chair of jurisprudence in that university. Wolmar, while technically a professor of law, continued to pursue his first love, Hellenism, although he published nothing further save a letter to Blauer on the Greek grammars in use in the schools.

The tribute to Wolmar already quoted indicates clearly Calvin's indebtedness to his first Greek teacher: not only did Wolmar lay the foundation for Calvin's knowledge of Greek; he inspired him to undertake that study. Although Calvin still had a long way to go to reach the consummate linguistic skill displayed in the New Testament commentaries, a beginning had been made.

12. John Calvin, *The Second Epistle of Paul the Apostle to the Corinthians and the Epistles to Timothy, Titus and Philemon*, trans. by T. A. Smail, ed. by David W. Torrance and Thomas F. Torrance (Grand Rapids: Eerdmans, 1964), 1.

Guillaume Budé (1531–32?). The literary dependence of Calvin on Guillaume Budé has been extensively examined for the works of Calvin written after his conversion in Josef Bohatec's classic study *Budé und Calvin.*[13] In my work on the Seneca commentary I have tried to perform a similar task on that first book of Calvin. The details of these published studies will therefore not be duplicated in this essay. Rather, Budé's career will be lightly sketched and some conclusions offered on when Calvin probably came under his influence.

Guillaume Budé was born in Paris in 1467. It was not until he was twenty-four years of age that he began to find himself when he was led to undertake with passion the study of the Greek language under the instruction of Jean Lascaris. This concentration on Greek made him an elegant stylist in his Greek correspondence but a crabbed and obscure Latinist, in which language most of his writings were of course composed. His was not the accustomed career of a university professor, but rather of a man of letters and civil servant. Successive offices he held included secretary to King Francis I, master of requests, master of the royal library (actually, founder, so to speak, of what is now the Bibliothèque Nationale), provost of merchants, ambassador to Pope Leo X, etc. He was the first great modern economic historian, his learned work *De Asse* being a study of ancient classical coinage and measures. His *Annotations on the Pandects,* while only a partial annotation of the corpus of Roman law, brought immense historical, literary, and philosophical erudition to the understanding of the text of Justinian. His *Commentaries on the Greek Language* provided a sort of nucleus for the later Greek lexicon of Stephanus. He also wrote on French law and edited a number of classical texts. Elsewhere I have shown how these writings were tapped by Calvin in the Seneca commentary. His *Institution du Prince,* posthumously published, was one of the most famous guides to statecraft in this period. Instinct with classical wisdom and history, it endeavored to raise the political tone of the French monarchy and pled the cause of humane letters with the sovereign.

It was this man, no university professor himself, who planned and persuaded Francis I to establish four lectureships at the University of Paris, to which we have already referred, and which eventuated in the prestigious Collège de France. These champions of humanistic and scriptural learning posed a terrible threat to the tight control of the university exercised by the theological faculty.

When did Calvin come under the spell of Budé? In our introduction to the Seneca commentary, my colleague Professor Hugo states:

---

13. Josef Bohatec, *Budé und Calvin* (Wien: Verlag Hermann Böhlaus Nachf, 1950).

> Calvin had had the privilege, some years previously, of moving in those circles of Parisian society in which the great Budé, foremost Hellenist of France and Counsellor to the King, was a prominent figure.[14]

While the phrase "some years previously" could be taken to refer to the time of Calvin's first sojourn in Paris (1523–27), this early time seems unlikely. We are left, presumably, with either the short Parisian stay of March 1531 or the longer one of June 1531 to mid-May 1532, but I have found no precise details on this. Calvin's familiarity with the Cop family in Paris is sometimes extended to include a personal acquaintance with Budé. The internal evidence of the Seneca commentary suggests, by early April 1532, an extensive knowledge of Budé's writings. Calvin may have made the acquaintance of some of them (the *De Asse* or the *Annotations on the Pandects*?) when he was sitting under Alciati in Bourges, if Quirinus Breen's interpretation of the evidence in du Chemin's *Antapologia* is correct.[15] Alciati and Budé were engaged in a similar enterprise, and, as we have stated, the Italian had borrowed material from the Frenchman; also Budé is known to have recommended Alciati as a teacher to several students.

In the Seneca commentary Calvin calls Budé "the first ornament and pillar of literature," and mentions him by name seven times. I have traced at least ninety passages in Calvin's commentary that clearly or probably rest on Budé. The young Calvin depended chiefly on Budé for the explanation of legal terms, Roman institutions, political philosophy, and literature. Unquestionably, Budé was quantitatively speaking the most impressively influential of all of Calvin's teachers.

And the closeness of Calvin to the Budé household persisted even after Budé's death in 1540. His widow, with three of his sons (Jean-Louis, Mathieu, and Jean), embraced the Reformed faith and settled in Geneva. Jean-Louis became professor of oriental languages at Geneva and published a French translation of the Psalms (1551). Mathieu became learned in Hebrew. Jean rose rapidly among the magistrates of Geneva, and went as ambassador with Guillaume Farel and Theodore Beza to the German princes to plead the cause of the French Calvinists. He translated into French Calvin's *Commentary on Daniel* (1552).

Pierre Danès (late fall 1531?). The final teacher of Calvin among the six we have chosen to look at, Pierre Danès, was one of the royal readers, appointed to the chair of Greek by Francis I in 1530. He was born in Paris in 1497 and studied under Budé and Lascaris. A foremost French Hellenist, he taught many who became famous scholars. Later in life he was sent by Francis I to the Council of Trent (1546), and was named by his successor Henry I as bishop of LaVaur (1557) and tutor

14. *Comm. Sen. De Clem.*, 4*.
15. See Breen, *John Calvin*, 44ff.

to the dauphin. Before his death in Paris in 1577 he had resigned his episcopal see. Herminjard[16] states that Danès' career as royal reader began *inter alia* with lectures on Aristotle's *Ethics*, held in 1530 at the Collège de Cambrai.

We know from Calvin's letter of 27 June 1531 to Francis Daniel that he intended to attend Danès' lectures. My colleague, Dr. Hugo, has shown, however, that Calvin—because of the summer holiday, the outbreak of the plague in the fall of 1531 (when he took refuge in suburban Chaillot), and his concentration on the Seneca commentary—could not have attended very many if any at all of Danès' lectures or those of any other royal reader. Thus, Calvin was for a second time frustrated in his attempt to study Greek. We cannot then, either from external evidence or from the internal evidence of the Seneca commentary, discern the effect of Danès on Calvin. We may therefore have literally to subtract him from the roll of Calvin's actual teachers. Yet such contact as Calvin had with Danès and the other royal readers was to have a definite influence on his later educational plans at Geneva.

Summary. What may we at this point say in summary concerning these six men? (1) Calvin studied under most of them for a very short time, but at a critical time both in his own life and in history; (2) almost all these men were educational innovators whose ideas contributed both to Calvin's career as a reformer, and, as we have already suggested, to his educational philosophy; (3) humanists or jurisconsults or both, they assured that law was to have a lasting influence on the shape of Calvin's thought and on the institutions he helped found; (4) some of them, or their families, found their way to Protestant lands, notably Switzerland, and were subsequently associated with the Reform.

Calvin's Educational Plan for Geneva of 1559 in Light of His Own Humanist Formation

The fortunes of education in Geneva (1536–59). Before looking specifically at Calvin's 1559 plan for the Geneva schools, it may be helpful to look briefly at the fortunes of the schools of Geneva as discussed in Doumergue's exhaustive biography of Calvin.[17] Space does not permit us to set forth in detail the earlier plan as printed in 1538.

The pre-Reformation Genevese school of Versonnex, which had lasted for 106 years, was replaced with the coming of the Reformation to Geneva in May 1536 by the Collège de Rive, approved by the general council on 21 May of that year. Antoine Saunier, one of the Geneva ministers, was named the first rector, to be assisted by Calvin's old

---

16. Herminjard, *Correspondance des Réformateurs,* 2:348.

17. E. Doumergue, *Jean Calvin—Les hommes et les choses de son temps,* 7 vols. (Lausanne, 1899–1928).

Latin teacher Mathurin Cordier and others. With the banishment of Calvin from Geneva in April 1538, the school nevertheless remained under the domination of those friendly to Calvin. Predictably, however, on 26 September the anti-Calvin forces banished two younger teachers, and then on 26 December Saunier and Cordier were exiled from Geneva. After Calvin's restoration to Geneva on 13 September 1541, he undertook to rebuild what had fallen into disrepair. As already noted, Calvin endeavored to call Cordier back to head his school in that year and again in 1545, but mainly financial problems with the city council seem to have blocked his plans. The Collège de Rive was hardly a great success: the period under Sebastian Castellio (1542–44) ended in the exile of Castellio after a conflict concerning the Song of Songs. Under Louis Enoch (1550–57) the school had vigorous direction, but by a principal who was rough and given to harsh treatment of the children. Furthermore, the location of the school and the buildings were very unhealthful.

The tide did not begin to turn until the January 1559 exodus of ministers and teachers from Lausanne, brought on by a quarrel over the independent right of the church to excommunicate, between the pastors and the city government (supported by Berne). Geneva was suddenly given a boost by this "brain drain" from her neighbor city to the east. Theodore Beza and Mathurin Cordier, among others, now settled in Geneva. Cordier was now a man of eighty, but he assisted in planning the educational reform.

The Académie, as it was called, was organized into two departments, the *schola publica* and the *schola privata*. The former was staffed by three professors from Lausanne: François Berauld in Greek, Jean Tagaut in philosophy, and Antoine Chevalier in Hebrew, with Theodore Beza as rector. The lower department, the *schola privata,* divided into seven grades each with a regent, was headed by Jean Randon as principal. The school was inaugurated at Saint-Pierre on 5 June 1559. Thus began the most potent educational force for the Reformed faith, destined to produce leaders and pastors not only for Geneva but for Protestant France and for the other countries that accepted Calvinism.

The curriculum of the schola privata. You will find in my *Analysis of the Institutes*[18] a summary of the plan of studies that you may peruse at your leisure. Note, however, the following features: (1) the instruction was trilingual, with Latin and French from the start and Greek introduced in the fourth year; (2) great emphasis was laid on the careful study of the Greek and Latin classics; (3) from the beginning grammatical drill, ear training through oral reading, and writing were used in concert; (4) translation and retranslation, oral and written, between

18. The plan is found in F. L. Battles, *Analysis* (1976 ed.), available at The H. H. Meeter Center for Calvin Studies, Grand Rapids, Mich.

Latin and French and subsequently Greek, were stressed; (5) the ancient medieval disputation and the Renaissance declamation were both put to use in the teaching of the higher forms; (6) while the content seemed to be predominantly drawn from secular literature, this was framed by Christian prayer, psalm singing, and catechesis in the lower grades and by the study of the New Testament in Greek in the higher grades. The parish sermons of Sunday and Wednesday were also explicitly drawn into the curriculum.

Unquestionably, this regimen is the fruit not only of the earlier Strasbourg and Nîmes curricula, as is commonly asserted, but also exemplifies Cordier's pedagogical views and Calvin's reflection on his own youthful educational experience as well as the frustrating trial and error of 1536–59 in Geneva itself. In short, the program is typical of Christian humanism in the Erasmian tradition, with a special Calvinian stamp.

The curriculum of the schola publica. Again, the program of the five public professors is set forth for one to study. From September 1536 Calvin himself had lectured assiduously, thereby producing commentaries on almost the entire Bible; and some of his colleagues had assisted in this higher public instruction. Thus, the two levels of instruction at Geneva had long been recognized. With the school reform of 1559, however, a coherent scheme of public lectures by five professors offered an integrated curriculum of classics and Christian theology.

Doumergue has remarked, and you have by this time probably noted for yourself, that the public professors of Geneva are molded after the royal readers of Paris, contact with whom had, as we have seen, marked the end of Calvin's formal education in 1532.

The educational formation prescribed by Calvin in the Leges Academicae compared with his own formation. The most striking contrast between Calvin's own youthful experience and what he hoped would be the experience of the students of Geneva was the deliberate deep integration of the Reformed faith and practice into a strong classical curriculum of the humanist type as over against Calvin's own evangelical conversion, which had come only after his formal education and with great struggle. Compare also Calvin's two premature attempts to learn the Greek language with the orderly introduction of that tongue to pupils at age eleven or twelve. Calvin himself probably did not master Greek until he was twenty-five years of age. He realized how crucial a knowledge of Greek was for the understanding of the New Testament. And his fluency in Hebrew probably came to him still later than that in Greek; the typical Geneva student, on the other hand, was to undertake the study of Hebrew, if he moved without delay from the *schola privata* to the *schola publica,* in his middle teens. Even instruction in French was more ordered and supported by the early juxtaposition of Latin in the Geneva plan, while Calvin's own introduction as a child to his mother tongue must have lacked such a solid grammatical base. His long years of writing and speaking in French had established canons for modern French prose, and these are reflected in his curricular principles here expounded.

The late medieval arts curriculum to which he had been subjected at the Collège de Montaigu was here transformed into a much broader humanist study of antiquity that clearly mirrors, even in the elementary grades, the teaching of Budé and Alciati. Calvin's legal education thus gave him more of a grasp of the ancient world out of which the Christian faith had emerged than any merely theological curriculum could give. And the lasting stamp of his legal studies is on the ordered yet unlegalistic grasp of both the Scriptures and the laws of nations. Finally, Calvin's long pilgrimage—for his faith was not fully formed at his conversion (as many like to think) but only at the end of his life—led him almost impatiently to telescope into an all-too-brief space the planned formation of his Christian scholars. With all his theological emphasis on predestination and the grace of God in Christ as the sole shaper of our lives, yet he also strove mightily, through a carefully prescribed educational process, to lay a right ground for the working of that divine grace and for the personal acceptance of the gospel. Such was the Reformed Christian humanism of John Calvin.

2

The Sources of Calvin's
Seneca Commentary[1]

There are in the *Institutio Christianae Religionis* many clear echoes of Calvin's earlier concentration on classical antiquity. The heavy dependence on Cicero's philosophical treatises in *Institutio* 1.1–4 is well known; scattered throughout Calvin's master work are quotations from the chief Latin and Greek writers. Furthermore, his very vocabulary and style are steeped in ancient culture. Yet there are two passages that more than any others seem to sum up his verdict, after conversion, on classical culture and his own humanist studies.

The first of these, at *Institutio* 2.2.15, eloquently asserts the Spirit of God to be the sole fountain of truth and calls on humankind not to despise the truth wherever it shall be found; Calvin then turns to the sciences and the arts themselves:

> What then? Shall we deny that the truth shone upon the ancient jurists who established civic order and discipline with such great equity? Shall we say that the philosophers were blind in their fine observation and artful description of nature? Shall we say that those men were devoid of understanding who conceived the art of disputation and taught us to speak reasonably? Shall we say that they are insane who developed medicine, devoting their labor to our benefit? What shall we say of all the mathematical sciences? Shall we consider them the ravings of madmen? No, we cannot read the writings of the ancients on these subjects without great admiration. We marvel at them because we are compelled to recognize how pre-eminent they are. But shall we count anything praiseworthy or noble without recognizing at the same time that it comes from God? Let us be ashamed of such ingratitude, into which not even the pagan poets fell, for they confessed that the gods had invented philosophy, laws, and all useful arts. Those men whom Scripture calls "natural men" were, indeed, sharp and penetrating in their investigation of things below. Let us, accordingly, learn by their example how many gifts the Lord left to human nature even after it was despoiled of its true good.

1. From G. E. Duffield, ed., *John Calvin* (Grand Rapids: Eerdmans, 1966), 38–66.

In this simple catalogue is the sum of Calvin's preparatory studies, and of the content of the commentary on Seneca's *De Clementia,* his first published treatise. Law, philosophy, rhetoric, medicine, mathematics, and poetry are mentioned by name. He could well have added history.

He had studied the *Pandects* and its chief commentators, traditional and contemporary, including what Budaeus called "the triumvirate"— Alciatus, Zasius, and Budaeus.[2] He had become reasonably well versed in ancient philosophy through Cicero and Seneca, Plutarch, and other writers. Yet at this time—in the midst of his humanist studies at Paris[3]—he had not read Plato[4] and Aristotle[5] in Greek. He had laid a foundation in rhetoric and dialectic as evidenced not only by his use of technical terms but also by his perceptive criticisms of Seneca's style and thought, and by his own excellent Latin style as well. His interest in and sympathy for medicine are reflected in the pages of the commentary,[6] and he had had occasion to compare various ancient views of the nature of the human body and soul.[7] Even mathematics is represented by a reference to Euclid,[8] and other useful arts, such as agriculture[9] and warfare,[10] are not unmentioned. The poets are copi-

2. Budaeus, Epist. to Claudius Contiuncula ICtus, 16 August 1518, *Opera* (Basel, 1557), 261–62. There have been two recent studies of Calvin's background of classical humanism. Josef Bohatec in *Budé und Calvin* showed Calvin's debt to the French humanist, but did not deal in detail with the impact of Budaeus on the Seneca commentary. André Malan Hugo in *Calvijn en Seneca* (Groningen: J. B. Wolters, 1957) surveyed the extent of Calvin's classical learning, his work on the text of Seneca, and the achievement of the commentary itself, but did not examine fully Calvin's sources. My own studies began independently but I am now working with Dr. Hugo on a new edition of Calvin's Seneca commentary.

3. Calvin's studies before conversion fall into four periods: (1)University of Paris (1523–28)—arts; (2) University of Orléans (1528–29)—law; (3) University of Bourges (1529–31)—law; (4) under the royal readers at Paris (1531–33)—literature.

4. Plato is mentioned approximately twenty times in the commentary; of these references, at least four come through Cicero and two through Aulus Gellius. Where Plato is directly quoted (three times) Calvin uses the translation of Marsilius Ficinus. Four references are incorrect. A number of others have been derived from humanistic intermediate sources.

5. Some twenty contexts where Aristotle is mentioned suggest about thirty-two references, many of which are commonplaces frequently mentioned by the humanists to which Calvin had recourse. There is some evidence that Calvin knew and used Theodore of Gaza's translation of the *Problemata,* but the translation of his one direct Latin quotation of *Politics* (3.5.2) has not been identified.

6. *Comm. Sen. De Clem.,* 66 (21:lines 22–24 and note).

7. Ibid., 92 (32).

8. Ibid., 52 (15:line 27 and note).

9. There is also the category of natural science and technology, which must include such miscellaneous matter as notes on Seneca's references to lampreys, to pruning fruit-trees, and to bees as well as to allusions to the habits of animals and such natural phenomena as lightning. The Auctores Rei Rusticae, Varro, Columella, Virgil, Pliny the Elder, Aristotle, and Alexander Aphrodiseus are cited on such points. These references are those of an educated person, familiar with the ancient writers and with contemporary humanist use of them.

10. See note 39.

ously quoted,[11] but always to make some lexical, philosophical, moral, or historical point. The preponderance of Latin over Greek poets gives evidence of Calvin's essentially secondhand knowledge of Greek literature.[12] While his use of Latin literature shows some independence, even here he used, as we shall see, contemporary compilations and commentaries for much of his material. The historians are richly represented: not only had he read with some care the chief Latin writers (notably Suetonius, Tacitus, and Livy) but also the lesser Scriptores Rei Augustae, and was to some extent familiar with the main Greek historians of Rome—Plutarch, Arrian, Herodian, Dio Cassius, and Dio Halicarnassus. However, these last were consulted almost entirely in Latin translations, when references to them were not of secondary derivation.

These writers do not exhaust Calvin's sources, but they suggest the chief authors he had in mind when he penned his tribute to ancient learning. But to stop with this one quotation would give a false impression of Calvin's mature judgment of classical antiquity. The second quotation, from *Institutio* 1.8.1, traces in a phrase or two Calvin's pilgrimage:

> Read Demosthenes or Cicero, read Plato, Aristotle, and others of that tribe. They will, I admit, allure you, delight you, move you, enrapture you in wonderful measure. But betake yourself from them to this sacred reading. Then, in spite of yourself, so deeply will it affect you, so penetrate your heart, so fix itself in your very marrow, that, compared with its deep impressions, such vigor as the orators and philosophers have will nearly vanish. Consequently it is easy to see that the sacred Scriptures, which so far surpass all gifts and graces of human endeavor, breathe something divine.[13]

11. The chief Latin poets used, in descending order of frequency, are Virgil, Ovid, Horace and Juvenal, and Terence. Virgil and Terence are used mainly through the commentaries of Servius and Donatus, respectively.

12. Epist. 2 (1530, Calvin to Franciscus Daniel, *OC*, 10a:3–6) refers to his copy of Homer's *Odyssey*, lent to Charles Sucquet, a Flemish jurisconsult. In the Seneca commentary, Calvin alludes three times to the *Iliad*, quotes it twice in Greek (once with Latin translation); at least two of these references are from Erasmus. The *Odyssey* is quoted in Greek twice, both times from Erasmus' *Adagia;* a third quotation is paralleled from other contemporary proverbial literature. How well did Calvin know Homer at this time? The scattered references to other Greek poets tell the same story.

13. The same idea of the innate superiority of the Scriptures to the writings of pagan philosophers is expressed when Calvin introduces (1539) his short treatise on the Christian life (*Inst.* 3.6–10): "As philosophers have fixed limits of the right and honorable, whence they derive individual duties and the whole company of virtues, so Scripture is not without its own order in this matter, but holds to a most beautiful dispensation, and one much more certain than all the philosophical ones. The only difference is that they, as they were ambitious men, diligently strove to attain an exquisite clarity of order to show the nimbleness of their wit. But the Spirit of God, because he taught without affectation, did not adhere so exactly or continuously to a methodical plan; yet when he lays one down anywhere he hints enough that it is not to be neglected by us."

It is with this divided judgment of the Graeco-Roman world, penned by Calvin for the second Latin edition of the *Institutio,* clearly before us, that we turn to a more detailed examination of his commentary on Seneca's *De Clementia.*

The Two Modern Pillars: Erasmus and Budaeus

Once I penetrated the façade of "74 Latin and 22 Greek Authors," long uncritically attributed to the classical competence of the young Calvin, I realized that the question to answer was not "What Greek or Latin writers did Calvin cite?" but rather "How did he come by these citations?" Just as important as finding out *what* Calvin read was to learn *where* he read it.

Calvin actually suggests, or at least hints, *where* he read. Twice he uses the figure of "pillar" to pay tribute to the chief contemporary and ancient authorities for his commentary. Gulielmus Budaeus (1467–1540) is called "the first ornament and pillar of literature,"[14] while Desiderius Erasmus is named "the second ornament of literature."[15] In another place, Calvin speaks of Seneca as "second only to Cicero a veritable pillar of Roman philosophy and literature (eloquence)."[16] Calvin's preference for Budaeus over Erasmus was not only a reflection of his own national pride, but Budaeus had indeed brought the palm of learning to France.[17]

Erasmus. That he was indebted to Erasmus, nevertheless, Calvin was quick to acknowledge. Erasmus, in Calvin's phrase, had "twice sweated in the arena"[18] in preparing editions of Seneca in 1515 and 1529. The need to correct and supplement Erasmus' work was one reason for choosing to comment on the *De Clementia.* "There are certain things which have escaped the notice of even Erasmus himself . . . and which I say without any ill-will."[19] Although in the body of the commentary Calvin refers to Erasmus by name only five times on textual matters, Dr. A. M. Hugo, with whom I am working on a new edition of the Seneca commentary, has listed some sixty-eight points where Calvin discusses Erasmus' reading in arriving at his own. A reference to Erasmus' use of Virgil is praised as "learned."[20] But at other points Calvin takes issue with Erasmus. For example, against Erasmus' assertion that the word *licentia* has only a bad meaning in classic Latinity,

14. *Comm. Sen. De Clem.,* 114 (42:line 37 and note).
15. Ibid., pref., 6 (ii:line 3, note).
16. Ibid., pref., 10–12 (iii:lines 16–18 and note).
17. Ibid., 116 (42:line 38).
18. Ibid., pref., 6 (ii:lines 2–3).
19. Ibid., pref., 6 (ii:lines 4–5).
20. Ibid., 318 (132:lines 1–2).

Calvin cites instances where it has a good meaning.[21] Even Erasmus' edition of Suetonius draws a small criticism.[22]

Of actual Erasmian sources Calvin mentions the *Adagia* three times,[23] even though there may be as many as twenty-six uses of it. The *Apophthegmata* may have been quoted six times, but not by name. Erasmus' *Panegyric of Philip* is referred to once,[24] but was certainly used at several other points. His *Education of a Christian Prince* (1515–16), drawn from the standard Greek and Roman writers on the princely office (including Seneca's *De Clementia*), doubtless challenged Calvin to comment independently on the Seneca text.[25] No effort has been made to determine what Erasmian editions of classical and patristic writers Calvin used, but in addition to Suetonius he doubtless knew Augustine and other Fathers in Erasmian editions.[26] No scholar of the time could avoid becoming indebted to Erasmus.

There is, on the other hand, some evidence that Calvin, at certain points, studiously avoided using Erasmus. Though the commentary is crammed with proverbial wisdom, it is surprising that so little of it has been drawn from the *Adagia*. It would have been easy for Calvin to turn to this enormous compend for material, but he seldom used it. Of more than passing interest is the fact that, while Calvin's Seneca commentary went virtually unnoticed, it was extensively plagiarized by Gilbertus Cognatus (Gilbert Cousin), who had been Erasmus' secretary from 1530 to 1535, in preparing a supplement to the *Adagia* that was printed much later. That Cognatus could so use it was a tribute to the relatively independent character of Calvin's work as much as to the aphoristic character of Seneca.

Budaeus. When one turns to Budaeus, however, Calvin's dependence gradually emerges. Budaeus is cited by name seven times in the text of the commentary, although only the *Annotationes in Pandectas* and its sequel or continuation are identified. Bohatec's study, *Budé und Calvin*,[27] concentrates mainly on parallels between Budaeus and Calvin's later writings; he refers only a few times to the *De Clementia* commentary. By contrast, in the course of the present investigation

---

21. Ibid., 60 (19:line 3).

22. Ibid., 374 (154:lines 25ff. and note on line 25).

23. Ibid., 46 (13:lines 6ff.), 294 (121:lines 39–40); 350 (144:line 21).

24. Ibid., 102 (36:line 24).

25. See Lester K. Born, ed. and trans., *Education of a Christian Prince by Desiderius Erasmus* (New York: Columbia University Press, 1936; reprinted New York: Octagon Books, 1965), and the introduction in *Comm. Sen. De Clem.*, 100*–114*.

26. Luchesius Smits, *Saint Augustine dans l'Oeuvre de Jean Calvin*, 2 vols. (Assen: Van Gorcum, 1957), 1.201f.

27. Josef Bohatec, *Budé und Calvin*, 406, note 2, lists Calvin's citations of the *De Asse* in the commentaries.

some ninety quotations or clear parallels have been identified. This number far from exhausts Calvin's dependence on Budaeus.

For many of the problems in annotation, Budaeus is Calvin's starting point. To explain the text of Seneca and to provide in a concise manner the necessary background material, some degree of versatility was demanded of the commentator. It is no wonder that the rich learning of Budaeus was unashamedly used by the young Calvin.

The material suggested by Budaeus[28] comes chiefly from two works: first, the *Annotationes in Pandectas,* and its continuation, *Annotationes Reliquae in Pandectas* (called by Calvin, *Annotationes Posteriores*); and, second, the interesting if somewhat miscellaneous treatise on ancient coinage, *De Asse et Partibus eius.* This material may be divided into five main classes: legal terms, Roman institutions and history, political philosophy, philosophy in general, and literature.

(1) *Legal terms.* Budaeus' *Annotationes in Pandectas* is an effort to explain a limited number of technical terms and concepts of Justinian's *Corpus Juris Civilis,* within the broadest sort of humanist framework. In fact, the select passages of the *Pandects* discussed in the *Annotationes* often served as an excuse for extended notes not only on legal terms and institutions, but also on political, theological, philosophical, moral, historical, and other questions. Budaeus' *Annotationes* differed markedly from traditional commentaries on Roman law, although imitated by jurisconsults like Alciatus. To understand Roman law, Budaeus felt, one must immerse oneself in Graeco-Roman history, and it is no wonder that Calvin found this work attractive. Hence, as Calvin came upon legal usages in his text, he turned to Budaeus for assistance.

Such technical terms as *manum iniicere,*[29] *index (indicium),*[30] *fidem praestare,*[31] *hereditatem adire/cernere,*[32] *aestimare litem,*[33] and the like had been copiously discussed by Budaeus, with historical, oratorical, and even poetic parallels from Roman literature. Procedural terms like *deprecatio*[34] and *cognitio*[35] had been similarly treated. Many of Calvin's numerous Ciceronian and other citations actually stem from Budaeus' juridical exegesis.[36] More important, however, than these isolated

---

28. While the editions of Budaeus' works published prior to 1532 were used initially in preparing the present study, references are given to the Paris edition of 1557, since this is fairly complete and more widely available in libraries. References to single works not included therein (e.g., *Commentarii Linguae Graecae*) are to pre-1532 editions. Budaeus' works are subsequently abbreviated as follows: AP, ARP, and DA.

29. AP 81B–82C; cf. *Comm. Sen. De Clem.,* 114 (42:lines 28–29).

30. ARP 309B–310C; cf. *Comm. Sen. De Clem.,* 156 (62:line 16).

31. AP 40C; cf. *Comm. Sen. De Clem.,* 168 (67:lines 29ff.).

32. AP 52C; cf. *Comm. Sen. De Clem.,* 250 (103:line 25).

33. ARP 326; cf. *Comm. Sen. De Clem.,* 378 (157:line 6).

34. AP 87B, 95B; cf. *Comm. Sen. De Clem.,* 378 (157:line 4).

35. ARP 337B; 338B–339A; cf. *Comm. Sen. De Clem.,* 248 (102:line 33).

36. E.g., *Comm. Sen. De Clem.,* 246 (102:line 14 and note), 378 (157:lines 9ff.).

terms is Calvin's grasp of the contrast between *aequum et bonum* and *summum ius*,[37] as expounded by Budaeus,[38] for this concept tempered his critique of Seneca's definition of *clementia*.

(2) *Roman institutions.* Closely related to legal terminology is the copious material on Roman institutions and society, found in the *Annotationes in Pandectas* and the *De Asse*. These two treatises overlap at many points, and Calvin drew from both, often for the same context. To sketch the background of Seneca's essay on the political instruction of the young Nero, Calvin needed a clear conception not only of the early empire, but of the whole course of Roman history. Technical questions on the size of Roman legions,[39] the population of imperial Rome,[40] the political offices of Republic and Empire,[41] and the social classes[42] had to be answered. Fleeting allusions to Actium, Sulla,[43] etc., called for brief notes.

Calvin found statistical material on Roman population and wealth already assembled by Budaeus in the *De Asse*.[44] Budaeus had, in his exposition of select passages in the *Pandects*, dealt at length with the office of dictator,[45] quaestor,[46] centurion,[47] tribune,[48] and the like. But more important, Budaeus demonstrated to Calvin a sound method of historical criticism. Budaeus had painstakingly compared Latin and Greek writers on Roman history and suggested canons of evidence.[49] Calvin, apt pupil that he was, treated critically, with use of Latin and Greek sources, many events of the second triumvirate and of Augustus' reign. However, unlike Budaeus (who was a consummate Hellenist), Calvin depended largely on recent Latin translations of Greek writers, yet not without at least one attempt to check translation.[50]

(3) *Political philosophy.* It was fashionable during the Renaissance for the humanists to write instructive essays for young princes and moving panegyrics for rulers. To prepare these, the ancients were plundered. Besides Erasmus' *Education of a Christian Prince* there is to be

---

37. Ibid., 68–72 (22–23), 270 (111:line 4).
38. AP 1 A–B.
39. DA 124; AP 56C; cf. *Comm. Sen. De Clem.*, 98 (35:lines 10ff.).
40. DA 124; cf. *Comm. Sen. De Clem.*, 122 (46:lines 29ff.).
41. See notes 46–49, below.
42. On social classes, see *Comm. Sen. De Clem.*, 310 (128:lines 3–12), 216 (88:lines 8–37), 122–25 (46:lines 31–47), and 310–13 (128:line 19–129:line 8).
43. On Actium, see *Comm. Sen. De Clem.*, 194 (78:lines 23–26). On Sulla, see *Comm. Sen. De Clem.*, 204–13 (83–86) and 240–43 (99).
44. *Comm. Sen. De Clem.*, 122–25 (46:lines 31ff.), using Jerome's translation of Eusebius, *Chron.*, through Budaeus, *De Asse*, 124.
45. AP 103B, 111B; cf. *Comm. Sen. De Clem.*, 206–8 (84).
46. AP 111–116; cf. *Comm. Sen. De Clem.*, 124–27 (47).
47. AP 54D; cf. *Comm. Sen. De Clem.*, 260–63 (107).
48. Ibid.
49. DA 120, 124–25.
50. E.g., Politianus on Herodian, 140–41.

noted the political teaching of Budaeus in the *Annotationes* and the *De Asse*, even if his posthumously published *L'Institution du Prince* (1547)[51] may not have been known to Calvin in 1532.

Since Calvin had access to a variety of political wisdom in preparing his commentary, one cannot at a particular point always state his source with certainty. But there is good evidence that the Christianized Plutarch of Budaeus, with Platonic, Aristotelian, and Stoic elements (as well as material from Cicero) was determinative in forming Calvin's political philosophy. The Seneca commentary is an important link between Budaeus' ideas in the *Annotationes in Pandectas* and Calvin's fully formed views at the beginning and end of the *Institutio*. Among the themes common to all three works is the following: rulers as ministers of God or as images of God.[52] Budaeus' understanding of the relation of the ruler to the law is carried over, by way of the Seneca commentary, to the *Institutio*.

(4) *Philosophy*. Budaeus was probably Calvin's starting point for certain lines of philosophical inquiry. The nature of the soul and its relationship to the body had engaged Budaeus' attention in both treatises, and he made a particularly detailed study of this subject in the *De Asse*.[53] Calvin quoted at length from Budaeus' own translation of Plutarch's *De Placitis Philosophorum*.[54] For the Stoic concept of *euthymia*, drawn from Democritus, Calvin first turned to Budaeus.[55] While Calvin used Cicero more than any other ancient writer for philosophical material, the Seneca commentary suggests that he was largely dependent on Budaeus for his initial contact with Greek philosophy. In fact, Budaeus' use of Cicero was doubtless instructive for the young scholar.

(5) *Literature*. Budaeus taught Calvin the relevance not only of the historians, jurists, and philosophers, to the understanding of life, but also the relevance of the poets and rhetoricians. Budaeus had mined the ancient commentators before him. Thus Calvin came to the Latin poets not less as a literary critic than as a moralist and philosopher, not blind to their beauty of language, but bent on gaining insight into meaning through a comparative study of their vocabulary, with the assistance of their ancient and latter-day commentators. What seems at first a rather strange and utilitarian application of poetry to exegesis when one reads it in Calvin's Seneca commentary, becomes clear after reading Budaeus' legal commentaries or those of his imitator, Andreas

51. Chapters 9–16, dealing with the place of history in the education of the prince, afford some parallels.
52. See also Erasmus, *Education of a Christian Prince*, 157ff., 171, 191.
53. DA 1 (*Opera*, 15); cf. Philippus Beroaldus, *Comm. Cic. Tusc. Disp.*, 7[a–b] *Comm. Sen. De Clem.*, 102 (36:line 37 and note).
54. *Comm. Sen. De Clem.*, 92 (32:note on line 21).
55. DA 284, 294; AP 281D–282C; cf. *Comm. Sen. De Clem.*, 40 (10:note on line 28).

Alciatus. The practice of careful word study learned early by Calvin served him well in his later career as theologian and scriptural exegete.

Two other works of Budaeus should be mentioned. While not referred to in the commentary, Budaeus' vast *Commentarii Linguae Graecae* (Paris, 1530) has presumably been used in at least five places for Greek parallels. Notable among these is Calvin's discussion of *bona fides*,[56] which undoubtedly reflects Budaeus' extended note on *fides*;[57] Budaeus deals in detail with *pistis/fides* in classical antiquity. Budaeus' *Forensia* (posthumously published) may have been available to Calvin in manuscript form. It is a glossary of Roman legal terms with their Latinized French equivalents. In several places in the Seneca commentary, Calvin has recourse to the same mode of defining meaning.[58] In the absence of definitive modern editions of Budaeus' treatises and of his classical texts, we can only suggest the nature of Calvin's borrowings; we cannot set the extent. In view of the frequent repetition in Budaeus (a quality shared with the other humanists), one cannot always be sure of precise literary relationships between Budaeus and Calvin. The picture of Calvin's use of Budaeus can for the most part be traced in terms of Budaean works published before the year of Calvin's treatise (1532); whether Calvin, as has been suggested, had access also to then unpublished ones cannot be answered.

That Calvin was deeply indebted to Budaeus is beyond question. That he did not, even as a young man, follow him slavishly must also be asserted. Seldom does Calvin quote Budaeus verbatim, unless it be a quotation from another author. Not only does he often rephrase, but he also selects from widely scattered contexts, and often puts his borrowed treasure to new and quite different uses. Even when Calvin praises Budaeus as the *decus et columen*,[59] he is preparing on the evidence of Horace and Curtius to take issue with Budaeus' flat assertion that *iniicere manus* is never used in the sense of *offerre* or *inferre manus*.[60] Most important of all, Calvin never succumbs to the easy allegorical appropriation of things pagan to Christian truth that Budaeus already betrays in the *Annotationes* and *De Asse*, and was later much more explicitly to express in the *De Transitu*. Calvin remained true to the exacting philological discipline of the humanists without practicing their excesses. (This is perhaps because he first held his classicism free of Christian piety and made no hasty amalgam before his conversion.) He could not say with Erasmus, *O sancte Socrates, ora pro nobis*;[61] he

---

56. *Comm. Sen. De Clem.*, 174 (70:line 5 and note).
57. Budaeus, *Commentarii Linguae Graecae* (1530), 145ff.
58. E.g., *tollere filios = elevare filios (élèver les fils); nuncupare vota = facere vota (faire des voeux)*.
59. See note 14.
60. See *Comm. Sen. De Clem.*, 114–17 (42:line 28–43:line 5).
61. Erasmus, *Colloquia*, 683DE.

could not with Budaeus see Christ in the ancient god Hermes;[62] he could not with Zwingli find a place in the Christian afterlife for ancient pagan worthies.[63] As our two initial quotations from the *Institutio* show, he respected, as divinely given, the great achievements of the ancient philosophers and poets, but he had, by 1539, come to take with uncompromising seriousness the superiority of the Bible over all mere human learning—a note frequently struck, one must admit, by Erasmus as well. Yet despite Calvin's profound change of life, his deep study of classical antiquity left an indelible mark on all that he later wrote.

Philippus Beroaldus the Elder (1453–1505)

While Calvin never graced Philippus Beroaldus the Elder with the title "third modern pillar," use of the noted Bolognese humanist is sufficiently extensive to warrant treating him beside Erasmus and Budaeus. Among the references to various humanist writers scattered throughout the Seneca commentary is the following note on the active sense of the adjectival suffix -*bilis* as used in the word *favorabilis:* "Yet the active sense is found, against the observation of Valla and Beroaldus, in Livy" (AUC 22.26.4) etc.[64] In examining this and other allusions I decided to look beyond the works obviously alluded to in Calvin's text. Apart from Erasmus and Budaeus, Beroaldus proved to be the most fruitful indicator of probable literary dependence. His short treatise on the princely office, *De Optimo Statu Libellus* (Basle, 1509), yielded forty-five close parallels, many of them proverbs not found in Erasmus' *Adagia* or *Apophthegmata*. Next I turned to Beroaldus' commentaries on classical writers, concentrating on three: the Suetonius, Apuleius, and Cicero *(Tusculan Disputations)* commentaries.

The combined Beroaldus–Sabellicus commentaries on Suetonius' *Lives of the Caesars* (Paris, 1512) afforded thirty-three parallels from Beroaldus and one from Sabellicus. Beyond this, clusters of other references at these points suggested that Calvin closely studied this commentary in developing his documentation for the historical passages in the *De Clementia*. The commentary on Apuleius' *Golden Ass (Metamorphoses)*, in its twenty parallels, demonstrated that every acknowledged and unacknowledged reference of Calvin to Apuleius had in fact been copied from Beroaldus. The commentary on Cicero's *Tusculan Disputations*, studied in the Bologna edition of 1496, provided nineteen parallels that "rounded out" the philosophical sources of Calvin: the materials not traceable (and some that were traceable) to Cicero, Seneca, Plutarch, Erasmus, or Budaeus could largely be found in this learned

---

62. Budaeus, DA 5 (*Opera*, 294ff.). See *Comm. Sen. De Clem.*, 40 (10:note on line 28).
63. Zwingli, *Fidei Christianae Expositio*, 12, "Vita Aeterna," SS Opera 4:65, lines 29–37.
64. *Comm. Sen. De Clem.*, 186 (74:lines 34–36).

work. And the duplicate parallels suggested alternate tracks for Calvin's source materials.

A learned quibble of Calvin on a point of translation in Angelus Politianus' Latin version of Herodian[65] gave a hint that all Calvin's Latin quotations of the Greek historians of Rome should be checked. Here I discovered that Calvin had used Beroaldus' translation of Appian, *De Civilibus Romanorum Bellis* (fifteen references).

How may we sum up the place of Beroaldus in the making of Calvin's commentary? First, Beroaldus provided a store of references that Calvin not only used directly but through which he was led to still others; second, the Suetonius commentary was the backbone of Calvin's comparative study of the historians of the early empire; third, the form and method of Beroaldus' commentaries taught Calvin a great deal. He did not fall into the vices of Beroaldus' excessively archaizing style or penchant for long digressions,[66] but the types of notes—historical, rhetorical, philosophical, lexical—of Beroaldus were taken into account by Calvin in developing his own format.

The Two Ancient Pillars

Seneca. "Our Seneca was second only to Cicero, a veritable pillar of Roman philosophy and literature (eloquence)." With these words Calvin in his preface sums up his defense of Seneca against the ancient critics, Quintilian and Aulus Gellius, and against the low opinion in which the philosopher was held by some contemporaries. Calvin gives Seneca high praise, calling him "a man of vast erudition and signal eloquence." In his "Short Life of Seneca, Drawn from the Best Authors," which he sets at the head of the commentary, Calvin leans almost entirely on Tacitus for biographical details, while ignoring Dio Cassius' less flattering picture.

Competent as Seneca was in "physics" (doubtless a reference to the *Quaestiones Naturales*), Calvin recognized Seneca's supreme gift to be in ethics, and this judgment is certainly borne out in the course of the commentary. Of history, Seneca (in Calvin's view) had wide knowledge, but he was guilty of occasional slips, as Calvin points out in the commentary.[67] His style Calvin finds elegant but perhaps a trifle too luxuriant, and this judgment, too, is borne out in the commentary. In his prooemium to the second book of the *De Clementia*, Calvin notes the contrast between the two books. In the first Seneca accommodated

65. See note 50.

66. For the life of Beroaldus, see Jean Pierre Nicéron, *Memoires pour servir à l'histoire des hommes illustrés dans la république des lettres, avec un catalogue raisonné de leurs ouvrages . . .* , tome 25 (Paris: Briasson, 1729–45), 374ff.

67. Calvin recognizes different uses of history (138.6–9): "Yet to the philosophers and orators, whose job is not to weave lasting history, it is permitted to put to their own use matters of doubtful authenticity, as this passage demonstrates."

himself to popular understanding; the second he sprinkled with Stoic paradoxes and scholastic subtleties.[68] A real hint of what sort of writer Calvin himself was to become is found in these words: "I also miss the orderly arrangement of matter, which is certainly not the least quality of a good style."[69]

Here we confine our attention to Calvin's use in his commentary of Seneca's other writings. Dr. Hugo has shown that he consulted all the then extant editions in establishing his text. That he read the rest of Seneca with some care is evident from his annotations. The tragedies are quoted twenty-three times by name; the philosophical writings, some seventy-four times. By far the most common citations are of close verbal parallels between the *De Clementia* and Seneca's other works. The *De Clementia* is almost obsessed with the contrast between the tyrant and the clement ruler;[70] nearly every quotation Calvin gives from the tragedies has this theme as well. The parallels are especially close between the *Octavia* and the *De Clementia*, as both writings deal with Nero.

The citations of Seneca's remaining works fall into several well-defined categories. There are the usual philological notes on Latin idioms, chosen not because they express the same thought but rather because they adumbrate some point of syntax or word usage: *ex facili*,[71] *sub manu*,[72] *verba dare*,[73] and *ex destinato*[74] are examples. These are part of the general reservoir of Latinity on which Calvin draws for clarification of doubtful points.

A second class of Senecan citations, already mentioned in connection with the tragedies, is that of close parallels of word or thought. Not only general references to tyrants, but actual historical allusions to Dionysius of Syracuse,[75] Alexander Phalerus,[76] etc., show us the reduplication of subject matter in Seneca as he used his stock of materials again and again. The *De Clementia* suggested a number of themes that Calvin enlarged on from other Senecan contexts (and from other writers too). Among these are the following: human beings as social and political animals,[77] the relation of vices and virtues,[78] the sinfulness of all humankind *(peccavimus omnes)*,[79] and the wise man's serenity of mind in adversity and prosperity alike. The favorite motto of Caligula *(oder-*

68. Seneca, *De Clem.* 2.1.1; *Comm. Sen. De Clem.*, 336 (139:lines 5f.).
69. See pref., *Comm. Sen. De Clem.*, 10 (iii:lines 13ff.).
70. See *Comm. Sen. De Clem.*, 200–3 (81ff.).
71. See *Comm. Sen. De Clem.*, 136–39 (53:lines 5–14).
72. Ibid., 32 (7:lines 3–22).
73. Ibid., 320–23 (132:lines 32–40).
74. Ibid., 128–31 (49:lines 19–33).
75. Ibid., 202ff. (82ff.).
76. Ibid., 358 (148:note on line 19).
77. Ibid., 82f. (28f.).
78. Ibid., 110–13 (41).
79. Ibid., 128–31 (49).

int dum metuant), twice repeated in the *De Clementia*,[80] calls forth a number of analogues from Seneca, Cicero, and others. Cruelty of rulers is abhorred; gentle-dealing enjoined.

The content of the *De Clementia* determines, to a large extent, Calvin's choice of material. The additional references to Seneca amplify and at points sharpen the reader's understanding of the text. On the whole, they underline Calvin's favorable verdict on Seneca and express admiration for Seneca's psychological insight.

Cicero. If Seneca is the "second pillar," Cicero is for Calvin the "first pillar of Roman philosophy and literature."[81] This is not surprising in an age of Ciceronians. He is cited far more than any other author. Not counting unmarked quotations, one finds about sixty references to the letters; ninety-five to the speeches and to their commentator, Asconius Pedianus; fifteen to the rhetorical writings; and some eighty to the philosophical treatises. Unquestionably, by sheer bulk, this total is impressive. Even where he is unmentioned, Cicero speaks through Calvin both in direct quotation and in paraphrase.

Calvin's rhetorical and logical terminology is a skillful blend of Cicero and Quintilian with some additions from other rhetoricians such as Rutilius Lupus, Julius Rufianus, and Romanus Aquila. Cicero is also, at this stage in Calvin's career, his main direct source for ancient philosophy.

When we come, however, to examine where Calvin amassed this Ciceronian material, we must single out a fair-sized group of citations that were either part of the traditional "grist" of the jurisconsults or of the rhetoricians. When, for example, one discusses the terrible Roman punishment for parricide, the sack, one always quotes a certain passage from Cicero's *Pro Roscio*.[82] Every commentary on Roman law repeats these famous lines. When one wishes to give an instance of *deprecatio*, one turns to the *Pro Ligario*, following Quintilian himself.[83] If one adds to these references a group of philological notes amassed by the earlier humanists from the ancients, the number of Calvin's "original" citations of Cicero is further reduced. While this may temper our estimate of his knowledge of Cicero, it enhances our respect for his knowledge of contemporary humanist writing and his discrimination in using it.

As intimated above, many of the same references made by Calvin to Cicero can be found in the *Annotationes* or the *De Asse*.[84] Legal expres-

---

80. Seneca, *De Clem.* 1.12.4; 2.2.2.
81. See note 16.
82. *Pro Roscio* 25.70 at *Comm.* 1.23.1.
83. *Pro Ligario* 10.30 at *Comm. Sen. De Clem.*, 68 (22:lines 1ff.).
84. E.g., the classic definitions of *religio* and *superstitio* by Cicero, Lactantius, and Augustine, later used by Calvin in *Inst.* 1.12.1 and foreshadowed in the *Comm. Sen. De Clem.* [362–65 (150:line 21–151:line 5)], are conveniently presented in Budaeus, AP 252D–254C.

sions, as one would expect, were tested by Ciceronian usage;[85] numerous quotations from Cicero are used similarly by both writers.

We can now categorize Calvin's use of Cicero, whether direct or through some intermediate source. There is, first of all, the usual substantial number of purely philological notes, at those points where Calvin seeks unimpeachable authority for some of Seneca's turns of phrase.[86] A number of these, together with several grammatical and syntactic annotations, reflect contemporary learned controversies among the humanists.[87] Such notes frankly do not add much to the understanding of Seneca's text, but were obviously included in the commentary to establish Calvin's reputation as a humanist. All of this, while dealing with minutiae of grammar and rhetoric, does give us a glimpse of the young scholar, painstakingly forming his consummate Latinity.

Second, the system of argument set forth in the *Topica* of Cicero is utilized by Calvin in his analysis of Seneca's logic.[88] We have already noted that Calvin drew his extensive rhetorical terminology from a comparative study of Cicero, Quintilian, and lesser writers.

A third group of Ciceronian materials comes mainly from the philosophical treatises; these serve to supplement and temper the Stoic teachings of Seneca. Political philosophy, psychology, and ethics are represented. Calvin's discussion of ultimate blessedness at the beginning of the commentary[89] stems mostly from Books II–III of the *De Finibus:* when he speculates on the seat of the soul, Calvin turns to Cicero and Plutarch for useful compends of ancient philosophy.[90] Epi-

85. Both Budaeus and Calvin cite the same Ciceronian references for the following terms: *aestimare litem* [ARP 326C–D; *Comm. Sen. De Clem.,* 378 (157:line 6)]; *cognitor, cognitio* [ARP 337Bff.; *Comm. Sen. De Clem.,* 248 (102:lines 30–36 and note)]; *cernere hereditatem* [AP 52C; *Comm. Sen. De Clem.,* 250 (103:lines 25f. and note)]; *iudex quaestionis* [ARP 317; *Comm. Sen. De Clem.,* 126 (48:line 2)]; *ius imaginis* [AP 53B; *Comm. Sen. De Clem.,* 172–75 (69:lines 20–21 and note on line 20); 210 (85:line 29)].

86. Some examples: *id aetatis* (71.9–15); *animum abicere demittere* (71.14; 124.4; 159.42); *animum contrahere* or *animi contractio* (157.44); *bene male/audire* (156.36); *auribus dare* (145.42); *gratium referre/deferre* (25.52–54; 63.34–36); *manus retinere/abstinere* (41.14–15); *nemo homo* (26.6); *se dare/applicare* (28.39–52).

87. Laurentius Valla, whose knowledge of Latin Budaeus had found far superior to that of Greek, is several times "twitted" by Calvin for his pedantic assertions and hairsplitting distinctions, usually with Ciceronian evidence. Examples are Calvin's assertion that *licentia* has both good and bad meanings, and is not used exclusively in the bad sense, in the best classical authors (32.9), and that the use of *quam* as "how much" is legitimate (66.51ff.). A study of the *Elegantiae* of Valla suggests the background for some of Calvin's philological notes.

88. Of the thirteen classes of *argumenta extrinsecus,* the first *(coniugata)* and fourth *(ex comparatione maiorum aut parium aut minorum)* are employed, together with three others: *a circumstantiis* and *ab utile* (from Quintilian) and *ex remotione* (from Sextus Victor or Quintilian).

89. See *Comm. Sen. De Clem.,* 22–27 (3:line 1–4:line 40).

90. Ibid., 92 (32:note on lines 21f.).

curus' analysis of *cupiditas* is borrowed from the *De Finibus*.[91] The *Tusculan Disputations* provide Plato's analysis of the mind. The concepts of love as the binding force of human society and of mutual interdependence come from the *De Officiis*.[92]

Far more important, though, than the comparatively small stock of philosophical borrowings is the evidence of Calvin's intellectual formation. Calvin was later to make a far fuller use of Cicero's philosophical treatises: notably, in *Institutio* 1.1–4, where, having asserted the innate awareness of Deity in all men, he yet finds them inexcusable in their unregenerate state. Also, when one compares the rather sketchy statement of psychology in the commentary with *Institutio* 1.15.2–8; 2.2.10–27, one sees not only the source of the latter passages, but the further intellectual and spiritual development our author underwent between the two writings.

Three Layers of Tradition

The two ancient and three humanist writers just discussed do not exhaust the sources of Calvin's Seneca commentary. The cumulative tradition of the ancient world, mediated through late classical and recent humanist compilers (whose interests were predominantly philological and moral), colored for our author and for other authors of his time the understanding of the past.

Three levels of contact with the classics may be discerned in the Seneca commentary: classical authors, classical intermediaries, and humanist compilers. These categories are not completely exclusive: Cicero, as already indicated, was both an author in his own right and a prime channel, for the Latin world, of the Greek philosophical and rhetorical tradition. The same may be said even more strongly of Seneca. Furthermore, one cannot always say with confidence that Calvin has read a particular classical author directly even though he may quote extensively from him. The philological or lexical use to which he puts his classical allusions and the particular combinations of references are often a clue to the derivative character of these citations. More often than not Calvin is tapping the common reservoir of Latinity, used by all his classicizing contemporaries.

Classical Authors Directly Used by Calvin

We cannot say with assurance that certain references to the classics were of Calvin's own original selection; on the contrary, evidence

91. Ibid., 58 (17:note on lines 30ff.), using Cic., *Fin.* 1.13.45ff. and *T.D.* 5.33.93ff.

92. On peace of mind, see *Comm. Sen. De Clem.*, 368 (152:lines 14–17 and note on line 14), using Cic., *T.D.* 3.6.12; 4.23.51. On love as the binding force of society, see *Comm. Sen. De Clem.*, 84 (28:line 34), using Cic., *Off.* 2.3.12–2.4.15; *Fin.* 2.14.45ff.

abounds that most were obtained through intermediate authors. A few general principles can, however, be stated concerning his knowledge of the original writers.

(1) At this time Calvin was much less versed in Greek than in Latin literature[93] (by contrast Erasmus, Budaeus, and Beroaldus move freely from one language to the other). All or nearly all of Calvin's Greek references have been garnered from secondary authors. And where he cites some Greek author more fully—for example, Plutarch or one of the Greek historians of Rome—he is using a known Latin translation. We can therefore rule out Calvin's Greek references and concentrate on his Latin in considering direct use of classical authors.

(2) The following Latin poets, infrequently quoted, may be eliminated from the category of directly used classical writers: Catullus (two references), Claudian (four plus one Pseudo-Claudian), Lucretius (one), Martial (three), Persius (three), Propertius (six), and Statius (seven). Among the Latin poets to whom Calvin may be referring directly out of his own reading of them are probably to be included Horace (thirty-seven), Juvenal (thirty-four), Lucan (fourteen), Ovid (fifty-nine plus three Pseudo-Ovid), Plautus (eight), Terence (thirty-one), and Virgil (seventy-six). The character of his references and the known use of intermediaries may eliminate further all or many of the following: Juvenal, Lucan, Plautus, and Terence. There remain Horace, Ovid, and Virgil.

(3) Among the historians, Calvin knew especially well Suetonius first and Tacitus second, for they cover the period of Roman history encompassed by the *De Clementia*. Yet Calvin's extensive use of Suetonius was in part mediated by Beroaldus' commentary. Plutarch's *Lives* and Appian's *History* (in Latin translation) are also used. Of Latin historians employed mainly for nonhistorical (i.e., lexical) annotations one must mention Curtius, Livy/Florus, Sallust, Ammonianus Marcellinus, and the Scriptores Historiae Augustae; Herodian (in Latin translation) is similarly utilized. A third group of historians includes those referred to by name only in strings of citations: Arrian, Dionysius Halicarnassus, Xenophon, Justinus/Trogus, and Dio Cassius.

(4) The rhetoricians, in their analysis of orators and other writers, seem in a sense to be intermediaries, although in our summary they will be included as primary authors. Next to Cicero, Quintilian stands preeminent; Calvin's use of him evidences thorough familiarity, even though some references can be attributed to the humanist intermediaries. The "rhetorici minores"—Romanus Aquila, Julius Rufianus, Rutilius Lupus—were also directly used by Calvin. Together these writers provided a major critical tool for the young commentator in his

93. On Calvin's knowledge of Plato, Aristotle, and others, see notes 4, 5, and 7, above.

analysis of meaning and style. Varro's *On the Latin Language* may be included in this class; the references to it seem derivative, although probably Varro's treatise was used as bound in Perottus' *Cornucopia*.

(5) Among the various prose writers who do not fall into the above classes are Apuleius (see under Beroaldus, above), the Auctores Rei Rusticae—obviously consulted in the study of the "King Bee"[94]—the Panegyrists, and the two Plinies. These last were studied closely, I believe, by Calvin, although some references are secondhand. The Younger Pliny's *Panegyric* (thirty) was liberally excerpted by Calvin for political maxims and an occasional historical judgment. The *Natural History* of the Elder Pliny (thirty-three) was, with the Auctores Rei Rusticae, a chief source for animal and plant lore, and (more important) for history, but many of the references were commonplaces. The scattering of other Latin prose writers does not suggest direct use of them by Calvin.

In sum, then, the number of authors used in their original published form by Calvin is far smaller than the impressive list of seventy-four Latin and twenty-two Greek alluded to in the commentary. The basic catalogue of these prime authors is further reduced by the large proportion of derived citations.

Classical Intermediaries

Before offering any general comments on "classical intermediaries," we must speak once again of Plutarch, who, with Cicero and Seneca, serves as an important channel of Greek philosophy, proverbial wisdom, political theory, and ancient biography. Calvin knew Plutarch's *Lives* (forty-one) in the Florentine Latin translation; the *Moralia* (fifteen) he used in the various Latin translations or excerpts of Budaeus, Pirckheimer, Erasmus, etc. Since Plutarch was himself a compiler and widely plundered by the humanists, it is often difficult to determine by what route a Plutarch reference finds its way into the commentary.[95] The longer quotations from the *Moralia* were probably directly obtained (e.g., the extended passage on the seat of the soul); also, the evidence is clearly in favor of Calvin having collated historical matter directly from Plutarch's *Lives* with that of other historians. A number of the shorter proverbs, on the other hand, were drawn from the common store of the humanists.

The two chief sorts of classical intermediaries are: (1) the commentators and grammarians and (2) the compilers or excerptors. Three of the commentators are of especial importance. Calvin read Terence through the eyes of his commentator, Donatus; Virgil through Servius'

---

94. The analogy of the "King Bee" is developed by Seneca in *De Clem.* 1.19.
95. This fact is often emphasized by variant Latin renderings of Plutarch's Greek.

eyes; some of Cicero's speeches through Ascanius Pedianus'. Well-printed and copiously indexed editions were available to him, containing the text of the poet framed by ancient and modern commentaries. Thus these commentators served a double purpose: they suggested to Calvin a preponderantly philological approach to the poets; they also, in the additional material adduced, greatly expanded Calvin's documentation. Of the seventy-six references to Virgil, more than twenty-nine contain twin citations of Virgil and Servius. Eighteen of the thirty-one references to Terence also explicitly mention Donatus. The use of Acron and Porphyrion, Horace's commentators, is minimal and clearly derivative, although similar combined editions of Horace and his commentators were available. Calvin's references to Priscian's *Grammar* give us no hint of the way by which he knew this standard work. Writers like Servius and Priscian treated Greek and Latin as virtually one body of language and literature—a practice later revived by the humanists.

Five Latin writers may be classed as compilers or excerptors: Aulus Gellius (thirty-five), Macrobius (ten), Pompeius Festus (seven), Nonius Marcellus (twelve),[96] and Valerius Maximus (twenty-one). All these authors were well thumbed by the humanists, and may be considered, with the humanist compilers themselves, to constitute a common pool of lexical matter as well as a guide to the determination of word meanings. It is said that Zwingli memorized Valerius Maximus to provide illustrations for his sermons;[97] Calvin uses this writer mainly for historical anecdotes. The others are employed as lexical authorities in defining terms. They are also the source of some quotations of Sallust, Cicero, Servius/Virgil, and others.

Humanist Compilers

The invention of printing in western Europe called into being a flood of classical materials: texts, translations, commentaries, anthologies, glossaries, specialized treatises, and miscellanies. Calvin enjoyed the fruits of two generations of this intense literary effort. We have already

96. Pompeius Festus, Nonius Marcellus, and Varro's *De Lingua Latina* were sometimes printed together, twice with Nicolas Perottus' elaborately indexed *Cornucopia* (Venice, 1513; Paris, 1529).

97. Oswald Myconius, *Life of Zwingli* 4: "He became a priest [at Glarus], devoted himself to studies, especially theological studies, for henceforward he made little account of the heathen classics, unless they assisted him in the sacred things, and in preaching. With this end in view, it should be said in passing, that for the sake of the illustrations he committed Valerius Maximus to memory, and did not forget him" [trans. from Samuel M. Jackson, *The Latin Works of Zwingli*, 1:5]. After coming to Zürich in 1519 Zwingli continued his studies: "In the midst of these anxious labors he never omitted his reading of the Greek authors, and went through Homer, Aristotle, Plato, Demosthenes, Thucydides, and in lighter vein Lucian, Theocritus, Hesiod, Aristophanes, and others" [ibid., 8:10.]

seen how he employed Erasmus, Budaeus, and Beroaldus, his chief humanist mentors, and the shape of his literary dependence is clear. It remains for us to summarize his use of the humanist writers as a group.

Calvin's explicit references to the humanists are meager and somewhat misleading. Andreas Alciatus is castigated five times in a single context, and refuted in another place.[98] Baptista Egnatius, while styled *vir de studiis humanioribus bene meritus*, is corrected on a point of Roman history.[99] Angelus Politianus' translation of Herodian is, as mentioned above, unjustly criticized.[100] Nicolas Perottus (the excerptor of Phaedrus' *Fables* and a humanist highly respected by Erasmus) is caught in an *insignus error*[101] in his definition of *muraena* (lamprey). Even the great Laurentius Valla is taken to task four times.[102] Caelius Ludovicus Rhodiginus is pitted against Erasmus on the spelling of "Vedius."[103] "Gabbling" Porcius Latro Vincentinus is bested by Budaeus on Roman coinage.[104] Zasius is praised for an emendation of Justinian's *Digest*.[105] It is quibbles of this sort that delighted the humanists as they waged their pen-and-paper war among themselves. One sees here, for example, the French standing against Italians when the fair name of Marseilles is at stake.[106]

Beneath these explicit points of difference lies a solid, if largely unacknowledged, dependence on the part of Calvin on at least some of these writers. Undoubtedly, most of the references to military, agricultural, and medical subjects came through humanist compilations. Laurentius Valla seems to have been used at least ten times on questions of syntax and meaning.[107] Rhodiginus, mentioned but once, is probably employed in three additional places on lexical matters.[108] Alciatus and Zasius, beyond Budaeus' *Annotationes*, offer interpretations of the Roman law.[109] These few references provide only a taste of Calvin's reading in his contemporaries.

98. See note 107.

99. *Comm. Sen. De Clem.*, 188 (75:lines 34–37).

100. Ibid., 340 (140:line 29).

101. Ibid., 274 (112:lines 38–39).

102. On Laurentius Valla, see ibid., 62 (19:line 26); 144 (56:line 23); 186 (74:lines 34–36); 206 (83:line 33).

103. On Rhodiginus, see ibid., 274 (112:lines 20–22).

104. On Vincentinus, see ibid., 250 (103:line 24).

105. On Zasius, see ibid., 254 (104:line 28).

106. See ibid., 246 (102:lines 7–17).

107. Reference to Valla's *Elegantiae* that have been traced include 1.13, 17; 3.83; 4.17, 101; 5.34; 6.26, 33, 58. See also *In Pogium Antidoti* 3.

108. Caelius Ludovicus Rhodiginus, *Lectionum Antiquarum Libi* 16 (Basel, 1517), 8.7; 12.52; 14.5.

109. Andreas Alciatus, *De Verborum Significantiae* (ed. Opera, Basel) (1558), cols. 143f., 161, 203, 257; *Comm. in ff. tit. de liberis et posthum* (ed. Frankfort) (1617) 1.624; *De Praefectio Praetorio*; in ibid., 3.508; *Dispunctionum Libri*, 3.7 (in ibid., 2.53f.).

We have not in our examination of these traditions mentioned the comparatively few patristic references used in the commentary. But the same generalizations can be made of them: most have come by way of the Decretals of Gratian, and repeat the same errors of attribution; a few can be noted in the humanist writings used by Calvin.

A Key to Calvin's Later Work

Except for the extensive plagiarism by Gilbertus Cognatus in his supplement to Erasmus' *Adagia*, the commentary went unnoticed among his contemporaries. Yet its effect on Calvin's own formation was considerable. In the commentary can be seen the beginnings of Calvin the exegete. The same attention to the close study of the text will later mark Calvin's Christian writings. The tools of exegesis—grammatical and rhetorical analysis, a wide background in history, philosophy, literature, science, and other studies—characterize the young Calvin as they will more fully the later Calvin. The "creative assimilation" of his sources is even at this early stage a trait of our author, for he seldom merely parrots his authorities despite a demonstrable dependence on them. The same "free literal" handling of sources will later be observed in his extensive use of such writers as Augustine.

As one reflects on Calvin's "pagan apprenticeship" to the Christian life evidenced in the commentary on Seneca's *De Clementia*, one is reminded of the ambitious classical curriculum that Calvin prescribed for the youth of Geneva in the *Leges Academicae Genevensis* (1559).[110] The same writers that he had read are here perhaps presented in a more systematic and carefully graded manner. Making due allowance for the widely held humanist educational views of the time, one may yet ask: Was not Calvin, perhaps unconsciously, commending his own path to Christian belief to the children of his followers? The only difference—and it is a very significant one—is that these youth were to be effectively catechized in the evangelical doctrine from the start; yet the serious study of the Scriptures was to come only after almost the whole of Greek and Latin literature had been mastered.

In conclusion, one must say that the commentary—slight though it is when measured by the standard of Calvin's later work—illuminates the latter. Here is a well-formed, disciplined, but not yet full-matured mind at work. Conversion was to bring not an utter repudiation of Calvin's classical learning, but a transformation of it, tested by God's Word. The result was no loose allegorical binding together of classical and Christian; Calvin could not repeat Budaeus' confident assertion that Alexander worshiped Jesus Christ. Rather, the message of Seneca's

110. *OS*, 2:366–70.

De Clementia—that the mighty should rule with mercy, accountable to God—was recast in the passionate essays in Christian political teaching that introduce and conclude the *Institutio Christianae Religionis*.[111] And something of the high seriousness of the Stoic ethic, also transformed by Christian faith, prevailed at least for a time in Geneva and in her spiritual daughters.[112]

111. In the dedicatory letter to Francis I and *Inst.* 4.20.

112. See *Consilium De Luxu* [*OC*, 10a:203–6] and my article and translation of this interesting document, "Against Luxury and License in Geneva: A Forgotten Fragment of Calvin," *Interpretation* 19 (April 1965): 182–202; reprinted herein as ch. 9.

Table A
The Sources of Calvin's *Commentary on Seneca's De Clementia*

	No. of Refs.	Use[a]	Source[b]
Aeschines	1	P	C
Aesop	1	P	C
Alciatus	7	J	C
Alexander Aphrodisaeus	2	Ph	C/D
Ambrose	1	P	C
Ammianus Marcellinus	7	PHL	B/C
Appianus Alexandrinus	15	H	D
Apuleius	20	L	B/C
Aristophanes	2	L	C?
Aristotle	35	PhLRM	C/D
Arrian	1	H	C
Augustine	23	PhHLJ	A/C
Ausonius	1	L	C
Beroaldus:			
Comm. in Suetonium	34	HL	C
Comm. Cicero Tusc. Disp.	19	PhL	C
De Optimo Statu Libellus	45	P	C
Bible	7	PM	
Budaeus	91	JHLPh	C/D
Julius Capitolinus	7	H	A/C
Cato	10	HPL	B/C
Catullus	2	P	C
Celsus	2	M	C
Cicero:		LPRPhJHM	A/C
Letters	60		
Speeches	95		
Rhetoric	15		
Philosophy	80		
Claudian	5	P	C
Columella	5	M	A or C
Corpus Juris Canonici	4	P	A or C
Curtius	45	LHP	A/C
Cyprian	2	P	C?
Demosthenes	1	P	C?
Dio Cassius	8	H	C/D?
Diogenes Laertius	5	Ph	C?
Dionysius Halicarnassus	1	H	C?
Erasmus	44	PPh	C
Euclid	1	L	C
Euripides	3	P	B/C
Eusebius	11	H	C?
Gaius	3	J	B/C

Aulus Gellius	35	LHPM	B/C
Gregorius Magnus	2	P	B/C
Herodian	23	PHL	C/D
Hesiod	1	P	C
Homer	10	P	C
Horace	37	LP	A/C
Isidore of Seville	1	P	B/C?
Isocrates	1	L	C
Jerome	8	PL	A(B)/C
Justinian:			
Corpus Juris Civilis	57	J	B/C
not found	6	J	B/C
Justinus	4	H	C
Juvenal	34	PL	A/C
Lactantius	3	ML	C
Aelius Lampridius	2	H	A/C
Livy	61	LH	A/B/C
Lucan	14	LHP	A/C
Lucretius	1	L	C
Macrobius	10	LPR	B/C
Martial	3	PH	C?
Nonius Marcellus	12	L	B/C?
Ovid	54	LHPR	A/B/C
Panegyrici	12	LP	A/C
Asconius Pedianus (Cicero)	10	L	B/C
Nicolas Perottus	6	L	C
Persius	3	P	C
Phalerus	1	P	C
Phocylides	1	P	C
Plato	19	PhPL	B/C/D
Plautus	8	PL	A?/B/C
Pliny the Elder	33	HML	A/B/C
Pliny the Younger	30	PhL	A/B/C
Plutarch:			
Lives	41	HPL	C/D
Moralia	15	PPh	C/D
Pompeius Festus	7	LP	B/C
Pomponius Mela	1	H	C
Priscian	3	L	C?
Propertius	6	PLH	C?
Publilius Syrus	11	P	A
Quintilian	93	RLP	A/B/C
Caelius Ludovicus Rhodiginus	4	LP	C
Romanus Aquila	9	R	A
Rutilius Lupus	9	R	A
Sallust	19	LPPh	B/C?
Seneca the Elder	6	LHP	A or C?
Seneca the Younger:		PhPLMH	A/C

Tragedies	23		
Philosophical Works	74		
Solon	3	P	C
Sophocles	1	L(P)	C
Aelius Spartianus	1	HL	A?
Statius	7	PL	C
Strabo	2	M	C
Suetonius	120	H	A/B/C
Suidas	1	L	C
Sulpicius Victor	1	R	C?
Synesius	1	L	C?
Tacitus	69	HL	A/B/C
Terence/Donatus	31	LP	A/B/C
Ulpian	1	J	B/C
Valerius Maximus	21	HLM	B/C
Laurentius Valla	10	L	C
Varro	9	LM	A/B/C
Vegetius	3	M	C
Porcius Latro Vincentinus	1	M(H)	C
Virgil/Servius	76 (V)	LPM	A/C (V)
	29 (S)	B/C (S)	
Vitruvius	1	M	C
Flavius Vopiscus	1	H	A/C?
Xenophon	1	L	C
Zasius	2	J	C

    a. *Use:* H—historical or institutional allusions. L—lexical use or literary parallel. P—proverbial saying or political maxim. Ph—philosophy. J—juridical (legal). M—miscellaneous.

    b. *Source:* A—direct use of classical authors (Latin) by Calvin. B—direct use of ancient compilers by Calvin. C—humanist compilers used by Calvin. D—humanist translations of classical writers used by Calvin.

Table B
The Classical Tradition in John Calvin's
Commentary on Seneca's De Clementia

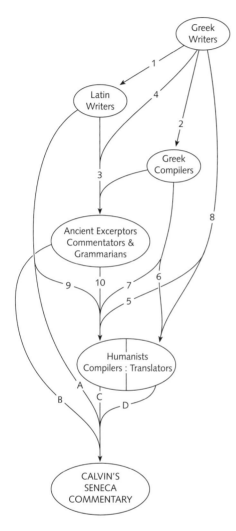

Legend

The Layers of Tradition

I. Original Classical Authors

1. Greek Writers used by Latin Writers

A. Direct use of Classical Authors (Latin) by Calvin

II. Classical Compilers, Excerptors, Grammarians, Commentators, &c.
2. Greek Writers used by Greek Compilers
3. Latin Writers used by Ancient Latin Compilers, &c.
4. Greek Writers used by Ancient Latin Compilers, &c.
B. Direct use of Ancient Compilers by Calvin

III. Humanists
5. Greek Writers used by Humanist Compilers
6. Greek Writers translated by Humanists
7. Greek Compilers used by Humanist Compilers
8. Greek Compilers translated by Humanist Compilers
9. Latin Writers used by Humanist Compilers
10. Latin Compilers, &c., used by Humanist Compilers
C. Humanist Compilers used by Calvin
D. Humanist Translations of Classical Writers used by Calvin

3   The First Edition of the *Institutes of the Christian Religion* (1536)[1]

Catechism or Apology?[2]

The Original Catechetical Intent

One of the results of Calvin's conversion was the demand placed on him, almost as soon as he began his new scriptural studies, as a teacher of those hungry for the true faith. His new popularity had already been set forth in the words of the preface to the *Commentary on the Psalms*. Despite his own comparative inexperience, seekers flocked to him for true doctrine. He concludes with the characteristic phrase: "God never left me at peace in any place."

There are scattered references to Calvin's early preaching in France, but these are fragmentary and impossible to date in a coherent way. They do suggest, however, that what Calvin says of his unsought popularity as a preacher and teacher is true. Unquestionably, his mind was drawn to the need for a good catechism that might answer the demands of his acquaintances. It was in the brief leisure of Basel, where the unknown French exile who knew no German lived in 1535 and early 1536, that he found time to write down the firstfruits of his theological studies. The long title tells the story: "Institutes of the Christian Religion, Embracing almost the Whole Sum of Piety, and Whatever is Necessary to Know of the Doctrine of Salvation: A Work most Worthy to be Read by All Persons Zealous for Piety. . . ." How much of his projected cate-

---

1. From *Inst. 1536b*, xxxvi–lix. Used by permission.

2. Luchesius Smits, in his work *Saint Augustin dans l'Oeuvre de Jean Calvin*, 1:28, notes the lack of "homogeneity" in the 1536 edition due to the combined catechetical and apologetic purposes of the work. He suggests that this double purpose has an example in Seneca's *De Clementia*. Smits quotes Calvin's *Comm. Sen. De Clem.*, 336 (139:lines 1–6), to this effect: "It seems, moreover, that Seneca's plan in this book was different from his plan in the first. While in the first Seneca accommodated himself to the popular understanding, the second he sprinkled with Stoic paradoxes and scholastic subtleties." Frankly, I think this "parallel" falls short of the mark.

chism he brought already written or in notes from France one cannot say. Some older authorities thought that the dedicatory letter to the French king and possibly chapters 5–6 were written at Basel, the first four chapters coming from his earlier intervals of leisure, especially in the library of his friend Louis du Tillet at Claix in Angoulême. Ganoczy, the most recent writer on this period of Calvin's life, credits the whole book (although not necessarily the entire preparatory study for it) to the first seven months of Calvin's Basel sojourn, pointing out the incredible speed with which the Reformer worked. We will not try to settle this question here.

In the French Reformed tradition, Calvin did not have many predecessors as catechism-writers. Besides translations of Luther, there had appeared in the French language Guillaume Farel's *Sommaire et briefve declaration dauscuns lieux fort necessaires a ung chascun chrestien pour mettre sa confiance en dieu et ayder son prochain*, first published at Basel in 1525 at the urging of the Basel Reformer Oecolampadius.[3] An English translation of the long title would read: "Summary and brief declaration of some passages very necessary for each and every Christian to put his confidence in God and help his neighbor." The *Sommaire* went through numerous editions. A second French summary of the Reformed faith was written in 1529 by Francis Lambert of Avignon, entitled *Somme Chrestienne*. It was to this rather meager store that Calvin proposed to add his own "short" work.

Farel's *Sommaire*, Piaget tells us, was "the first work in French to expound the principal points of Reformed Christian doctrine, in a simple and popular fashion for the use of those 'who knew no Latin.'" It was written "in order that all those of the French language could have a more correct understanding and knowledge of Jesus, who by so few is purely known and served." Based on Holy Scripture, "which contains God's plan and will," it was addressed to all those who "love truth."[4] While there may be some echoes of Farel's tone and general position, Calvin's work seems to owe nothing to it in style, structure, or even content, although two such works, covering as they do the same field from the same general theological vantage point, would necessarily overlap.

Calvin very clearly describes his literary intention on the first page of the letter to Francis I:

> When I first set my hand to this work, nothing was farther from my mind, most glorious King, than to write something that might be offered to your Majesty. My purpose was solely to transmit certain rudiments by

---

3. N. Weiss identifies a 1523 imprint, *La Summe de l'Escriture Saincte*, as likely Farel's. See *Bulletin de l'Histoire du Protestantisme Français* 68 (1919): 63–79.

4. A. Piaget, ed., *Guillaume Farel, Sommaire et Briefve Declaration* (Paris: Droz, 1935), 7–8.

which those who are touched with any zeal for religion might be shaped to true godliness. And I undertook this labor especially for our French countrymen, very many of whom I saw to be hungering and thirsting for Christ; very few who had been imbued with even a slight knowledge of him. The book itself witnesses that this was my intention, adapted as it is to a simple and, you may say, elementary form of teaching.[5]

This, then, was Calvin's catechetical intent. If we take his words at face value, he must have planned a French version to follow soon after, for a Latin work, however simply conceived, would be a closed book for most of his "French countrymen . . . thirsting for Christ." That he put it first in Latin may in part be due to the fact that he wanted it as an apology to reach foreign nations that they "might at least be touched with some compassion and concern" for the persecuted French Protestants. Latin was the lingua franca of the time, the logical medium to bring his case before the world. A lively debate among scholars of a generation ago discussed whether in fact such a French work was ever published. The first extant French edition of the *Institutes* is dated 1541, a translation of the second Latin edition of 1539. However, Calvin adapted from the 1536 Latin the Geneva *Catechism* of 1537. Obviously, he found the 1536 *Institutes* too long and complicated for a mere catechism; in fact, even the 1537 *Catechism* proved too learned for this popular use and was replaced, as Calvin gained pastoral experience at Geneva and Strasbourg, by the familiar Genevan question-and-answer type of catechism.[6]

The *Institutes* Becomes an Apology

But Calvin's plan for a simple catechism was not to be. History dictated otherwise, and at the heart of the bloody events that changed the book was Francis I, Most Christian King of the French.

The stirring of religious reform in the early sixteenth century brought a wide variety of movements, from a most conservative effort to cleanse the existing church to radical attacks on the entire social fabric. George H. Williams has well shown the almost hopeless complexity of the varied personages who put forward their plans for the amelioration of humanity during the first half of the century.[7] In church history it had long been characteristic of the supporters of the establishment not to differentiate too precisely between moderate and radical critics. To offer but one example of many, the medieval church lumped the simple Bible faith of the early Waldensians with the Manichaean dualism

---

5. *Inst. 1536b*, 1.

6. For the relationship among the 1536 *Institutes*, the 1537 (French) and 1538 (Latin) *Catechism*, and the 1539 *Institutes*, see *Catechism 1538* (1972), x, xii. A comparison of the *Catechism* with the 1536 and 1539 editions of the *Institutes* is found in *Analysis 1980*, 16.

7. George H. Williams, *The Radical Reformation* (Philadelphia: Westminster, 1962).

of the Cathari of the thirteenth century. And in actuality it has always been difficult to differentiate movements of religious reform: there are shades and combinations of all kinds. The defenders of the establishment, too, have reasons of their own for perpetuating such confusion. The most reasonable demand for reform of corrupt or outmoded institutional forms and practices can be blunted and discredited if it can be attached to more exaggerated and dangerous demands for change. Perhaps this failure to discriminate is only partly conscious and deliberate: the beleaguered supporters of the status quo may in fact see the threatening forces as a single entity.

In both Luther and Zwingli we see a certain effort to prove their essential orthodoxy to Rome, especially in their forcible repudiation of radical movements that seemed to threaten their own recently constructed establishment. Luther against the Peasants' Revolt; Zwingli against the nascent Anabaptist movement in Zürich; in fact, Luther over against Zwingli's more radical handling of the Lord's Supper—all may serve to illustrate our point.

When Lutheran ideas reached France in the 1520s, moderate reform was already represented by Jacques Lefèvre d'Étaples, Bishop Guillaume Briçonnet,[8] and the so-called Cercle de Meaux. But travelers brought more radical views from the Low Countries, from Germany and Switzerland. There was already a ferment at work in France; medieval sectarian ideas had been kept alive underneath the surface. Thus, there was ample evidence of revolutionary tendencies that might prove subversive to church and state. The spreading of French translations of the Bible through printing encouraged even uneducated persons to reflect on the meaning of Scripture. The Sorbonne saw all these tendencies as one threat to the ecclesiastical establishment and labeled them all heretical. The impressive machinery for the suppression of heresy inherited from the thirteenth/fourteenth-century fight to extirpate the Cathari was brought into action to cope with "Lutheranism," the name under which all dissident movements were now lumped.

Francis I, who in his humanist sympathies had earlier resisted Sorbonne attempts to suppress Erasmus and other advocates of Christian humanism, went along with the Sorbonne's demands to purge France of heresy. This internal campaign of persecution, particularly as it threatened Germans resident in France, became an embarrassment to Francis' negotiations with the German Protestant princes and their theological advisers. The diplomatic accomplishments of 1534 were dashed by

---

8. On Bishop Briçonnet's tragic recantation of the evangelical cause, see Herminjard, *Correspondance des réformateurs* (Genève: H. Georg, 1878), tome 1, nos. 77, 78. He officially decreed against Luther and his doctrines on 15 October 1523. On the work of Lefèvre d'Étaples, see P. E. Hughes, *Lefèvre: Pioneer of Ecclesiastical Renewal in France* (Grand Rapids: Eerdmans, 1984).

the affair of the Placards in October of that year. So, in the continued negotiations with the Lutherans of early 1535, in the midst of persecutions
at home, it became expedient to picture the whole matter as an affair of
national security and to isolate the French evangelical party from the re-
spectable Protestants outside France. Three groups of supporters of this
reading of French Reform emerged: Catholic theologians like Cochlaeus
and Ceneau wrote what Calvin was to call "lying pamphlets, tarring all
French evangelicals with the same dire Anabaptist brush"; otherwise re-
spectable humanists like Budé and Sadolet snobbishly treated the whole
movement as that of an ignorant rabble; finally, Francis' memorandum
to the German Protestant princes on 1 February 1535 (drafted by his
diplomatic envoy Guillaume du Bellay) presented this view of the whole
movement toward Reform in France. To summarize the memorandum:
the sovereign attempted to justify to his Protestant allies the persecutions undertaken in France following the affair of the Placards, an act of
anarchy and revolt against the internal order of the kingdom. The government not only had the right but the duty to take vigorous steps. The
French evangelicals, the memorandum asserted, unlike the German
Protestants, were seditious persons in no respect different from the Anabaptists. Were not such persons quite justly put to death even in Protestant Germany?

So went the reasoning of the royal memorandum. It did not serve its
purpose of allaying the fears and misgivings of the Germans, but it did
convince the more conservative spokesmen of the French evangelical
party of the need to dissociate themselves, theologically and politically,
from more radical forces of reform, and to make their distinction very
clear not only in the minds of their fellow Protestants outside France
but to their own monarch and his advisers. The immediacy of this was
borne out by the tragic events of Münster now approaching their apoc-
alyptic climax: the polygamous kingdom of Münster was to fall on 25
June 1535.

Calvin's response to the question of how the true evangelicals could
be proved of a different stamp from their more radical brethren took
two forms. He first set out to deal with what he considered the most
damning theological aspect of the question in his *Psychopannychia*,
written in 1534–35 and finally published in 1542. He then mounted a
more comprehensive literary campaign in the 1536 *Institutes*. Let us
look at each of these documents in turn.

The *Psychopannychia* poses considerable critical problems. Against
what groups or group was it originally intended? How much of the
1542 published version represents, actually, what Calvin originally
wrote in 1534–35? Fortunately for us, these questions are not central to
our present task, so they can be laid aside. We are concerned only with
the message of the book.

Why did Calvin choose for his first theological essay obscure questions of what happened to soul and body at the time of physical death? If the book is directed against the Anabaptists, the doctrine of soul-sleep or soul-death was not one widely held in that movement.[9] By whatever groups it was held, unquestionably the doctrine was accepted more in France than in other lands that had been touched by Reform. Calvin must have felt the need to refute it in the interests both of protecting his fellow religionists from it and in assuring the Catholics that this heretical notion was not held by the authentic evangelicals of France.

Among the Catholic doctrines rejected by the Protestants were purgatory, prayers for the dead, and the intercession of the saints. The Catholics who supported these doctrines thought their opponents must of necessity be rejecting the continued existence of the soul after the death of the body, a doctrine dictated to Pope John XXII by the University of Paris in the fourteenth century, and reiterated recently at the Fifth Lateran Council, against dangerous Aristotelian tendencies of Averroist origin stemming from the University of Padua. Did the evangelicals in fact, by rejecting prayers for the dead, assume the death of the soul?

This question was posed to Calvin by Cardinal Sadolet in 1539:

> Nor will I say anything either of the prayers of the saints of God for us, or of ours for the dead, though I would fain know what these same men would be at when they despise and deride them. Can they possibly imagine that the soul perishes along with the body? This they certainly seem to insinuate, and they do it still more openly when they strive to procure for themselves a liberty of conduct set loose from all ecclesiastical laws, and of a license for their lusts. For, if the soul is mortal, Let us eat and drink, says the Apostle, for tomorrow we die; but if it is immortal as it certainly is, how, I ask, has the death of the body made so great and so sudden a disruption, that the souls of the dead have no congruity, in any respect, no communion with those of the living, and have forgotten all their relationship to us and common human society? And this, especially, while charity, which is the principal gift of the Holy Spirit to a Christian soul, which is ever kind and fruitful, and which, in him who has it, never exists to no purpose, must always remain safe and operative in both lives.[10]

Just as the rejection of prayers for the dead, invocation of the saints, etc., was the key to overcoming the whole oppressive Catholic system of indulgences against which Luther had already taken his stand, so the

---

9. On this question, now see Willem Balke, *Calvin and the Anabaptist Radicals*, trans. by William J. Heynen (Grand Rapids: Eerdmans, 1981), 25–33.

10. "Letter by Cardinal Sadolet to the Senate and People of Geneva," in John Calvin, *Tracts and Treatises*, trans. by Henry Beveridge (Grand Rapids: Eerdmans, 1958), 1:15.

continued assertion of the life of the soul, independent of the body, was requisite to dissociate the evangelicals from fantastic and subversive tendencies that could, theologically, be tied to a doctrine of soul-death and soul-sleep. We shall later take up the sacramental and political consequences of this.

And so, in his first theological essay, Calvin had set out, through painstaking word studies of "soul," "spirit," and other scriptural terms, to assert the immortality of the soul against those who claimed either that it died or went to sleep until the general resurrection. The theological presupposition upon which Calvin's view rests is that the soul, preeminently, is to be identified with the image of God. If this be so, to assert that that image is destroyed for a time or even for a period sleeps, is unthinkable. As God never dies, never sleeps, so God's image in humanity must be ever watchful until the blessed reunion of soul with body at the general resurrection. To this essentially Christian doctrine, however, Calvin was to add the Protestant insistence that communication between the souls in living bodies on earth and the disembodied souls of the dead awaiting the day of resurrection was impossible. To postulate such would be to detract from Christ's sole mediatorship.

The *Psychopannychia* itself went through several literary stages; we are primarily concerned with the first one at this point. Writing on 3 September 1535 to his friend Christopher Libertet, Calvin speaks of his first draft in these terms:

> As for that essay . . . it contained my first thoughts, rather thrown together in the shape of memoranda or commonplaces than digested after any definite and certain method, although there was some appearance of order.[11]

The first draft bears a preface dedicated to a certain friend (unidentified) who stands "firm in prudence and moderation" "amid those tumults of vain opinions with which giddy spirits disturb the peace of the church." In the preface Calvin anticipates the charge that his writing will disturb the unity and charity of the church, to which he responds: "We acknowledge no unity except in Christ, no charity of which he is not the bond; and therefore, the chief point in preserving charity is to maintain faith sacred and entire."[12] This in 1534 at Orléans, perhaps in the late summer. Calvin sent a copy of the first draft to the Reformer Wolfgang Capito at Strasbourg for his advice on publishing it. Capito's response, which Herminjard dates toward the end of 1534, dissuaded Calvin from this and sent him "back to the drawing board" so to speak. Here are Capito's words:

11. *OC*, 10:51–52.
12. *Psychopannychia*, in John Calvin, *Tracts and Treatises*, 3:416.

As to publishing it, if you pay attention to us, you will by all means make plans for it at a more appropriate time. Now sects are raising an uproar everywhere, and the Germans in the great religious calamity have found that fighting errors makes them better known; that the surest way to take care of the afflicted churches is to depict Christ most carefully. . . . I would prefer that you begin your literary endeavors in a more praiseworthy matter . . . To sum up: the tortured state of the French churches demands that you rather withdraw from all contentions.[13]

Capito suggests that constructive scriptural exegesis would be more appropriate, pointing to his own work on Hosea. But this advice came during the negotiations of the German princes and Reformers with the French authorities looking toward a religious peace and a reforming council. October 1534 was to see the affair of the Placards at Paris, the bloody persecutions of the French evangelicals in the months that followed, then the cataclysm of Münster and the official justification of internal religious oppression by the French Crown, that the offenders were all, indiscriminately, subversives. Calvin took Capito's advice concerning the *Psychopannychia* (which he, however, revised in 1535 during his Basel sojourn after completing the *Institutes*). But remain silent he could not to the charge that he and his compatriots were trying to destroy political order in France. And so in his preface to the French king, having alluded to his original catechetical intent—which we have already quoted—he immediately and passionately launched on why he decided to give his work a second purpose:

But I perceived that the fury of certain wicked persons has prevailed so far in your realm that there is no place in it for sound doctrine. Consequently, it seemed to me that I should be doing something worthwhile if I both gave instruction to those I had undertaken to instruct and made confession before you with the same work. From this you may learn the nature of the doctrine against which those madmen burn with rage, who today disturb your realm with fire and sword. And indeed I shall not fear to confess that I have here embraced almost the sum of that very doctrine which they shout must be punished by prison, exile, proscription, and fire and be exterminated on land and sea. Indeed, I know with what horrible reports they have filled your ears and minds, to render our cause as hateful as possible to you. But, as fits your clemency you ought to weigh the fact that if it is enough merely to make accusations, then no innocence will remain either in words or deeds.[14]

Essentially the same story is told by Calvin in his preface to the *Commentary on Psalms*, but perhaps even more pointedly:

13. Herminjard, *Correspondance des Réformateurs*, 3, no. 490.
14. *Inst. 1536b*, 1.

But it happened that while I was dwelling at Basel,
Hidden there as it were, and known only to few people,
Many faithful, holy men were burned in France,
And reports of this having spread to foreign countries,
A great part of the Germans
Reacted with grave disapproval
So as to conceive a hatred
Toward the authors of that tyranny.
In order to quiet things down,
It was arranged to circulate
Certain shameful pamphlets
Full of lies, to the effect
That only Anabaptists and seditious persons
Were being treated so cruelly,
Who by their dreams and false opinions
Were overturning not only religion
But the whole political order.
It appeared to me that these tools of the court[15]
Were by their disguises trying
Not only to keep this shameful shedding
Of innocent blood
Buried under false charges and calumnies
Brought against the holy martyrs after their death,
But also that thereafter they might have a means
Of proceeding to the ultimate extremity
Of murdering the poor faithful
Without anyone having compassion for them.
Unless, then, I strongly opposed them
To the best of my ability,
I could not justify my silence
Without being found lax and disloyal.
This was the reason that roused me
To publish my *Institutes of Christian Religion:*
First, to answer certain wicked charges
Sowed by the other,
And to clear the memory of my brethren
Whose death was precious
In the presence of the Lord; [Ps. 116:15]
Secondly, as the same cruelties
Could very soon thereafter
Be exercised against many poor people,
That foreign nations might at least
Be touched with some compassion
And concern for them.
For at that time I did not publish
The book as it now is,
Full and laborious,

15. *ab aulicis artificibus* . . . See Bohatec, *Budé und Calvin,* 128.

But it was only a little booklet
Containing in summary form
The principal matters.
I had no other purpose
Than to acquaint others
With the sort of faith
Held by those
Whom I saw
These wicked and faithless flatterers
Villainously defaming.[16]

We see, then, that two things led Calvin to write his first edition of the famous *Institutes:* the catechetical needs of his religious brethren and the need to plead their case before the king, that persecution might cease. And the latter purpose called forth a double theological response from Calvin: the rejection of institutionalized Roman Catholicism and at the same time of its extreme opposite, the revolutionary, disruptive spiritualism of what at that time he lumped under the name "Catabaptists." Hence, Calvin's future theological course was determined: to hold a middle direction between the right and left. This was not a prudent compromise, but a judgment securely grounded on Calvin's own independent study of Scripture. The later development of his theological system is an extending and perfecting of this initial polarity.

The Dedicatory Letter to the French King

An Apology among Christian Apologies

A study of the classic apologies of the Christian religion, particularly those early writings of the Church Fathers prompted by pagan Roman persecutions of the infant Christian church, will demonstrate the creative impulse apologetic gave to Christian theology. The church found itself caught between Jew and Gentile, and more intimately between tendencies within its ranks that sought on the one hand to perpetuate its Jewish heritage and on the other to repudiate that heritage. Already in the experience of Paul these forces are at work; by the second century the future of the faith lay in holding to the unity of the Testaments against the Jews who would deny the New and the Gnostics who would reshape the New shorn of its historic roots in the Old. The apologists also had to convince the authorities that the Christian movement did not wish to destroy the Roman state and that its refusal to go along with official paganism and the emperor cult was not an act of political sedition but a religious preference that in no way weakened the Christian's support of the state. Even in Paul, and especially in the Pastoral

16. *Piety 1978*, 31–32.

Epistles of the New Testament, this assurance of peaceful, nonrevolutionary coexistence is sounded.

In trying to bridge the gulf that these conflicts seemed to open, the apologists, Justin Martyr notably, began the long process of the domestication of Greek philosophy in the Christian tradition, following Philo Judaeus, in the first century of our era.

It may seem an unwarranted digression to speak of these early writers here but for the fact that a significant parallel in literary tone and even in argument may be pointed out between their writing and Calvin's. To mention but one striking item: the early apologists were faced with the pagans' question, What authority does this new cult born a little over a hundred years ago have in comparison with other faiths such as the Egyptian that goes back thousands of years? To this the apologists, insisting on Christian continuity with the Jewish Scriptures, said: "Our faith is as old as creation itself." To the charge that they were plotting to overthrow established religion and in fact the whole political establishment, they pointed to the purity of their life, the exemplary character of their worship, and their loyalty to the emperor. To the charge that their faith was a thing of patches hastily sewn together from bits filched from ancient philosophy, they asserted that on the contrary their faith was the original from which these later pagan aberrations derived.

No wonder that Calvin eagerly scanned the whole history of the church and especially its earliest centuries! Like his fellow apologists of the early church, Calvin was by his apologetic effort really constructing a new synthesis of the faith. To the charge of novelty leveled by the Sorbonnists, Calvin asserted his faith was the authentic apostolic message, theirs the late medieval aberration. To the charge that the French evangelicals were plotting to topple the monarchy, Calvin pledged the political loyalty of the evangelical party. No one ever put to better use the force of history in the service of the faith.

The letter to Francis I is, therefore, to be set beside the apologies of Justin Martyr and his mid-second-century contemporaries, as well as beside the apologies of Tertullian, Origen, and Eusebius.

The Content of the Dedicatory Letter

Let us look at the structure of the letter. Calvin does not break it up into sections as he did the chapters of the latest editions of the *Institutes*. The printers set it in solid type. But one may discern eight parts, already noted in our translation of the 1559 edition, and here reproduced.

(1) We have already quoted from and discussed the first section, which we may entitle "Circumstances in which the book was first written." Here, after outlining his double purpose, Calvin asks Francis I, a

truly Christian king (as his title claims), for a full and fair inquiry into the evangelicals' case.

(2) Next Calvin pleads for the persecuted evangelicals, casting in stark relief their scriptural faith and heroic martyrdom over against the Romanists' neglect of that scriptural faith and insistence on the Mass, purgatory, pilgrimages, and like trifles.

(3) Thereupon Calvin takes up four basic charges of the Catholics against the Reformed faith: that it is new, unknown, uncertain, and unsupported by miracles. The antithetical approach once again had come to Calvin's aid: God's Word is hardly new! Unknown the Reformed faith may be, but the reason is that true doctrine has long lain buried and forgotten through man's impiety. How can you call our faith "uncertain," seeing our assurance over against their doubt? As for supporting miracles, you should sift the difference between true and false miracles.

(4) In the next section, Calvin disposes of the oft-repeated argument that the evangelicals have thrown out the Church Fathers because they fail to support their teaching. Calvin has read his Fathers and the standard historians of the church. From them he produces an impressive series of sharp antitheses. We summarize them here:

(a) God doesn't need gold or silver / Look at their lavish rites
(b) Christians may either eat meat or abstain from it / Lenten fasts
(c) monks must work / idle, licentious monks of our day
(d) no images of Christ or saints / churches crawling with images
(e) after burial of the dead let them rest / perpetual solicitude for the dead
(f) bread and wine remain in the Eucharist / transubstantiation
(g) all present must partake of the Lord's Supper / public and private Masses put grace and merit of Christ up for sale
(h) rash verdicts without basis in Scripture disallowed / jungle of constitutions, canons, etc., not based on God's Word
(i) marriage affirmed for clergy / celibacy enjoined
(j) God's Word to be kept clear of sophistries / look at their speculative theological brawls!

(5) After this heavy cannonade of the Roman Catholic position, Calvin turns to the next circle of defense of the papal stronghold, the appeal to custom. Most Roman Catholic polemicists had stood firm in the assertion that these Protestant Johnny-come-latelies were sacrilegiously mangling the established and hallowed customs of Mother Church. Here, Calvin's humanist training shows its clearest strength. Most customs, he asserts, are the result of the private vices of the majority that become public error and wrongly take on the force of law. Over against such public error stands the eternal justice of God's kingdom, which we are called on fearlessly to follow. In ringing terms

Calvin asserts that, though the whole world may fall into the same wickedness, strength of numbers does not sanction or excuse it.

(6) Where, then, is the true church to be found? The Romanists have asserted that the form of the church is always observable; that this form of the church rests in the Roman Church and its hierarchy. To this Calvin makes rejoinder with the Pauline marks of pure preaching and lawful sacraments—the same marks Luther had earlier asserted in the ecclesiological debate with Rome. Historically, both in the Old Testament and in subsequent Christian history, this true church often went underground and was without visible form. Yet though it seemed to disappear, a thin line of true witnesses to it was marvelously preserved by God even through the darkest times. When Elijah asked where the true worshipers were, God told him there were seven thousand who had not bowed the knee to Baal. The remnant still lived when mankind as a whole lay in spiritual slumber.

(7) Now, one of the most telling criticisms of the Romanists against the Reformed preachers, an argument to which harassed monarchs were especially sensitive, was that the renewed preaching of the gospel was destroying peace and bringing in its train tumult and revolution. Calvin's reply to this rather strong argument is to postulate a twofold satanic strategy. For centuries Satan kept the church asleep in worldly luxury. When, however, it started to wake up, in this new apostolic age so to speak, he countered with a new strategy. He raised up contentions of all sorts, prompted religious strife, especially centering his ingenious new strategy on those Calvin calls the "Catabaptists." In this time of strife, we are in the same boat as the apostles, but like them we have assurance of our faith.

(8) In the last section Calvin realistically sizes up the likelihood that his appeal will actually reach the king and, if it does, whether it will sway him in the least. Whether their earthly king listens or not to their plea, really recognizes them as loyal Frenchmen, the evangelicals will ultimately put their faith in the King of kings, whose rule is perfect justice and who will hear their plea. So ends the letter to Francis I.

If we now turn from this impassioned appeal, to the very end of the *Institutes*, whether the third portion of the sixth chapter of the 1536 edition, or Book IV, chapter 20 in the 1559 edition, we see a final plea of obedience to the earthly monarch, but at the very last the ringing assertion that obedience to human authority must not become disobedience to God. "We must obey God rather than men." This is the "political frame" of the *Institutes*.

At the heart of this letter, then, is the acute sense of contrast, not only between the evangelical faith and the doctrine and practice of the Roman Church, but also a contrast, not elaborated here but to be worked out more fully later, between the evangelicals and the loose congeries of extremists (from Calvin's point of view) that he here conveniently if inaccurately labels "Catabaptists"—the very term Zwingli had made current in his famous *Elenchus* and Bucer used in his commentaries to denominate that group. We may conclude that the *Institutes* took shape between these two opposing religious tendencies. We now turn to the six chapters that comprise the 1536 *Institutes*.

Analysis of the "Catechetical" Chapters (1–5)

The catechetical literature of the Later Middle Ages, both in Latin and in the vernacular, took the form of simple expositions of the law, Apostles' Creed, Lord's Prayer, etc. Luther found this form ready at hand when he compiled his *Small Catechism* of 1522 and *Large Catechism* of 1529. It was natural, then, that Calvin would construct his first edition of the *Institutes* from the successive expositions of the Ten Commandments (ch. 1), the Apostles' Creed (ch. 2), the Lord's Prayer (ch. 3), and the sacraments (ch. 4). To this he appends first a refutation of the papal Mass (end of ch. 4) and a long chapter rejecting on scriptural and historical grounds the so-called five false sacraments (ch. 5). The concluding chapter contains three related essays, on Christian freedom, ecclesiastical power, and political power, which we propose to treat separately as really a part of the apologetic aspect of the book, more perhaps than the catechetical.

In dealing with these basic documents of the faith, Calvin quite often seems to follow, but always in his own independent way, Martin Luther. This is especially true in his treatment of the Decalogue. (Later editions of the *Institutes* will show a greater independence of treatment of the separate commandments.) Yet we must candidly remark that the well-known difference between Luther and Calvin on the law is already apparent. Our analysis of these chapters will not be exhaustive but will concentrate on the polarities they present.

Chapter 1: On the Law

After the theological restatement of Calvin's faith that serves as a preface and that we have already discussed, Calvin launches into an exposition of the Decalogue. Most of the commandments are paraphrased in the briefest of terms, but four of them call for fuller discussion: the Third evokes an essay on images and idolatry with application to the Roman Catholic cultus; the Fourth offers an opportunity to reject the Anabaptist teaching on oaths; the Fifth on Sabbath observance, since it stands between the moral and ceremonial law, calls for something other than a literal exegesis; the Tenth or "Deuteronomic" Commandment is more extensively discussed because of its practical consequences: if the family is extended to include the larger political groupings (one is reminded here of Aristotle's *Politics*) one may subsume under it the honoring of the king, prince, magistrates, etc. Here is a scriptural restatement of the classical notes on the *Pater Patriae* as set forth in the Seneca commentary.[17]

The concluding discussion of the chapter moves on to the uses of the law and to justification: this logically brings in the contrast between faith-righteousness and works-righteousness, and such subsidiary Roman Catholic notions as works of supererogation. The influence of Luther (and of Paul) is obvious here. In later editions fuller support will be drawn from Augustine as this material is broken up, expanded, and distributed to new chapters.

Chapter 2: On Faith

This chapter, containing an exposition of the Apostles' Creed, was the chief casualty of the later editions, being fragmented to provide substance for a radically altered structure. The centrality, existentially speaking, of faith to Calvin's whole religious view demanded more than a mere reliance on an ancient and postscriptural epitome of evangelical teaching, such as the Apostles' Creed.

Basically, in 1536, the chapter consists of a theological essay on the nature of faith and the Trinity, an exposition of the Creed, and a concluding section on the relation of faith, hope, and love. Strong antitheses, some against the Roman Catholics and others against the Anabaptists and Antitrinitarians, mark the chapter.

Let us look at the chapter in more detail. True versus false notions of faith mark the opening pages, largely against the Roman Catholics. The section on the Trinity seems to be directed against unnamed contemporary Antitrinitarians, who are credited with "mocking us for confessing one God in three persons"; the indiscriminate use of "Spirit" by some, the criticisms of others leveled against the use of technical non-biblical theological terms are refuted by Calvin with the help of ancient church history parallels. Some authorities think that the proposed meeting of Calvin with Servetus in Paris in 1534(?) (which never occurred) may be hinted at here; at any event, these kernels of refutation were later reused and expanded in the Servetus quarrel as reflected in the latest edition of the *Institutes* (1559). Our notes mark points of contact with Servetus' two earliest treatises.

In discussing the Creed, Calvin utilizes the first article to assert God's omnipotence and providence against any vestigial Pelagianism of the Sorbonne.

The second article carries a strong critique by Calvin of an unidentified position that had asserted Christ was God's Son only according to

17. See *Comm. Sen. De Clem.*, 105, 121, 171, 237, 107.

his humanity (by the virgin birth) and charged Calvin and his party with "two-Christ" doctrine.

Calvin in dealing with descent into hell reiterates the nonliteral interpretation of the *Psychopannychia*, thus setting a further antithesis with the Anabaptists; but this position of Calvin is also taken implicitly over against the Roman Catholics. The session at God's right hand is simply stated in a way that presages the remarks on Christ's risen body in chapter 4 ("On the Sacraments"): "Therefore, although lifted up to heaven, he has removed the presence of his body from our sight, yet he does not refuse to be present with his believers in help and might, to show the manifest power of his presence." Here we see his distinction not only from the Roman Catholics but from Luther and Zwingli as well. This affords the clue to Calvin's christological difference from the Lutherans.

The fourth article is chiefly a brief positive statement of Calvin's view of the church, based on a thoroughgoing theology of grace, marked by election and predestination, but the most corporate and least developed statement of his doctrine in all of Calvin's voluminous writings on this hotly contested doctrine.[18] It is very much here a churchly doctrine, cast as it is in the midst of the discussion of the ecclesiastical article of the Apostles' Creed. Not all of Calvin's ecclesiology is confined to this chapter, however; aspects are dealt with in chapters 3–6 as well.

The concluding essay of chapter 2, on faith, hope, and love, argues the primacy of faith and rejects the Roman Catholic notion of *fides informis* as well as the Roman Catholic teaching that we are justified by love rather than faith.

It is interesting to note that the antitheses sketched here against the "left wing" of the Reformation are utilized in much expanded form later against Servetus, other Antitrinitarians, and certain Anabaptists (as Menno Simons on Christology).

Chapter 3: On Prayer

This chapter owes a great deal to Martin Bucer's *Commentary on the Gospels* (1530), as Alexandre Ganoczy has shown and as is documented in our notes. Here let us be content with summing up the antitheses it contains. The most obvious antithesis is between Christ as sole Mediator and the many human mediators in the invocation of the saints. Implied throughout the chapter is the general antithesis between the false aspects of Roman Catholic worship and the purity of evangelical worship, a subject to be more polemically treated in the following chapters. This included the localization of the holy, the superstitious use of set

---

18. Smits, *Saint Augustin,* reveals that Calvin does not quote *On the Predestination of the Saints* until the 1539 edition.

times (cf. Calvin's earlier exegesis of the Fifth Commandment, and his later adiaphoric treatment of rites in the second essay of chapter 6), the use of Latin rather than the vernacular, and passivity versus action of the congregation (implied in his remarks on singing). These points were later to be greatly expanded by Calvin.

Chapter 4: On the Sacraments

This chapter is divided into four sections, the first three corresponding roughly to the order of the sacramental chapters of the 1559 *Institutes* (4.14–18): the initial essay deals with the sacraments in general; it is followed by essays on baptism and the Lord's Supper, and the short concluding piece discusses the administration of the two dominical sacraments. In the marriage of physical with spiritual which is a sacrament, Calvin uses the exegetical principle of accommodation.

Parenthetically, we would like to note that many years later, in 1556, when Calvin was writing his Second Defense against Westphal, his chief Lutheran opponent on the Lord's Supper, he referred to his early reading on this topic:

> Beginning gradually to leave the darkness of the Papacy and having taken a little taste of healthy doctrine, when I read in Luther that Oecolampadius and Zwingli left nothing in the sacraments but bare figures and representations without truth, I confess that I turned from their books, with the result that I abstained from reading them for a long time. But before I began to write they had conferred together [1529] at Marburg.[19]

That Calvin had read Zwingli, or through some other source knew his position when he wrote this chapter, will be apparent from the position our Reformer took. In defining a sacrament, Calvin rejects, on the one hand, "those who weaken the force of the sacraments and completely overthrow their use," and, on the other hand, "those who attach to the sacraments some sort of secret power with which one nowhere reads that God had endowed them." This latter tendency embraces two groups: those who teach that the sacraments of the new law justify and confer grace, "provided we do not set up a barrier of mortal sin" (obviously referring to the Roman Catholics); and those who believe a hidden power is "joined and fastened to the sacraments to distribute in them the graces of the Holy Spirit, but only if the Holy Spirit accompanies them." Calvin does not identify this last group. So we may see that Calvin's general sacramental position lies between Zwinglianism and Roman Catholicism, emphasizing as it does the sacraments as "seals"

---

19. "Second Defense . . . to the Calumnies of Joachim Westphal," John Calvin, *Tracts and Treatises*, 2:252–53.

on the document of faith, as God's accommodation to our weak capacity to understand.

Calvin's chief opponent in his discussion of baptism would seem to be the Anabaptists, whose demand for believer baptism and Donatistical insistence on rebaptism he rejects; but Calvin also refutes the Roman Catholic view, resting on a defective grasp of original sin, that baptism releases us from original sin and restores us to the righteousness and purity of Adam before the Fall. Briefly alluded to is the Zwinglian minimal view of baptism as "but a token and mark by which we confess our religion before men." That Calvin senses his mediating position may be seen in his refutation of the Anabaptist demand for rebaptism by identifying them with the ancient Donatists: "Such today are our Catabaptists who deny that we have been duly baptized because we were baptized by impious and idolatrous men under the papal government."

Calvin's essay on the Lord's Supper sets forth in a briefer fashion the essential points made at greater length in his mature theological expression. There are several striking features of this earliest eucharistic discussion: first, it shows remarkably wide reading and independent reflection on the infinitely varied views previously expressed on the Lord's Supper. While deeper study of Augustine and Chrysostom was to be evidenced in the 1539 edition, Calvin had in the edition of 1536 canvassed historically the development of the Lord's Supper, had examined the pertinent scriptural passages deeply, and had reviewed the various positions on the Supper expressed in his own time. Two testimonies to this preparation for his task come from later writings. We have the text of two speeches he gave at the Colloquy of Lausanne in early October 1536, a discussion organized by the Bernese authorities between Roman Catholics and Reformed on the Lord's Supper.[20] In this, Calvin quoted extensively from the Church Fathers. In 1556 in writing his *Second Defense* against the Lutheran Westphal he made the statement previously quoted about his early reading on the sacraments. Taken literally as some scholars do, this statement in the Westphal essay would push Calvin's theological awakening back to his days at Bourges and associate this interest with the influence of his teacher Melchior Wolmar. But it probably refers rather to Calvin's postconversion religious studies in 1534–35.

A second feature of Calvin's earliest eucharistic statement is that it enters the debate not as a new voice just beginning its labors, but as if Calvin had long been debating the points at issue, either as spokesman for a party he does not identify or possibly as the self-appointed continuator of true Christian orthodoxy as he, fresh from his initial studies, understands it.

20. *OC*, 9:877–86.

A third feature is that Calvin's grasp of the various tendencies, combinations, and alignments of parties is so deep that he in brief anticipates later full-blown developments of theological controversy; in fact, much of his material here possessing a general application is later adapted and augmented to apply to specific controversies in which he is subsequently engaged.

Without entering into all the subtleties and details of Calvin's eucharistic teaching, one may ask the question, Where does his position lie with regard to the major alignments of parties? He sees two opposing faulty views on the Lord's Supper, expressed perhaps more succinctly in his exposition of the *Consensus Tigurinus* (1551): if the dignity of the sacraments is too highly extolled, superstition easily creeps in; on the other hand, a cold and less elevated discussion of their virtue and fruit leads to profane contempt of them. The main cause of controversy over the Supper, he asserts in the *Institutes* of 1536, is that theologians have asked the wrong question: "How do we eat Christ's body?" They should have asked: "How does Christ's body become ours?" He rejects the idolatry of the Mass. He rejects a discipline that allows only the perfect (Anabaptists) or the perfectly shriven (Roman Catholics) to communicate. He rejects the rationalistic reductionism of Zwingli but sides with him on the limits of the glorified body against the real presence (differently advanced by the Roman Catholics on the one hand and by the Lutherans on the other); he accepts an "as if" physical presence, a sort of ubiquity of God's power that marvelously bridges the otherwise unbridgeable spiritual gulf between heaven and earth. These are subtle distinctions taken in conscious differentiation from the manifold positions taken by other theologians both of the past and of his own time, but dictated primarily by a living faith proclaimed to humankind in the Scriptures but fortified, "sealed," by the sacraments for the sake of man's weakness and incapacity. Faith does not make the sacraments mere signs, nor do the sacraments by themselves do the work of faith: they work together—faith and sacraments. At bottom, these differences in eucharistic theology mark corresponding differences in theology and Christology.

The strong pastoral intent of Calvin is seen in his rejection of any theological position or liturgical practice that denies the benefits of the sacraments to the faithful.[21] He therefore concludes his chapter with a discussion on the administration of the sacraments. Briefly but succinctly he sets forth the evidence from the New Testament for sacramental practice, then discusses details that can be varied according to time and place without harm to sacrament or receiver. The touchstone

---

21. One of the worst features of the Roman Mass, in Calvin's view, is that it makes the laity into "second-class citizens" of the kingdom.

of true versus false sacramental theology and practice is scriptural authority: all else is of human invention.

Chapter 5: On the Five False Sacraments

This chapter was perhaps to be in later editions the least altered in basic content and structure of all the chapters of the 1536 *Institutes.* From the copious sidenotes of the original text at this point it is clear that Calvin has both the Scriptures and Gratian's *Decretum* and Peter Lombard's *Sentences* beside him as he writes this chapter. It is of course directed against the false sacramental teachings and practices of the Roman Church, and draws at least some of its initial inspiration from Luther's *Babylonian Captivity of the Church* (1520). Each "sacrament" is examined in terms of the claims made for it, its actual history, and the true teaching that should replace it. While Calvin lives up to his promise of brevity in discussing confirmation, extreme unction, and marriage, he deals with penance and orders at length. Under penance he treats such related topics as repentance, confession, absolution (the power of the keys), indulgences, the treasury of merits, satisfaction for sins, and purgatory. In later editions these will be detached to separate chapters, leaving only the original nucleus. Over against this false ecclesiastical structure Calvin lays the scriptural view of repentance and forgiveness. In like manner, he deals at length with the "sacrament" of orders and its various divisions, setting over against it the scriptural doctrine of ministry, a topic to be much more fully dealt with in the edition of 1543, after Calvin's pastoral experience at Strasbourg.

We have in this chapter, in a sense, the nucleus of Calvin's detailed refutation of the foundations of the medieval church order, if we add to it some details from the middle essay of chapter 6, "On Ecclesiastical Power." These two portions, taken together and skillfully patched, were to become the first half of Book IV in the final edition of 1559. In reaction to the ecclesiastical abuses of his time Calvin reaches back through history for a better way. Much of what he says here is an expansion of the lean antitheses already set forth in the letter to Francis I.

Chapter 6: Conclusion of the Letter to Francis I?

General Considerations

A comparison of the dedicatory letter to Francis I and the final chapter of the 1536 *Institutes* suggests that this, and not the end of the letter itself, is the real conclusion of the apology to the king. Chapters 1–5 are primarily the catechism Calvin initially had set out to write, although chapter 5, as we have seen, is a careful examination of the unscriptural sacramental structure and related features of the Roman Catholic Church as well as a catechetical chapter. The threefold structure of chapter 6, however, particularly relates to the appeal to Francis I. The first essay, on Christian freedom, claims on a scriptural basis freedom for Christians in the spiritual (ecclesiastical) as opposed to the political (temporal) sphere. The second essay, on ecclesiastical power, both rejects humanly devised ecclesiastical laws and customs as violations of this freedom, and also tries to demonstrate to the monarch the fact that the Roman Catholic ecclesiastical establishment has usurped some portion of the secular power. There ought to be two kings: Christ over his church and the earthly monarch over his domain. This latter topic is the subject of the third essay, on civil government, designed to assure Francis of the evangelicals' political loyalty, and apprise him of their utter rejection of the false political views of the Anabaptists, and to warn him that the ultimate spiritual stakes are in the hands of God, the King of kings. While many details summarily covered in the dedicatory letter are dealt with in other chapters in passing, the chief arguments of the letter are formally rehearsed in chapter 6 and rounded out.

In chapter 6 Calvin specifically alludes to arguments of the Sorbonne theologians in support of the current Roman Catholic ecclesiastical structures and practices. By skillful scriptural and historical arguments set antithetically against their views, Calvin seeks to refute them, justify his own religious party in the king's eyes, and also (by implication) detach Francis from his malign ecclesiastical advisers.

Specific Content

It will be useful, perhaps, to look in more detail at the three essays that comprise the final chapter.

Christian Freedom. In a sense the problem of freedom is the central theme of chapter 6. Later editions, in fragmenting this chapter and distributing its elements to widely separated contexts, have sacrificed the pointed message. But, as the immediate apologetic task of the first edition receded into the past, new and more multifarious questions arose that called for the expansion and regrouping of the thought of this chapter.

Calvin throughout chapter 6 is steering a middle course between the piling up of laws and the rejection of all laws; he is pleading for a spiritual freedom even in the midst of civil tyranny, unburdened by the yoke of illicit church regulations and at the same time unplagued by wild, unbridled license.

Christian freedom means three things: (1) freedom from the law, (2) freedom of conscience willingly obeying without compulsion of the law, (3) freedom in "things indifferent." Such freedom must never be exercised to the harm of the poor or the weak. We should avoid offensive opulence in living, and sometimes show our freedom by abstaining from exercising it, especially when by so doing we may endanger weak

consciences. But the final determination is not offense against neighbor but offense against God. In pressing the freedom of the Christian
conscience from human traditions and laws, Calvin postulates the distinction between spiritual and political government, more or less par-
alleling his distinction between soul and body.

This first essay on Christian freedom, which with little alteration is
ultimately moved to a new context (between justification and prayer)
in the 1559 edition, serves in the 1536 edition as the introduction to the
discussion of the two kingdoms, a concept already familiar in Luther.
The constitutions of the Roman Church enslave consciences, and thus
deprive Christians of their God-given spiritual freedom.

Ecclesiastical Power. Calvin lays down his views of church order between the radical rejection of all church laws (currently evidenced in
the revolutionary kingdom of Münster) and the senseless heaping up of
all sorts of doctrinal, disciplinary, and ritual requirements which (however recently originated) are claimed by the Romanists to have an apostolic or even dominical origin. The radical or Anabaptist notions are
but mentioned in passing here; the main butt of Calvin's argument in
his second essay is the Roman Church. Against claims that the faith
rests solely on the church's decision, that the clergy and councils of the
church are inerrant, Calvin brings both scriptural and historical coun-
terevidence. In an interesting digression he displays the patrimony of
the church—its usurpation of temporal power and perquisites—as due
to the misguided but pious generosity of princes. Was this an oblique
appeal to Francis I?

The church needs laws to govern itself, to achieve concord in the diversity of human customs; but such are not necessary for salvation:
consciences are not to be bound by them. Here Calvin's view of Christian freedom, already enunciated in the prior essay, is reiterated. And
so Calvin distinguishes between impious ecclesiastical constitutions
and legitimate church ordinances made either for public decency or
based on common usage—hours of worship and the like. The details
are not important; that definite procedures are set is important. We see
here how his adiaphoric principle, elucidated in the previous essay on
Christian freedom, is put to use.

Civil Government. In the final essay, on civil government, the Anabaptists figure much more prominently. As we read these final pages of
the book we clearly see Calvin lecturing the French king both on what
the loyal evangelical French believe and how he as monarch of the
French ought to conduct himself in his office. Calvin first discusses the
necessity of civil government.

Earlier, we mentioned in passing that the defective teaching of the
Anabaptists on soul and body, already criticized in the *Psychopannychia,* has political implications as well.

> Certain men, when they hear that the gospel promises a freedom that ac-
> knowledges no king and no magistrate among men, but looks to Christ
> alone, think that they cannot benefit by their freedom so long as they see
> any power set over them. They therefore think that nothing will be safe
> unless the world is shaped to a new form where there are neither courts,
> nor laws, nor magistrates, nor anything similar which in their opinion re-
> stricts their freedom. But whoever knows how to distinguish between
> body and soul, between this present fleeting life and that future eternal
> life, will without difficulty know that Christ's spiritual kingdom and the
> civil jurisdiction are things completely distinct.[22]

The distinction between body and soul, and the distinction between
the spiritual and political realms are all of one piece. Also, the contrast
between perfectionism held by at least some Anabaptist groups and by
Calvin attributed to them all, and the Calvinian notion of gradual spiritual growth during the present life, is to be associated with this general
antithesis.

Calvin's picture of the function of the establishment and protection
of true religion by the civil authority is consciously constructed against
Anabaptist repudiation of all government but also against Romanist
usurpation of temporal functions to the ecclesiastical sphere. Yet we
must admit that in his delicate balancing of church and state, Calvin
laid himself and the city of Geneva open to frequent conflict between
council and consistory.

> Let no man be disturbed that I now commit to civil government the duty
> of rightly establishing religion, which I seem above to have put outside of
> human decision. For, when I approve of a civil administration that aims
> to prevent the true religion which is contained in God's law from being
> openly and with public sacrilege violated and defiled with impunity, I do
> not here, any more than before, allow men to make laws according to
> their own decision concerning religion and the worship of God.[23]

Calvin's second topic, a discussion of civil government, is divided
into three parts: magistrates, laws, and people.

What, then, does Calvin have to say on the office of *magistrate?* In
what sense may the word "god" be applied to man? In their perfectionism the Anabaptists fancied themselves "god," or so Calvin inferred; in
their ecclesiastical usurpations, the Romanists took unto themselves,
their saints, and their images and eucharistic hosts the name of "god."
To Calvin, like Luther, following especially Psalm 82 and Romans 13,
the only human beings who could scripturally bear the name of "gods"
were the magistrates. And so explicitly against the Anabaptist rejection

22. *Inst. 1536b*, 207.
23. Ibid., 208–9.

of kings and civil authorities, and implicitly against Romanist incursions into the civil sphere, Calvin ringingly asserts the "godship" of the ruler. We are shocked by this sort of teaching until we read the high demands Calvin laid on his civil magistrate. For him "civil authority is the most sacred calling before God, and the most honorable of all callings in the life of mortal men." As if reminding Francis I of his superlative title "Most Christian," Calvin pictures the high office:

> This consideration ought continually to occupy the magistrates themselves, since it can greatly spur them to exercise their office and bring them remarkable comfort to mitigate the difficulties of their task, which are indeed many and burdensome. For what great zeal for uprightness, for prudence, gentleness, self-control and for innocence ought to be required of themselves by those who know that they have been ordained ministers of divine justice? How will they have the brazenness to admit injustice to their judgment seat, which they are told is the throne of the living God? How will they have the boldness to pronounce an unjust sentence by that mouth which they know has been appointed an instrument of divine truth? With what conscience will they sign wicked decrees by that hand which they know has been appointed an instrument of divine truth? With what conscience will they sign wicked decrees by that hand which they know has been appointed to prescribe the acts of God? To sum up, if they remember that they are vicars of God, they should watch with all care, earnestness, and diligence, to represent in themselves to men some image of divine providence, protection, goodness, benevolence, and justice. And they should perpetually set before themselves the thought that "all are cursed who do in deceit the work of God" [Jer. 48:10].[24]

Revolutionaries who rail against this holy ministry as abhorrent to Christian religion and piety are reviling God himself. It is quite apparent that the conflict between Calvin and the Anabaptists is one concerning the use of Scripture. The Anabaptists rest their case primarily in Jesus' sayings viewed apart from their Jewish roots; for Calvin the teachings of Jesus must be seen in the light of the Old Testament as well as the New; and the Pastoral Epistles, at the other end of the Scriptures, also buttress his case. You confuse the office of apostle and king, Calvin warns the Anabaptists. Applying to Scripture the ancient classical distinction between the private and public person (on which Calvin had laid so much emphasis in his Seneca commentary), he uses this in the remaining pages of the chapter as the foundation principle in discerning the interworking of magistrate, laws, and people.

The sole endeavor of the magistrate should be to provide for the common safety and peace of all. In fulfilling his function the magistrate has the power of judicial murder, for in sentencing to death he is but

24. Ibid., 210.

carrying out God's judgments. This would be an unpopular stand to take in modern penology! Here again, an exegetical principle is at stake. The pacifist Anabaptists took a simple biblical prohibition against killing both as a Christian repudiation of the judicial process and especially of capital punishment and the right to wage war. Other radicals were not pacifists, but still repudiated worldly government. It is not improbable that Calvin had in mind the chaos of Münster when he wrote:

> Now if their [the magistrates'] true righteousness is to pursue the guilty and the impious with drawn sword, should they sheath their sword and keep their hands clean of blood, while abandoned men wickedly range about with slaughter and massacre, they will become guilty of the greatest impiety, far indeed from winning praise for their goodness and righteousness thereby.[25]

Throughout this essay on the civil government, there are strong echoes of the Seneca commentary. Earlier, we tentatively spoke of the former as the "first draft" of Calvin's apology to Francis I; unquestionably Calvin is here reworking from this new evangelical Christian vantage point the whole classical teaching on the monarch. This connection between the two writings is especially close as he turns to clemency, clue to the best king, and *epiekeia*, the well-spring of law giving and its application.

True leadership in the state lies between excessive cruelty and exaggerated gentleness. Thus, the use of war must be only as a last resort. Kings must restrain their wrath; they must also restrain their greed and their passion for magnificence; for ultimately the public chest, raised through the right to tax his subjects, is "almost the very blood of the people."

Calvin now turns to the *laws*, the second aspect of civil government, reworking again materials already familiar to readers of the Seneca commentary. As he often does, Calvin begins with the repudiation of an exaggerated position. Jacob Strauss, Andreas Carlstadt, and others had proposed literally substituting the entire Mosaic code of the Old Testament for the civil laws of the European nations. In response to this Calvin sets forth his famous distinction (shared with Melanchthon) of law into three layers: moral, ceremonial, and judicial or civil. Moral law, which has already been discussed in chapter 1 (but without benefit of this tripartite distinction), is nothing else than a testimony of natural law and of that conscience which God has engraved in the minds of men. In his discussion of the Fourth Commandment in chapter 1 and of rites and ceremonies in chapter 5 and chapter 6, part 2, Calvin has al-

25. Ibid., 213.

ready dealt with the ceremonial law. He now concentrates on judicial law. *Epiekeia* (equity) and adiaphora are two principles that inform his discussion of the topic. Equity is the goal and limit of all laws, determining their right framing and their right application in later generations. Among the nations of the world there is and always has been an incredible variety of laws and punishments to be meted out; these varying details are adiaphoric. Fundamental to all laws, however, is their identical end: to punish those crimes that God's eternal law has condemned, but according to the specific needs of particular times and places.

The final topic is the *people*, for whom magistrates and laws exist, and who are to respond in obedience to him. Again, Calvin sets the stage for his discussion by sketching exaggerated views: in 1 Corinthians Paul had referred to the passionate litigiousness of certain Corinthian Christians. These constitute one extreme—the persons who use the law courts to excess. At the other end are the Anabaptists, who hold the courts of law to be superfluous among Christians. Calvin's exposition of the Christian people's course is a mean between these two extremes. Use the law courts? Yes, with Christian love toward one's legal opponent. To repudiate the courts is for Christians to repudiate God's holy ordinance. Do not lust for revenge, but with equity and moderation of mind use the God-given office of magistrate and court to seek justice.

Calvin reserves to the very end of the *Institutes* the vexed question of what sort of obedience the subjects owe their sovereign. Here he is speaking both to Francis I and to his own countrymen. To the magistrate (under whatever political system one lives) is owed obedience because the magistrate is the vicegerent of God. Amassing evidence especially from the Old Testament history (e.g., Daniel, Jeremiah) Calvin argues for obedience not only to the just ruler, but even to the unjust, for the latter is a judgment of God on the people. Private individuals have no right to take the law into their own hands.

However, God does provide some relief from oppression, in his own good time. He raises up, history teaches us, two kinds of avengers against unjust rulers: his public servants, lesser magistrates whose task it is to defend the people (ephors in Sparta, tribunes in Rome, and the three estates in France are given as examples); second, others who in their rage unwittingly do God's will.

Lastly, Calvin reminds Francis I and the persecuted evangelical French that there is but one King of kings. When obedience to the ruler leads away from obedience to God, then "We must obey God rather than men." The last lines of the Book then reecho and amplify the closing words of the dedicatory letter.

4 God Was Accommodating Himself to Human Capacity[1]

Any study of Calvin as scriptural exegete that failed to examine his frequent appeal to the principle of accommodation would be incomplete.[2] Yet, at least in the *Institutes of the Christian Religion* and presumably elsewhere, he never uses the noun *accommodatio*, but always either the verb *accommodare* or *attemperare*, when he has recourse to this principle. Thus, it would be incorrect to entitle this short essay, "Calvin's Use of Accommodation." Our title, therefore, by using the verb instead of the noun, reflects both Calvin's usage and his intent.

In the Battles–Hugo edition of *Calvin's Commentary on Seneca's De Clementia* I have traced the roots of Calvin's rhetoric in the rhetoricians of classical Greece and Rome. The ancient rhetoricians evolved the principles of their art both to clothe in suitable language what they wrote and spoke and also to interpret what had been written and spoken by others. Trained in this school, Calvin served his apprenticeship in commenting on classical texts, notably the *De Clementia* of Lucius Annaeus Seneca. After his conversion, all of Calvin's classical learning was transmuted. In a sense, he exchanged for human rhetoric a divine rhetoric (*Inst.* 1.8.1f.). He saw the task of the theologian no longer as speculative, primarily philosophical, but rather as pasto-

1. From *Interpretation: A Journal of Bible and Theology* 31 (1977): 19–38. Used by permission.

2. I know of only one contemporary study explicitly devoted to accommodation: Clinton Ashely, "John Calvin's Utilization of the Principle of Accommodation and Its Continuing Significance for an Understanding of Biblical Language" (Ph.D. diss., Southwest Baptist Theological Seminary, 1972). It has not been used in preparing this essay. While the evidence of Calvin's biblical commentaries has been examined, this essay rests primarily on the *Institutes* in which every aspect of accommodation has apparently been set forth. Nowhere, however, is it the topic of a separate locus: rather, it is everywhere assumed as a working principle.

ral, pedagogical (*Inst.* 1.14.4) and making large if guarded use of the rhetorical discipline.[3]

As in human rhetoric there is a gulf between the highly educated and the comparatively unlearned, between the convinced and the unconvinced, a gulf which it is the task of rhetoric to bridge so that through simple, appropriate language the deeps of human thought yield up their treasure, or at least the views of the speaker are persuasively communicated—analogously in divine rhetoric the infinitely greater gulf between God and man, through divine condescension, in word and deed, is bridged. And the divinely appointed human authors and expositors of Scripture express and expound the divine rhetoric under the Spirit's guidance for the benefit of all.

In so espousing the divine rhetoric, Calvin was no innovator; before him went a cloud of patristic witnesses who, in response to the destructive critique of the Scriptures by pagan and heretic alike, had contended that God in revelation was adjusting the portrait of himself to the capacity of the human mind and heart. But, unlike an Origen, or an Augustine, or a John Chrysostom, or a Hilary of Poitiers, Calvin makes this principle a consistent basis for his handling not only of Scripture but of every avenue of relationship between God and man. Thus, the starkest inconsistencies in Scripture are harmonized through rhetorical analysis, within the frame of divine accommodation, to human capacity; but, more than merely serving as an apologetical device, this method unlocks for Calvin God's beneficent tutelage and pedagogy of his wayward children.

Such a method can be little more than an intellectual exercise unless it is grounded in a firm faith. With Paul, Calvin sees human beings—even before the Fall—as creatures far removed from their Creator. He sees human language as utterly insufficient to bridge this gap. Therefore, in Calvin's picture of God three biblical themes especially stand out: God is first and foremost our *Father,* our divine parent exceeding all human parents. Second, he is our *teacher,* who well knows his pupils. Third, he is our *physician,* who skillfully diagnoses our diseases. Thus, at the outset we have the three analogies: of parental care, of instruction, and of healing. The weakness and inexperience of childhood, the ignorance of the schoolboy, and the disease of the sick, respectively, correspond to these three divine roles.

But the rhetorician's task is not merely to bridge the gulf of weakness or ignorance. As in the law court, the advocate seeks to sway the judge

---

3. Calvin refused to use rhetoric for its own sake or for illegitimate purposes. In *Comm. Sen. De Clem.*, 38 (9:line 38), he says: "I have no desire here to indulge in long-winded conceited ostentation; I leave declamation to the rhetoricians." At *Comm. Ps.* 95:3, he spurns "the lying panegyric with which rhetoricians flatter earthly princes." See *Comm. Sen. De Clem.*, 76*, note 1.

to either mercy or punishment, so God has to deal not only with inexperience and ignorance but with willful stubbornness and disobedience. The divine rhetoric then becomes a rhetoric of violence, or exaggeration, of unbelievable heightening. Scripture exhibits all shades and moods of divine rhetoric, from the physician's soothing balm to the surgeon's scalpel. We should therefore add to our self-portraits of God that of the judge; and to our figurative institutions of nursery and family, school and hospital, that of the law court.

Here we begin to see that, for Calvin, accommodation has to do not only with Scripture and its interpretation, but with the whole of created reality to which, for the Christian, Scripture holds the clue. The entire created universe and all its parts are naught but a grand accommodation on God's part of himself to the crowning glory (and subsequent shame) of that creation, namely, man. The six days of creation bear the message of God's tender care of his human offspring. The unfolding of subsequent history within that universal theater and all the structures of society that mark that history—these, too—decode the message of a just and merciful God to his errant offspring. Here we have in mind preeminently the institutions of state and church, whose divinely ordained symbiosis Calvin recognizes.

But more specifically we see in the political sphere, ordered by law however imperfectly and governed by divinely ordained leaders even in their misrule, a reflection of the divine tutelage. Parallelly, in the ecclesiastical sphere we see the God-given realities of Word and sacrament set within a structure of discipline and worship and administered by human functionaries as a prime instance of divine accommodation, of *adminicula* (helps) to salvation.

At the center of God's accommodating himself to human capacity, however, is his supreme act of condescension, the giving of his only Son to reconcile a fallen world to himself. If accommodation is the speechbridge between the known and the unknown, between the infinitesimal and the infinite, between the apparent and the real, between the human and the divine, the Logos who tented among us is the point from which we must view creation, Fall, and all history, before and since the incarnation. For Calvin, then, in every act of divine accommodating, the whole Trinity—Father, Son, and Holy Spirit—is at work.

Accommodation in Classical Rhetoric

The classical rhetoricians recognized five "offices" in their discipline: invention, disposition, elocution, pronunciation, memory. These are actually stages in the preparation of an oration or of other literary forms. *Invention* consists in the finding out or selection of topics to be treated or arguments to be used—the analysis of the topic for discourse and the assembling of materials. *Disposition* is the due arrangement of the parts of an argument or discussion into an ordered discourse. *Elocution* is more or less synonymous with our word "style"—the choice of language appropriate to the topic and the intended audience. *Pronunciation* (cf. *Inst.* 2.7.11) is what we would call the delivery of the speech. In each of these stages accommodation takes place; in fact, the whole process of rhetorical construction of discourse is one continuous act of accommodation. This is well brought out in the Pseudo-Ciceronian treatise, *Rhetorica ad Herennium* (1.2.3): "Elocution is the accommodation of suitable words and sentences to invention" (cf. Cicero, *De Inventione Rhetorica* 1.9). Also, another rhetorician uses the same word in reference to *pronunciation:* "Pronunciation is worthiness of words, accommodation of the voice to the sense, and moderation of body" (Albin., *Rhet.* 546:12). The corresponding verb *accommodare* is widely found in the Latin rhetoricians in the same sense of fitting, adapting, adjusting language, of building a speech-bridge between the matter of discourse and the intended audience. For example, Cicero (*De Orat.* 2.159) states that "the oration is to be accommodated to the ears of the multitude." Quintilian (*Inst. Orat.* 8.2.6; 9.1.15) quotes Livy to the effect that words are to be accommodated to the things to which they refer. Cato speaks of accommodating a fit form of matter, senses, sentences, and words to the use of the reader (cf. *Agr.* 21.5; 22.1; 135.7). The rhetorical uses of this verb could be multiplied. It was also a technical term among the jurisconsults with reference to legal actions (judicial forms) that were adapted to certain definite cases. Calvin uses also a synonymous verb, *attemperare,* but classical Latin did not apparently employ it as a technical term of rhetoric. The earliest uses of the latter word similar to Calvin's are found in Tertullian.

However *accommodare,* then, was used in Latin rhetoric, it always had to do with the adaptation of the verbal representation of the matter under consideration to the persons being addressed, with full regard to their situation, character, intelligence, and emotional makeup. In his reading of the classics, Calvin frequently came across *accommodare* in Cicero, Quintilian, and the minor rhetoricians.

The Use of Accommodation by the Church Fathers

Whenever a religious tradition is translated from one language to another, an enormous act of accommodation takes place. Such accommodation began in the Septuagint version of the Old Testament, with the initial restatement of Hebrew religious concepts in Greek, continued in the New Testament itself, and moved (as Christianity became a religion of the Gentile world) into the heterodox and orthodox formulations of the patristic era of the church. The Gnostics and Marcionites in their dehistoricization of the gospel were in fact radical accommodators of Scripture, even though they laid the very same charge of hypocrisy against the apostles (according to Irenaeus): the apostles, they said, were guilty of hypocrisy for they framed their teaching to the capacity of their hearers, tailoring their answers to the opinions and prejudices of their questioners, thus subverting the truth. No, says Irenaeus, the apostles actually taught the true and unaccommodated doctrine that leads to salvation (*Adv. Haer.* 3.5.2). Yet Irenaeus himself seems to hint at accommodation when he states that "the unmeasurable Father was Himself subjected to measure in the Son, for the Son is the measure of the Father, since He also comprehends Him" (*A.H.* 4.4.2). Calvin (*Inst.* 2.6.4) interprets this to mean "the Father, himself infinite, becomes finite in the Son, for He has accommodated himself to our little measure lest our minds be overwhelmed by the immensity of His glory." Irenaeus shows himself a master of scriptural accommodation in his teaching on Christ. Taking a mediating position between the two extremes of Gnostic Docetism and Jewish Ebionism (*A.H.* 3.16ff.), he emphasizes Christ's human characteristics against the former, and his divine against the latter, with the virgin birth a crucial proof. He denies both the Gnostic doctrine of two Christs and the "pusillanthropous" view of Judaizing Ebionism.

The principle of accommodation seems to emerge more explicitly in the exegetical work of the School of Alexandria, grounded in the prior thought of Philo Judaeus, whose hermeneutical rules included a way of dealing with the anthropomorphisms of Scripture: "The lawgiver talks thus in human terms about God, even though he is not a human being, for the advantage of us who are being educated, as I have often said in other passages" (Philo, commenting on Gen. 11:5). This principle is repeated in Clement of Alexandria (*Strom.* 2.16.72): "But in as far as it was possible for us to hear, burdened as we were with flesh, so did the prophets speak to us, as the Lord accommodated himself to human weakness for our salvation."

For Origen, accommodation (the Greek term is *symperiphora*) can, through the allegorical senses of Scripture, work in two opposing ways: it can reveal divine truths to the godly; it can conceal them from the godless. The meaning of *symperiphora* is often illustrated by an image later used by Augustine, Calvin, and others—that of an adult stooping to a child: "He condescends and lowers Himself *accommodating Himself* to our weakness, like a schoolmaster talking a 'little language' *(symphellizon)* to his children, like a father caring for his own children and adopting their ways."[4] The same analogy is used by Ori-

---

4. Frag. on Deut. 1:21, *Patrologiae Graeca* 17.24, quoted by R. P. C. Hanson, *Allegory and Event* (Richmond, Va.: John Knox, 1959), 226.

gen in his reply to Celsus' attacks on the anthropomorphism of the Old Testament:

> Just as when we are talking to very small children we do not assume as the object of our instruction any strong understanding in them, but say what we have to say accommodating it to the small understanding of those whom we have before us, and even do what seems to us useful for the education and bringing up of children, realizing that they are children: so the Word of God seems to have disposed the things which were written, adapting the suitable parts of his message to the capacity of his hearers and to their ultimate profit.[5]

Even more detailed is Origen's use of this analogy when he endeavors to explain how God can be said in the Bible to repent or change his mind:

> But when the providence of God is involved in human affairs, he assumes the human mind and manner and diction. When we talk to a child of two we talk baby-talk because he is a child, for as long as we maintain the character appropriate to an adult age, and speak to children without adapting ourselves to their speech, children cannot understand us. Now imagine a similar situation confronting God when he comes to deal with the human race, and particularly with those who are still "babes." Notice too how we who are adults change the names of things for children, and we have a special name for bread with them, and we call drinking by some other word, not using the language of adults. . . . And if we name clothes to children we give other names to them, as if we were inventing a child's name for them. Do we suffer from arrested development when we do this? And if someone hears us talking to children, will he say, "This old man is losing his mind, this man has forgotten that his beard is grown, that he is a grown-up man?" Or is it allowable for the sake of *accommodation*, when we are associating with a child not to talk the language of older and mature people, but to talk in a child's language?[6]

Origen's chief theological work, *On First Principles*, is really a textbook in accommodation: how Scripture is to be interpreted for human salvation. His system of allegorical senses rests on the conviction that God, taking cognizance of human limitations, has fashioned Scripture in three levels of meaning, corresponding to the three parts of man: body, soul, and spirit (4.2.4). Spiritual truth finds its vehicle in physical language about God and in the literal crudities of biblical history. In all this, God as our physician and teacher is couching his truths in language we can understand.

5. Hanson, *Allegory and Event*, 226, from *Contra Celsum* 4.71; 5.16.
6. Ibid., 227, from *Homilies on Jeremiah* 18.6.

The Holy Spirit does not depend on feeble human eloquence. No created mind can by any means possess the capacity to understand all; this is true even of higher beings than man. Let everyone, then, who cares for truth, care little about names and words, for different kinds of speech are customary in different nations. Let him be more anxious about the fact signified, particularly in questions of difficulty and importance. This should be the controlling rule of interpretation: "There are certain things, the meaning of which it is impossible adequately to explain by any human language, but which are made clear rather through simple apprehension than through any power of words" (4.3.14).

The School of Antioch, which developed in reaction to the excessive allegorism of Alexandria, reached its peak in the exegete Theodore of Mopsuestia and the preacher John Chrysostom. Yet even in this more historically oriented school of interpretation, accommodation was an important principle. One sees it, for example, in their discussion of the varied styles of the biblical writers, or in the pedagogy of our Lord, especially in the parables. Berkouwer sums up Chrysostom's view of Christ's use of accommodation: "Christ often checked himself for the sake of the weakness of his hearers when he dealt with lofty doctrines and he usually did not choose such words as were in accord with his glory, but rather those which agreed with the capability of men."[7] This is seen in Christ's deliberate delay in performing miracles in order to catch the attention of his hearers and thus heighten the faith-giving force of those miracles.

Since the time of Tertullian, accommodation has frequently been appealed to in the Latin West. Hilary of Poitiers, trained in classical rhetoric, devoted his career largely to the combatting of the Arian heresy. In his chief work, *On the Trinity,* he frequently adverts to the limitations of human speech in handling divine truth and eloquently portrays God's supreme act of condescension in Christ. Actually, against the crass literalism of Arius ("there was a time before the creation of the Son when God was not yet Father") accommodation of the scriptural language was a powerful weapon. Hilary in his *Tractates on the Psalms* (Ps. 126:6) explicitly refers to accommodation: "For the divine Word *tempers* (*temperare*) itself to the habit and nature of our understanding, by common words of things adapted to the signification of his doctrine and institution."

It is in Augustine, however, and notably in his *On Christian Doctrine,* that the "scaling down" of the divine speech to human capacity is laid out. Augustine, as a teacher of rhetoric, was put off repeatedly by what seemed to him the rude and barbarous style of Scripture. As he por-

---

7. G. C. Berkouwer, *Holy Scripture,* trans. and ed. by Jack B. Rogers (Grand Rapids: Eerdmans, 1975), 175f.

trays his pilgrimage to faith in his *Confessions*, he did not come to full Christian belief until he realized that sublimity of style and depth of truth are very often not found together. This insight is developed at length in *On Christian Doctrine*, the first Christian rhetoric.

In freeing himself from the Manichees, Augustine had early to come to terms with the Christian doctrine of creation and with the Book of Genesis. The Manichees had, like the Gnostics and Marcionites before them, amassed antitheses between the Old and New Testaments. These he endeavors to resolve in his reply to Adimantus, often using accommodation as his means. And in his *Genesis according to the Literal Sense*, he picks up the familiar figure of a mother stooping down to her child to illustrate the way of scriptural language with our weakness. Calvin's reading of Augustine clearly familiarized him with accommodation as a hermeneutical principle; yet he did not accept the excessive allegorism that Augustine had bequeathed to the medieval West.

We may conclude our brief survey of the patristic use of accommodation with a reference to Maximus the Confessor, who explained the prime anthropomorphism of the Old Testament, God's "repentance," "as an accommodation of biblical language to human ways of speaking. Scripture spoke in a way that was not literally accurate, in order to enable its readers to grasp what transcended literal accuracy."[8]

Some Scriptural Inconsistencies That Calvin Resolves through Accommodation

Accommodation begins as an apologetical tool against hostile critics of Scripture; it ends as a pastoral instrument for the edification of believers. Both these notes are struck in Calvin's frequent use of accommodation. Let us first illustrate the former use by four examples, taken from Book I of the *Institutes;* these we shall set out in propositional fashion for the sake of emphasis:

God's Nature (1.13.1)

Apparent teaching of Scripture: God has a mouth, ears, eyes, hands, and feet.

True teaching: God's infinite and spiritual essence.

Accommodation: As nurses commonly do with infants, God speaks "baby talk" to us: thus such forms of speaking do not so much express clearly what God is like as accommodate the knowledge of him to our slight capacity. To do so he must descend far beneath his loftiness.

---

8. *Patrologia Graeca* (hereafter PG) 90.621, 812, cited by Jaroslav J. Pelikan, *The Christian Tradition*, 5 vols. (Chicago: University of Chicago Press, 1974), 2:14.

The Creation of the Angels (1.14.3)

Apparent teaching of Scripture: The angels are not mentioned in the scriptural account of creation, yet they are afterward introduced as ministers of God.

True teaching: Unquestionably, angels are creatures of God.

Accommodation: Moses, accommodating himself to the rudeness of the common folk, mentions in the history of the creation no other works of God than those that show themselves to our own eyes.

The Function of the Angels (1.14.11)

Apparent teaching of Scripture: God uses angels to carry out his commands.

True teaching: God has no need of angels to carry out his commands; in fact, he sometimes disregards them and acts directly.

Accommodation: God uses angels to accommodate to our feeble capacity and show us more intimately his loving protection of us.

Fate (1.16.9)

Apparent teaching of Scripture: The same fate awaits man and beast, good man and sinner, wise man and fool (cf. Eccles. 2:14f.; 3:19; 9:2–3, 11).

True teaching: Fate, fortune, chance are pagan terms inadmissible to Christians; nothing is fortuitous, but all things live under God's secret plan.

Accommodation: The sluggishness and limits of the human mind see as fortuitous those things that are actually ordered by God's purpose: Scripture uses "fate" and "fortune" to explain seemingly contingent events, but known to faith to derive from a secret impulse of God.

God's Ways with Man: Does He Repent? (1.17.12f.)

Apparent teaching of Scripture: Since God repented of having created man, of having put Saul over the kingdom, and of the evil he determined to inflict on his people, therefore he has not determined the affairs of humankind by an eternal decree, but, according to each individual's deserts or according as he deems him fair and just, he decrees this or that each year, each day, and each hour.

True teaching: God's ordinance in the managing of human affairs is both everlasting and above all repentance: his plan and will proceed unchangeably from eternity.

Accommodation: God represents himself to us not as he is in himself, but as he seems to us, to accommodate to our weak capacity his description of himself.

In each of these instances, Calvin began as apologist for Scripture, but in his recourse to accommodation he seized upon instruction. Thus the two uses with which we began are actually one.

Scriptural Portraits of God and Humanity:
Ground of Accommodation

A. God's Self-Portraits: The greatest apparent inconsistencies in Scripture, long recognized by believers and nonbelievers, by Jews and Christians alike, are those between the Old and New Covenants. Hence a major effort of Christian exegetes has always been, by some means, to harmonize or at least explain such discrepancies. Calvin's appeal to accommodation has therefore very often to do with the differing dispensations of the Old and New Testaments. Building especially on the apostle Paul (physical/spiritual Israel; law as tutor to Christ) and the author of Hebrews (shadow/reality) as their thought was elaborated by Augustine, Calvin (without explicitly postulating a doctrine of progressive revelation) saw a spiritual growth, an advance toward spiritual maturity, in the pilgrimage of Israel to Christ. Two portraits of God metaphorically share the depiction of this upward movement from childhood to adulthood: God as father and God as teacher. In some Calvinian contexts, it would be difficult to determine which of the two is the ruling metaphor, for both family and school concern themselves with the growth of children.

1. God as Father. Yet the Fatherhood of God, so often referred specifically to the history of Israel, also has a universal reference in the creation itself:

> we ought in the very order of things diligently to contemplate God's fatherly love toward mankind, in that He did not create Adam until He had lavished upon the universe all manner of good things. For if He had put him in an earth as yet sterile and empty, if He had given him life before light, He would have seemed to provide insufficiently for his welfare. Now, when He disposed the movements of sun and stars to human uses, filled the earth, waters and air with living things, and brought forth an abundance of fruits to suffice as foods, in thus assuming the responsibility of a foreseeing and diligent father of the family He shows His wonderful goodness toward us (1.14.2).

Summing up his doctrine of creation in the same chapter of the *Institutes,* Calvin adverts once more to the same theme, that by the order of creation God shows that he created all things for man's sake: "the dispensation of all those things which He has made is in His own hand and power and . . . we are indeed His children, whom He has received into His faithful protection, to nourish and educate" (1.14.22).

In taking up the differences between the Old and New Testaments (*Inst.* 2.11), Calvin warns us not to consider God changeable "merely because He accommodated diverse forms to different ages, as He knew would be expedient for each." This Calvin illustrates by the simile of the farmer and of the householder; of the latter he says: "if a householder instructs, rules, and guides his children one way in infancy, another way in youth, and still another in young manhood, we shall not on this account call him fickle and say that he abandons his purpose. Why, then, do we brand God with the mark of inconstancy when He has with apt and fitting marks distinguished a diversity of times?" (2.11.13). Calvin then relates this comparison to Galatians 4:1ff., where Paul likens the ancient Jews to children, Christians to young men. He sums up with the assertion that such varied dispensation does not show God subject to change. "Rather, He has accommodated Himself to men's capacity which is varied and changeable" (2.11.13).

As we have pointed out in our note to *Institutes* 2.7.2, Calvin frequently describes the spiritual development of the ancient Hebrew vis-à-vis Christ as a childhood "that rendered necessary the accommodation of revelation to an elementary mentality in the Old Testament" (cf. 1.11.3; 2.11.2; 2.10.6; *Comm. Gen.* 1:16; 2:8).

As in the larger sweep of history from ancient Jew to Christian, so in the personal history of the believer, in his growth in the faith, Calvin uses the same analogy of Father and child, even as Paul had distinguished between the milk suitable for the childhood of belief and the strong meat digestible by the mature Christian. Underlying the short treatise on the Christian life (*Inst.* 3.6.10), which describes the restoration of the image of God in humanity as a growing process throughout life, is the same sense of God's fatherly accommodation to, and tutelage of, humanity's feeble capacity. The cross, for example, which we must bear, is described as "fatherly chastisement" (3.8.6).

The father of the household also portrays the providence with which God guides his earthly family. In his commentary on Psalm 11:6, Calvin states that the metaphor of the householder is used to teach the carnal mind that calamities and mercies do not happen by chance, but according to God's just distribution.

Among the other Calvinian passages that portray accommodation in terms of a father's care for his children, we can take up here only Calvin's gloss of the opening words of the Lord's Prayer, "Our Father." Commenting on the parable of the prodigal son, he says:

in setting forth this example of great compassion to be seen in man, He willed to teach us how much more abundantly we ought to expect it of Him. For He is not only a father but by far the best and kindest of all fathers, provided we still cast ourselves upon His mercy, although we are ungrateful, rebellious, and forward children. And to strengthen our assurance that He is this sort of father to us if we are Christians, He willed that we call Him not only "Father" but explicitly "our Father" (3.20.37).

2. God as Teacher. In discussing the ancient portraits of God as father and as teacher, our emphasis is not on Calvin's originality in using these well-worn figures of speech, but rather on their functioning as foundation images for his conviction that in all his ways with man, God is accommodating his infinity to our small measure. The parabolic method of the prophets and of our Lord often utilizes a qualitative or quantitative difference between high and low within human society as the clue to the infinitely greater contrast between God and man. This is the force of the "How much more . . . ," "How much greater . . . ," so frequently on Jesus' lips. As the parent stands higher than the infant, so the teacher is above his pupil. But this superiority is not one of tyranny but of tutelage. The instruction fits the pupil where he is. This "scaling down" is at the center of Calvin's appeal to accommodation: for him, the Christian spends his life in the school of Christ.

This metaphor dominated the theology of Alexandria. The second treatise in Clement of Alexandria's great trilogy, *The Instructor,* sees Christ as our tutor unto salvation. For his successor, Origen, the curriculum extends from our earthly life to our future life in heaven, where we shall be educated in ever-new secrets of God. One senses also in the *Confessions* of Augustine a teacher–pupil relationship in his divinely directed pilgrimage to faith. The insights of the *De Magistro* doubtless draw on Augustine's awareness of God as teacher.

In the Reformation era, too, Calvin was not alone in picturing the locus of Christian growth as a school. Among other Reformers who employed the analogy was the Silesian nobleman, Caspar Schwenckfeld von Ossig, and the Nuremberg radical reformer, Hans Denck. The latter used the term "School of the Spirit";[9] Schwenckfeld prefers "School of Christ."[10]

Calvin (*Inst.,* 3.21.3) calls Scripture the "School of the Holy Spirit"; in his *Sermons on the Epistle to the Galatians,* 12, 26 (*CR,* 50:424, 597), the "School of God." Sometimes Christ is called the teacher (*Inst.* 2.15.2; 3.2.4,6; 3.20.48), or the Holy Spirit is "the inner teacher" (1.9.1; 3.1.4; 3.2.34; 4.14.9) or "the schoolmaster" (4.17.36). Let us content ourselves with but one illustration of this common Calvinian comparison; in searching out scriptural limits to the doctrine of predestination, he says: "For Scripture is the school of the Holy Spirit in which, as nothing is omitted that is both necessary and useful to know, so nothing is taught but what is expedient to know (3.21.3). . . . We are to fol-

---

9. From Denck, "Divine Order," ch. 6, in Edward J. Furcha, with Ford Lewis Battles, *Selected Writings of Hans Denck* (Pittsburgh: Pittsburgh Theological Seminary, 1975), 89; it also appears in E. J. Furcha, *Selected Writings of Hans Denck 1500–1527,* rev. ed. (Lewiston, N.Y.: Edwin Mellen, 1989), 258.

10. Edward J. Furcha, with Ford Lewis Battles, *The Piety of Caspar Schwenckfeld* (Pittsburgh: Pittsburgh Theological Seminary, 1969), 13.

low God's lead always in learning, but, when He sets an end to teaching
. . . stop trying to be wise."

Calvin attends not only to the teacher, but also to the pupil and to his
course of study. The organizing principle of the *Institutes* is not philosophical or even theological (in the traditional scholastic way): it is primarily pedagogical. From his earliest steps after conversion, Calvin
was himself marked as a teacher. It is therefore understandable that he
has ordered the *Institutes* after the "right order of teaching." For him
doctrina resumes its rightful and root meaning of teaching, *didache*. As
one chosen of God to expound the Scriptures, he saw this human task
to be a reflection or rather a recapitulation of the divine work of revealing, through scaled down and carefully planned teaching, what is needful of God's nature and purposes for human salvation. That Calvin was
sensitive to the limits God the accommodator had set in Scripture to
the knowledge of divine things—the parameters of accommodation—
is frequently brought to our minds, particularly when boundaries are
set to human speculation, notably in his discussion of predestination,
as suggested above.

3. God as Physician. The Latin word for salvation (in fact, the parent
word from which our English term takes its origin) is *salus*. *Salus* has
two root meanings: safety and health. Christian salvation partakes of
both notions—Christ both provides a safe haven for souls buffeted on
the sea of the world and heals our spiritual illnesses. It would be point-
less here to amass the countless references, within or without the
Judeo-Christian tradition, to the divine healer: the uses of this obvious
metaphor are legion. Certainly, from earliest patristic times full use of
it was made from biblical sources. One is reminded of the ancient description by Ignatius of Antioch of the Eucharist as the "medicine of
immortality." If death was the dread disease brought on humankind by
their primordial disobedience, the work of Christ was to heal that disease and bring humanity to *aphtharsia, immortalitas,* deathlessness.
God the physician is frequently mentioned by Origen: the divine physician accommodates his treatment to the nature of the sinner's spiritual
ailment.

The analogy of physician, as one would expect, is put to good (if less
frequent) use than that of father or teacher by Calvin. Even as the two
former analogies are used to express the divine accommodation effected in the transition from the Old to the New Dispensation, so is the
portrait of God as physician thus used. When critics object, in commenting on the contrast between the Old and the New Covenants, that
it is "not fitting for God, always self-consistent, to permit such a great
change—afterward disapproving what He had once commanded and
commended," Calvin replies: "If a physician cures a young man of disease in the best way, but uses another sort of remedy on the same per-

son when he is old, shall we then say that he has rejected the method of cure that had pleased him before? No—while he perseveres in it, he takes into account the factor of age" (2.11.14). God ought not to be considered changeable merely because he accommodated diverse forms to different ages, as he knew would be expedient for each. What is changeable is man's capacity.

Again it is the portrait of God the physician that Calvin has in mind when he speaks of election as "God's healing hand": "Therefore, though all of us are by nature suffering from the same disease, only those whom it pleases the Lord to touch with His healing hand will get well. The others, whom He, in His righteous judgment, passes over, waste away in their own rottenness until they are consumed" (2.5.3). The cross of Christ is God's medicine for us: "Some are tried by one kind of cross, others by another. But since the heavenly physician treats some more gently but cleanses others by harsher remedies while He wills to provide for the health of all, He yet leaves no one free and untouched, because He knows that all, to a man, are diseased" (3.8.5).

B. Man: Portrait of Insufficiency—Vocabulary of Weakness: Over against the scripturally derived portraits of God as father, teacher, and physician, we must of course set mankind as child, schoolboy, and sick person. Yet the picture of human beings in their weakness bursts the bounds of these three sketches. We shall not here itemize the rich vocabulary of weakness that Calvin uses to paint humanity not only in their fallenness but even in the Pauline contrast of Creator/creatures. Romans 1 provides the key, as has been suggested in my reflections on Calvin's conversion (*Inst. 1536*, xvi–xvii). Calvin also affords us a summary of humanity's insufficiency in the long prayer of confession that begins the Strasbourg/Geneva liturgy.

The key word for Calvin is *captus*, capacity. Frequently (as already noted) the verb *accommodare* or *attemperare* is associated with this noun: "accommodated to our capacity." The same idea is also expressed by *measure*. We try to measure God's immeasurableness by our small measure. But it is God who knows the incalculable difference in measure between his infinity and our finiteness, and accordingly accommodates the one to the other in the way in which he reveals himself to us.

Our *captus* is described in many and varied ways. Sometimes it is our vision that is singled out—we suffer from *lippitudo*, blearedness. Sometimes it is our *hebetudo*, our sluggishness, which stands in the way. One could multiply the words that bespeak for Calvin our human condition: let that be the theme of a separate investigation. It is our *captus* that God knows so well. As Calvin, commenting on Psalm 78:60, puts it: "God, it is true, fills both heaven and earth; but as we cannot attain to that infinite height to which He is exalted, in descending among us by the exercise of His power and grace, He approaches as near to us as is needful, and as our limited capacity will bear" (CTS Ps. 3.270). The effect of the Fall on human *captus* is concentratedly described in the opening lines of *Institution 1536,* chapter 1 (20f.).

God's Avenues of Accommodation

Assuming the contrast between Creator and creatures, between God and human beings (*Inst.* 1) and the even greater gulf between divinity and fallen human nature (*Inst.* 2), what bridges has God thrown across that gulf? There is a sense in which the entire visible creation is such a bridge or avenue of revelation, even though for man in his fallenness and insensitivity these clear evidences leave him inexcusable before God. God clothes, so to speak, his invisible, inaccessible nature with the visible, palpable raiment of the universe in which we live (*Inst.* 1.5.1). In these lineaments small or vast—yet still finite—he condescends to our *captus.* And more narrowly, man, the apex of God's creation, also in his own divinely fashioned physical body is an evidence of God's accommodation of himself to the measure of human understanding (*Inst.* 1.5.2).

Hence if we but look around us at the ordered motion of the heavens, the procession of the seasons, the ordinary and extraordinary miracles of human existence, we see in this theater, in this mirror, accommodated to our creaturely selves, the ways of God to us. For Cicero the universe was a *temple.* Not so for Calvin: with Plutarch he chooses as his ruling metaphor the *theater.* As a stage play is itself an accommodated representation of the playwright's inspiration and insight into human existence to the more limited vision of his audience, so in the vast theater of heaven and earth the divine playwright stages the ongoing drama of creation, alienation, return, and forgiveness for the teeming audience of humanity itself. Or, to change the metaphor, God whose brightness is beyond human seeing vouchsafes to us a dimmed, reflected image of himself, accommodated to our creatureliness.

It may be that we have succumbed to the temptation of putting the concept of accommodation too much at the center of Calvin's thought and of trying to organize everything around this notion. Yet, if this be a faithful interpretation, accommodation would seem (even when Calvin does not explicitly advert to it) his fundamental way of explaining how the secret, hidden God reveals himself to us. Everything of which our senses bring knowledge to us—from our puny bodies to the stars, microcosm, and macrocosm—is the work of a beneficent Creator who for our sakes thus shows himself in these ways, varied, faceted, yet altogether a unity. That, however, we may not give the impression of Calvin as a natural theologian, we must quickly assert that this picture of creation as accommodated revelation of God to us takes its scriptural starting point not in Genesis 1 so much as in Romans 1. The *Institutes* is constructed backward from the incarnation through the law, the Fall to the creation, from the second Adam to the first Adam. The theater is built, the stage set, wherein the audience, inexcusable in its blindness, may at last view its true destiny in Christ. Step by step, calculated to our capacity, God moves the drama forward to its heavenly dénouement.

We have spoken of the created universe and of the human body as physical, scaled down, accommodatory avenues between God and man. To a degree a similar reading may be given of the two chief modes in the human ordering of creation—the civil and ecclesiastical structures of society. These are so depicted at the beginning and end of Book I of the *Institutes*. In fact, Book IV in its totality describes God's accommodation to the weakness of his people. The very choice of a human ministry to proclaim the saving message and to nurture us in spiritual growth is in itself an act of accommodation by God to our capacity. And its varied forms throughout times and places are divinely ordained accommodation to varied human needs. To paraphrase Calvin: all the outward helps that the church provides, and in fact is, accommodate to our sluggishness the acceptance of Christ, who becomes ours through faith in the gospel (4.1.1).

Similarly, the peace that a well-ordered civil administration—as necessary to human beings as sun or air or water or bread—is an accommodatory work of God. It provides a protective form within which spiritual government (which gives us a foretaste of immortal and incorruptible blessedness) can function. We may infer from the six ends that Calvin assigns to civil government and from his general views of the political order that it is to accommodate man's obedience to the King of kings to whom ultimately loyalty is owed. Calvin's particular application of his views to the government of Geneva is a bold effort truly to crown God as the King of his people (4.20.22ff.; cf. 3.20.43; 4.20.32). The great variety of legal and political forms in human history, again, are calculated to the differing capacities of mankind (4.20.8). But beyond the convenience and welfare of men, these civil and churchly structures are, so to speak, a parable of God. Through them and the economy they represent, God accommodates himself to us in our weakness.

Scripture as Accommodation

A. Scriptural Language in General: Classical Christianity affords a number of instances of individuals who came with great reluctance to the acceptance of the faith. For some of these at least, trained in ancient rhetoric, it was the rude and barbarous language of Scripture that offended their aesthetic sensibilities. Notable among these was (as we have previously noted) Augustine of Hippo. For Calvin, however, there is no thirty-three-year pilgrimage to Christian faith; in his brief but intense sounding of the classics we may rightly read his discovery (painful for a humanist) that sublimity of style and sublimity of thought are not necessarily coterminous. This is the burden of the celebrated passage (at *Inst.* 1.8.1f.) where the finest authors of classic Greece and Rome are found to fall far short of the prophetic eloquence, "far exceeding human measure." The several styles of the scriptural writers are, under the guidance of the Spirit, accommodated to varied human capacities.

As the visible creation itself was the book wherein Adam as yet upright might read his destiny, so in the revealed Scriptures, and preeminently in the law for the ancient Jews, God was accommodating himself to his fallen creation. Early in his Christian pilgrimage Calvin grasped this essential Pauline reading of the history of salvation. It is rehearsed, from Adam to Christ ("help from another quarter"), first in his French preface of his cousin Robert's translation of the New Testament, then in the compressed initial pages of the first chapter of the *Institution* of 1536. Patiently God, through our history, accommodates his ways of revelation to our condition. Thus, par excellence, the Word made flesh and the written Word from which he speaks is God accommodating himself to us.

B. Three Specific Instances of Accommodation: In Scripture, and in the church that flows forth from the Word, we may select for brief analysis three instances wherein God has chosen to accommodate his truth to us. Again we must return to human *captus*. When that *captus* is marked primarily by ignorance, divine accommodation takes the character of "scaled down" language: the mother stooping to her child, God talking the language of babes. When, however, that ignorance is stiffened by stubbornness, the language of accommodation takes on added rhetorical heightening. Let us first look at a single example of this from Psalm 78:65, where God is shockingly depicted as a drunken man. This anthropomorphism is commented on by Calvin in these words: "The figure of a drunken man, although somewhat harsh, has not without reason been put forward, for it is accommodated to the stupidity of the people *(accommodatur ad populi stuporem)*." Only shocking language will sometimes penetrate through our stubborn and perverse stupidity. At such an occasion, as we have said before, the divine rhetoric becomes a rhetoric of violence, of exaggeration, of unbelievable heightening.

It is this point, and not the general observation that for Calvin the law is an instance of accommodation, which is made here. In his reading of the Decalogue, Calvin starts not in Exodus 20 but in Matthew 5–6. The true, interior spiritual meaning of the law is at last expressly stated by Christ in the Sermon on the Mount. But Moses' pedagogy anticipates Jesus'. There is a divine synecdoche in "thou shalt not kill" or "thou shalt not commit adultery." Of all the instances of one class of sins, the law giver has chosen the most heinous instance to be the shocking vehicle of all the rest (*Inst.* 2.8.39, 41). Under the divine inspiration, Moses is singling out the worst crimes in society to stand for all.

God's moral pedagogy is thus accommodated to a stiff-necked people. Yet, before we leave the accommodatory aspect of the law, it is necessary to pit against one another two fundamentally opposed views of wherein it exemplifies God's accommodating to human needs. At issue (in *Inst.* 2.5.6) is the question of whether God's precepts are beyond our strength to keep. Calvin's Roman Catholic opponents, including John Eck,[11] say the law would have been given in vain if it were impossible to observe. Surely God has so accommodated the commandments to our capacities that we are able to fulfill their requirements: what they enjoin is within our power. No, says Calvin. The accommodation God has made in framing the law is, by putting its requirements so far above our power, to show clearly our own weakness and thus point our way, through love, to grace.

Another instance of accommodation is to be seen in the language of the Lord's Prayer. The phrases "Our Father," "in heaven," "hallowed be thy name," to mention only the beginning of the prayer, are interpreted by Calvin so to speak synecdochally in pointing beyond their limited human meaning to the larger sphere of reality to which their accommodated language speaks. "In heaven" does not mean that God "is bound, shut up and surrounded, by the circumference of heaven, as by a barred enclosure," "but not confined to any particular region." He "is diffused through all things." Yet in the crassness of our minds, we cannot otherwise conceive his unspeakable glory. The sublimity conjured in our minds by "heaven," the most mighty, lofty, incomprehensible thing we know, raises our thoughts to God, that we may avoid "dreaming up anything earthly or physical about Him, or try to measure Him by our small measure or to conform His will to our emotions" (*Inst.* 3.20.40). What is this but the recognition that in the synecdoche on Jesus' lips as he teaches us to pray is accommodation of his Father's greatness to our *captus*? The scriptural language in which we couch prayer, "the chief exercise of faith," is already accommodated speech when we take it up to use it.

---

11. See John Eck, "Concerning Free Will," in *Enchiridion of Commonplaces: Against Luther and Other Enemies of the Church,* trans. by Ford Lewis Battles (Grand Rapids: Baker, 1979), 210–19.

Calvin sees in the sacraments a third instance of accommodation. Taking his cue perhaps from Bucer, he applies to them the analogy of the sealed document. As we have souls engrafted in bodies, God imparts spiritual things to us, not in direct incorporeal form, but under visible things, that is, sacraments (4.14.3). God accommodates to our weakness by sealing the "document" of the proclaimed Word with the "seals" of physical sacraments. This is why God gives us Word *and* sacrament. This is why the Pauline marks of the true church are the correct preaching of the Word and the due administration of the sacraments.

To speak of the Lord's Supper: the mystery of Christ's secret union with the devout is incomprehensible, ineffable; therefore God shows it to us—thrusts it before our very eyes—under signs adapted to our small capacity (4.17.11). By the physical rite of the Supper man's weak mind is helped to rise heavenward that he may apprehend Christ in the Supper (4.17.36). In refuting the papal Mass—in Calvin's view a wrong interpretation of Old Testament sacrificial and ceremonial practice to justify the Mass' physical character—Calvin proceeds analogically between the Testaments, adverting to the changing form of the divine pedagogy as it proceeds from spiritual infancy to maturity (4.18.12–18). Yet Calvin sees the accommodating character of the Lord's Supper not as exemplifying a completely spiritual reality in mere physical terms, but in the God-given physical lineaments of the Supper in as-if-physical presence of the risen Lord at table with us. The act of accommodating to our weakness is not mere rhetoric clothed with the physical, but divine energy, power, spirit, channeled through the physical. In this the divine rhetoric utterly transcends the rhetoric of the human orator or writer.

The Incarnation as Accommodation

We come now to the most perilous part of this essay. If all the evidence we have sifted so far may be denominated under divine condescension to human weakness, surely the incarnation, to which (for the Christian) all this evidence points and from which it takes its meaning, must be the accommodating act par excellence of our divine father, teacher, physician, judge, and king. Yet we run the danger, in too glibly inferring this, of making the whole Christian gospel a mere exercise in rhetoric. Let us therefore pause here to take seriously Calvin's warning about theological language.

At two points in the *Institutes* Calvin draws back from what might otherwise seem a too-easy reliance on human language. The first passage is at 1.13.5, where Calvin, goaded by the critique of Servetus and others against the use of nonscriptural terms to describe the Trinity (itself a nonscriptural term), stops to comment that it were better to get along without such terms; but when we are called on in controversy or in teaching to defend orthodoxy, they are not to be rashly repudiated, but to be used with all humility as holding sound scriptural teaching if they concisely express the simple truth of God's Word (1.13.5, 3).

Again, in reluctantly undertaking the writing of his chapter on the Supper, Calvin lays bare the utter inadequacy of his and all human thoughts and words (4.17.7) to deal with this, the greatest mystery of all. Wonder is the only proper response to this life-giving communion. But if we may imperfectly interpret his view: accommodation, divine accommodation is at work in the Supper, but (as we have suggested) it is neither accommodation of physical to spiritual nor of spiritual to physical. It is rather accommodation of spiritual *in* physical. Not like Zwingli should we insufficiently regard the physical signs, thus divorcing them from their mysteries; nor like the Roman theologians should we immoderately extol them, thus obscuring the mysteries themselves (4.17.5).

We are here, cautioned by Calvin's own self-warning, to seek after a definition of divine accommodation that neither repudiates the anthropomorphisms of Scripture in our quest of pure Spirit, nor so clings to the anthropomorphic mode of thought and worship as ourselves, veiled by flesh, to lose sight of our God. In the divine rhetoric accommodation as practiced by the Holy Spirit so empowers the physical, verbal vehicle that it leads us to, not away from, the very truth. Thus accommodating language and the truth to which it points are really a unity. One cannot say this of the tempered speech of human rhetoric.

Thus warned, we can perhaps see in the short but critical chapter 6 of Book II, added in 1559 under the revised organization of the *Institutes* into the "twofold" knowledge of God and of ourselves, an accommodation of the supreme and most substantive character. This chapter links the previous chapters on the Fall of man, by way of Christ, to the chapters on the law and on the relation of the Old and New Covenants; thus we are prepared for the concluding christological chapters of Book II. As Calvin says:

> The natural order was that the frame of the universe should be the school in which we were to learn piety, and from it pass over to eternal life and perfect felicity. But after man's rebellion, our eyes—wherever they turn—encounter God's curse. . . . For even if God wills to manifest his fatherly favor to us in many ways, yet we cannot by contemplating the universe infer that he is Father. . . . This magnificent theater of heaven and earth, crammed with innumerable miracles, Paul calls the "wisdom of God" (1 Cor. 1:21). Contemplating it, we ought in wisdom to have known God. But because we have profited so little by it, he calls us to the faith of Christ, which because it appears foolish, the unbelievers despise (*Inst.* 2.6.1).

Thus, after the Fall of Adam, there is no salvation apart from the Mediator. The accommodatory act of Christ's intermediation is even more expressly stated in Calvin's *Commentary on I Peter* (1:20):

There are two reasons why there can be no faith in God, unless Christ put himself as it were in the middle *(quasi medius interveniat),* for we must first ponder the vastness of the divine glory and at the same time the slenderness of our understanding. Far from certain is it that our keenness could climb so high as to apprehend God. Therefore all thinking about God, apart from Christ, is a bottomless abyss which utterly swallows up all our senses. . . . The other reason is that when faith ought to join us to God, we shy away from and dread all approach, unless the Mediator meets us to free us from fear. . . . Hence it is clear that we cannot trust in God *(Deo credere)* save through Christ. In Christ God so to speak makes himself little *(quodammodo parvum facit),* in order to lower himself to our capacity *(ut se ad captum nostrum submittat);* and Christ alone calms our consciences that they may dare intimately *(familiariter)* approach God.[12]

We may then conclude that all means of divine accommodation—from the vast reaches of the created universe to the characteristic turn of phrase of a prophet calling a stubborn people to repentance (to all of which Scripture holds the clue)—point to the supreme act of God's intermediation in Christ.

---

12. *Commentary on I Peter, OO,* 1667, tome 7, p. 8.

5

Calculus Fidei:
Some Ruminations on the Structure
of the Theology of John Calvin[1]

The theology of John Calvin has long been the subject of analysis. Many gifted minds have plumbed its profundities and have thought themselves to have arrived at its essence, only to be contradicted or corrected by their successors. In making yet another effort to wrestle with the structure-problem of Calvin's theology, my sole justification is the path whereby God has seen fit to bring me to some familiarity with the faith and piety of a great Christian.

As a translator and teacher, my chief concern was pastoral: to present the thought of the Geneva Reformer in the most direct, practical, and living way to generations of students preparing for the Christian ministry. If, then, my remarks in this essay seem to be little touched by the impressive accumulation of scholarly interpretation, in the ocean of which these lines will soon merge as a forgotten ripple, the fault is to be charged to a pastor-teacher who has tried to exemplify the *ad fontes* pedagogy.

Ad fontes: In this case the fons is the writings of Calvin: the *Institutio,* the commentaries, the sermons, the letters, the treatises, the prayers—all of which point to the *fons primordius,* the Scriptures. In my view, most of the wrong inferences drawn from Calvin rest on a partial reading or defective understanding of his thought. How many Calvinists are Calvinists of only Book I of the *Institutio,* or of even only a part of that book? Early in my teaching career I realized that the whole of the *Institutio* must initially be read, if not at a single sitting, at least within the limits of a single course. For the inexperienced student this is difficult,

1. *Calculus Fidei* was prepared for the International Congress on Calvin Research held in Amsterdam on 28 September 1978. Except for very small printings intended for class distribution, the work has never been published in its entirety. An edited portion of the work appeared in W. H. Neuser, ed., *Calvinus Ecclesiae Doctor* (Kampen: J. H. Kok, [1980]).

not to say impossible, without some help. Although Calvin gives his readers frequent guideposts in the course of the *Institutio*, a more concise overview, a road map showing points already passed and points yet to be reached in the reader's journey, seemed to be called for. And so, with the help of several students, I prepared *An Analysis of the Institutes*. Yet even in outline form this came to 291 pages! Gradually in translating and in analyzing the *Institutio* the truth was brought home to me that the shaping of that work was profoundly influenced by the many controversies that tried Calvin's faith, patience, and ingenuity throughout his life. As a church historian, in teaching the struggle of orthodoxy against the heresies of left and right that shaped the creeds in the early church, I had already learned the affirmative function of polemical theology. And when those by-gone heresies were relived by twentieth-century students, the orthodoxy emergent from these conflicts not only became clear to them, but they were also helped to see in our own day comparable wrong-turnings to which the Christian faith is vulnerable and against which we must struggle to a living faith.

Was there, then, a single principle that could sum up the experience of Calvin in a way that might speak to our time? A principle began to emerge: I tentatively called it the "antithetical structure" of the *Institutio*. Its birth pangs were already discernible in the *Psychopannychia* and the preface to Calvin's cousin's translation of the New Testament; the dedicatory letter to Francis I seemed to set forth the right and left limits of the stage wherein the *Institutio* was to enact the history of its life. Every Christian apologist thinks he is walking in the middle way of truth between the extremes of false faith; but in Calvin, I came to find, there was a truly authentic discerner of the *via media*. The successive editorial embodiments of the *Institutio*, achieving in the author's judgment at last a satisfactory literary form in 1559, graphically illustrate how Calvin sorted and resorted the dialogues with his opponents, and in so doing came to an ever more adequate and satisfying (to him) formulation of his reading of the Christian gospel. For him this was a *via media* between the Scylla of aberrant Romanism and the Charybdis of the radical tendencies of his time, whatever name he might give to them.

What, then, is that single principle (cf. theses 1–5b, below)? There is in Calvin a single principle, but it is expressed in many ways: every fundamental notion of his thought is defined in a field of tension—a true middle between false extremes. One can call that a true/false principle, nothing new in the history of theology, and most recently used by Erasmus, Luther, and Zwingli. But for Calvin, in this life, the expression of truth never exhausts the possibility of falsehood; unfaith is always present in faith; false worship always lurks beneath true worship; the face of the true church is always potentially distorted with falsity. Hence we cannot simply and flatly characterize Calvin's master-principle as true versus false. It is rather a concept of truth emergent from bondage to falsehood, or conversely, of the lie ever seeking to engulf truth; it is the history of salvation at once enacted in the chronicle of creation, in the chronicle of mankind, and in the chronicle of the individual. It is the notion of the false approaching the negation it truly is; and of the true approaching the infinity of God, its beginning and its end. This is why, cognizant of all the dangers involved, I have chosen to take at least one of my exemplars of the structural principle of Calvin's thought from the field of mathematics—the theory of limits.

Our plan will be (1) to discuss four basic assumptions concerning the nature of Calvin's conversion and initial theological reflection on it; (2) to then discuss five theses concerning the structure and organizing principles of Calvin's thought, particularly as adumbrated in the *Institutio Christianae Religionis.* To this essay will be attached six appendixes.

Four Assumptions Concerning Calvin's Conversion

Assumption 1: The scriptural passage that "triggered" Calvin's conversion was Romans 1:18–25, or more narrowly, Romans 1:21 and/or 1:25 (cf. thesis 3a)

Calvin's Latin translation of Romans 1:18–25 (1539) reads as follows:

> 18   Revelatur enim ira Dei
>   e coelo super omnem impietatem
>   et iniustitiam hominis,
>   veritatem Dei iniuste continentium;
> 19   quia quod cognoscitur de Deo,
>   manifestum est in ipsis.
>   Deus enim illis manifestavit
> 20   Siquidem invisibilis ipsius,
>   ex creatione mundi,
>   operibus intellecta,
>   conspiciuntur:
>   aeterna quoque eius potentia et divinitas:
>   ut sint inexcusabiles.
> 21   <u>Quoniam, quam Deum cognovissent,</u>
>   <u>non tanquam Deo gloriam dederunt,</u>
>   <u>aut grati fuerunt,</u>
>   <u>sed exinaniti sunt in cogitationibus suis,</u>
>   <u>et obtenebratum est stultum cor eorum,</u>
> 22   Quum se putarent sapientes,
>   stulti facti sunt:
> 23   et mutaverunt gloriam incorruptibilis Dei
>   similitudine imagines corruptibilis hominis,
>   et volucrum, et quadrupedum, et serpentum.

24   Propterea tradidit illos Deus
      in cupiditates cordium suorum in immunditiem:
      ut ignominia afficerent corpora sua in se ipsis.

25   Qui transmutarunt veritatem eius in mendacium:
      et coluerunt ac venerati sunt
            creaturam supra creatorem:
      Qui est benedictus in saecula.
      Amen.[a]

> a. Commentary on Paul's Epistle to the Romans, *OC*, 49:22–28. See also *Iohannis Calvini commentarius in epistolam Pauli ad Romanos*, ed. by T. H. L. Parker (Leiden: E. J. Brill, 1981). For ET, see *The Epistle of Paul to the Romans and to the Thessalonians*, trans. by Ross Mackenzie, ed. by David W. Torrance and Thomas F. Torrance (Grand Rapids: Eerdmans, 1961), 29.

Classic accounts of conversion usually cite some verse of Scripture as triggering the change.[2] Augustine's experience of "Tolle! Lege!" ("Take up and read!") in the garden near Milan (*Confessions*, 8.12.28–30) led him through Romans 13:13f. to Bishop Ambrose and Christian baptism. Luther was captivated by Romans 1:17 ("The just shall live by faith"). We have no such definite information on the specific Scripture that caused Calvin's change of heart. A study of the evidence has, however, led me to suggest that it very probably was Romans 1:18–25. More narrowly, we may underline especially verses 18 and 25:

v. 18   Although they had already known God,
              yet they did not give God the glory,
              or thank him
              but became empty in their thinking,
              and their foolish hearts were darkened
                . . .
v. 25   who transmuted God's truth into a lie,
              and worshiped and venerated
              the creature rather than the Creator.

The central themes of Calvin's piety are the honoring of God and being thankful to him; they are interwoven in the recital of his conversion in the preface to the *Commentary on the Psalms*,[3] and the account of the Reformed Christian's confession before God's judgment seat in Calvin's *Reply to Cardinal Sadolet* [see assumption 2]. Also, the central feature of Calvin's piety is the two knowledges, of God and of humanity (sketched in *Institutio 1536*, ch. 1; and elaborated in *Institutio 1539*, chs. 1–2).[4] In summing up the knowledge of God, Calvin lists the *virtues*

2. Battles, *Piety 1978*, 16.
3. For an annotated strophic translation of this, see ibid., 27–42.
4. *Inst. 1536a*, introduction, xvii; *Inst. 1536b*, xxvii.

Dei, the excellence or powers of God, revealed in the *theatrum mundi* [see appendix C]; the knowledge of man, he summarizes in terms of the contrasting traits of human emptiness in his discussion of the *descensus in se* [see appendix D]. The list of *virtues Dei* given at the head of chapter 1 of the *Institutio 1539*[5] is almost identical with those given in the *Commentary on Romans* (1540) at 1.21 [OC 49.24f.]. The same Romans passage is alluded to in Calvin's *Reply to Cardinal Sadolet* (1539),[6] when Calvin sets forth his true confession of faith before God's judgment seat, to replace the false one Sadolet had in his letter to the people of Geneva put, so to speak, into Calvin's mouth. Calvin is speaking of the false faith against which he had reacted:

> The people . . . indeed called him
> the only God,
> but they did so
> while transferring to others
> the glory which thou hast claimed
> for thy majesty.
> They imagined for themselves
> and esteemed as many gods
> as they had saints to worship.

Clearly there are echoes here of the Romans passage.

There is another piece of indirect evidence for the place of Romans 1:18–25 in Calvin's conversion: while Paul is not here alluding to human philosophy per se, what he says of turning truth into falsehood, of knowing God but not giving him the glory, can be identified with philosophical reflections on Deity. The passage in the *Institutio* that I have in mind is 1.15.6–8. Calvin drafted this critique of the classical philosophical view of the human soul in 1539, but sharpened it in 1559.[7] He was probably too close to his conversion in 1535, when he was writing his first edition, to examine his old masters dispassionately and so remained largely silent about them. But the evidence of 1539 points to a marked disenchantment that had occurred earlier with respect to his old Stoic and Platonic leanings (however judiciously selective they had been even in his Seneca period).[8] When Calvin grasped the reality of the Fall, everything began to make sense for him: his former muted rejection, for example, of Stoic *apatheia* or *pronoia (fatum),*[9] or his laconic note on the hopeless disagreement among the philosophers concerning

---

5. *Inst.* 1.2.1.

6. *OS,* 1:481.

7. This sharpening, in 1559, of his 1539 attitude against the philosophers can be paralleled in other contexts of the *Institutio.*

8. *Comm. Sen. De Clem.,* 128*.

9. *Comm. Sen. De Clem.,* 28–31 (6:lines 8f.); 364f. (151:lines 5f.); cf. *Piety 1978,* 85 (note on line 896), 87 (note on lines 1473ff.).

the origin of the soul, as expressed in the Seneca commentary,[10] now matured into a real Christian understanding of the failure of pagan thinkers to take the Fall into account in assessing the present state of the soul. Calvin had already found Augustine (as well as Cicero) helpful in leading him to draw back from the Stoic passionless wise man.[11] Now the Augustinian distinction between original righteousness before the Fall and the state of the human soul after the Fall helped Calvin free himself from the vestigial control heretofore exercised on his view of the soul by the philosophers, who are now "weighed in the balance and found wanting." He is now able to group the vulgar ignorant with the most sophisticated philosophers as equally corrupters of the truth of God,[12] equally idolatrous,[13] equally deluded in their views of Deity[14] and of the creation.[15]

This is why the ancient philosophers[16] (although Plato explicitly,[17] and some aspects of Stoicism implicitly,[18] more lightly condemned), together with their later champions as well as their latter-day theological users, take their place in the dichotomous scheme which, in this study, we are endeavoring to trace.

To look at this probable scriptural base of Calvin's conversion more broadly: as with Luther, so with Calvin, it is the constellation of Psalms and Romans that holds the secret of their faith.[19] Luther's first com-

10. *Comm. Sen. De Clem.*, 92f. (32:lines 13f.); cf. *Inst. 1536a*, introduction, xiii; *1536b*, xxiii–xxiv.

11. *Comm. Sen. De Clem.*, 366f. (152:lines 4f.); *Piety 1978*, 86 (note on lines 1306ff.).

12. *Inst.* 1.10.3.

13. *Inst.* 1.11.1.

14. *Inst.* 1.13.1.

15. *Inst.* 1.14.1.

16. *Inst.* 1.8.1 (1539) asserts the superiority of Scripture, with its handling of grand themes in lowly language, over the elegance of classical writers. *Inst.* 1.8.2 (1559) heightens this contrast. One is reminded of Augustine the rhetorician, who came slowly and reluctantly to Scripture because of its seemingly vulgar style.

17. *Inst.* 1.15.6.

18. Cf. F. L. Battles, "Against Luxury and License in Geneva," 182–202. This article deals with the *Consilium de Luxu*.

19. See F. L. Battles, review of W. Pauck, *Luther's Lectures on Romans*, Library of Christian Classics 15, *Interpretation* 16 (1962): 322: "Perhaps one should remark especially the constellation of Old Testament and New Testament—of Psalms and Romans—that clearly emerges here. Nurtured first as a child and then as a monk in the piety of the Penitential Psalms (xi), Luther's earliest exegetical efforts were directed toward the Book of Psalms, the *Dictata super Psalterium* (1513–), wherein (WA vols. 3–4) he makes explicit connections with Paul's Letter to the Romans. Then, in the *Lectures on Romans* (1515–), one sees the partnership of the two books developing further. The Psalms are quoted far more than any other book of the Bible, and certain Psalms (32 and 51) are repeatedly cited. By 1519 Luther referred to the Psalms with newfound insights and began his *Operationes in Psalmos*, but was unable to complete it because of controversies with his papal opponents (xxxvi).

This "constellation" of Psalms and Romans is far wider than Luther: Faber Stapulensis had already in Luther's day pointed the way through his exegetical work on the

mentary was on the Psalms; his second on Romans, some years before the 1517 experience but leading to it. Calvin's first biblical commentary was on Romans; in fact the *Institutio* itself may be thought of as an extended commentary on Romans. While his Psalms commentary came much later (1555–57), it is his most explicitly personal commentary (with sometimes veiled references to his own spiritual states under those attributed to David) and, as mentioned before, contains in its preface the one explicit testimony to Calvin's conversion. Also, statistically—whatever mere quantities mean in religious scholarship—we find the following interesting shift in frequency of use of biblical books between the first and last editions of the *Institutio:*[20]

	1536	1559
Psalms	67 (IX)	580 (II)
Isaiah	78 (VII)	324 (VI)
Matthew	185 (I)	542 (III)
John	139 (III)	466 (IV)
Romans	162 (II)	598 (I)
1 Corinthians	133 (IV)	428 (V)

By 1559 Psalms indeed comes into its own as the second most-cited book, relegating Matthew, which had originally occupied first place, to third. Thus, when Calvin in his preface to the Psalms commentary characterizes the Psalter as ANATOMHN *omnium animae partium,*[21] we see what a high place he gives to it; add to this the fact that he makes the Psalter the hymnbook of the Reformed Church.

While not as impressively represented in the frequency count (89, 244), the Epistle to the Hebrews was for Calvin, as for the authors of the Placards,[22] the key to the relationship between the Old and New Covenants and the bulwark against both those who would confuse the New Testament with the Old and those who would sever the New from the Old.

---

two books (used by Luther). Augustine had long before grasped the marriage of the two books. In fact, Paul himself drew copiously from the Psalms in his original letter!

"This Psalter-based medieval piety, steeped in monastic discipline, but conversely Pelagianized thereby too, was freed, descholasticized, deepened and universalized via Augustine (especially the anti-Pelagian writings), to Paul. Our editor is quick to hint at the parallel between Luther's grappling with the Pharisaism of the observants of the Augustinian Hermits (lix–lx), and Paul's own struggles. Luther was not the only Reformer to grasp this grand unity of Old Testament–New Testament: Calvin rested the piety of the *Institutes* solidly upon the Psalms and Romans, and in the most existential passages of the *Institutes* identified himself religiously with David as understood through Paul's eyes (especially *Inst.* 3:2). Herein lies, this reviewer thinks, a secret spring of the Reformation, and, in fact, of all Christian piety."

20. See appendix 4, "Tabulation of Biblical Citations in the *Institutes.*"
21. *Piety 1978,* 27, 39 (note to line 15).
22. *Inst. 1536a,* appendix 1, 437f.; *Inst. 1536b,* 339–42.

Assumption 2: To the explicit account of this religious experience given in the preface to the commentary on the Psalms 1555 (1557) may be added the oblique account, in terms of the confession of the evangelical layperson before God's judgment seat, given in Calvin's *Reply to Cardinal Sadolet* (1539). (Cf. thesis 3a.)

To the discussion already presented in support of assumption 1, I invite the reader to compare the following passages in the epistolary exchange between Cardinal Jacopo Sadolet[23] and Calvin:[24]

Sadolet, *Epistola ad Genevenses*	Calvin, *Responsio*
(1) The confession of the faithful Catholic before God's judgment seat (*OS* 1.451.42–452.26)	(1) The confession of the Reformed pastor before God's judgment seat (*OS* 1.480.31–484.2)
(2) The confession of the "convert" to the "new" faith before God's judgment seat (*OS* 1.452.32–453.23)	(2) The confession of the evangelical layperson before God's judgment seat (*OS* 1.484.9–486.31)

Quite clearly, Sadolet has falsified Calvin's religious experience and the motives for his allegiance to the Reformed cause. Calvin, in response, has in a generalized way reviewed his own pilgrimage to the year 1539.

Elsewhere,[25] from the evidence of the Seneca commentary,[26] I have suggested the three religious questions that seem to have concerned Calvin on the eve of his conversion: (1) the contrast between paganism and Christianity—or, more broadly stated, between superstition and true religion; (2) the origin and nature of the human soul;[27] (3) the question of governance, divine and human, or in other words, the place of human authority within the divine providential frame.[28] The second question, on the origin of the human soul, leads Calvin to the doctrine of the image of God, early defined by him in the *Psychopannychia:* "Whatever philosophers or these dreamers [the Anabaptists] may pretend, we hold that nothing can bear the image of God but spirit, since God is a spirit."[29]

23. ET, John Calvin, *Tracts and Treatises,* 1.16–18.
24. ET, John Calvin, *Tracts and Treatises,* 1.56–64; J. K. S. Reid, *Calvin: Theological Treatises,* Library of Christian Classics, 22 (Philadelphia: Westminster, 1954), 246–53. For a stropic translation, see *Inst. 1536a,* introduction, xviii–xxiv; *Inst. 1536b,* xxviii–xxxiv.
25. *Inst. 1536a,* introduction, xii; *Inst. 1536b,* xxii–xxiii.
26. *Comm. Sen. De Clem.,* 75, 32, 6.
27. See note 10, above.
28. *Inst. 1536a,* introduction, xii–xiv, with discussion; *Inst. 1536b,* xxiii–xxiv.
29. *Psychopannychia,* ed. by W. Zimmerli (Leipzig: D. Werner Scholl, 1932), 29, lines 6–8. See *Inst. 1536a,* introduction, xv; *Inst. 1536b,* xxv.

Already (1534–35?) Calvin is ranging himself not only against the pagan philosophers and the papists, but against the Anabaptists as well (cf. assumption 4). Later, the defective teaching of the spiritualist sect on spirit will in its turn come under Calvin's critical eye.[30]

Assumption 3: Two theological "restatements" of Calvin's conversion experience were written around 1534–35: the preface to the French translation of the New Testament by his cousin Pierre Robert; and the initial pages of chapter 1, *De Lege,* of the *Institutio* of 1536 (cf. thesis 1).

We have here to deal with what I have elsewhere[31] called "two theological restatements of Calvin's religious experience": the French New Testament preface (of late 1534 or early 1535) and the early pages of the first chapter of *Institutio 1536* ("The Kernel of Calvin's Faith"),[32] written probably at the same time. Together with *Psychopannychia* in its original form, they serve as a bridge between Calvin's conversion and his later theological career. My earlier discussion of these texts is here summarized.

Preface to the French Translation of the New Testament of Pierre Robert

The preface to the New Testament expresses in a succinct fashion the familiar Pauline-Augustinian summary of human history: Adam was made in the image of God, but through pride fell; the image was defaced, and God turned against him and his corrupt offspring. Yet as a God of mercy, he still loved humankind and did not utterly destroy them, but revealed himself so as to move human beings to find him. This he did through the whole of nature, but especially through a special people, Israel. But, despite these gifts of mercy, the human race continued to be false to God, thus making a new covenant necessary for the restoration of humanity. The Gentiles, though endowed with conscience, failed to heed God's manifest tokens of himself; the Jews, even though provided with Law and Prophets, forsook their God. Thus humankind needed a new covenant and a Mediator. Through prophecies and rites, the new covenant and Mediator were heralded from the promise of Abraham on. The event of his coming was revealed in the New Testament, a book that fulfills the Old Testament prophecies in a complete unity and sets forth the Savior's power in accounts of his miracles and other acts. The gospel calls humanity to salvation, showing the weak-

---

30. E.g., in Calvin's treatise of 1545: *Contre la secte phantastique et furieuse des Libertins qui se nomment Spirituelz, OC,* 7:145–252.

31. *Inst. 1536a,* introduction, xxiv–xxvii; *Inst. 1536b,* xxxiv–xxxvi.

32. *Inst. 1536a,* 20–25; *Inst. 1536b,* 15–18; *Piety 1978,* 43–49.

ness of mere human wisdom compared with the divine wisdom of Christ and depicting the joy of Christians in his service even in the midst of persecution. Jesus Christ is at the center, key to eternal life and perfect wisdom. All Old Testament types of great men converge in him:[33]

> This is life eternal:
> to know one true God,
> and Him whom He has sent,
> Jesus Christ,
> in whom He has set
> the beginning, middle and end
> of our salvation.
> It is He who is Isaac,
> the beloved Son of the Father,
> offered as a sacrifice,
> yet He never gave in to the power of death.
> He is the watchful shepherd Jacob,
> taking such great care
> of the flock entrusted to Him.
> He is the good and merciful brother Joseph,
> who in his glory was not ashamed
> to recognize His brothers,
> lowly and abject as they were.
> He is the high priest and bishop Melchizedek,
> who once for all made eternal sacrifice
> for all men.
> He is the sovran lawgiver Moses,
> writing His law on the table of our hearts
> by His Spirit.
> He is the faithful captain and guide Joshua,
> to conduct us to the promised land.
> He is the noble and victorious King David,
> subjecting to His hand
> all rebellious power.
> He is the magnificent and triumphant King Solomon,
> governing His kingdom
> in peace and prosperity.
> He is the brave and powerful Samson
> who by his death has routed
> all His enemies.

All that we think or desire, all that we experience, is to be found in Jesus Christ, whom to know the whole of Scripture calls us.

Calvin concludes the preface with an appeal to those who can see to the right preaching of the gospel and to the health of the church: kings and magistrates, bishops and pastors.

33. *OC*, 9:813, lines 3–24.

From this reading of the gospel Calvin moves out from personal experience to reflect on the whole history of salvation. It is all in this brief preface, Calvin's first theological reflection on his conversion.

Calvin's faith, then, is a salvation-history faith; it must be told as the story of Israel, narrowly begun in the Old Testament, but in Christ embracing all nations. If Calvin were asked to reduce his theology to a single principle, he would probably point to this oft-repeated summary of the history of salvation as succinctly reflecting both his own experience of Christ and that of the authentic church of every generation.

We turn now to the second "bridge-text."

Initial Pages of Chapter 1 of the *Institutio* of 1536: "The Kernel of Calvin's Faith"

At the head of the first chapter of the *Institutio 1536,* "On the Law," there is a brief passage which, because it seems to sum up Calvin's theology, I have elsewhere[34] entitled "The Kernel of Calvin's Faith." It affords a second and more explicitly theological bridge between Calvin's own reflection on his conversion[35] and his elaboration of it in the *Institutio.* It commences with the two "knowledges," of God and of man, passes to the law, unwritten and written, and concludes with "another way," Christ.

> . . . Unless he has first looked upon God's face,
> and then descends from contemplating Him
> to scrutinize himself[36]

Or:

> As often as I descended into myself
> or raised my mind to thee. . . .[37]

These two movements of the human mind lead to the knowledge of God and the knowledge of ourselves, set in antithesis to one another: the gulf between the all-holy God and the fallen sinner which only the incarnate Son of God can bridge. Calvin felt this deeply in his conversion and sought to express it in concentrated form in these first few pages of his critical chapter on the law, with which he begins the first edition of the *Institutio.* Successive editions of the *Institutio* were to see these thoughts dispersed to the growing bulk of the work, ultimately of-

---

34. *Piety 1978,* 43–49; Latin text: 43–50 *(Inst. 1536); OS,* 1:37–41; ET, *Inst. 1536a,* 20–25; summary in *An Analysis of the Institutes of the Christian Religion of John Calvin,* 3rd rev. ed. (Pittsburgh: Pittsburgh Theological Seminary, 1976), 17*.

35. Preface to the *Commentary on the Psalms,* as cited in note 3, above.

36. *Inst.* (1539), 1, lines 30–32; *Inst.* 1.1.2 (1559); *OS,* 3:32.10–12.

37. *Reply to Cardinal Sadolet, OS,* 1:485.8–10.

fering for it a kind of organizing principle. But here, and here alone, they stand in a coherent brief theological summary of Calvin's religious experience.

What is the knowledge of God? God is infinite wisdom, righteousness, goodness, mercy, truth, power, and life; all things have been created for his glory; he is a just judge; he is merciful and gentle.

What is the knowledge of ourselves? Adam, our common parent, was created in God's image with all the virtues; by his fall into sin this image was effaced and cancelled; he was stripped of the virtues, which were replaced by the corresponding vices. As a result, all of us born of Adam are ignorant and bereft of God, powerless to do his will, deserving of eternal death.

Into this impasse in his creation, the merciful Father brings the law—the unwritten law on the conscience, and then the written law. To keep us from ignorance of our true condition, God stamped on our hearts a witness of what we owe him: because conscience, the law within, is still blinded by self-love, we have been provided by God with a written law to teach us how to keep perfect righteousness; since, however, we do not, and cannot in our condition, perform the law's requirements, we still deserve the curse of eternal death.

To this second impasse of man, God in his infinite mercy offers another way. In our despair we must seek help from another quarter, in deepest humility: in Christ God gives us all the gifts we cannot earn for ourselves; but we must grasp Christ with a true and living faith in order to avail ourselves of his benefits; through him is the only way to reach eternal blessedness in the Father.

Stamped on this summary is not only Calvin's fresh study of the Scriptures, but the memory of his so recently experienced crisis of faith. Here are the deep currents of faith that issued in a life of dedication to Christ and his church. Here are the sources of Calvin's *Institution of the Christian Religion*, of his exegesis, of his preaching, and of all his other multifarious activities in behalf of the Reform. To summarize:

A
1. Human beings are made in the image of God (791)
2. Humankind through pride falls, God's image is defaced, and God turns against them and their corrupt offspring (791)
3. As a God of mercy, he still loves humanity and does not utterly destroy them, revealing himself so as to move human beings to find him (793)
   a. through the whole of nature
   b. especially through a special people, Israel
4. Despite these gifts of mercy, the human race continues to be false to God, thus making a new covenant necessary for the restoration of humanity (795)

    a. the Gentiles fail to heed God's manifest tokens of himself
    b. the Jews, even though provided with Law and Prophets, forsake their God

5. The coming of the Savior (797)
    a. the need for a new covenant and for a Mediator
    b. long heralded from the promise to Abraham on, through prophecies and rites
    c. the event of his coming revealed in the New Testament, a book that fulfills the Old Testament prophecies in a complete unity and sets forth the Savior's power in accounts of his miracles and other acts

6. The call of the gospel (807)
    a. the weakness of mere human wisdom compared with the divine wisdom of Christ
    b. the joy of Christians in his service even in the midst of persecution
    c. the centrality of Jesus Christ, key to eternal life and perfect wisdom
      (1) all Old Testament types of great men converge in Jesus Christ
      (2) all that we think or desire, all that we experience, is to be found in Jesus Christ, whom to know the whole of Scripture calls us

7. Final appeal to those who can see to the right preaching of the gospel and to the health of the church (817)
    a. to kings and magistrates
    b. to bishops and pastors

B
1. The knowledge of God
    a. God is infinite wisdom, righteousness, goodness, mercy, truth, power, and life (cf. appendix C: *Virtutes Dei*)
    b. All things have been created for his glory
    c. He is a just judge
    d. He is merciful and gentle

2. The knowledge of humanity (ourselves)
    a. Adam: Adam, our common parent, created in God's image with all the virtues
    b. Fall: by his fall into sin this image was effaced and cancelled; he was stripped of the virtues, which were replaced by the corresponding vices
    c. Original sin: all of us born of Adam are ignorant and bereft of God, powerless to do his will, deserving of eternal death

3. The Law
    a. Conscience: to keep us from ignorance of our true condition, God stamped on our hearts a witness of what we owe him—conscience, the law within
    b. The written law: still blinded with self-love, we are provided by God with a written law to teach us how to keep perfect righteousness
    c. Curse: since, however, we do not perform the law's requirements we still deserve the curse of eternal death

4. Another way: forgiveness of sins through Christ
    a. Humility: in our despair we must seek help from another quarter in deepest humility
    b. Gifts: in Christ, God gives us all the gifts we cannot earn for ourselves

   c. Faith: but we must grasp Christ with a true and living faith in order
to avail ourselves of his benefits

   d. Blessedness: through him is the only way to reach eternal blessedness
in the Father

To recapitulate the summary of the two "bridge-texts":

A	B
1	2a
2a	2b
2b	2c
3	3a
4b	3b
5	4

Together these early texts of Calvin constitute, in our view, the *duplex
exemplar fidei suae*.

Assumption 4: Upon his conversion to evangelical Christianity,
Calvin was faced with finding a *via media* between papalism and spiritualism (radical tendencies initially lumped together in his mind under
the label "Anabaptist" or "Catabaptist" [cf. thesis 2])

In his dedicatory epistle to Francis I, "Most Christian King of
France" (which heads the *Institutio* in all its editions during Calvin's
lifetime), Calvin devotes sections 2–6 to the fundamental contrasts between the papalist and evangelical positions on the Christian faith. In
section 7 he turns briefly to the "Catabaptist" radicals with whom also
he is in disagreement. As I have discussed elsewhere,[38] there is a twofold direction that Calvin's critique of false religion and defense of true
religion takes:

> two things led Calvin to write his first edition of the famous *Institution*:
> the catechetical needs of his religious brethren; and the need to plead
> their case before the king, that persecution might cease. And the latter
> purpose called forth a double theological response from Calvin: the rejec-
> tion of institutionalized Roman Catholicism and at the same time of its
> opposite, the revolutionary, disruptive spiritualism of what at that time
> he lumped under the name "Catabaptists." Hence, Calvin's future theo-
> logical course was determined: to hold a middle direction between the
> right and the left. This was not a prudent compromise, but a judgment
> securely grounded on Calvin's own independent study of Scripture. The
> latter development of his theological system is an extending and perfect-
> ing of this initial polarity.

38. *Inst. 1536a*, introduction, xxxvii–xxxviii, and pp. 325f. (note to p. 16, line 1); *Inst.
1536b*, xliv–xlv, and pp. 242–43 (note to p. 12)

Luther had already tried to account for the rise of the Reformation in terms of the thousand-year sleep of the visible church, a charge refuted by the Roman Catholic controversialist, John Eck, in chapter 1 of his *Enchiridion.*[39] Calvin explained the rise of the radical groups during the Reformation era as a second strategy of Satan:

> Thus for some centuries during which everything was submerged in deep darkness,[40] men were the sport and jest of this lord of the world, and, not unlike some Sardanapalus, Satan lay idle and luxuriated in deep repose. For what else had he to do but jest and sport, in tranquil and peaceable possession of his kingdom? Yet when the light shining from on high in a measure shattered his darkness, when that "stronger man" had troubled and assailed his kingdom [cf. Luke 11:22], he began to shake off his accustomed drowsiness and to take up arms. And first, indeed, he stirred up men to action that thereby he might violently oppress the dawning truth. And when this profited him nothing, he turned to stratagems: he aroused disagreements and dogmatic contentions through his Catabaptists and other monstrous rascals in order to obscure and at last extinguish the truth. And now he persists in besieging it with both engines. With the violent hands of men he tries to uproot that true seed, and seeks (as much as lies in his power) to choke it with weeds, to prevent it from growing and bearing fruit. But all that is in vain, if we heed the Lord our monitor, who long since laid open Satan's wiles before us, that he might not catch us unawares; and armed us with defenses firm enough against all his devices. Furthermore, how great is the malice that would ascribe to the very Word of God itself the odium either of seditions, which wicked and rebellious men stir up against it, or of sects which imposters excite, both of them in opposition to its teaching.[41]

The elaboration of this bipolar critique of false religion, and the complex task of locating the true faith between these two historical positions, of spelling out the *via media,* will be the subject of thesis 2.

The Sorbonnist theological advisers of Francis I perceived, without discrimination, all reformatory tendencies within the kingdom of France to be heretical efforts to overthrow the true papal religion, and, as a consequence, seditions against the monarchy itself. Calvin set himself the task of distinguishing the true gospel from the false gospel of the papal church, and at the same time to disassociate the party of Reform from the radicals, against whom (at least in the light of the Muenster experiment) the charge of sedition had been laid by the papalists. No, the advocates of true ecclesiastical reform in France were not subversive of the state, but were most loyal supporters of the Crown. One

---

39. John Eck, *Enchiridion,* trans. by F. L. Battles (Grand Rapids: Baker, 1978), 8f.
40. Luther, according to Eck (*Enchiridion,* ch. 1), taught that falsehood and error reigned in the church for a thousand years.
41. *Inst. 1536a,* 15 (line 23)–16 (line 12); *Inst. 1536b,* 11–12.

might sketch this fundamental difference in perceiving the true from the false as follows:

Table C. The true gospel of the Reformers distinguished from the false gospel of the papal church

Sorbonnists:	True Faith		False Heretical Faith	
	that of the Roman Church	Party of Reform		All Revolutionary Sects
Calvin:	False Faith	True Faith		False Faith

In terms of our later dichotomous analysis (thesis 4a), Calvin's view would appear as follows:

Table D. The party of reform distinguished from the radicals

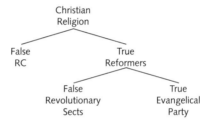

```
              Christian
              Religion
         ┌───────────┴───────────┐
      False                     True
       RC                    Reformers
                         ┌───────────┴───────────┐
                      False                     True
                  Revolutionary             Evangelical
                     Sects                     Party
```

A possible philosophical source for Calvin's search for a *via media* may be seen in his application of the Aristotelian concept to the analysis of seemingly conflicting pairs of virtues in relation to vices, in terms of reciprocal defect and excess. In his first published book, the *Commentary on Seneca's De Clementia*, at *De Clem.* 2.4.1, he is expounding Seneca's statement: "The ill-informed think that the opposite of clemency is strictness, but no virtue is the opposite of a virtue." Calvin comments:

> For since every virtue is a sort of mean between extremes, of which the one tends to defect, the other to excess, the defect as it were is diametrically opposed to the virtue to which it refers, the excess rather imitates the virtue. Here therefore it is a question of extreme in defect, which certain people think to be strictness. Seneca shows that such people are deceived in their opinion, for strictness is a virtue, and virtues cannot contend against virtues. For virtues can be diverse, not contrary: as clemency and strictness indeed have a varied character, but can still stand at the same time: whence also they have the same extremes, but in different ways. For cruelty is the defect of clemency, the excess of strictness; but pity is the defect of strictness, the excess of clemency.[42]

42. *Comm. Sen. De Clem.*, 354f. (146:lines 30f.).

Expressed in terms of a diagram, this discussion would appear as follows:

Table E. Virtues in relation to vices

$$\text{cruelty} \left\{ \begin{array}{l} \text{defect} \longleftarrow \text{clemency} \longrightarrow \text{excess} \\ \\ \text{excess} \longleftarrow \text{strictness} \longrightarrow \text{defect} \end{array} \right\} \text{pity}$$

Calvin applies this Aristotelian principle of excess defect not only to the analysis of virtues (e.g., *frugalitas,* at *Inst.* 3.10.5, etc.) but to the major theological doctrines; this will become apparent as we move to thesis 2. We shall see in theses 3 and 4 the double character of falsity: in terms of this classical model as expounded in the *Commentary on Seneca's De Clementia,* it includes both defect (in diametrical opposition to truth) and excess, in false imitation of truth. From this it is not a far distance to the notion of limits (theses 5a–b).

Five Theses Concerning the Structure of Calvin's Theology

Thesis 1: The structure of *Institutio Christianae Religionis* was the outworking through successive editions (1536–59) of the *exemplar* (cf. assumption 3).

The *exemplar fidei suae,* which we have abstracted, so to speak, from the first two "theological restatements" of Calvin's conversion experience (assumptions 2 and 3), is, we contend, the true model to which the ordering of its parts moved in the successive editions of the *Institutio* (1536–59). Insofar as the *exemplar* partook of a creedal pattern or reflected the *duplex cognitio,* these two contributed to the ultimate disposition of the parts in the edition of 1559, of which Calvin said, in commenting on the unexpected success of the first edition and his conscientious effort, through successive editions, to respond to it:

> each time the work has been reprinted since then, it has been enriched with some additions. Although I did not regret the labor spent, I was never satisfied until the work had been arranged in the order now set forth.[43]

Perhaps the best way to summarize this "labor of enrichment" of which Calvin speaks is to display it in a diagram (see table F), and then tabulate briefly the editorial process, chapter by chapter. Thereupon the successive placement of one or two heads of doctrine will be examined in exemplification of thesis 1.

43. "John Calvin to the Reader," *Inst.,* 3–5.

Table F. Shifts and additions of material in the five chief Latin editions of the *Institutio*

(boxes indicate new material; only main editorial blocks are shown)

1536

1. law
   a. knowledge of God
   b. knowledge of man
   c. law and decalogue
   d. justification
2. faith
   Apostle's Creed
   a. part 1
   b. part 2
   c. part 3
   d. part 4
   election and predestination
3. prayer
4. sacraments
   a. in general
   b. baptism
   c. Lord's Supper
5. false sacraments
   repentance, satisfaction
6. Christian freedom
   a. Christian freedom
   b. ecclesiastical power
   c. civil government

1539

1. knowledge of God
2. knowledge of man
3. law
4. faith; Apostle's Creed
   a. part 1
   b. part 2
   c. part 3
   d. part 4
5. repentance
6. justification by faith
7. O.T./N.T.
   a. likenesses
   b. differences
8. predestination
   providence
9. prayer
10. sacraments
11. baptism
12. Lord's Supper
13. Christian freedom
14. ecclesiastical power
15. civil government
16. five false sacraments
17. life of the Christian man

1543–50

1. knowledge of God
2. knowledge of man
3. law
4. on vows; monasticism
5. faith; Apostle's Creed
6. creed 1
7. creed 2
   creed 3
8. creed 4
9. repentance
10. justification by faith
11. O.T./N.T.
    a. likenesses
    b. differences
12. Christian freedom
13. human traditions
14. predestination
    providence
15. prayer
16. sacraments
17. baptism
18. Lord's Supper
19. five false sacraments
20. civil government
21. life of the Christian man

1559

- chs. 1–10 — Book I
- chs. 11–12
- chs. 13–14
- ch. 15
- ch. 16
- ch. 17
- ch. 18
- chs. 1–5 — Book II
- ch. 6
- chs. 7–8
- ch. 9
- ch. 10
- ch. 11
- chs. 12–16
- ch. 17
- ch. 1 — Book III
- ch. 2
- chs. 3–5
- chs. 6–10
- chs. 11–18
- ch. 19
- ch. 20
- chs. 21–24
- ch. 25
- chs. 1–9 — Book IV
- ch. 10
- chs. 11–12
- ch. 13
- ch. 14
- chs. 15–16
- chs. 17–18
- ch. 19
- ch. 20

This diagram is reproduced from *Analysis* 1980, 15.

Editorial Account of *Institutio* 1559

Book I

1 1539, revised 1559
2 nucleus from 1536, enlarged 1539, reworked 1559
3 1539, reworked 1559
4 1539, reworked 1559
5 1539, reworked 1559 (plus one quotation from Augustine, 1543)
6 1539, revised 1559
7 1539 plus 1550, revised 1559
8 core from 1539, enlarged 1550, retouched 1559
9 1539, retouched 1559
10 1539, reworked 1559
11 1539 (plus 1536), augmented 1550
12 1539, enlarged 1550, reworked 1559
13 nucleus 1536, reworked 1539, revised and augmented 1559
14 largely 1543
15 largely 1559; reflects controversies with Osiander and Servetus
16 mainly 1559, with some material, reworked, from 1539
17 largely 1539, reworked 1559
18 almost entirely 1559, with a bit from 1539

Book II

1 1539 plus small portions of 1543, 1550, retouched 1559
2 largely 1539, with a few quotations added in 1543, a couple of words in 1545, then retouched in 1559
3 1539, with some patristic additions of 1543, retouched 1559
4 1539, with an addition (Augustine) 1543, retouched 1559
5 1539, with some patristic augment 1543, 1550, retouched 1559
6 1559 (transitional chapter)
7 largely 1539, plus some 1543, revised 1559
8 the 1536 chapter on the law was completely rewritten in 1539 with richer patristic citations (with some augment in 1543), then the whole was retouched and relocated 1559
9 1559 (added partly to refute the views of Servetus and the Anabaptists); also for transition
10 1539, slightly retouched in 1559
11 largely 1539 with augment from 1543 at end, slightly retouched 1559
12 core of 1536, reworked 1539, expanded 1559, in answer to Osiander
13 elements from 1539, 1543, completely reworked and amplified 1559
14 core of 1536, reworked in 1539, with augment of 1543, then reshaped 1559
15 fragments from 1536, 1539, completely reworked 1559
16 core from 1536, reworked 1539 plus Augustine augment 1543, revised 1559
17 1559: chapter directed against Laelius Socinus

Book III

1 1559, with fragments from 1536, 1539, worked in
2 1559, rewritten from 1539, with bits from 1536 and 1543 (1550, Pighius addition, sec. 30)

3   1559, rewritten from 1539, with bits from 1536, 1543
4   1536, enlarged 1539 with additional patristic citations also in 1543, then re-
    worked 1559
5   1536, rewritten 1539, augmented 1543, 1550, retouched 1559
6   1539, retouched 1559
7   1539, retouched 1559
8   1539, retouched 1559
9   1539, retouched 1559
10 1539, slightly retouched 1559
11 3 elements:
    (a) introduction: 1539 plus 1543, retouched 1559
    (b) Osiander refutation: 1559: secs. 5–12
    (c) scholastic refutation: 1539 plus touches from 1543, 1553, retouched 1559
12 nucleus of 1536, redone 1539, with augment 1543, retouched 1559
13 largely 1539, with bits from 1536, 1543, retouched 1559
14 1536, thoroughly revised 1539, with augment 1543, retouched 1559
15 nucleus 1536, redone 1539, with patristic additions; ditto 1543
16 1536, reworked 1539, retouched 1559
17 nucleus 1536, thoroughly redone 1539, slightly augmented 1543, retouched
    1559
18 largely 1539, with bits from 1536, 1543, retouched slightly 1559
19 largely 1536, with additions of 1539, 1543, 1550, 1559
20 3 editions of this chapter: 1536, 1539, 1559 (plus 1543, on church music)
21 1539, revised 1559
22 1539, revised 1559, with key quotation from Augustine (1543)
23 1539, rewritten 1559, with touch from 1543
24 1539, rewritten 1559
25 completely rewritten 1559, from materials of 1539 (plus fragment of 1536)

Book IV

1   nucleus 1536, redrafted 1539, expanded 1543, reworked 1559
2   nucleus 1536, enlarged 1539, revised 1543, retouched 1559
3   nucleus 1536, augmented 1539, rewritten 1543, slight alteration 1545
4   1543, with a few elements from 1536
5   1543, with a few fragments from 1536
6   1543, retouched 1559
7   1543
8   1536, greatly expanded 1543, slightly retouched 1559
9   1536, rewritten 1543, with touches 1550, 1559
10 1536, revised 1543, with augments 1550, retouched 1559
11 nucleus 1536, composed 1543, with a few touches of 1559, to bring in new
    materials
12 1543, with a few elements from 1536, 1539, slightly retouched 1559
13 entirely 1543, except for a fragment of 1536, 1539, in sec. 3, and touches of
    1559 in secs. 1–3
14 elements of 1536, 1539; chapter rewritten 1543, with some retouching 1559
15 1536, slightly expanded 1539, redrafted 1543, with additions 1545, 1550, re-
    touched 1559

16   chapter written 1539, one slight addition 1550 (sec. 19) and touches 1559; sec. 31 (1559) a detailed analysis of Servetus' arguments in the *Restitutio* (1553)
17   nucleus 1536, some additions 1539, revised 1543, slight addition 1550, reworked 1559
18   1536, enlarged 1543, retouched 1559
19   1536, with slight additions 1539, revised and enlarged 1543, retouched 1559
20   1536, with slight additions 1539, 1543, retouched 1559

If our diagram in table F were to be more comprehensive, we would have to insert the first *Catechism* of 1537–38[44] between the *Institutio 1536* and *Institutio 1539*, for the reason that a number of features new to the *Institutio* in 1539 are actually anticipated in 1537–38, as if the smaller document contained working notes for the enlarged second Latin edition.[45]

Aside from that suggested improvement, let us peruse some of the details of our diagram. Note especially the shift in topics and the blocks of additional material inserted in each of the four major subsequent Latin editions. Some of the evidence for claiming a more experiential/salvation-historical frame as the initial pattern of Calvin's earliest theological reflections and also as the ultimate shape of the *Institutio* of 1559 may be suggested by our diagram. Three points should be noted.

First, prominent in the *exemplar* is of course the contrasting *duplex cognitio*, of God and of man. This is merely hinted at in the *Institutio 1536*. In 1539, the two knowledges emerge as the subjects of the two initial chapters (1 and 2).

Second, there is gradually a clearer and fuller assertion of Christology in the Old Testament, under the goad of Servetus' (and the Anabaptists') severance of Old Testament and New Testament. This assertion is perhaps also in response to the excessive Lutheran contrast of law and gospel, but especially under the continuing prompting of the original assertion of Christ in the patriarchal types.[46] A major step in this shift of emphasis is to be seen in both the insertion of chapter 7 (1539), "On the Likenesses and Differences between the Old and New Testaments," and its ultimate placement in the christological sequence at 2.10–11 (1559). There, too, the original *De Lege* (ch. 1, 1536), quite markedly influenced in its exposition of the Decalogue by Luther's *Small Catechism*,[47] is revised, enlarged, and slightly redistributed by 1559, but (most significant of all), radically relocated within the christological sequence at 2.7–8 by means of the short but crucial transi-

44. *Catechism 1538* (1972, rev., 1976).
45. Ibid., x: "The literary relationship of the editions of 1536, 1537/38, and 1539." See also the critical notes and indexes for a detailed comparison of the three documents.
46. See assumption 3, discussion, and note 33, above.
47. *Inst. 1536a*, 20, 327f. (note on "Title law"); *Inst. 1536b*, 15, 243–44 (note on "Law").

tional chapters 6 and 9. A further brief touch added to the 1559 *Institutio* is the triumphant claim for Christ of every article of the Apostles' Creed.[48]

Third, the true doctrine of the church must lie between the false denial in practice of the true marks of the church (Roman Catholic)[49] and the distorted perfectionist notions that led the Anabaptists Donatistically to reject the prior baptism of the reformed mother church as well as continued fellowship within a less-than-perfect congregation.[50]

Thus as Calvin, in successive reworkings of this model for the *Institutio,* incorporated into this continuum of theological types the varied positions of his time, he at the same time set down ever more precisely the parameters of his own teaching.

Thesis 2: The new additions to subsequent editions (1539ff.)—from further reading and from various controversies—were fitted within a spectrum, gradually castigated, of:

Table G. Spiritualist/papist spectrum in the *Institutio*

Only a summary statement can be given here in support of our second thesis. As Calvin came, after 1536, to a more intimate knowledge of the Anabaptists, he tempered his judgment of them somewhat, and (to use our terminology) began to identify the left extremity of his theological spectrum not so much with them as with more radical groups—spiritualists, Libertines, or the position of Servetus.[51] This is not to say, however, that his rejection of the Anabaptist views on pedobaptism or on the state, for example, were softened; rather, he found in their emphasis on church discipline, as he developed this topic in *Institutio* 1543, much in common,[52] leading him almost to accept discipline as a third mark of the church.[53]

48. *Inst.* 2.16.19 (1559). For strophic translation, see *Piety 1978,* 174f.

49. *Inst.* 4.2.

50. *Inst.* 4.1.13.

51. This appears, *passim,* in his *Short Instruction against the Anabaptists* (1544), *OC,* 7:49–142.

52. See William E. Keeney, "An Analysis of Calvin's Treatment of the Anabaptists in the *Institutes,*" in *Analysis 1980,* 74*–84*, especially 83*. Cf. also *The Writings of Dirk Philips, 1504–1568,* trans. and ed. by Cornelius J. Dyck, William E. Keeney, and Alvin J. Beachy (Scottdale, Pa.: Herald, 1992).

53. See F. L. Battles, *New Light on Calvin's Institutes: A Supplement to the McNeill-Battles Translation* (Hartford, Conn.: The Hartford Seminary Press, 1966), additional note on 4.1.9 (LCC 21.1023, note 18), quoting *Supplementa Calviniana,* 2.365.13–16 (1557) and 2.381.3–10 (1557).

The right extremity, the Roman Catholic position, already set forth in the dedicatory epistle to Francis I (*Institutio* 1536),[54] was consolidated by a variety of influences at work on Calvin in the years 1536–59. Before the Council of Trent, while there was still a faint hope for reunion of the church, repeated efforts were made by the imperial power using the deliberative machinery of the Diet (the *Interim,* for example), and various unitive schemes were discussed. Calvin's own literary output on the relation of the Reform to the papal church took four chief forms: (1) pastoral pieces intended for individuals or groups to guide them vis-à-vis Roman Catholicism; (2) reprints of various Romanist documents with Calvin's comments or "antidote"; (3) refutations of specific doctrines directed to individuals; and (4) ecumenical blueprints or refutations of unitive efforts of others.

The various polemical tracts, some of the dedications of his biblical commentaries, and relevant letters evince a growing clarity in his expounding and refuting of the differences between himself and his opponents. This growing clarity is, of course, reflected also in the changes made in successive editions of the *Institutio.*[55] Some persons who chose to remain with the Roman Church were not to be placed at the extreme right of his spectrum of theological positions, although their continued allegiance to the old way was no less to be deplored than the intransigence of their more extreme and vocal brethren. More to be excoriated were those turncoats who, after briefly joining the Reform, chose to return to the old mother;[56] more to be contended against, too, were those weak evangelicals who chose to hide their Reformed faith under a cloak of seeming Catholicism, those styled by Calvin "Messrs. the Nicodemites."[57]

While Calvin's increased contact with opposing groups as a result of the Strasbourg experiences and his increasing reputation as a religious leader during the second Geneva sojourn did much to clarify his statement of his own position and his placement of their positions in relation to his own, there is a sense in which much that later became explicit was already anticipated in the first edition of the *Institutio.* The Antitrinitarian party, which caused Calvin so much agony in his

54. See discussion of theses 3 and 4, 6, and note a, p. 165, below.
55. See thesis 1, discussion, above.
56. Calvin had a special Latin term for such people: *versipellis* ("turncoat"), applied to his faithless former intimate, Franciscus Ralduinus (*OC,* 9:525–60).
57. See Calvin's tract, *Excuse à Messieurs les Niocodeites, OC,* 6:589–614; critical text by F. M. Higman (1970). Repeatedly in Calvin's writings the creative value of controversy is to be marked. If he had not been driven by his opponents to treat the scriptural prooftexts that they set forth in support of their contrary positions, many insights would have been lost to him. At *Inst.* 3.3.24, where he is trying to distinguish true from false repentance, there is a good instance of how he was led to a deeper understanding of the problem at hand than would have been possible had there been no controversy.

later life, is already described in outline form in 1536.[58] In the same first edition, the spectrum of eucharistic positions,[59] including Luther's, is set forth with a truly independent judgment in a comprehensive typology, later to be thoroughly revised, to be sure, but already marking Calvin as one clearly aware of the issues. The later extensive debate with the Lutherans on this topic, while forcing Calvin to rigorous restatement and clarification at some points, does not gainsay the initial insight of 1536.

Every contact Calvin had with disagreeing brethren, every treatise he read, ancient or modern, was sifted and analyzed and the resulting insights incorporated into what we may call a spectrum. The permutations within the spectrum might shift from doctrine to doctrine, as he found himself closer to one group or one Church Father on one point, to another on a second, and so on. Obviously, he did not call this ordering of theological positions a spectrum in so many words. But his application of the true/false principle by means of dichotomy leads inexorably to a series, shading from more to less, with his own position at the midpoint.

Thesis 3a: A true/false principle was employed to organize and articulate the materials in the successive editions; this reached its fullest and most perfect application in the Latin edition of 1559 (cf. assumptions 1 and 2).

Thesis 3b: An examination of Calvin's use of the true/false principle discloses certain underlying presuppositions and analytical procedures that impart coherence to his theology.

In examining Calvin's development of a true/false principle we have made no attempt here to trace its origins either in prior theologians or in the philosophical traditions wherein Calvin received his earliest instruction. Let such investigation be the work of another time.

58. See *Inst. 1536a,* 65 (lines 19f.); 341f. (note p. 65); introduction, xliv: "These kernels of refutation were later reused and expanded in the Servetus quarrel as reflected in the latest edition of the *Institution* (1559)." *Inst. 1536b,* 48; 256f. (note on p. 48); introduction, l.

59. *Inst. 1536a,* xlviii. Calvin's initial eucharistic typology (*Inst. 1536a,* 141f. [ch. 4., § 27]; 369 [notes 141f., with identifications]) is sixfold:

1. really and substantially present
2. same dimensions of body of Christ as he had when he hung on the cross
3. wondrous transubstantiation
4. bread itself is the body
5. body is under the bread
6. only a sign and figure of the body is set forth

This scheme was abandoned in later editions of the *Institutio,* 1539ff. Cf. also *Inst. 1536b,* liii; 104 (ch. 4, § 27); 280f. (notes, pp. 104f.).

This working principle is, in my view, squarely based on the Pauline contrast between truth and falsehood, already noted in the crucial verses of Romans 1. The rootage, in turn, of the Pauline contrast in the Hebraic polemic against idolatry is most dramatically expressed in the prophetic antithesis between אֱלִיל (idols, things of weakness, nought) and אֱלֹהִים (the God of might and power). This Hebrew play on words is most appropriately rendered in a western European language by the German *Goetze* and *Gott*. Following in this biblical and patristic tradition, idolatry for Calvin is a term whose meaning extends far beyond the making and worship of physical idols. The constructs, too, of the human mind can be as much the objects of idolatry as can physical representations of Deity.[60] Calvin makes a direct application of the Old Testament critique of idolatry to the comparable idolatry of the papists of his own day (*Inst.* 1.11.10); this is repeated throughout the *Institutio* and in the commentaries, in a variety of ways.

Thus an idol can be either a construct of the human mind that reduces the majesty of God and his ways of revelation to a mere shadow, or it can be a physical, palpable construction of the human hand that itself becomes the object of that worship and honor due God alone. The one is a defect of the truth; the other, an exaggerated imitation of it. Both are false; truth lies in between. Let us illustrate.

Calvin's defense of the reality of angels (*Inst.* 1.14.3–12; see appendix C) illustrates both his use of dichotomy and the way it produces not a bifurcation, but a trifurcation, with determination of the *via media*. If, to use the Aristotelian notion that *defect* is diametrically opposed to a virtue, while *excess* falsely imitates the virtue,[61] the contention of the Libertines that angels are nonexistent corresponds to *defect;* the adoration of angels by the Roman Catholics corresponds to *excess,* which is a false imitation of the truth. The dichotomization would be represented as follows (table H).

The true/false principle is already manifest in the lengthy antithesis between false (Roman Catholic) and true (evangelical) beliefs and practices in section 4 of the dedicatory epistle to Francis I.[62] Against the charge that his party is "transgressing the limits" (Prov. 22:28), Calvin

---

60. Cf., e.g., *Inst.* 1.10.3.

61. See assumption 4, discussion, above, and note 42.

62. Another striking use of the true/false dichotomous principle is to be seen in Calvin's Latin preface to his cousin's French translation of the New Testament (late 1534?). The patristic argument is advanced for putting the Scriptures into the hands of the people in their own language (*CR,* 9:788). After the long drought of scriptural teaching, at long last the gospel is beginning to be taught to the people. But certain persons would deny the saving message to their flock. Why? Because such knowledge, they say, will endanger the souls in their charge. Others, while not denying the right to translate the Scriptures, would lock such versions up in scholars' studies away from the common people. Why? Because, they say, novelty is a bad thing. But is this novelty? Dichotomized, these positions would appear as follows (see table I, next page):

Table H. The reality of angels

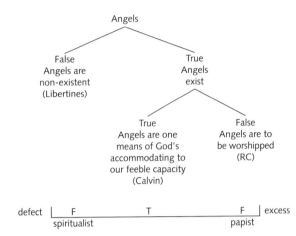

sets forth the chief aberrations of the sixteenth-century papal church, in contrast to the true teaching of the early Church Fathers:

What the Fathers said	versus	What the Romanists practice[a]
1. God doesn't need gold or silver		Look at their lavish rites
2. Christians can either eat meat or abstain from it		Lenten fasts
3. Monks must work		Idle, licentious monks of our day
4. No images of Christ or saints		Churches crawling with images
5. After burial of dead, let them rest		Perpetual solicitude for the dead
6. Bread and wine remain in the Eucharist		Transubstantiation

Table I. Should the Scriptures be given to the people?

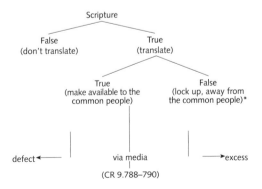

7. All present must partake of Lord's Supper	Public and private Masses put grace and merit of Christ up for sale
8. Rash verdicts without basis in Scripture disallowed	Jungle of constitutions, canons, etc., not based on God's Word
9. Marriage affirmed for clergy	Celibacy enjoined
10. God's Word to be kept clear of sophistries	Look at their speculative theological brawls

a. *Analysis* 1980, 27f.; cf. *Inst. 1536a,* introduction, xl; also, *Inst. 1536b,* xlvii. Cf. Luther, *Passional Christi & Antichristi.*

The thirteen "strophes" of this extended contrast between the tradition of the Fathers and the practice of Calvin's Romanist contemporaries are cast in bipartite rhetorical structures, the anaphora of each commencing with:

(1) *Pater erat qui . . .* or *Patres erant qui . . .*

and the second member of each commencing with:

(2) *Transgrediuntur . . . limitem quum . . .*
    or *. . . fines transiliunt quum . . .*
    or *. . . hunc limitem transgressi sunt, quum . . .* &c.

Thus, in each is expressed a limit within which true patristic orthodoxy as viewed by Calvin rests, and beyond which (in Romanist practice) lies false religion. Thus, the proof-text, Proverbs 22:28, of which Roman Catholic controversialists had made so much use against their Protestant opponents, is roundly turned against them by Calvin.

Among other conscious uses of *limits* on Calvin's part, one may cite his basic touchstone for the testing of eucharistic teaching on the presence of Christ in the Supper. In a passage dealing with the Lutheran doctrine of ubiquity, Calvin asserts that our thinking about that presence must subscribe to two limits: (1) what we say about that presence must withdraw nothing from Christ's heavenly glory; (2) it must ascribe nothing inappropriate to human nature, to his body.

No, says Calvin to the papists: you cannot appeal to custom, for most custom is the result of the private views of the majority that become public error and wrongly take on the force of law.

How this initial description (of 1536) of the false features of the Roman Church (together with other details in chs. 4–6, especially), over against the true ones of the Reformed Church, was polished and elaborated into what became Book IV of the *Institutio* of 1559 can be seen in bare outline in our *Speculum Institutionis* (appendix A), tables 19–34.

By way of illustration, see tables 20–21, covering *Institutio* 4.1–7. Table 20, "The Marks of the Church," illustrates the true/false principle in terms of defect-excess. A church of God undoubtedly exists wherever[63]

(1)   the Word of God is purely preached and heard
(2)   the sacraments are administered according to Christ's institution

Diagrammatically, generalized from Calvin's critique of false aspects of both spiritualism and Romanism, our analysis is presented as follows:

63. *Inst.* 4.1.9.

Table J. Spiritualism and Romanism

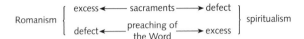

The Romanists, in overemphasizing the physical aspects of the Eucharist in the Mass, are guilty of excessive (hence, false) imitation of the true, while those spiritualists who overspiritualize the Supper are guilty of defect. Conversely, the spiritualists who exaggeratedly go beyond the Word in their preaching are guilty of excess, while the Romanists in omitting or debasing the proclamation of the Word, or at least in cutting the vital nexus between Word and sacrament, are guilty of defect.

How does the true/false principle work in various contexts? Sometimes the principle implicitly underlies the discussion, sometimes it very explicitly sorts out particular questions. For example, the position of Calvin's scriptural exegesis can be sketched as follows:[64]

Table K. Calvin's scriptural exegesis

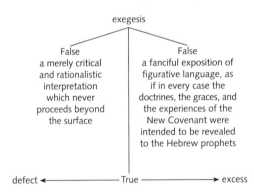

While this dichotomy was intended to set Calvin between tendencies as they were manifested in the sixteenth century, it is sufficiently accurate to represent Calvin's critique, here and there, of his opponents. Zwingli's exposition of the words of institution of the Supper is cold and defective; in different degrees and ways, the Romanist and Lutheran readings of *hoc est corpus meum* represent exegetical excess.

The larger dichotomy from which Calvin apparently adduces the true nature of prayer is simply expressed (see table 15). Here again the

64. Thomas Myers, "Calvinus Judaizans an Orthodoxus," in Calvin, *Commentaries on the First Twenty Chapters of the Book of the Prophet Ezekiel,* 2 vols. (Edinburgh: Calvin Tract Society, 1849–50), 2:418.

defect is represented by the philosophical rejection of prayer as superfluous; the excess, by the exaggerated extension to other mediators of
the invocation that should be made in the name of Jesus alone.

Alternatively, in terms of defect/excess:

Table L. The nature of prayer

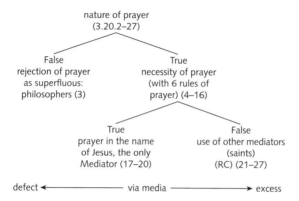

Thesis 4a: Successive dichotomies of the true/false principle, applied
in varied ways in different contexts, might be schematized, in general
form, as follows:

Table M. The true/false principle

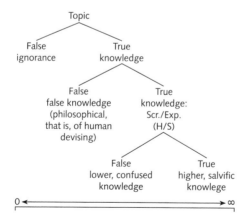

In our thesis 4a we have given a general schema of the successive
dichotomizations through which Calvin sorts through conflicting
teachings to arrive at what for him is the true midpoint. This may be
illustrated by his discussion of the final resurrection in *Inst.* 3.25 (see
table 18).

As table 18 illustrates, the general schema enables Calvin to encompass in his discussion, in a unified way, a widely divergent field of authorities. This, I believe, gives him a unique place among the major Reformers of the sixteenth century.

Thesis 4b: These dichotomies correspond to the tripartite working of the Holy Spirit in providence (cf. *Inst.* 1.16–18; "Against the Sect of the Libertines," ch. 14—appendix E, below).

Table N. The working of the Holy Spirit in providence: represented by concentric circles

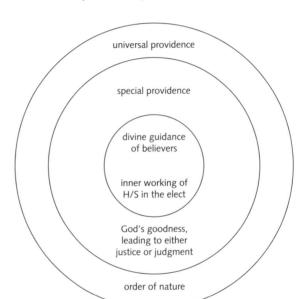

Evidence for this thesis will take the form of (a) a note on the working of the Spirit, gleaned largely from the *Institutio;* (b) a translation of chapter 14 of Calvin's tract, *Contre la secte phantastique des libertins* (1545), carried in appendix E. My note envisions a bipartite working of the Spirit. The chapter in the anti-Libertine tract divides the same range of activity into three levels or layers. We have attempted diagrammatically to show this "layering," in the form of ever-narrowing concentric circles.

I start from *Institutio 1536,* where Calvin often expresses his ideas most succinctly, if in unelaborated form:

Persuasi, non alium esse nobis ad patrem ductorem ac directorem quam spiritum sanctum, quemadmodum non alia est via, quam Christus. Nihil nobis gratia a Deo esse, quam per spiritum sanctum cum *gratia ipsa sit spiritus virtus alque actio.*

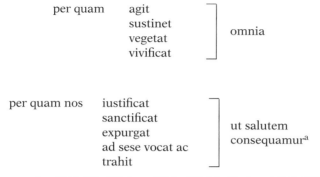

> per quam   agit
>   sustinet
>   vegetat   } omnia
>   vivificat
>
> per quam nos   iustificat
>   sanctificat
>   expurgat   } ut salutem
>   ad sese vocat ac   consequamur[a]
>   trahit

a. See *OS,* 1:85f.; ET, *Inst. 1536a,* 77f. (ch. 2); *Inst. 1536b,* 57f.

This passage corresponds to *Institutio* 1559:[65]

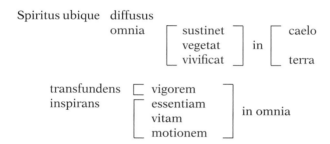

> Spiritus ubique   diffusus
>   omnia   ⌈ sustinet ⌉   ⌈ caelo
>   │ vegetat │ in   │
>   ⌊ vivificat ⌋   ⌊ terra
>
> transfundens   ⌈ vigorem ⌉
> inspirans   ⌈ essentiam
>   │ vitam   in omnia
>   ⌊ motionem

auctor regenerationis

These two passages indicate a two-level activity of the Holy Spirit: *praesens vegetatio/futura regeneratio.*
   Now turn to *Institutio* 1.13.18:

> Pater   ⌈ principium agendi
>   ⌊ fons et scaturigo rerum omnium
>
> Filius   ⌈ sapientia
>   │ consilium
>   ⌊ dispensatio in rebus agendis
>
> Spiritus ⌈ virtus ⌉ actionis
>   ⌊ efficacia

65. *Inst.* 1.13.14.

Now turn to *Institutio* 2.2.17. Here the familiar distinction between *gratai generalis* and *gratia specialis* is made. If *gratia est spiritus actio,* here is a further layering of that action.

In my view, Calvin had a clear spectrum of the range of the Spirit's activity in his mind at all times, but did not specifically and expressly set forth this structure in a sustained and explicit section of the *Institutio*. This is true of very many of Calvin's fundamental notions; they are taken for granted, used as working principles, but not elaborated. Sometimes, when under the stimulus of controversy, he will state such notions more explicitly, as in *Contre la secte phantastique des libertins*.

In his pursuit of portraying a totally active God, not passive in any aspect of his being, Calvin loves words like *actio, efficacia, virtus, potentia, operatio,* etc.[66] The whole range of his thought about God, from the most general principle to the most specific act, is summed up in the action of the Holy Spirit. The Father is the source, the Son the plan, the Spirit the outworking.

Now, to embrace the totality of God's activity in the cosmos, Calvin envisions a sort of "ladder" of two stages.[67] The lower stage moves from the Spirit's tending of the as yet shapeless mass on the first day of creation to the highest stage of intelligent, good, heroic, but unregenerate man. The upper stage of the ladder has to do with the rungs of man's redemption. *All is the work of the Spirit.* We may call the first the more general or "lower" work. But all these activities are inseparable from one another and equally essential for God's creation.

Seen in this broad way, Calvin's doctrine of the Holy Spirit (and of providence), includes, each in its place, such activities as creation, growth, nourishment, anointing and sending of Christ, performance of miracles, illumination, sending of prophets and ministers, working in the church, regeneration, justification, revivification, glorification.[68]

In the *Institutio,* as more explicitly in the anti-Libertine tract, Calvin is concerned to defeat the unhypostatic views of the spiritualist Libertines on the Holy Spirit. Thus he claims for every aspect of God's work in the cosmos the hypostasis of the Holy Spirit.

To enlarge on the "lower" and the "higher" workings of the Holy Spirit, it can be put in this way: for Calvin, God's working in his creation is of two kinds: (1) undifferentiated, general; (2) special, particular. This twofold working is a principle that can be illustrated repeatedly in Calvin's thought. For example, at 3.2.11f., Calvin describes a "lower" working of the Spirit among the reprobate, eventuating in false or impermanent faith. Again, at 3.2.32, we learn of a twofold effect of God's benefits, in the elect and in the reprobate. The passages

66. Cf. appendix C.
67. Or three stages, as at (b), below, and appendix E.
68. See especially appendix A, tables 10–14.

Table O. The working of God's Spirit in the cosmos

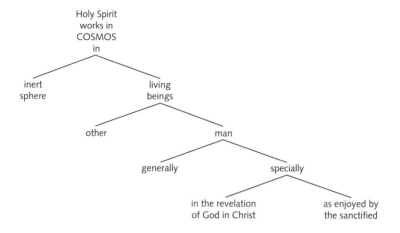

could be multiplied. Our "ladder" elaborated a little might look like table O.

For the lowest rung of the ladder, the general working of God's Spirit in the cosmos, the chief scriptural texts seem to be Genesis 1:2 and Psalm 33:6, as well as Acts 17. The commentaries and sermons provide yet other references.[69]

(b) The tripartite exposition of providence, as set forth in the anti-Libertine tract, chapter 14,[70] is summarized by Wendel.[71]

(1)   Order of nature in which God leads all creatures according to the condition and property that he gave to each one when they were formed (universal operation)

(2)   Special providence, through which God works in his creatures (especially man) and makes them of service to his goodness, justice, and judgment, according as he wills, sometimes to help his servants punish the wicked; sometimes to try the patience of the faithful or to administer fatherly chastisement to them

(3)   God governs his believers, living and reigning within them by his Holy Spirit, that is, practically indistinguishable from the interior witness of the Holy Spirit

The *bonitas Dei* thus works in a twofold manner among mankind:

69. Cf. *Comm. Gen.*, 1.11 (*OC*, 23:20); sermon 59 sur le Deuter., ch. 8 (*OC*, 26:601); *Comm. I Cor.*, 12:4 (*OC*, 44:498); *Comm. Act.*, 2:2f. (*OC*, 48:26); *Sermons de la Pentecoste*, sermon 1 (*OC*, 48:625); etc.

70. ET, appendix E, 241–44, below.

71. François Wendel, *Calvin: The Origins and Development of His Religious Thought*, trans. by Philip Mairet (New York: Harper & Row, 1963), 179.

Table P. *Bonitas Dei*

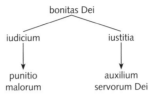

We may summarize, alternatively to the representation in concentric circles, the teaching of chapter 14 of *Against the Sect of the Libertines,* in a dichotomy:

Table Q. Providence of God expressed in a dichotomy

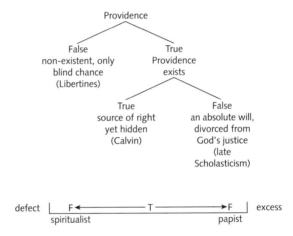

Thesis 5a: In successively "fractioning off" false from true, on a scriptural-experiential datum, Calvin displays a method more akin to that which later emerged in the Newtonian calculus than the traditional scholastic method, concerned as the latter was with the harmonizing by formal logic of discordant authorities.

Thesis 5b: The "fractionings off" schematized in thesis 5a exemplify a concept of truth emergent from bondage to falsehood, or conversely, of the lie seeking to engulf truth; it is the notion of the false approaching the negation it truly is, and of the true (as perceived by divinely aided man) approaching the infinite perfection of God, its beginning and its end.

Calculus Fidei. The theory of limits, on which modern mathematics, and as a corollary, all modern science and technology depend, is actually a secularized form of the scriptural view of reality. Mathematics and Scripture both view the human grasp of reality as increasingly approximated to, but never identified with, the human symbols we use to represent reality. Even our system of numbers, when faced, for example, with defining the ratio of the side of a square to its hypotenuse, or of the circumference of a circle to its radius or diameter, cannot do more than approximate relationships given in the realm of creation. The mathematical discipline is in this sense as much historical as it is philosophical.

Assuredly, the scriptural account of the creation—its beginning, continuance, and end—and its account of men and nations, is a history. When we try to absolutize this history in scholastic philosophical concepts that exhaust truth, we tend to break its dynamic character. Things incomplete are alive, have energy, have history; things completed, filled up, are dead, lifeless. Only divine perfection is alive, is in fact life itself. This history, whose midpoint is the incarnation, is best seen as a pathway toward truth which, throughout its length, is fraught with turnings to either side, which to take is disaster. Faithful listening to Scripture prevents us from turning to either side. Truth, then, is an approaching, by human creatures, under divine guidance, to the goal of God their Creator, Redeemer, and Judge.

Our grasp of all Christian truth has this dynamic bipolarity—between absence and presence, between nothing and infinity, between Creator and created—growing toward perfect comprehension but in this life not reaching it.

This movement toward the truth of God is seen in the agonizing effort to grasp the cardinal doctrines of our faith; the once dead but ever recurring heresies of the past clearly illustrate both the pitfalls of the search and the limits of the human mind in groping toward the truth.

The relational character of our knowledge of God and of self exemplifies this movement toward understanding. For Calvin this relational character of the *duplex cognitio* is marked both by the terms on which his theology is built—*pietas, religio, fides,* and all the rest (see appendix B)—and by the principle of accommodation, to which he adverts in resolving the apparent anomalies in Scripture.[72]

The necessity of accommodation as an exegetical principle rests on the notion of *captus,* the limited capacity of the human mind—both inherent from the very beginning in our creatureliness and after the Fall in our denatured condition. And *captus* asserts that the human intellect, however brilliant, has limits beyond which it cannot go. Between ignorance (the underuse of our rational faculty) and speculation (its

72. See Ford Lewis Battles, "God Was Accommodating Himself to Human Capacity," ch. 4 herein.

overuse, unrestrained by Scripture), lies the narrower zone where human rationality may function, in Calvin's view. Those limits can be breached only in the act of adoration, of giving honor and gratitude to the majesty of God, and this act itself is God's gift through Christ, in the Spirit. The two extremes of ignorance and speculation are, conversely, the dishonoring of God.

When we pray, we breathe out toward infinity.

This is why the *Institutio* is strewn with caveats against human speculation. At 1.6.3, Calvin describes how men's powerful tendency to move away from God made written proof of heavenly doctrine necessary; and how we will always wander in error and never reach our goal if we leave the scriptural path, which alone truly and vividly describes God to us from his works. In exposing the false, extrascriptural teaching of the Libertines on the Holy Spirit at *Institutio* 1.9.1, he shows how their touted freedom from "the letter that kills" leads them to dream up a new kind of doctrine that leads away from the gospel. Explicit warnings against extrascriptural speculations, whatever the source of their inspiration, are given, for example, when Calvin undertakes the discussion of the Lord's Supper (4.17) or of the doctrines of predestination and election (3.21–24).

But there is still another way in which Calvin exemplifies a doctrine of limits, at which we have already hinted. Like all great theologians, he was concerned with the problem of nothing and infinity. In asserting with Paul, and with an Augustine emancipated from Manichaean dualism, a doctrine of the goodness of creation, he sensed in the flight from the world of politics and law and war by the Anabaptists an underlying dualism, which he explicitly relates in his critique to ancient Manichaeanism. At the other end of the theological spectrum he saw in the Romanist two-tiered view of the Christian life (active/contemplative) a preference for a world-denying asceticism. Between two such asceticisms and their opposite, libertinism, Calvin strikes a superb balance.

> Our contempt for the present life (a gift of God's goodness to us) should not lead us to a hatred of it or ungratefulness toward Him; rather, hope of the future life should feed our present life and give it meaning and purpose.[73]

Nothing in creation is annihilated: even the reprobate in the utter alienation from God that is eternal death have continued existence. The image of God (preeminently the rational faculty in humankind) was not effaced by the Fall, although it is gravely impaired in all its faculties. Human beings may, in pursuing love of self, approach nothingness, an-

---

73. *Piety 1978*, 87, line 1662, note.

nihilation, but as a creation of God they can never cease to exist. On the other hand they cannot in self-adulation breach the barrier of finitude in their investigation of theological questions. The human quest, set in trinitarian terms of *Institutio,* Book III, may be summarized:

Apart from
- Christ—no knowledge of God
- H/S—no XP within us, that is, no faith
- God's choice of us in election,
- no effective working of the H/S within us

Expressed in terms of limits:

Table R. The human quest expressed in terms of limits

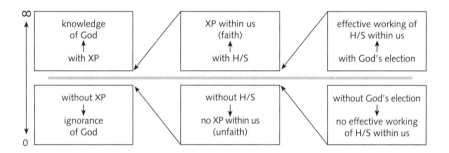

How, then, do these notions of limits relate to the calculus? We propose here no rigorous mathematical demonstration, but an analogy expressed in literary rather than mathematical language.

It would be difficult to choose a point in the history of mathematics at which to make our comparison of the calculus with Calvin's notion of how faith may be examined and described in language. More or less arbitrarily, we have set upon Isaac Newton (1642–1727), whose theory of fluxions was one of the starting points of modern calculus. Assuredly, we would disassociate Calvin from the Newtonian worldview: our comparison of the two is confined to the theory of limits.

The operation of long division—to take a simple example—where the resultant quotient is a surd or irrational number, when carried to a series of decimal places, illustrates the theory of limits. We never arrive at the perfect answer, but we approach, with each succeeding decimal, closer to that answer. In other words, we approximate it. The same is true of extracting roots, determining the area of circles, the volume of cylinders, cones, or spheres, etc. And there is in the determination of successive decimal points an oscillation between more and less. This phenomenon might be said to correspond, in Calvin's working, to suc-

Table S. True and false religion

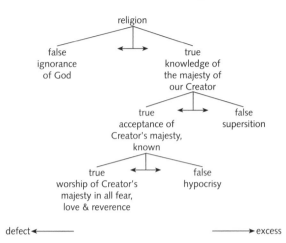

cessive fractionalization by dichotomies of the true from the false. The word "religion" (see appendix B) encompasses in its broadest sense both *true* and *false* religion; *true* religion, in turn, encompasses both a *true* and a *false* form of *true* religion; finally, the *true* form of *true* religion encompasses both a *true* and a *false* practice of the *true* form of *true* religion. Diagrammatically (table S).

This diagrammatic representation emphasizes Calvin's *via media;* in this diagram we have alternated *true* and *false* between *right* and *left.* If instead, the diagram is cast (in the form of our *Speculum Institutionis*) with the *true* always on the *right,* the *false* on the *left,* and laying aside the Aristotelian notion of *defect-excess,* we will see zero and infinity as the limits toward which falsity and truth, respectively, approach, through successive dichotomizations.

To turn once more to Isaac Newton: building on the ancient Greek consideration of the "area of a rectangle" as produced by the "motion of one of its sides along the other," Newton extended

> this principle to all kinds of mathematical quantities. The conception is very easy and natural: we see by continual experience that all kinds of figures are actually described by the motion of bodies. But it is evident, that quantities generated in this manner in a given time become greater or less, in proportion as the velocity with which they are generated is greater or less. These were the considerations that led the author to apply himself to the finding out of the magnitude of finite quantities by the velocities of their generating motions, which gave rise to the method of fluxions.[74]

74. Isaac Newton, *Mathematical Works,* ed. by Derek T. Whiteside, 2 vols. (New York: Johnson Reprint Corp., 1964–67), 1:33f. The quotations are taken from a facsimile of the first English edition.

To put this in theological terms: the rectangle, one of whose sides might be likened to the human condition, turns upon its other, the incarnate Christ as its axis; when its full rotation is accomplished, it has attained its complete area, that is, its full, divinely ordained stature in Christ.

Or, to change the metaphor, with Calvin, our pursuit of Christian truth moves through time to the end point, the eschaton. Perfection is not instantaneously achieved at conversion, but is a gradual struggle between faith and unfaith[75] in which, if God's electing grace be present, there is movement (at different rates for different individuals) toward the full enlightenment that can come only at the end. Rather than the model of Jacob's ladder used by Origen to picture the progress of souls toward and away from God, according as they use their free will rightly or wrongly,[76] Calvin has chosen to see the line of salvation history, in both its microcosmic and macrocosmic aspects, as the attraction toward, or repulsion from, God, of human souls and the church, by necessity, but not by compulsion. Thus Calvin can claim human responsibility for acts committed by a will bound by the necessity of sin.[77] Thus he can answer the synergistic argument of the Romanists, that such a view of the working of God's grace makes human beings like mere stones,[78] and hence not responsible.

Working in this historic frame that extends from creation to judgment and future life, Calvin sees Scripture as the key: God, in accommodatory language, has given his written revelation to us as the key to our salvation. We strive to understand his purposes for us not in absolute terms, but in relational categories that approach the infinity that is divine truth, and conversely, recede from the nothingness that is error. The false turnings that the Spirit of Falsehood counterfeits as true, to lead us astray, are to be fractioned off and away from the *really true.*

Let us close with a cautionary note from Newton himself, through his first editor and translator, as he introduces the theory of fluxions and endeavors to anticipate the busybodies who will make

> enquiries into the precise magnitude, the exact form and nature of infinite quantities. In all our reasonings about infinity, there are certain bounds set to our finite and limited capacities, beyond which all is dark-

75. *Inst.* 3.2.16–28.
76. Origen, *On First Principles* 1.3ff.
77. *Inst.* 2.3.5.
78. John Eck, *Enchiridion,* ch. 31, p. 210: "Here the heretics have revived the once extinct heresy of Mani who first indeed denied free will functions actively on good works, because such are wholly and totally done by God: thereupon Luther, having become insane, denied free will completely, because all things happen out of absolute necessity—something once said by the stupid Stoics, Empedocles, Critolaus, Diodorus and other mistaken ones."

ness and confusion. And it is the distinguishing mark of true philosophy to know where to stop. This is certain, we can know nothing of it but by comparison only. However, such conclusions as are fairly deduced from principles taken in a sense that we can comprehend, ought not to be rejected, on account of any difficulties that may arise for want of a complete and adequate understanding of the whole extent and nature of such principles.[79]

With a few changes of terms, Calvin could have written these lines. In giving this humble suggestion that Calvin, in a sense, anticipates in a general way the notion of the calculus, it is my prayer that no one will busy himself with enquiries into the precise magnitude, the exact form and nature of infinite truths. Our proper response is doxological, a hymn to the wisdom, goodness, and majesty of God best known to us in this life when, under Christ, we compare these *virtues Dei* with our own folly, wickedness, and wretchedness.

---

79. *The Mathematical Works of Isaac Newton*, 1:34.

Appendix **A**

Speculum Institutionis
Prolegomena

In essaying a "mirror of the *Institutes*" in terms of the true/false principle (theses 3ff.), I did not achieve a uniform analysis. Book I and part of Book II, it will be noted, are expressed for the most part in simple, undetailed dichotomies.[1] In subsequent books, where larger blocks of lightly reedited material had been incorporated from earlier editions into the final Latin edition by Calvin, it seemed necessary to expound the content of the structure more fully, as in the christological passages (tables 6–8); in still other places, as in the exposition of the law (2.8) or that of the Lord's Prayer (3.20), it seemed more useful for our purpose, on the basis of the presumed underlying dichotomy, to generalize diagrammatically the great bulk of this part of the *Institutio* (table 5). Each of the four Books has been presented also in a briefer, generalized form (tables 1, 9, 19). In some cases where there is a large sequence of material (within a particular book), illustrating true/false dichotomies within dichotomies, as in the case of the sacraments (4.15–19), the more detailed analysis of the contents is preceded, or accompanied (as a recurrent running head), by a generalized scheme. Thus, this *speculum* does not purport to be a definitive, rigorous exposition of the content of the *Institutio*.[2]

Another limitation of the *speculum* should be mentioned: because of its serial character, it does not pick up explicitly the many interconnections or sym-

---

1. This study of Calvinian dichotomy has been made without reference to Peter Ramus (1515–72), whose addiction to the dichotomy is well known. See W. Ong, *Ramus: Method, and the Decay of Dialogue: from the Art of Discourse to the Art of Reason* (Cambridge, Mass.: Harvard University Press, 1958). Even a superficial comparison of Calvin's use of the dichotomy in elucidating theological truth over against Ramus and his Reformed imitators in England and elsewhere will demonstrate the utter difference of purpose, method, intent, and religious tone of the two. An examination of the adaptation of the Ramean dichotomy by the English Puritans to the teaching of Reformed theology (Ramus devoted only one of his sixty-odd works to theology!) would probably reveal a displacement of the scriptural-historical-experiential dichotomy of Calvin by a philosophical-rhetorical form that could hardly prove a worthy vehicle for Calvinian piety in later generations.

2. For that sort of detailed presentation, the reader is invited to examine my *Analysis 1980.*

metries of the various parts of the *Institutio*. To have attempted such a statement of interconnections would have made the analysis here presented unduly complicated, thus defeating its purpose. Such should be the work of another time.

A further limitation is that the false member of each dichotomy has not always been identified in terms of an actual opponent of Calvin. To be sure, the basic positions of the Roman Catholics and of the various radical factions (to which Calvin was opposed) are generally labeled, with enough detail to indicate the function of controversy in shaping Calvin's theology (thesis 2).[3]

In many cases, the true/false dichotomy, which is muted in the *Institutio*, is forthrightly expressed in a tract, often with valuable details.[4]

The *mirror* also does not detail the scriptural exegesis or the analysis of church history that underlies the true/false dichotomization. Calvin, scripturally, had to deal not only with the prime texts on which his theology rests but with the texts set forth by his opponents.[5]

Calvin successively (1536–43, especially) reviewed the development of various doctrines through the history of the church, and at the same time applied the ancient classification of the major heresies to some of the theological tendencies of his opponents.[6] This is most extensively to be observed in his devel-

---

3. Readers wishing to explore this aspect in more detail with reference to the pre-Tridentine Roman position should consult my annotated English translation of John Eck's *Enchiridion*. On his relation to the Anabaptists, see William Keeney's brief essay, "An Analysis of Calvin's Treatment of the Anabaptists in the Institutes," *Analysis* (1976), 74*–84*, and his subsequent book, *The Development of Dutch Anabaptist Thought and Practice from 1539–1564* (Nieuwkoop: De Graaf, 1968). The larger question of all the dissident groups and tendencies—Anabaptists, Spiritualists, Libertines, Nicodemites, etc.—I attempted to address some time ago, but my work on this is incomplete. I have, however, in an unpublished form, analyzed and worked out a typology of many of Calvin's polemical tracts. Francis M. Higman's book, *The Style of John Calvin in His French Polemical Treatises* (London: Oxford University Press, 1967), while largely philological in character, is helpful. Further work on the true/false principle will require the completion of the study of all the polemical tracts.

4. Of course, the annotations in Barth-Niesel, *OS*, have done much to identify the putative opponents of Calvin, and Calvin has in the *De Scandalis* given his own classification of "despisers" of the gospel. Ganoczy, *The Young Calvin* (ET, 1987), gives in some detail the chief formative influences on the 1536 and 1539 *Institutio*. Smits, *St. Augustin dans l'oeuvre de Jean Calvin*, vol. 2, details the progress of Calvin's study of Augustine. The work of John Walchenbach has made a beginning in assessing the place of John Chrysostom in Calvin's theological development; see "John Calvin as Biblical Commentator: An Investigation into Calvin's Use of John Chrysostom as an Exegetical Tutor" (Ph.D. diss., University of Pittsburgh, 1974). In my annotated *Inst. 1536*, I have endeavored (in the introduction and end-notes) to detail the chief affirmative and negative influences in the formation of the first edition of Calvin's work. There it is noted how some later controversies were already anticipated in outline in the 1536 edition (e.g., the Servetus controversy over the Trinity).

5. The beginning of this lifelong labor is seen in the *Psychopannychia*, ed. by W. Zimmerli (1932). For the Roman Catholic arsenal of supporting texts, see, for example, John Eck, *Enchiridion;* Eck also details the proof-texts of his opponents (see *Enchiridion*, scriptural index, 285–94, for list).

6. Calvin's application of the Marcionite/Manichaean pattern to some aspects of the thought of Servetus and the Anabaptists is to be seen in the *Institutio*, and especially in relevant letters and treatises.

opment of ecclesiology[7] (table 21), but it contributes to his understanding of almost all the chief doctrines. At the same time that he selectively rejects views of his contemporaries, he sorts out the true from the false in the ancient Fathers and their scholastic successors. The notion of doctrinal deterioration (at varying rates for different doctrines) during the years between the New Testament and his own day leads Calvin to a scriptural datum, elaborated on the basis of an eclectic Augustinianism corrected chiefly from the Chrysostomic elements. To express this in a general dictum: Calvin takes his dogmatics chiefly from Augustine; his exegetics, chiefly from John Chrysostom.[8]

Tables 1–37

Summary of Tables

Table no.	Institutes
1	Books 1–2 (generalized)
9	Book 3 (generalized)
19	Book 4 (generalized)
2	1.1–14
2a	1.15
3	2.1–5 (with generalized linkage to Book 3)
4	2.6–7
5	2.8–9 (ch. 8, generalized)
6	2.10–14
7	2.15–16
8	2.17
10	3.2–10 (generalized)
11	3.11–13
12	3.14
13	3.15–18
14	3.19
15	3.20.1–27 (generalized)
16	3.20.28–33 (generalized)
17	3.21–24 (generalized)
18	3.25
20	4.1–2
21	4.3–7
22	4.8–9
23	4.10
24	4.11
25	4.12
26	4.13
27	4.14–19 (generalized)

7. For example, the chief sources for the periodization of church history presented in chs. 1ff. of Book IV, seem to have been: Cyprian, *Letters*, especially in chs. 4, 7, and 12; and Gregory the Great, *Letters*, especially in ch. 7; possibly also the papal histories of Platyna and Sleidan; Bernard of Clairvaux, *De Consideratione*, especially in ch. 7; and, of course, Cassiodorus, *Tripartite History*.

8. On this, see J. W. Walchenbach, "John Calvin as Biblical Commentator."

28   4.15.1–13
29   4.15.14–22
30   4.16
31   4.17 (generalized)
32   4.17 (in detail)
33   4.18
34   4.19
35   4.20.1–13
36   4.20.14–21
37   4.20.22–32

Table 1. *Institutes*, Books 1–2: knowledge of God and humanity

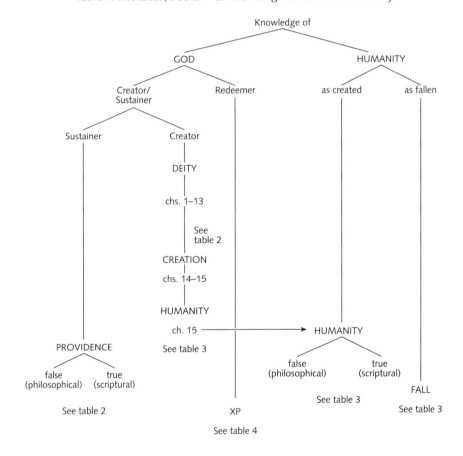

Table 2. The knowledge of God as Creator (*Inst.* 1.1–14)

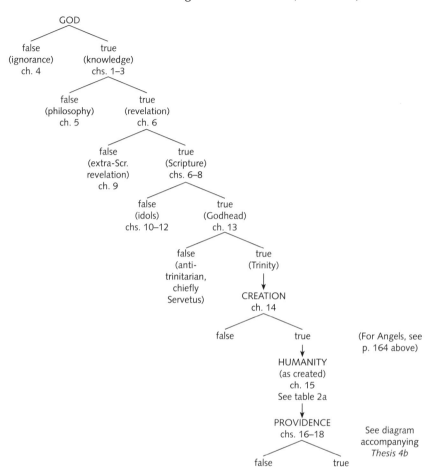

Table 2a. Humanity as created (*Inst.* 1.15)

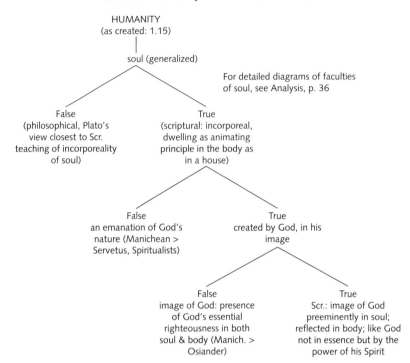

HUMANITY
(as created: 1.15)

soul (generalized)

For detailed diagrams of faculties
of soul, see Analysis, p. 36

False
(philosophical, Plato's
view closest to Scr.
teaching of incorporeality
of soul)

True
(scriptural: incorporeal,
dwelling as animating
principle in the body as
in a house)

False
an emanation of God's
nature (Manichean >
Servetus, Spiritualists)

True
created by God, in his
image

False
image of God: presence
of God's essential
righteousness in both
soul & body (Manich. >
Osiander)

True
Scr.: image of God
preeminently in soul;
reflected in body; like God
not in essence but by the
power of his Spirit

Table 3. Humanity after the Fall (*Inst.* 2.1–5; with generalized linkage to Book 3)

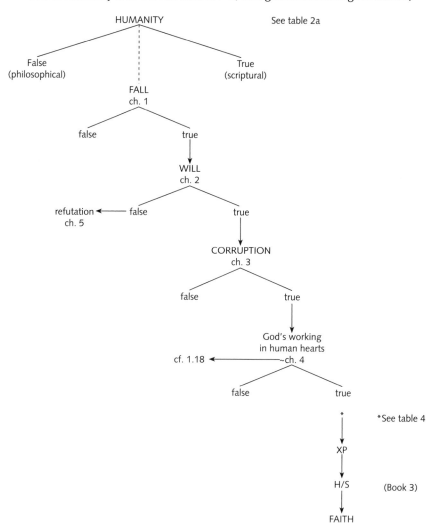

Table 4. The knowledge of God as Redeemer (*Inst.* 2.6–7)

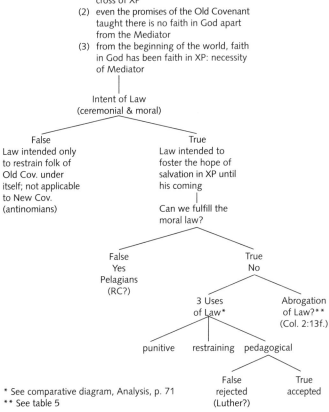

Transition from humanity as fallen (2.1–5) to
knowledge of God as the Redeemer (2.6)

(1) to the knowledge of God the Creator,
derived from the contemplation of the
created order (useless to us because of
our fallen condition) faith must be
added, through the preaching of the
cross of XP

(2) even the promises of the Old Covenant
taught there is no faith in God apart
from the Mediator

(3) from the beginning of the world, faith
in God has been faith in XP: necessity
of Mediator

Intent of Law
(ceremonial & moral)

False
Law intended only
to restrain folk of
Old Cov. under
itself; not applicable
to New Cov.
(antinomians)

True
Law intended to
foster the hope of
salvation in XP until
his coming

Can we fulfill the
moral law?

False
Yes
Pelagians
(RC?)

True
No

3 Uses
of Law*

Abrogation
of Law?**
(Col. 2:13f.)

punitive   restraining   pedagogical

* See comparative diagram, Analysis, p. 71
** See table 5

False
rejected
(Luther?)

True
accepted

Table 5. Abrogation of the law (*Inst.* 2.8–9; ch. 8 generalized)

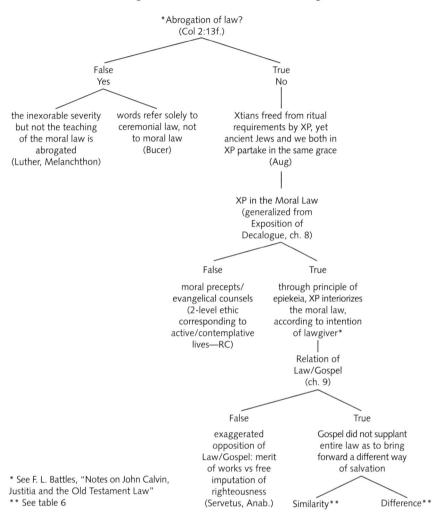

* See F. L. Battles, "Notes on John Calvin, Justitia and the Old Testament Law"
** See table 6

Table 6. Relation of law and gospel (*Inst.* 2.10–14)

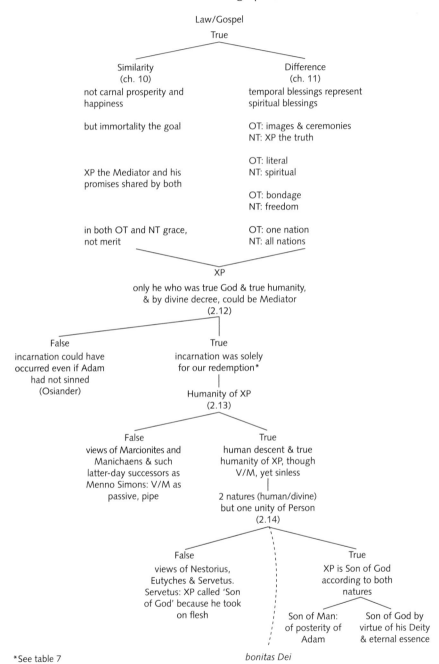

*See table 7   *bonitas Dei*

Table 7. Why was Christ sent? (*Inst.* 2.15–16)

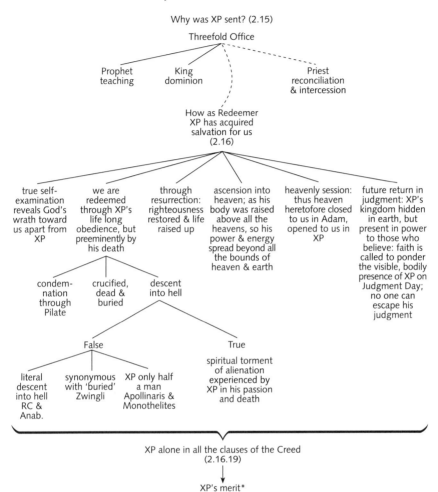

*See table 8

Table 8. Christ's merit (*Inst.* 2.17)

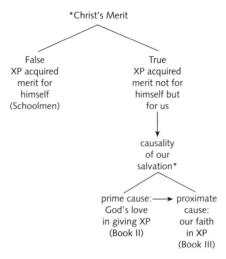

*See Analysis, p. 151: Diagram: The Causality
of Salvation (Calvin vs. the Council of Trent)

Table 9. *Institutes*, Book 3: Christ, Holy Spirit, and faith

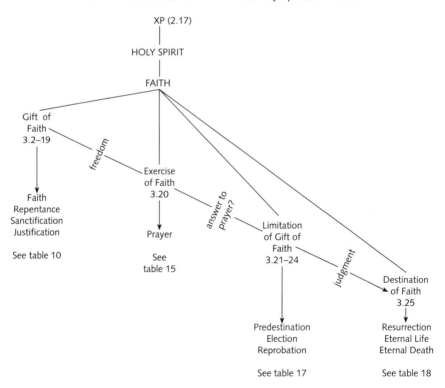

Table 10. Gift of faith (*Inst.* 3.2–10 generalized)

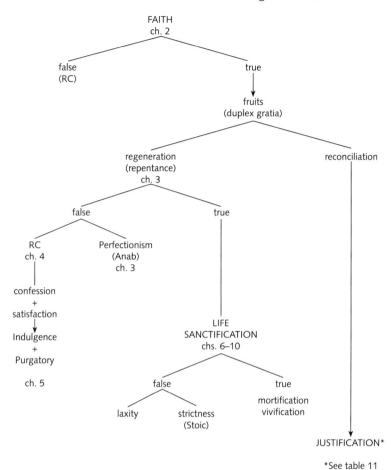

Table 11. Gift of faith (2) (*Inst.* 3.11–13)

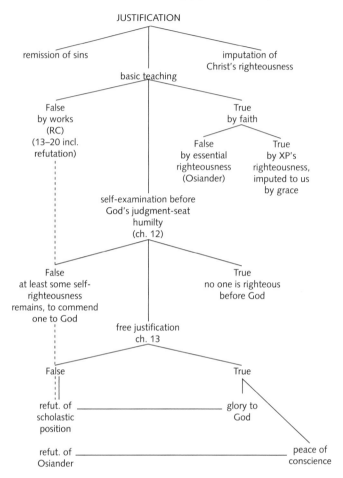

Table 12. Gift of faith (3) (*Inst.* 3.14)

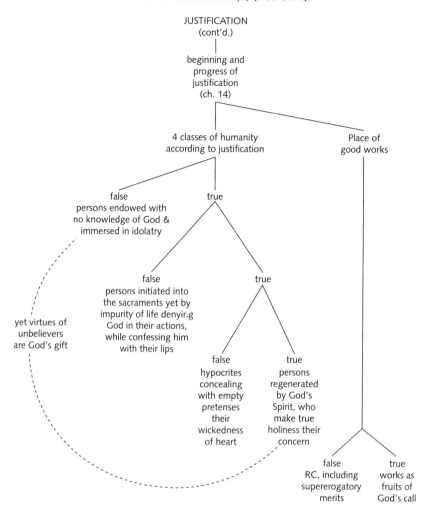

Table 13. Gift of faith (4) (*Inst.* 3.15–18)

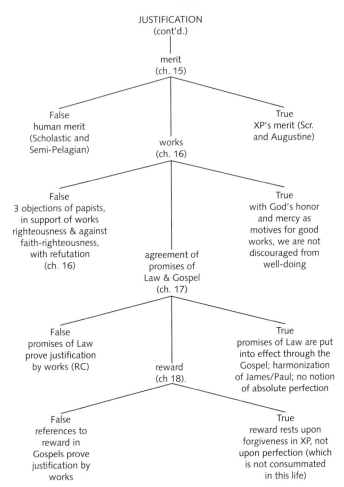

Table 14. Gift of faith (5) (*Inst.* 3.19)

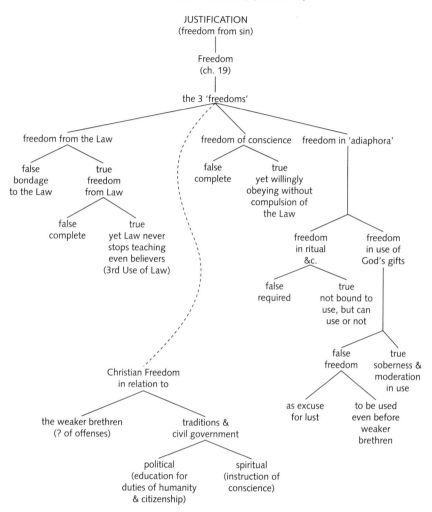

Table 15. Exercise of faith and nature of prayer (*Inst.* 3.20.1–27 generalized)

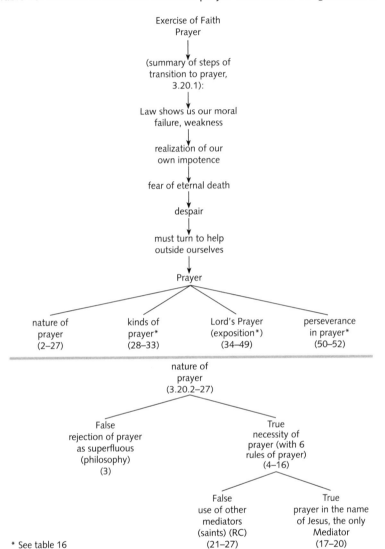

* See table 16

Table 16. Exercise of faith (prayer) (2) (*Inst.* 3.20.28–33 generalized)

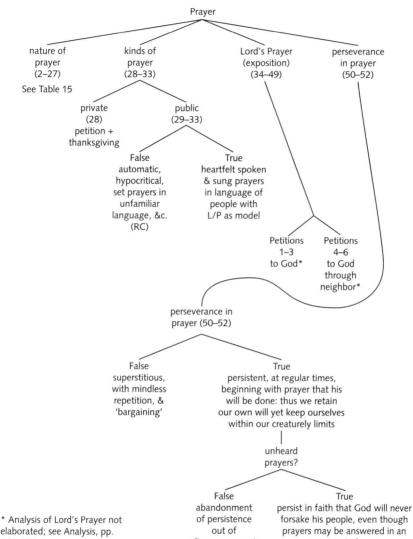

* Analysis of Lord's Prayer not
elaborated; see Analysis, pp.
164–174.

Table 17. Limitation of gift of faith (*Inst.* 3.21–24 generalized)

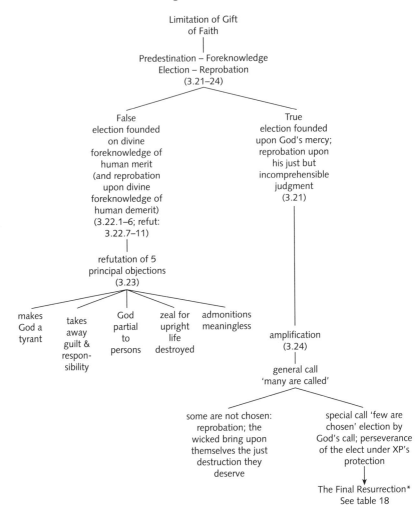

Table 18. Final resurrection (*Inst.* 3.25)

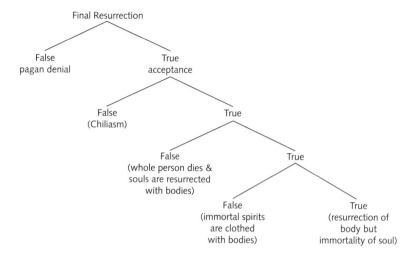

Table 19. *Institutes*, Book 4: Ecclesiastical and civil power

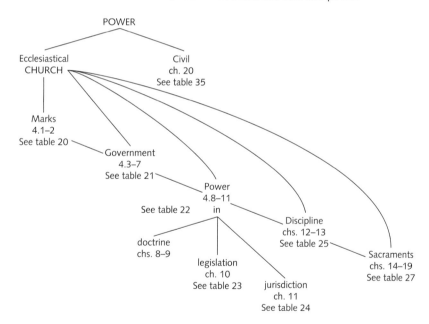

Table 20. Marks of the church (*Inst.* 4.1–2)

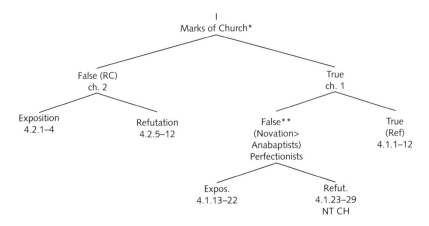

* In determining marks of Church; where true Church is, marks are to be applied to churches, not to individuals
** False, because marks are applied to individuals

Table 21. Government of the church (*Inst.* 4.3–7)

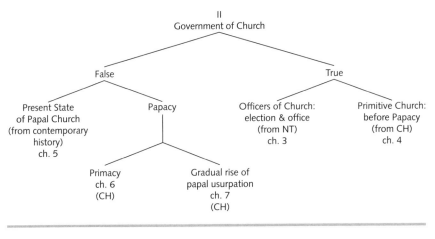

Table 22. Power of the church in doctrine (*Inst.* 4.8–9)

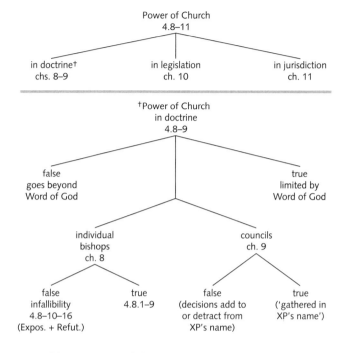

Table 23. Power of the church in legislation (*Inst.* 4.10)

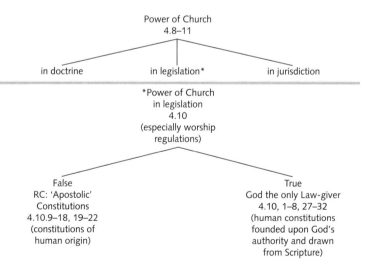

Table 24. Power of the church in jurisdiction (*Inst.* 4.11)

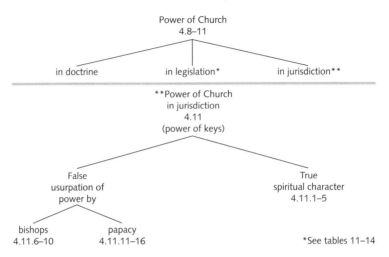

Table 25. Discipline of the church in censures and excommunication (*Inst.* 4.12)

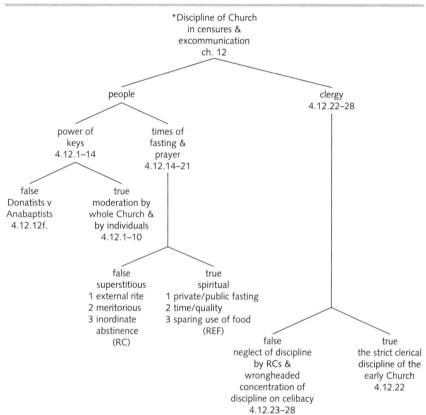

Table 26. Discipline of the church in vows (*Inst.* 4.13)

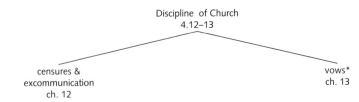

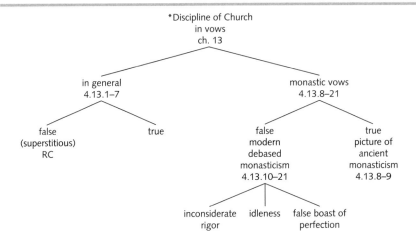

Table 27. Sacraments of the church (*Inst.* 4.14–19 generalized)

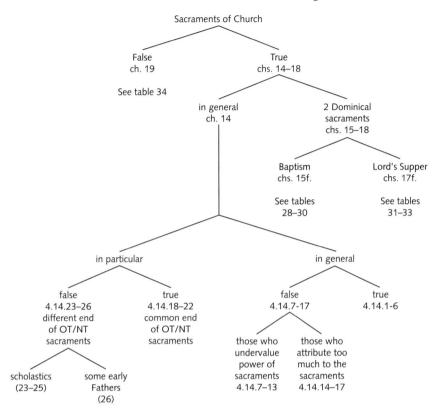

Table 28. Sacraments of the church: baptism (2) (*Inst.* 4.15.1–13)

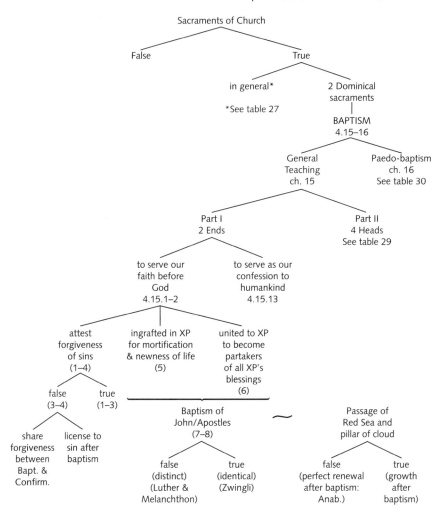

Table 29. Baptism (*Inst.* 4.15.14–22)

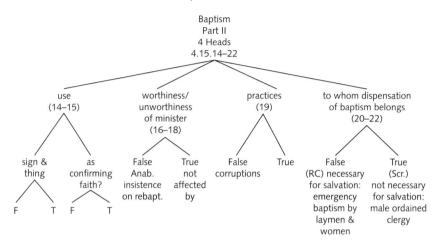

Table 30. Paedobaptism (*Inst.* 4.16)

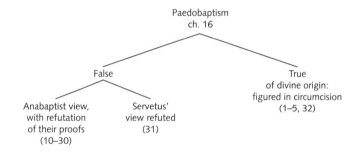

Table 31. Lord's Supper (*Inst.* 4.17 generalized)

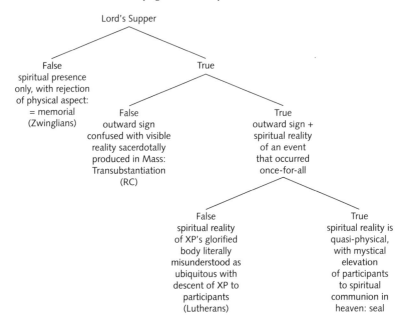

Lord's Supper*
4.17

Underlying T/F dichotomy inferred in ch. 17:

Lord's Supper

False
spiritual presence
only, with rejection
of physical aspect:
= memorial
(Zwinglians)

True

False
outward sign
confused with visible
reality sacerdotally
produced in Mass:
Transubstantiation
(RC)

True
outward sign +
spiritual reality
of an event
that occurred
once-for-all

False
spiritual reality
of XP's glorified
body literally
misunderstood as
ubiquitous with
descent of XP to
participants
(Lutherans)

True
spiritual reality is
quasi-physical,
with mystical
elevation
of participants
to spiritual
communion in
heaven: seal

*Note: for Calvin's earliest typology of the Lord's Supper, see *Institution* . . . 1536, 4.27
(Eng. tr. Battles, pp. 141f.)

Table 32. Lord's Supper (2) (*Inst.* 4.17 in detail)

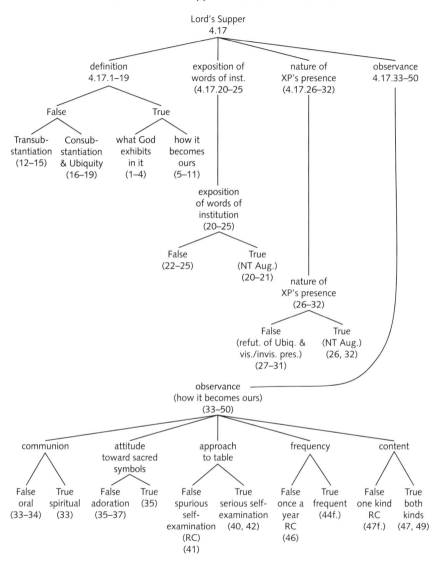

Table 33. The sacraments and the papal Mass (*Inst.* 4.18)

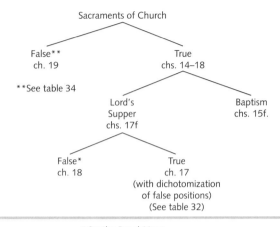

Sacraments of Church

False** ch. 19   True chs. 14–18

**See table 34

Lord's Supper chs. 17f   Baptism chs. 15f.

False* ch. 18   True ch. 17
(with dichotomization
of false positions)
(See table 32)

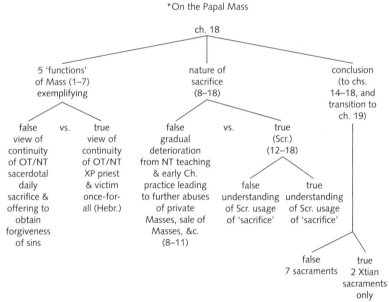

*On the Papal Mass

ch. 18

5 'functions'
of Mass (1–7)
exemplifying

nature of
sacrifice
(8–18)

conclusion
(to chs.
14–18, and
transition to
ch. 19)

false
view of
continuity
of OT/NT
sacerdotal
daily
sacrifice &
offering to
obtain
forgiveness
of sins

vs.

true
view of
continuity
of OT/NT
XP priest
& victim
once-for-
all (Hebr.)

false
gradual
deterioration
from NT teaching
& early Ch.
practice leading
to further abuses
of private
Masses, sale of
Masses, &c.
(8–11)

vs.

true
(Scr.)
(12–18)

false
understanding
of Scr. usage
of 'sacrifice'

true
understanding
of Scr. usage
of 'sacrifice'

false
7 sacraments

true
2 Xtian
sacraments
only

Table 34. Sacraments (2) (*Inst.* 4.19)

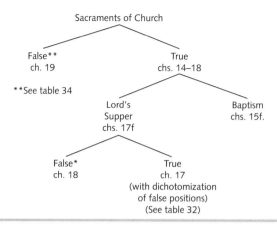

Sacraments of Church

False**   True
ch. 19   chs. 14–18

**See table 34

Lord's   Baptism
Supper   chs. 15f.
chs. 17f

False*   True
ch. 18   ch. 17
(with dichotomization
of false positions)
(See table 32)

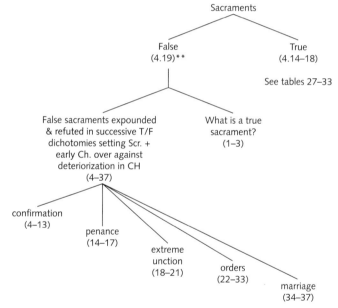

Sacraments

False   True
(4.19)**   (4.14–18)

See tables 27–33

False sacraments expounded   What is a true
& refuted in successive T/F   sacrament?
dichotomies setting Scr. +   (1–3)
early Ch. over against
deteriorization in CH
(4–37)

confirmation
(4–13)

penance
(14–17)

extreme
unction
(18–21)

orders
(22–33)

marriage
(34–37)

Table 35. Ecclesiastical and civil power (*Inst.* 4.20.1–13)

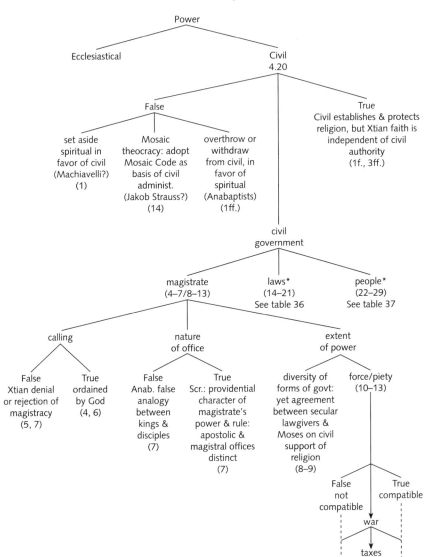

Table 36. Civil government (*Inst.* 4.20.14–21)

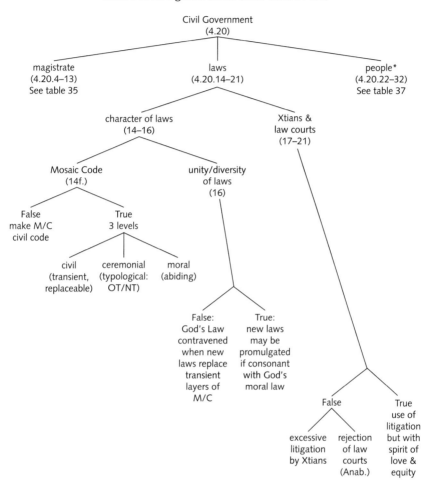

Table 37. Civil government (2) (*Inst.* 4.20.22–32)

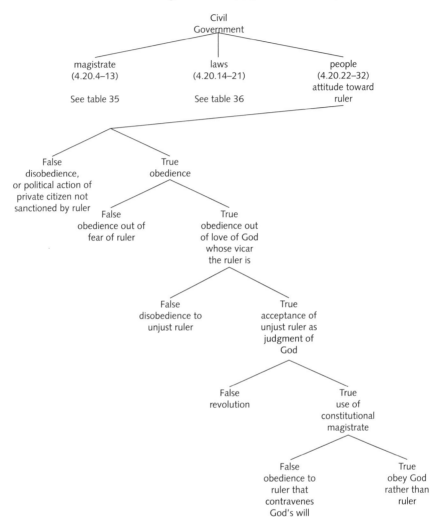

Appendix **B**   The Web of Meaning

A characteristic mark of Calvin's theological exposition is the interlocking of the definitions of the terms that make up his working vocabulary. A prime principle of lexicography is not to define a word in terms of itself, or to fall into circularity of meaning by reciprocally defining a limited number of terms without an external datum or reference point. The mark of a poor dictionary is that it takes the user on a merry chase through a series of entries, only to lead him back to his starting point without a clear grasp of the meaning of either the original word or the intermediate terms through which his search has passed.

Yet it is so to speak in defiance of such a lexical principle that Calvin lays the foundation of his theology on just such an articulation of basic terms. Now, such care in striving after consistency in terminology is not absent from any responsible philosopher or theologian. There is, however, in Calvin's "core of meaning" a dynamic resistance to formal, static, human-centered categorization, not always found in the annals of Christian theology. From his humanist apprenticeship he had learned precision in the use of language and in the determination of meaning.[1] His whole life was in a sense a search for that verbal vesture that was at once true, clear, and salvific for his readers. The *fons et origo*, the true datum of his theological language, is God's Word, the Holy Scriptures. Especially does he draw on the Psalms and Paul.[2] There he found that the whole of creation, of human existence and history, the beginning, middle, and end of all things, was a ring, closed in the mind and purpose of God, but still open, moving to closure in the ways of humankind.[3] Hence, his own basic terms in their almost ineffable interarticulation are fleeting yet eternally abiding reflections in the mirror that God in his fatherly accommodation to our feeble capacity[4] has set before our eyes. Calvin's use of the subjunctive, of the gerundive, of words like *coniungere, subicere, manare*, etc., strives to express the dynamic interrelatedness of his reading of reality.

If two words might be—almost arbitrarily—selected from this already select company of fundamental terms as representative, these would be *religio* and

1. *Comm. Sen. De Clem.*, introduction, ch. 5.
2. See note 19, pp. 144–45.
3. On ring-composition (or *inclusio*), see F. L. Battles, *The Theologian as Poet: Some Remarks about the Found Poetry of John Calvin* (1978), 2, and subsequent references in that essay, ch. 6 herein.
4. See F. L. Battles, "God Was Accommodating Himself to Human Capacity," ch. 4 herein.

pietas. Parenthetically, may I comment on the unhappy state of the English language cognates of these Latin words in contemporary usage? In reference to my translation of the *Institutes of the Christian Religion*, a learned Harvard professor of comparative religion lamented that the moth-eaten English word "religion" had been used to render *religio*. Why didn't the translator use the dynamic (and then currently acceptable) word "faith"? This was at the time when it was fashionable to speak of a "religionless Christianity." And as far as the words *pious* and *piety* go, they have long since lamentably received their decent internment in the graveyard of obsolete English.

Yet if one looks at the linkage of terms, the web of meaning, to translate *religio* as "faith" would initiate a great falling of dominoes (to use a current metaphor of global military strategy). How would Professor Smith, then, render the word *fides?* No, Calvin's terminology must be respected, not only as to each separate instance, but as to the whole *ensemble*. Elsewhere I have examined in detail the meaning of the crucial Calvinian term *pietas*.[5] Here let me merely sketch what seems to be the core of the far-extending web of meaning that marks the *Institutio*, and the biblical commentaries that support and adumbrate that book. It will take the form of a central diagram around which, like the spokes of a wheel, circle the interlocking definitions that Calvin perceived to be in living relationship with one another. To use the ancient patristic term *oeconomia*, Latinized by Tertullian (and inadequately glossed by him as *dispensatio*) as expressive of the inner life of the Trinity, we see in these words a household, a family of living, acting faith. At this stage, the false counterparts of each of these terms, over against which the true must ultimately be viewed, will not be examined. First, the chief texts will be set forth. Then the "hub" will be lightly sketched. The diagrammatic exposition of the whole "web" will not be attempted.

Texts:

A Vera autem pietas
   non in timore sita est
   qui Dei iudicium liberiter quidem fugiat,
   sed quia effugere nequeat, formidet:
   sed sincero magis affectu constat,
   qui Deum non secus ac patrem diligat
   perinde ac dominum timeat ac revereatur,
   iustitiam eius amplexetur,
   offensionem morte peius horreat.
   Et quicunque sunt ea praediti,
   non quam libet sibi Deum
   pro sua temeritate fingere audent:
   sed veri Dei cognitionem ab ipso petunt,
   non alium concipientes
   quam qualem se ipse exhibet ac declarat.[a]

   True godliness consists rather in a sincere
      feeling
   which loves God as Father as much as it
      fears
   and reverences Him as Lord,
   embraces His righteousness,
   and dreads offending Him worse than
      death.
   And whoever have been endowed with
      this godliness,
   dare not fashion out of their own rashness
   any God for themselves.
   Rather, they seek from Him the
      knowledge of the true God,
   and conceive Him just as He shows
   and declares Himself to be.

B Pietatem voco coniunctam
   cum amore Dei reverentiam
   quam beneficiorum eius notitia conciliat.[b]

   I call "piety"
   that reverence joined with love of God
   which the knowledge of his benefits
      induces.

5. *Piety 1978*, 13ff.

C Porro ex duabus notis
   quibus insignet fideles,
   discimus quae sit vera pietatis natura,
   timorem Dei vel reverentiam
   priore loco ponit:
   sed mox adiungit caelestis doctrinae
       scientiam,
   ut sciamus res esse coniunctas.
   Nam ut aliquem Dei timorem
   prae se ferant superstitiosi,
   nonnisi evanida est species.
   Deinde ludunt operam
   qui se fatigant in suis commentis:
   quia Deus non alia,
   nisi quae ex suo mandato praestantur,
   obsequia in rationes suas referet.
   Vera igitur religio et cultus Dei
   ex fide oriuntur,
   ut nemo rite Deo serviat,
   nisi qui edoctus fuerit
   in eius schola.[c]

Moreover, let us learn from the two marks,
by which he distinguishes true believers,
what is the nature of genuine godliness.
He puts the fear, or the reverence of God,
   in the first place;
but he immediately joins to it
the knowledge of Divine truth,
to teach us that these two things are
   inseparably connected.
The superstitious, indeed, exhibit a fear of
   God of a certain kind,
but it is a mere show, which quickly
   vanishes.
Besides, they weary themselves in their
   own inventions
to no purpose;
for God will take no account of any other
   services,
but those which are performed
in obedience to his commandments.
True religion, then,
and the worship of God,
have their origin in faith—
in the faith of what he has enjoined;
so that no person can serve God aright,
but he who has been taught in his school.

D Nunc iusta fidei definitio
   nobis constabit
   si dicamus esse
   divinae erga nos benevolentiae
   firmam certamque cognitionem,
   quae gratuitae in Christo promissionis
       veritate fundata,
   per Spiritum Sanctum
   et revelatur mentibus nostris
   et cordibus obsignatur.[d]

Now we shall possess a right definition of
   faith
If we call it a firm and certain knowledge
   of God's benevolence toward us
Founded upon the truth of the freely given
   promise in Christ,
Both revealed to our minds
And sealed upon our hearts through the
   Holy Spirit.

E En quid sit pura germanaque religio,
   nempe fides cum serio Dei timore
       coniuncta:
   ut timor et voluntariam reverentiam in se
       contineat,
   et secum trahat legitimum cultum
   qualis in Lege praescribitur.[e]

Here indeed is pure and real religion:
faith so joined with an earnest fear of God
that this fear also embraces willing
   reverence,
and carries with it such legitimate
   worship
as is prescribed in the law.

F Praecedat oportet
   vera religio
   qua in Deum viventem
   animi referantur,
   cuius cognitione imbuti,
   ad suspiciendam,
       timendam,
       colendam
           ipsius maiestatem,
   ad amplexandam bonorum eius
       communicationem
   ad opem ubique requirendam,

But true religion must come first,
To direct our minds to the living God.
Thus, steeped in the knowledge of Him,
They may aspire to contemplate, fear, and
   worship His majesty;
To participate in His blessings;
To seek His help at all times;
To recognize, and by praises to celebrate,
The greatness of His works
As the only goal of all the activities of this
   life.

ad recognoscendam
   laudisque confessione celebrandam
   operum magnificentiam,
in omnibus vitae actionibus
tanquam ad unicum scopum adspirent.[f]

G Etsi autem quae Deo debemus   Even though there are innumerable
    innumera sunt,   things that we owe to God,
    ad quatuor tamen capita   Yet they may be conveniently grouped in
    non inepte referuntur: four headings:
    Adorationem, cui tanquam appendix,   Adoration (to which is added as an
    spirituale conscientiae obsequium;   appendix, spiritual obedience of the
    Fiduciam, Invocationem, Gratiarum   conscience),
      actionem.   Trust, invocation, thanksgiving.
    Adorationem voco   Adoration I call the veneration and
    venerationem ac cultum   worship
    quem illi reddit quilibet nostrum,   That each of us, in submitting to His
    ubi se eius magnitudini submisit.   greatness,
    Quare non immerito eius partem facio, Renders to Him.
    quod nostras conscientias   For this reason, I justly consider as a part
    eius Legi subiiciemus.   of adoration
    Fiducia est, ex virtutum eius recognitione, The fact that we submit our consciences
    acquiescendi in eo securitas: to His law.
    quum in eo sapientiam,   Trust is the assurance of reposing in Him
    iustitiam, potentiam, veritatem,   That arises from the recognition of His
    bonitatem omnem reponentes,   attributes
    sola eius communicatione   When—attributing to Him all wisdom,
    nos beatos existimamus.   righteousness, might, truth, and
    Invocatio, sit mentis nostrae,   goodness—
    quoties urget ulla necessitas,   We judge that we are blessed only by
    in eius fidem atque opem receptus,   communion with Him.
    tanquam ad unicum praesidium.   Invocation is that habit of our mind,
    Gratiarum actio, est gratitudo,   Whenever necessity presses us, of
    qua laus bonorum omnium   resorting to His faithfulness and help
    illi tribuitur.[g]   as our only support.
                            Thanksgiving is that gratitude with which
                            we ascribe
                            Praise to Him for all good things.

H Docemur initium pietatis   . . . for we are by them taught
    esse in Dei cognitione.   that the beginning of religion is the
    postea adiungit fructum vel effectum,   knowledge of God.
    nempe invocationem.   He then mentions the fruit or the effect,
    Haec duo inter se cohaerent: which is invocation or prayer.
    sed ordo etiam tenendus est,   These two things are connected together:
    quia non potest invocari Deus,   but we must bear in mind the order also;
    nisi praeluceat eius cognitio.   for God cannot be invoked,
    . . . ergo . . . necesse est,   except the knowledge of him previously
    ut viam nobis praemonstret Deus ipse shines on us.
    quoties invocare ipsum oportet: Hence it is necessary
    ac proinde ubi nulla est Dei cognitio,   that God himself should show us the way
    nulla etiam est ratio precandi.   before we can rightly pray:
    Sed ubi Deus semel nobis affulsit,   and therefore where there is no
    tune via nobis aperta est   knowledge of God,
    ad ipsum invocandum.   there can be no way of praying to him.
    ergo invocatio fructus perpetuus est fides, But when God has once given us light,
    sicuti est testimonium pietatis.[h]   then there is a way of access open to us.

Invocation then is ever the fruit of faith,
as it is an evidence of religion;
for all who call not on God, and that
    seriously,
prove that they have never known
    anything of religion.

I   Sed hinc patet etiam,
    nos Deum timere
    ubi iuste vivimus
    cum fratribus nostris.
    Nam pietas est radix charitatis. . . .
    Quoniam ergo charitas manat
    a pietate et timore Dei,
    quoties secunda Tabulae officia
    videmus nobis poni in medium,
    sciamus ea esse
    testimonium cultus Dei.[i]

J   Ut in summa nihil aliud sit spes
    quam eorum expectatio,
    quae vere a Deo promissa fides credidit.
    Ita fides Deum veracem credit:
    spes expectat ut in temporis occasione
    veritatem suam exhibeat.
    Fides credit, nobis esse Patrem:
    spes expectat, ut se talem
    Fides datam nobis vitam aeternam credit:
    spes expectat, ut aliquando reveletur.
    Fides fundamentum est
    cui spes incumbit.
    Spes fidem alit,
    ac sustinet.[j]

But it is clear from this
That we fear God
When we live justly with our brethren,
For piety is the root of charity. . . .
Since, therefore, charity flows from piety
    and the fear of God
As often as we see the duties of the second
    table placed before us
We should learn them to be
The testimonies to the worship of
    God. . . .

To sum up, hope is nothing else
than the expectations of those things
that faith believed to have been truly
    promised by God.
Thus faith believes God to be truthful;
hope waits for Him
to show His truth at the right occasion.
Faith believes God to be our Father;
hope waits for Him ever to act as such
    toward us.
Faith believes eternal life has been given
    us;
hope waits for it sometime to be revealed.
Faith is the foundation on which hope
    leans.
Hope nourishes faith and sustains it.

a. *Catechismus* 1538, par. 2, 2.
b. *Inst.* 1.2.1; *OS*, 3:35.3–5.
c. Comm. in Psalm. 119:78f., *OO*, tome 3, 453b.
d. *Inst.* 3.2.7; *OS*, 4:16.31–35.
e. *Inst.* 1.2.2.; *OS*, 3:37.7–10.
f. *Inst.* 1539, ch. 3, p. 66, lines 10–15—2.8.16; *OS*, 3:358.7–14.
g. *Inst.* 1539, ch. 3, p. 65, line 45–p. 66, line 6—2.8.16 (1559); *OS*, 3:357.29–358.3.
h. Praelect. in Jerem., 10:25, *OO*, tome 4, 137a.
i. Praelect. in Ezech., ch. 18, v. 5, OO, tome 4, 168b.
j. *Catechismus 1538*, par. 21, 33.

Table 38. The 'hub': *religio/pietas*
(A, B, E above)

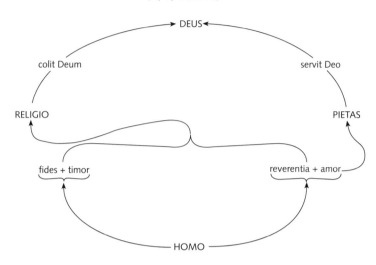

Table 39. The definition of *fides* and its detailed exposition

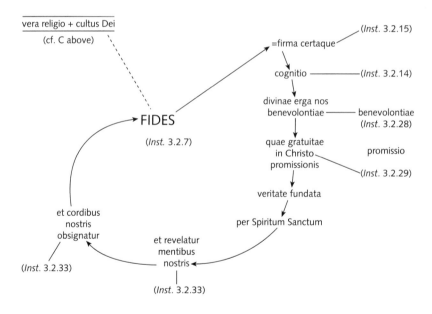

Table 40. *Legitimus cultus Dei*
(*Inst.* 2.8.16)
(cf. G above)

Gratiarum actio,
est gratitudo
qua laus bonorum omnium
illi tribuitur

Adorationem voco
venerationem ac cultum
quam illi reddit
    quilibet nostrum,
ubi se eius magnitudini
    sumisit
Quare non immerito
eius partem facio
quod nostrae conacientias
eius Legi subiieciemur

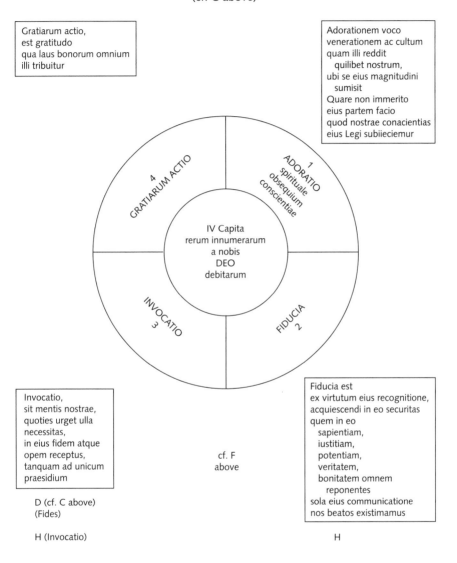

IV Capita
rerum innumerarum
a nobis
DEO
debitarum

Invocatio,
sit mentis nostrae,
quoties urget ulla
necessitas,
in eius fidem atque
opem receptus,
tanquam ad unicum
praesidium

Fiducia est
ex virtutum eius recognitione,
acquiescendi in eo securitas
quem in eo
    sapientiam,
    iustitiam,
    potentiam,
    veritatem,
    bonitatem omnem
        reponentes
sola eius communicatione
nos beatos existimamus

D (cf. C above)
(Fides)

cf. F
above

H (Invocatio)   H

Appendix C *Virtutes Dei: Theatrum Mundi*

Scattered throughout the *Institutio* and various commentaries of Calvin are lists of what Calvin calls the *virtutes Dei*. Taken together, these qualities of God perceived in the created universe and in the beneficent care showered on it by its Maker constitute the divine portrait as accommodated to our capacity. Calvin tells us that they are summed up in Psalm 145, but he ranges through the whole and through other books of the Old Testament as well; in the New Testament he most clearly attaches the *catalogus virtutum Dei* to Romans 1:21.[1] Two preliminary observations should be made about the lists: (1) they are primarily derived from Scripture and not from philosophical reasoning; (2) they display the traits of Deity as interrelated, flowing into one another in dynamic tension.

The dynamism can best be approached by studying first the probable reasons why Calvin chose the term *virtus;* then by examining the concept of *theatrum mundi* wherein the *virtutes Dei* are to be experienced by humanity. Finally, we shall attempt to sketch in diagrammatic form how Calvin perceives serially and together our apprehension of this portrait of God.

Why *Virtutes Dei?*

One of the characteristic phrases of Calvin, used to express what might in more scholastic language be termed "attributes of God" is *virtutes Dei/Domini*. Why did he use this expression, and how is it to be translated?

The roots of the phrase, I believe, are to be traced in the Psalms. One of the familiar Hebrew titles of God, "The Lord of Hosts" (יהוה צבאות), is rendered in the LXX usually as Κυριος [oΘεὸς] Σαβὰωθ, or as Κύριος [ὁ Θεὸς] τῶν δυνάμεων. The Vulgate translates, in the same passages, the phrase as *Dominus [Deus] exercituum,* where the usage is *Dominus [Deus] virtutum.*

But we do not find this Vulgate usage in Calvin's Latin rendering of the Psalms passages. Why? Probably as a result of the Blandrata incident of 1557(?) he substituted in the *Institutio* of 1559 for the earlier *Dominus* (as translation of the Tetragrammaton), or inserted new passages containing *Iehova*. This same change is reflected in his *Commentary on the Psalms* (1557), where the phrase יהוה צבאות is rendered always as *Iehova [Deus] exercituum*. In the commentary the phrase is glossed as *potentia Dei* (Ps. 46:8[7]), *virtus Dei*

---

1. Cf. assumption 1, and discussion, above.

(Ps. 48:9), *immensa potentia Dei* (Ps. 59:6[5]), etc. Calvin interestingly comments on the frequent juxtaposition of the titles "Lord of Hosts" and "God of Jacob (Israel)" as referring to God's universal power and at the same time his fatherly care of his people—the scriptural fundament of the twofold working of God's providence among humanity.

Yet צבאות refers to the angelic hosts, the armies of angels *(exercitus)* surrounding the throne of God and reaching, in their message-bearing mission, to the uttermost borne of creation. The Greek δυνάμεις (Latin, *virtutes*) is the name of what came in later Christian history to be designated as one of the orders of angels. Commenting on its use in Ephesians 1:21 and 1 Corinthians 15:24, Calvin states: "Indeed, since the Lord through this wonderfully sets forth and declares the power and strength of His hand, for this reason they are called *virtutes*. The names *Principatus, Potentates, Dominationes* (Col. 1:16; Eph. 1:21 and I Cor. 15:24) tell us that God "exercises and administers His authority in the world through them" (*Inst.* 1.14.5). In this part of the *Institutio*, Calvin is arguing for the actuality of angels against the Libertines, who deny their real existence (*Contre la secte* . . . , ch. 11),[2] and also against Osiander, whose speculations on whether the incarnation would have occurred if Adam had not fallen involved a defective view of the angels and of Christ's headship over them.[3] But Calvin is also, on the other hand, urging that the worship of angels or the use of them to justify the cult of saints (by the papists) be avoided. The angels represent, then, one aspect of God's grand accommodation of his self-revelation to mankind.[4]

Why does Calvin use *virtutes*, the name applied to angels and to praiseworthy human qualities (ἀρετή) in the Latin versions of the New Testament, to designate the *Eigenschaften Gottes?* Working primarily from the royal imagery and sovereign majesty and power of God as set forth in the Psalms, and also from the similar mood in Paul's letters, Calvin sees, under the various divine qualities, the energy, the effective working[5] of Deity in the universe and in human existence. Every aspect of the divine–human relationship is seen under the *virtus Dei:* this overarching notion (to which has been given the term "virtualism") may be seen, for example, in Scripture (*Inst.* 1.6), in the giving of Christ to us (2.12–17), in the giving of faith to us (3.2), in the sacraments (4.17.19), and in the likeness of man's soul to God (1.15.5). The *virtus Dei* is in fact the working of the Holy Spirit, apart from whose activity every aspect of the Christian faith would be cold and external and the *theatrum mundi* itself would not continue to exist. From the human side, there is more power, more energy, in scripturally inspired, incomplete, inchoate descriptive terms than in terms which in their very attempt to exhaust or fully express truth become, in their utter human presumption, static and dead.

The qualities of God which with clearer vision we can see in his universal working in the world and in mankind are not angels, not an army of celestial messengers at the divine beck and call. These *virtutes Dei* are the divinely accommodated, humanly perceived avenues of God's self-disclosure to us. Yet in

2. See theses 3a and 3b, above.
3. *Inst.* 2.12.6.
4. Cf. discussion of theses 2 and 3, above.
5. Cf. note 66, p. 70.

the accommodatory imagery of the heavenly host we can still believe in angels and, keeping their servanthood firmly in mind, *almost* identify the two notions of *virtutes Dei* with one another. In rejecting statically descriptive notions as expressed in such words as "attributes," "qualities," "characteristics," etc., and in boldly using an angelic model, Calvin is holding fast to the dynamic, personal scriptural teaching whose consummation is in Christ himself. Can there be any other adequate English translation of the word *virtus*, in this use, then, than *powers of God?*

Quoniam vero vim ac fortitudinem
    manus suae
Dominus per ipsos
mirabiliter exerit
ac declarat,
inde Virtutes nominantur.ᵃ
	Indeed, since the Lord
	    through them
	wonderfully sets forth
	and declares
	the power and strength
	of His hand,
	for this reason they
	are called Virtues.

    a. *Inst.* 1.14.5; Eph. 1:21; 1 Cor. 15:24; *OS*, 3:157.34–36.

Theatrum Mundi

The figure under which Calvin subsumes the traits of God that he deigns to make known to his human children is, as we have seen, *virtus*, power. The figure under which Calvin preeminently organizes the *virtutes Dei* is that of the *theatrum mundi* or theater of the universe. An examination of this metaphor may perhaps help us understand its meaning for Calvin and why he chose it as a vehicle for his teaching.

In four places in the *Institutio*[6] Calvin uses the metaphor of *theater* to describe the workmanship and ongoing activity of the universe wherein God vouchsafes to reveal himself to humanity.[7] In a fifth passage it is applied to the church.[8] Each of these first four references to the *theatrum mundi* was added in the final Latin edition of 1559. The word is absent from the earlier editions; in them the visual imagery was carried, for example, by the figure of the mirror *(speculum)*, as at 1.5.1 (1539) or 1.14.21 (1543), a figure that Calvin used in a wide variety of significations, but which usually remains beside *theatrum* in the final edition. There is a certain symmetry to the four passages:

I

sed quia maior pars
    erroribus suis imbuta,
in tam illustri theatro
    caecutit,
exclamat rarae et singularis
    esse sapientiae,
prudenter expendere haec
    Dei opera,
	But because most people,
	    immersed in their own errors,
	are struck blind in such a
	    dazzling theater,
	He exclaims that to weigh
	    these works of God wisely
	is a matter of rare and
	    singular wisdom,

    6. *Analysis 1980*, 40.
    7. *Inst.* 1.5.8; 1.6.2; 1.14.20; 2.6.1.
    8. *Inst.* 3.20.23.

quorum aspectu nihil
   proficiunt
qui alioqui videntur
   esse acutissimi.
Et certe quantumvis
   splendeat Dei gloria
vix centesimus quisque
   verus est eius spectator.[a]

in viewing which they who
   otherwise seem
to be extremely acute
   profit nothing.
And certainly however much
   the glory of God shines forth,
scarcely one human being in a hundred
   is a true spectator of it.

   a. *Inst.* 1.5.8; *OS*, 3:52.27–32.

II

Ergo quanvis hominem
   serio oculos
infundere conveniat
   ad consideranda Dei opera,
quando in hoc splendidissimo
   theatro locatus est
ut eorum esset spectator:
aures tamen praecipue arrigere
convenit ad verbum
ut melius proficiat.[a]

Therefore, however fitting
   it may be for man seriously
to turn his eyes
to contemplate God's works,
since he has been placed
   in this most glorious theater
to be a spectator of them,
   it is fitting that he prick up
his ears to the Word
   the better to profit.

   a. *Inst.* 1.6.2; *OS*, 3:62.20–63.2.

III

Interea ne pigeat
   in hoc pulcherrimo theatro
piam oblectionem capere
ex manifestis et obviis
   Dei operibus.[a]

Meanwhile let us not be ashamed
   to take pious delight
in the works of God open and
   manifest
in this most beautiful theater.

   a. *Inst.* 1.14.20; *OS*, 3:170.23f.

Parenthetically, it should be noted that this sentence replaced the following words, which had stood in the text from 1543 onward:

sequuntur deinde
   visibilia Dei opera,
in quibus opificem ipsum
recognoscere hic iubemur,

ad fidei aedificationem:
   coelum, terra, mare,
et quidquid in illis
   continetur.

There follow the visible
   works of God
in which we are bidden
here to recognize
The Artificer Himself,
for the upbuilding of faith:
   heaven, earth, sea,
and whatsoever is contained
   in them.

IV

Sapientiam Dei appellat
magnificum theatrum
   caeli et terrae,
innumeris miraculis refertum,
   ex cuius intuitu sapienter

This magnificent theater
   of heaven and earth,
crammed with innumerable miracles,
Paul calls the "wisdom of God,"

Dei cognoscere decebat:	Contemplating it, we ought
sed quia tam male illic profecimus,	in wisdom to have known God.
revocat nos ad fidem Christi,	But because we have profited
quae ob stultitiae speciem	so little by it,
incredulus fastidio est.[a]	He calls us to the faith in Christ,
	which, because it appears foolish,
	the unbelievers despise

a. *Inst.* 2.6.1; *OS*, 3:320.29–33.

The theater is *illustre, splendidissimum, pulcherrimum, magnificum:* the force of these epithets is to heighten clarity, order, beauty, perspicuity. But over against it is set our blindness to such clear evidences of God's workmanship and care. The substitution in 1.14.20 (for the 1543 passage) suggests that Calvin's introduction of *theatrum* in 1559 was to heighten human inexcusability before these manifest testimonies, and to remove the last vestige of inference (however wrong) of any direct causal relation between the seeing of God's works and the onset of faith.

The earliest use of *theatrum* yet found in the commentaries (in the *Comm. I Cor.* [1546]) seems to bear this out:[9]

Pulcherrimus locus,	This is a most beautiful passage
unde patet quanta sit	clearly revealing how great
humanae mentis caecitas,	is the blindness of the human mind
quae in media luce	which in broad daylight
nihil cernit.	discerns nothing.
Verum et enim,	For it is true
hunc mundum theatri instaresse	that this universe is like a
in quo nobis Dominus	theater
conspicuam gloria suae	in which the Lord shows to us
figuram exhibet:	a clear figure of His glory:
nos tamen, quum tale spectaculum	yet we, when such a spectacle
nobis ante oculos pateat,	is laid before
caecutimus:	our eyes,
	are blind,
non quia obscura sit revelatio,	not because the revelation is
sed quia nos mente alienati	obscure,
sumus.	but because we are estranged
nec voluntas tantum,	in mind.
sed facultas etiam ad eam	Not only the will
rem nos deficet.	but even the ability to do this
Nam utcunque Deus palam	fails us.
appareat,	For as often as God openly
non alio tamen quam fidei	appears,
oculo	yet we cannot see Him
ipsum possumus aspicere,	save with the eye
nisi quod tenuem divinitatis gustum	of faith,
concepimus,	except that we grasp a slight
qui nos inexcusabiles	taste of divinity
reddat.	to make us inexcusable.

9. *Comm. I Cor.*, 1:21; *OO*, tome 7, 119A–B.

Institutio 1.5.8 expresses our sin-bound blindness in this clear theater; 1.6.2 contrasts the *seeing* of God's wisdom in the theater of nature, as over against the *hearing* of God's Word in Scripture. 1.14.20 continues this by explaining how the creation narrative of Genesis 1–2 (more fully illustrated by such Fathers as Basil the Great and Ambrose) leads us to a right view of God's works and their benefits. The true response is one of joyous, grateful praise, expressed in 1.14.21 by Calvin in almost hymnic form.[10] Yet this newfound awareness in God's creation is not "the chief evidence for faith." In *Institutio* 2.6.1, which is the beginning of the crucial christological link (added in 1559) between the depiction of fallen humanity and the exposition of the law and gospel,[11] we are returned once more to the note of inexcusableness: "contemplating this magnificent theater of heaven and earth, we ought in wisdom to know God." But in our heedlessness of it, we are called to faith in Christ by the foolishness of the gospel, despised as it is by unbelievers.

Thus, through the references to the *theater* we trace the blinding of humankind and the restoration of their sight.

As in the notion of *virtutes Dei* we found it necessary to include the angels in our discussion, so in the figure of *theatrum* they must also be embraced. Now, as humankind was placed in the theater of the world to perceive and worship their Creator but, fallen, did not in truth do so until Christ the Word was proclaimed; so the angels frequent the theater of the church. But though they were created to live in the visible presence of God, yet new truth about their Creator is revealed to them, not by hearing the preached Word, but by observing its effect on the church. So Calvin interprets that fought-over passage, Ephesians 3:10:[12]

Voluit Deus Angelos curandae nostrae saluti praeficere;	God willed to appoint the angels to care for our salvation.
unde et sacros coetus frequentant,	Consequently, they attend sacred assemblies,
et Ecclesia illis theatrum est,	and the church is for them a theater
in quo mirantu variam et multiplicem Dei sapientiam.	in which they marvel at the varied and manifold wisdom of God.

This is made still more explicit in his commentary passage on the same verse:[13]

Ecclesia ex Iudaeis pariter ac Gentibus collecta,	The church gathered equally from the Jews and Gentiles
quasi speculum sit, in quo contemplantur Angeli	is as a mirror wherein the angels contemplate God's wondrous wisdom,

10. See *Piety 1978*, 169f.
11. See the discussion following table F, above.
12. *Inst.* 3.20.23; *OS*, 4:328.25–28.
13. *Comm. Eph.*, 3:10; *OO*, 7:334.

mirificam Dei sapientiam.
quam prius nescierant.
Opus enim vident sibi
   novum,
et cuius ratio in Dei
   latebat:
talis est profectus,
non quia ex ore hominum
aliquid discant.

which they knew not before.
For they see a work
   new to them,
whose reason lay hidden in God.
This, then, is the way
   they progress:
not because they learn anything
   from the lips of men.

Crudely expressed in graphic form:

Table 41. *Theatrum mundi*

Note that in these last two passages *theatrum* and *speculum* are synonymous for Calvin, a fact borne out both by his own, and by the Vulgate rendering of θέατρον in 1 Corinthians 4:9 as *spectaculum*.[14] The figure comprises not only the theater but the stage and the show taking place thereon.

Having examined representative uses of *theatrum* in the *Institutio* and in the commentaries, we may ask: What is the source of this favorite metaphor of Calvin? Perhaps it is so obviously suggested from common experience that the question is otiose. It is like tracing Shakespeare's words:

> All the world's a stage,
> And the men and women are merely players . . .

However, by looking at prior use of the metaphor, and at the distinctive way in which it is employed by Calvin, we may be able to understand it better.

Among Latin writers, the expression *theatrum mundi* is most tellingly used in Quintus Curtius Rufus, the author of *The History of Alexander*. As shown in our edition of *Calvin's Commentary on Seneca's De Clementia*, the young Calvin made a thorough study of Curtius, referring to him some forty-five times,[15] largely for lexical rather than historical purposes. Yet that Calvin gave considerable reflection to the character of Alexander the Great himself is clear.[16] In Book IX, Curtius represents Alexander, after a near-fatal wound sustained in leading an attack on a city of the Malli, beyond the River Hypasis, as reviewing publicly his conquests to date and his resolve to open to himself "a new world." He continues:[17]

14. *Comm. I Cor.*, 1:21; *OO*, 7:119A–B.
15. *Comm. Sen. De Clem.*, 93*.
16. Ibid., 131f.
17. "History of Alexander the Great of Macedon," in *Quintus Curtius*, trans. by John C. Rolfe, Loeb Classical Library, 2 vols. (Cambridge, Mass.: Harvard University Press, 1946), 2:420f.

Having conquered both continents in the ninth year of my reign and the twenty-eighth of my life, does it seem to you that I can pause in the task of completing my glory, to which alone I have devoted myself? I at least shall not be found wanting, and wherever I shall fight, I shall believe that I am in the theater of the whole world (in theatro terrarum orbis). I will give fame to unknown places. I will open to all nations lands which Nature had moved to a distance.

To Alexander the *theatrum mundi* is the stage on which his own glory is displayed for all to see.

Among Christian writers θέατρον is metaphorically used of Christian life as a contest in the theater (Clement of Alexandria, Origen, John Chrysostom). Closer to Calvin's usage is that of the theater as the world (Clement, Basil). In Gregory Nazianzus and John Chrysostom θέατρον can mean a spectacle or sight. Chrysostom also applies it to the heavenly host as spectators of Christians' activities in the world.[18] These seem to be the uses in patristic Greek closest to Calvin's own. But closest of all to his usage seems to be Basil of Caesarea (*Hexaemeron* 6.1).[19]

There is still another reference to the *theatrum mundi* (in *Comm. Gen.* 1:6) that seems to offer another reason for Calvin's choice of the phrase—the avoidance of idolatry. Calvin's attitude toward religious art,[20] reflected in his strictures against Gregory the Great's excuse for icons as *libri idiotarum* ("books of the uneducated"),[21] is elsewhere positively countered with God's painting[22] in the created world and the "painting" by the prophets of eternal blessedness under the lineaments of temporal benefits.[23] The critique and the affirmation are brought together in *Comm. Gen.* 1:6:

Hic Spiritus Dei	Here the Spirit of God
omnes simul sine exeptione	wills to teach all at once
docere voluit:	without exception:
atque adeo quod falso et	and therefore what Gregory
perperam	falsely and wrongly declares
de statuis et picturis	concerning statues and pictures
Gregorius pronunciat,	truly applies to the history
vere in hanc creationis historiam	of the creation:
competit,	
librum esse idiotarum.	it is the true "book of the unlearned"
Ergo quaecunque commemorat,	Whatsoever therefore he relates
ad ornamentum illius theatri	has to do with the adornment
spectant	of that theater
quod nobis ante oculos posuit.	which He sets before our eyes.

Calvin's preference, then, for *theatrum* as a figure for the created realm seems to rest on his desire for a single metaphor that expresses the ordered beauty of God's self-revelation to man, but which at the same time rejects any theater in which man's own acts are glorified or in which false representations

---

18. G. W. H. Lampe, *A Patristic Greek Lexicon* (Oxford: Clarendon, 1961), 617.
19. See appendix F.
20. *Inst.* 1.11; 2.8.17.
21. *Inst.* 1.11.7.
22. *Inst.* 1.5.10: *in tabulis depictas esse Dei virtutes.*
23. *Inst.* 2.10.10.

of Deity are depicted. By setting the *theatrum ecclesiae* alongside the *theatrum mundi*, bracketing men and angels in both, Calvin is approaching metaphorically the question of how rational beings can be instruments of God's will, yet operate for their own part as well.[24]

Virtutes Dei Secundum Joannem Calvinum

Texts:

I 1536 (Institutio): Haec vero de Deo nobis in praesentia descenda sunt. Primum, ut certa fide constitutum habeamus, ipsum infinitam esse, sapientiam, iustitiam, bonitatem, misericordiam, veritatem, virtutem ac vitam: ut nulla sit prorsus alia sapientia, iustitia, bonitas, misericordia, veritas, virtus et vita (Bar. 3; James 1). Et quidquid earum rerum ubivis spectatur, ab ipso sit (Prov. 16). Deinde, universa quae in coelo sunt et in terra, in eius gloriam creata esse (Ps. 148; Dan. 3). Idque iure illi serviant, eius imperium intueantur, maiestatem eius suspiciant, et parendo velut dominum ac regem agnoscant (Rom. 1). Tertio loco, iustum esse ipsum iudicem, itaque in eos severe vindicaturum, qui ab eius praescriptis deflexerint, qui non per omnia eius voluntati obsequuti fuerint: qui alia cogitaverint, dixerint, ac fecerint, quam quae ad eius gloriam pertinent (Ps. 7; Rom. 2). Quarto, misericordem esse ac mansuetum, et qui miseros ac pauperculos benigne sit accepturus, qui ad eius clementiam confugiant, et in eius fidem se conferant; qui parcere ac condonare paratus sit, si qui veniam ab eo postulent, qui velit succurrere ac opem ferre, si qui eius auxilium implorent, qui servare velit, si qui fiduciam omnem in eo reponant ac defigant.[a]

II 1539 (Commentarius in Epist. ad Romanos): Concipi Deus non potest sine sua aeternitate, potentia, sapientia, bonitate, veritate, iustitia, misericordia. Aeternitas ex eo liquet, quod auctor est omnium. Potentia, quod tenet omnia in sua manu, facitque ut in se consistant. Sapientia, ex ordinatissima dispositione. Bonitas, quia nihil causae erat cur consideret omnia, neque alia ratione moveri potest ut conservet quam ob illam ipsam. Iustitia, in administratione: quia sontes punit, innocentes vendicat. Misericordia, quod tanta patientia tolerat hominum perversitatem. Veritas, ex eo quod immutabilis est. Ergo qui conceptam Dei notitiam habet, iam illi laudem debet aeternitatis, spaientiae, bonitatis, iustitiae.[b]

III 1536 (Institutio): Dei nomine hic eius potestas indicatur, quae omnibus eius virtutibus constat: ut, eius potentia, sapientia, iustitia, misericordia, veritate, in hoc enim magnus et mirabilis est Deus, quia iustus, quia sapiens, quia misericors, quia potens, quia verax, etc. Hanc ergo maiestatem in huiusmodi virtutibus sanctificari petimus. non in Deo ipso: cui apud se nihil accedere aut decedere potest: verum ut ab omnibus sancta habeatur: hoc est, vere agnoscatur et magnificetur. Et quicquid agit Deus, omnia eius opera gloriosa, ut sunt, appareant. Ut sive ipse puniat, iustus: sive ignoscat, misericors: sive praestet quod promisit, verax praedicetur.[c]

IV 1555 (1557) (Commentarius in Psalmum CXLV, Argumentum): Propheta secum reputans admirabilem Dei sapientiam, bonitatem, iustitiam, primum in tota mundi gubernatione, praesertim vero in tuendo, fovendo, et regendo genere humano, effertur ad celebrandas eius laudes. Postquam autem in genere elogia providentiae eius recensuit, tandem descendit ad peculiarem gratiam qua dignatur suos fideles.[d]

V 1539 (Institutio): Virtutes porro easdem hic enumerari audimus quas notavimus in caelo et terra relucere: clementiam, bonitatem, misericordiam, iustitiam, iudicium, veritatem. Nam virtus et potentia sub titulo Elohim continetur. Iisdem

---

24. See appendix E (translation of *Contre la secte . . . , ch. 14*).

etiam epithetis illum insigniunt Prophetae quum ad plenum volunt sanctum eius nomen illustrare. Ne multa congerere cogamur, in praesentia nobis Psalmus unus sufficiat: in quo tam exacte summa omnium eius virtutum recensetur, ut nihil omissum videri queat (Ps. 145). Et nihil tamen illic ponitur quod non liceat in creaturis contemplari. Adeo talem sentimus, experientia magistra, Deum, qualem se verbo declarat. Apud Ieremiam, ubi pronunciat qualis agnosci a nobis velit, descriptionem proponit non ita plenam, sed eodem plane recidentem. Qui gloriatur, inquit, in hoc glorietur, quod me noverit Dominum qui facio misericordiam, iudicium, et iustitiam in terra (Jer. 9:23 or 24). Tria certe haec apprime nobis cognitu sunt necessaria: Misericordia, qua sola consistit nostra omnium salus: Iudicium, quod in flagitiosos quotidie exercetur, et gravius etiam eos manet in aeternum exitium: Iustitia, qua conservantur fideles, et benignissime foventur. Quibus comprehensis, te abunde habere vaticinium testatur quo possis in Deo gloriari. Neque tamen ita omittuntur aut veritas eius, aut potentia, aut sanctitas, aut bonitas. Quomodo enim constaret, quae hic requiritur iustitiae, misericordiae, iudicii eius scientia, nisi veritate eius inflexibili niteretur? Et quomodo crederetur terram iudicio et iustitia moderari, nisi intellecta eius virtute? Unde autem, nisi ex bonitate, misericordia? Si denique viae omnes ius sunt misericordia, iudicium, iustitia, in illis quoque et sanctitas conspicua est.[e]

VI   1539 (Institutio): (In primo genere operum Dei quae intra ordinarium naturae cursum sunt) . . . Iam potentia nos ad cogitandam eius aeternitatem deducit, quia aeternum esse, et a se ipso principium habere, necesse est: unde omnia trahunt originem. Porro, si causa quaeritur, qua et ad creanda haec semel omnia inductus sit, et nunc ad conservanda moveatur: solam illi suam bonitatem comperiemus pro causa esse. Quin etiam haec si una sit plus satis tamen sufficere debet, ad nos in amorem eius alliciendos: quando nulla est creatura, ut propheta monet, in quam non effusa sit eius misericordia (Ps. 145:9).[f]

VII   1539 (Institutio): In secundo genere operum eius, quae scilicet praeter ordinarium naturae cursum eveniunt, nihilo obscuriora se proferunt virtutum eius argumenta. Nam in administranda hominum societate, ita providentiam suam temperat: ut cum sit erga innumeris modis benignus ac beneficus: apertus tamen, ac quotidianis iudiciis, suam piis iustitiam, improbis ac sceleratis iudicium declaret. Non enim dubiae sunt, quas de flagitiis sumit, ultiones, quemadmodum non obscure tutorem, ac etiam vindicem se innocentiae esse demonstrat: dum bonorum vitam sua benedictione prosperat, necessitati opitulatur, dolores lenit ac solatur, adversitates sublevat, saluti per omnia consulit. Neque vero perpetuam iustitiae eius regulam obscurare debet, quod improbos et sontes, ad tempus, impunitos exultare saepiuscule sinit: Probos autem et immerentes multis adversitatibus iactari, impiorum etiam malitia et iniquitate premi, sustinet. Quin potius longe diversa cogitatio subire mentem debet. Quando in flagitium unum, manifesto irae indicio, animadvertit, omnia execrari: quando multa inulta praetermittit, aliud fore iudicium, quo punienda differantur. Similter misericoridiae suae considerandae quantam materiam nobis suppeditat? dum saepius miseros peccatores indefessa tamen benignitate prosequitur: donec eorum pravitatem, benefaciendo, fregerit: plusquam paterna indulgentia, ad se revocando.[g]

VIII   1543 (Institutio): Nec dubium quin velit nos Dominus in hac sancta meditatione continenter occupari: ut dum illas immensas sapientiae, iustitiae, bonitatis potentiae suae divitias in omnibus creaturis, velut in speculis contemplamur, non tantum eas fugiente oculo percurramus, et evandio (ut sic loquar) intuitu: sed in ea cogitatione diu immoremur: eam serio ac fideliter animis revolvamus, memoriaque identidem repetamus.[h]

a. Ps. 103; Isa. 55; Pss. 25 & 85; p. 42, line 10–p. 43, line 17; *OS*, 1:37.8–29. ET, Battles, 20.

b. *OO*, 1667, tome 7, p. 7.

c. P. 181, line 14–p. 182, line 2; *OS*, 1:108.20–30. ET, Battles, 106f. (First Petition).

d. *OO*, 1667, tome 3, p. 525.

e. P. 16, lines 1–23. *OS*, 3:86.19–87.14. ET, Battles, Library of Christian Classics, 20.98.

f. P. 7, lines 1–8 (cf. *OS*, 3:51.21–29). ET, Battles, Library of Christian Classics, 20.59.

g. P. 7, lines 9–27; cf. *OS*, 3:51.30–52.13. ET, Battles, Library of Christian Classics, 20.59.

h. *OS*, 3.171.25–32. ET, Battles, Library of Christian Classics, 20.180.

Summary

I.	Cf. Institutio (1559)	1.2.1
III.	Cf. Institutio (1559)	3.20.41
V.	Cf. Institutio (1559)	1.10.2
VI.	Cf. Institutio (1559)	1.5.6
VII.	Cf. Institutio (1559)	1.5.7
VIII.	Cf. Institutio (1559)	1.14.21

See also *Institutio* 1.15.1; 3.2.6; 3.20.13, 40; 1.5.2, 8, 10, 14f.; 1.10.3; 1.14.12; 3.13.4, &c. 2.18.16 (= Text G, *fiducia*)

Table 42. The *virtutes Dei* as to be perceived by humanity in the *theatrum duplex*

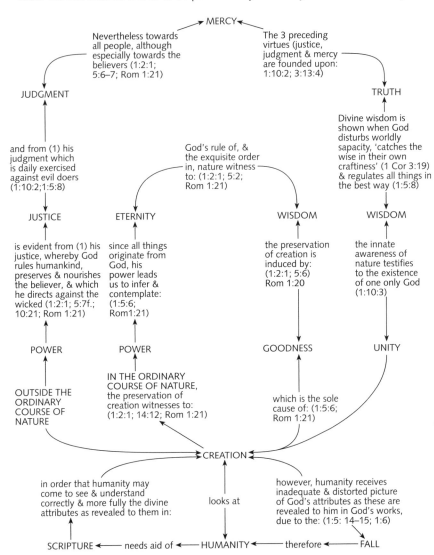

MERCY

Nevertheless towards all people, although especially towards the believers (1:2:1; 5:6–7; Rom 1:21)

The 3 preceding virtues (justice, judgment & mercy are founded upon: 1:10:2; 3:13:4)

JUDGMENT

TRUTH

and from (1) his judgment which is daily exercised against evil doers (1:10:2;1:5:8)

God's rule of, & the exquisite order in, nature witness to: (1:2:1; 5:2; Rom 1:21)

Divine wisdom is shown when God disturbs worldly sapacity, 'catches the wise in their own craftiness' (1 Cor 3:19) & regulates all things in the best way (1:5:8)

JUSTICE   ETERNITY   WISDOM   WISDOM

is evident from (1) his justice, whereby God rules humankind, preserves & nourishes the believer, & which he directs against the wicked (1:2:1; 5:7f.; 10:21; Rom 1:21)

since all things originate from God, his power leads us to infer & contemplate: (1:5:6; Rom1:21)

the preservation of creation is induced by: (1:2:1; 5:6) Rom 1:20

the innate awareness of nature testifies to the existence of one only God (1:10:3)

POWER   POWER   GOODNESS   UNITY

OUTSIDE THE ORDINARY COURSE OF NATURE

IN THE ORDINARY COURSE OF NATURE, the preservation of creation witnesses to: (1:2:1; 14:12; Rom 1:21)

which is the sole cause of: (1:5:6; Rom 1:21)

CREATION

in order that humanity may come to see & understand correctly & more fully the divine attributes as revealed to them in:

looks at

however, humanity receives inadequate & distorted picture of God's attributes as these are revealed to him in God's works, due to the: (1:5: 14–15; 1:6)

SCRIPTURE ◄──── needs aid of ◄── HUMANITY ◄──── therefore ◄──── FALL

Based on Texts I–VII, above and others.

Table 43. The *virtutes Dei* in and after the creation (*Catechismus 1538*, par. 3)

Text:

Contemplamur enim in hac rerum universitate, Dei nostri immortali tatem, e qua omnium principium origoque fluxerit, potentiam, quae tantam molem & condiderit, & nunc sustentet, sapientiam, quae tantam ac tam confusam varietatem ordine tam distincto composuerit, et perpetuo moderetur, bonitatem que ipsa sibi causa fuerit ut haec crearentur, et nunc consistant, justitiam, quae in defensione piorum, impiorum vero ultione mirifice se profert, misericordiam, quae ad resipiscentiam quo nos vocet, nostras iniquitates tanta mansuetudine tolerat.	For in this universe of things, we contemplate the immortality of our God, from which flows the beginning and origin of everything; we contemplate his power which both framed this great mass and now sustains it; we contemplate his wisdom which composed in definite order this very great and confused variety and everlastingly governs it; we contemplate his goodness, itself the cause that these things were created and now continue to exist; we contemplate his righteousness, marvellously proffering itself to defend the godly, but to take vengeance on the ungodly; we contemplate his mercy, which, to call us back to repentance, tolerates our iniquities with great gentleness.

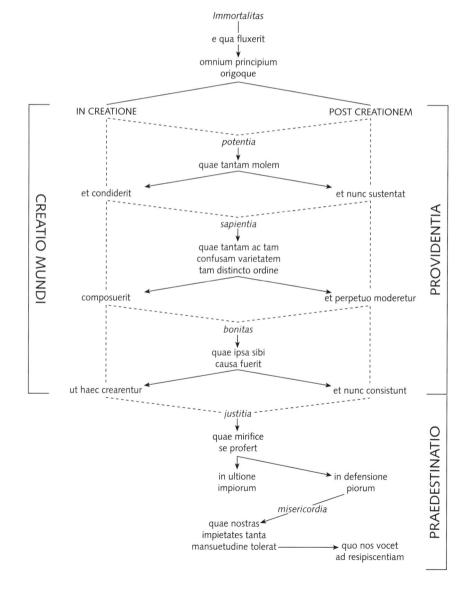

Table 44. The placing of providence and predestination in the
successive editions of the *Institutio*

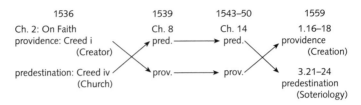

Appendix **D**   *Descensus in se*

Two movements, as we have seen,[1] mark for John Calvin the initial steps of the soul's return to God: our upward vision of God as he accommodates himself to our feeble capacity,[2] and our downward contemplation of ourselves within. It is in the *theatrum mundi* that God deigns to allow us to experience his powers: the metaphor of the *theater* serves for Calvin as the ruling image that gives coherence to the intimations of Deity provided by the Word and the world.[3] The contrasting human traits that we discern from our descent into the inner world of self, a microcosm of the universe in which we live out our brief lives,[4] are parallelly knit together by the metaphor of descent: the *descensus in se*.

The deepest religious experiences of mankind are often expressed in the figurative language of ascent and descent.[5] Clearly, Calvin's own conversion embraced both movements, and these are faithfully recapitulated in his theological elaboration of the faith. Now, the character of an individual's Christian piety is often most clearly displayed in his eucharistic teaching. For Luther, the *descensus Christi* to the worshiping flock, in terms of the glorified body of our Lord, infinitely extended in space, marked the essence of real sacramental communion. For Calvin, communion took literary expression rather in the mystical elevation of the worshiper, by the Holy Spirit's power,[6] to the heavenly presence of Christ. This *ascensus animae* could not occur without the *descensus animae*, the deep searching of conscience, which had to precede the Eucharist. There is a sense, then, in which that first descent[7] into the inner wasteland of alienation, the initial step in conversion, is repeatedly recapitulated in the eucharistic life of the Christian. It is no accident that Calvin chose the spiritual interpretation

1. See assumption 3, discussion of ch. 1 of the *Institutes,* above.
2. On accommodation, see Battles, "God Was Accommodating Himself to Human Capacity," ch. 4 herein.
3. See appendix C, above.
4. *Inst.* 1.1.2 (LCC 20.37, note 5); 1.5.3.
5. The commonplace metaphor of the *scala* or ladder, or the *gradus humilitatis,* comes to mind.
6. *Inst.* 4.17.18, etc. Robert Benedetto pointed out to me (1976) the parallel of this with Augustine (*Conf.* 1.3): "You do not come down to us but rather elevate us to Yourself." Also, 7.18: "lifts up to Himself those who were cast down."
7. See assumption 3, discussion, above.

of the *descensus ad inferos,* over against the contrasting literalism of a bodily descent into hell (of the Roman Catholics and Anabaptists) and of a mere burial in the earth for three days (of Zwingli).[8] The alienation from his Father that the sinless Christ in his passion and crucifixion suffered for our sakes is mirrored in the alienation we must come to know in all its agony before our return as adopted children in Christ can begin. In fact, the *descensus ad inferos* is, so to speak, the final stage in the incarnation itself, which Calvin describes in these words:[9]

> No child of Adam,
> no angel,
> but rather the very majesty of God
> had to descend to us,
> since it was not in our power
> to ascend to Him.

Calvin's metaphor of *descent* has both classical and Christian roots. In his *Adagia*[10] (well known to the young Calvin) Erasmus traces the sources of this phrase:

> *To descend into oneself* is for one to inspect his own vices. It is derived either from pits or storage places into which men descend so they can know what is stored or hidden there. Alluded to are the caverns and recesses of the human heart, to which Momus wished the door to be closed.

Erasmus quotes the same passage from Persius (*Satires,* 4.23f.) later used by Calvin (*Commentary on Seneca's De Clementia* 6.1):[11]

> *Prosopopoeia,* by which it is pretended that the emperor is talking to himself, and so to speak entering into meditation. Here is the reward of conscience which Seneca was promising him, if *he descended into himself* and saw to the composure of his mind.

The idea of descent into the heart for self-scrutiny is found elsewhere in the Christian tradition. For example, Augustine uses similar language:[12]

> But when a profound reflection had, from the secret depths of my soul, drawn together and heaped up all the misery before the sight of my heart, there arose a mighty storm, accompanied by a mighty shower of tears.

Martin Bucer applies the phrase to the self-examination enjoined in prayer:[13]

8. Calvin's first assertion of the spiritual interpretation of the descent into hell was in the *Psychopannychia.* See Zimmerli, ed., *Psychopannychia,* 98, 36. See notes on this in *Inst. 1536a,* 347f.; *Inst. 1536b,* 261. See also *Inst.* (1559), 2.16.8–13 (LCC 20.512, and notes).

9. *Inst.* 2.12.1, as cited in *Analysis 1980,* 92.

10. *Adagia* 1.7.86.

11. *Comm. Sen. De Clem.* 28f.

12. *Confessions* 8.12.28.

13. Bucer, *Enarrationes perpetuae in Evangelia* (1530), 1, fol. 63[V].6ff. For ET, see *Inst. 1536a,* appendix 2, 446; *Inst. 1536b,* 348.

Paul everywhere greatly urges his followers to be persistent in prayer, obviously desiring that *they descend into themselves*, recognize their own and others' diseases, rightly ponder God's unspeakable goodness, and thus more and more turn with desire for new life, a life established in conformity to God, that is continually and increasingly putting off humanity and putting on God.

Calvin who, in his exposition of prayer, largely followed Bucer, describes the beginning of true prayer as a *descensus in se:*[14]

> Since prayer is a sort of agreement between us and God whereby we pour out before Him all the desires, joys, sighs, in sum, thoughts of our hearts, we must diligently see to it, as often as we call upon the Lord, that we *descend into the innermost recesses of our hearts* and from that place, not from the throat and tongue, call God.

The *descensus*, then, bespeaks the examination we subject our conscience to (a) in conversion; (b) under the instruction of the law, as the standard;[15] (c) before communion;[16] (d) in commencing to pray.[17] It is also the basis of our true knowledge both of ourselves[18] and of the *virtutes Dei*.[19] Proud and arrogant human beings are reluctant to descend into themselves,[20] or, if they do, it is to search foolishly for their salvation within themselves.[21]

Here our chief concern is with the *descensus* as the revealer both of our false estimation of ourselves and of the true judgment of ourselves in God's eyes. Before the Fall, the image of God in Adam was marked by the God-like qualities of *sapientia, iustitia, sanctitas, virtus, vita;* after the Fall these were exchanged for the "fruits of sin" (Gal. 5:19–21): *ignorantia, iniquitas, impotentia, mors, iudicium*.[22] Or *iustitia, virtus, vita, salus*, gave way to *infelicitas, mors, inferi*.[23] Note the almost symmetrical pairing of opposites. When we view ourselves in our fallenness by our own standards, we possess *iustitia, sapientia, virtus:* but when we measure these qualities over against God's perfect holiness, we attribute them to him, and find in ourselves *iniquitas, stultitia, impotentia*.[24]

Calvin, like Paul, repeatedly lists the human traits that true self-examination reveals: all his lists underline the relative character of our traits—seen in our own feeble light they seem great, but in God's light they can be recognized for the emptiness that they are. The contrasts between the self-perceived and the God-perceived in *Institutio* 1.1.1f. are reminiscent of the downward movement of the soul, raised up in its own eyes in pride; and the contrasting spiritual upward movement, when it abases itself in true humility—as described in Ber-

14. *Catechism 1538*, para. 23, 34.
15. *Inst.* 2.8.3.
16. *Inst.* 4.17.40.
17. *Catechism 1538*, para. 23, 34.
18. *Inst.* 1.1.2.
19. *Inst.* 1.5.10.
20. *Inst.* 1.5.3; 2.8.1.
21. *Inst.* 3.22.6.
22. *Inst. 1536a*, 21; *Inst. 1536b*, 16.
23. *Inst. 1536a*, 22; *Inst. 1536b*, 16f.
24. Cf. Battles, "God Was Accommodating Himself to Human Capacity," 31f.; ch. 4 herein.

nard of Clairvaux, *Steps of Humility,* for example. Significantly, the opening paragraphs of Books I and II of the *Institutio* carry similar lists of our marks of fallenness:

1.1.1	1.1.2	2.1.1	2.1.2
ignorantia	iniustitia	imbecillitas	pauperies
vanitas	foeditas	miseria	ignominia
inopia	stultitia	vanitas	turpitudo
infirmitas	impuritas	foeditas	imbecillitas
pravitas			
corruptio			

Here, then, we see the other member of the *duplex theatrum:* humankind created in the image of God, a microcosm of the *mundus,* but showing, fallen, a defaced image of God.

Appendix **E**

Calvin,
Against the Libertines (1545)[1]

How appropriate it is for us to consider God's providence, by which he does all things; and how the Libertines confuse everything in speaking of it. The first consequence of the preceding article.

For our part, we do not deny that all things are done by God's will. And even when we explain how he is said to be *almighty*, we attribute to him a power active in all creatures: teaching that just as once he created the universe, so also he governs it, always having his hand on his work of maintaining all things in their condition, and of disposing them as it seems good to him. To express still more readily what this means, I say that we have to consider that God's care in governing the universe is of three kinds.

First, there is a universal operation by which he conducts all creatures, according to the condition and property he has given each of them in forming them. This conduct is simply what we call the order of nature. For while the unbelievers recognize in the disposition of the universe only what they see, and accordingly postulate Nature as a goddess ruling over all, we must needs credit this to God's will, which alone rules and governs all things. Accordingly, when we see the sun, the moon, the stars in their courses, let us ponder that they obey God, carrying out his commandment; and not only that, but [187] that God's hand conducts them, and it is by his power that all this takes place. Thus, when we see the ordinary course of earthly things, let us be advised to attribute the whole to God, and to understand creatures as instruments in his hand, to apply them to work as he pleases. This universal providence is often touched upon for us in Scripture, to the end that we may learn to glorify God in all his works. And especially does the Lord bid us recognize this power of his in us, to the end that we may be deprived of all presumption, which immediately arises in us when he no longer reminds us that we are in his hand. To this point St. Paul said at Athens: "It is in him that we are, that we live and have our movement" [Acts 17:28]. For by that he admonishes us that we cannot last for a moment of time, unless he sustains us by his hand, being the same thing [as to say] that it is in him that we subsist; and just as the soul, expanding its vigor throughout the body, quickens the members, so God quickens us and gives us whatever we have of capacity and ability. Yet this universal operation of God does not pre-

1. "Contre la secte phantastique des libertins," ch. 14; *OC,* 7:186–92. Trans. by F. L. Battles, July 1978.

vent each creature, whether in heaven or on earth, from having and retaining his own quality and nature and from following his own inclination.

The second kind or manner by which God works in his creatures is that he makes them serve his goodness, justice, and judgment, according as he wills sometimes to help his servants, sometimes to punish the wicked, sometimes to test the patience of his believers or to chastise them as a father. Thus when it pleases him to bless us with abundance of goods, he provides rain in its season, he gives warmth and fine weather by his sun, and uses all the other natural means as instruments of his blessing. When he withdraws his hand, the heaven is like brass and the earth like iron [cf. Deut. 28:23]. So it is with him when he thunders, freezes, causes hail, storm, and barrenness. Accordingly, what the pagans and the ignorant attribute to fortune, we must assign to God's providence—not only to this universal power, of which we have spoken, but to a special ordinance, by which he conducts things according as it seems expedient to him. That is what he means when he says by his prophets, [Isa. 45:7; Amos 3:6; Prov. 16:1, 2, 3, 4, 9, 33] that he creates darkness and light, that he sends death and life, that no good or evil comes save by his hand. In other words, he governs the chances and other things that seem indeed to be fortuitous, and if someone is killed by chance and not deliberately [unwittingly] that it is he who is the cause of his death, and that it is he who has so willed, to the end that we may realize that nothing happens by chance, but according as he has determined according to his plan. And one is bitterly irritated when one thinks that things come about otherwise or that one does not look to him to recognize him not only as the chief cause of all; but also as the author, who by his plan disposes it thus and so. Let us therefore resolve that prosperity as well as adversity, rain, wind, hail, frost, fine weather, abundance, famine, war, peace, are works of God's hand; and that the creatures who are the inferior causes thereof are but means whereby he accomplishes his will; and accordingly that he disposes and turns them when it pleases him, to lead them to this end, that what he has ordained may come to pass. Moreover, it is to be noted, that not only does he make use in this way of insensate creatures, to work and execute his will thereby, but also of men and even of devils. In this way Satan and the wicked are executors of his will. As he made use of the Egyptians to afflict his people, sometime later he raised up the Assyrians to chastise his people when they forsook him, and other like passages. As for the devil, we see that he was used to torment Saul [1 Sam. 16:14; 18:10], to deceive Ahab [1 Kings 22:22], and to exercise God's judgments on the wicked when he carried out his business on them [Ps. 78:49], or else on the contrary to test the constancy of his own, of which we have an example in Job. But the Libertines, hearing these passages, are staggered by them, and without looking further, conclude that the creatures therefore do nothing at all. But in this way they commit a terrible error. For not only do they confuse heaven and earth together, but God and the devil. That comes about by their failure to observe two exceptions that are essential. The first is that Satan and the wicked are not instruments of God in such a way that they do not operate also for their own part. For one must not imagine that God carries on his work by a wicked man, as by a stone or a trunk of wood; but he makes use of these as rational creatures, according to the quality of the nature he has given them. When therefore we say that God works through the wicked, that does not gainsay the fact that the wicked also work in their own place. This

[189] the Scriptures say very clearly and openly show us. For just as the Scriptures declare that God will hiss [Isa. 5:26] and as it were sound the drum to arouse the unbelievers to arms, and that he will harden or inflame their hearts, likewise Scripture does not fail to recount their own plan and the will that they had, and attribute to them the work that may have been by God's ordinance. The second exception to which these unhappy ones pay no attention is that there is a great difference between God's work and that of a wicked man, when he makes use of it as an instrument. For the wicked one is aroused either by his greed, or ambition, or envy, or cruelty to do what he does, and has regard for no other end. According to the root that is the affection of the heart, and the end whither it tends, the work is qualified and is rightly adjudged evil. But God regards it in quite the opposite way. It is to exercise his justice for the salvation and conservation of the good, to make use of his goodness and grace toward believers, to chastise those who deserve it. This, then, is how one must distinguish between God and man, to contemplate in the same work his justice, his goodness, his judgment; and on the other hand the ill will both of the devil and of unbelievers. Take a fine, clear mirror to see all I have said. When Job receives news of the loss of his possessions, of the death of his children, of so many calamities that have befallen him, he recognizes that it is God who is visiting him, saying: "The Lord has given me all these things; he has taken them away from me." And in truth he also had done it. But didn't Job know the devil had brewed this pottage for him? Wasn't he informed that the Chaldeans had stolen and pillaged his flocks? Did he praise the thieves and brigands or make excuses for the devil, because the affliction had come to him from God? No. For he knew that there was a great difference. Thus, in condemning the evil, he said: "May the name of the Lord be blessed." Likewise, David, being pursued by Shemei, said that he had received that from God [2 Sam. 16:11f.] and saw that this wicked man was a rod by which God chastised him. But in praising God, he did not fail to condemn thereafter Shemei [1 Kings 2:9]. And of this we must treat again in another place. For the moment, let it suffice to hold this: that God so takes care of his creatures, and makes them serve his providence, that the instrument of which he makes use may oftentimes itself be wicked, and the fact that he turns the ill will of Satan and wicked men to good is not to be regarded as excusing them or sanctifying them for their wrongdoing, or that their works are not evil and damnable; moreover, that every work is qualified by the intent of him who does it. Accordingly, those who do not distinguish this are like pigs who turn everything upside down with their snouts, and cause confusion when there was once the finest order in the world. Such are the Libertines, who not only make the devil God's companion, but change him into God, making his works praiseworthy, on the ground that he is only doing what God has ordained. And this heresy, if we believe the ancient teachers, took its origin from Simon Magus. On the contrary, we must note that creatures here below do their works according to their degree: these are to be estimated good or evil, according as they have been done to obey God or to offend him. However, it is God who directs things to a good end, and turns evil into good, or at least draws some good from what is evil, taking care according to his nature, that is, in justice and equity, and making use of the devil in such a way that he does not mix himself up with him so as to have anything in common with him, or to envelop himself in some society of evil, or wiping out the nature of evil by his justice.

For just as the sun, shining its rays on a corpse, or causing some putrefaction in it, does not derive therefrom any corruption or defect, and does not by its purity cause the corpse not to stink or be infectious, so God does his works by the wicked so that the holiness that is in him does not justify them, and the infection that is in them does not contaminate him at all.

The third kind of working of God lies and consists in the fact that he governs his believers, living and reigning in them by his Holy Spirit. For inasmuch as we are corrupted by original sin, we are like a dry and barren land, which cannot produce any good fruit. For our judgment is perverted, our will rebellious against God, inclined and given over to evil; all our nature, in sin, is vicious. Being such, not only do we have no power to apply ourselves to good, but, what is more, we are incapable of conceiving a single good thought, as St. Paul says [2 Cor. 3:5]: but our whole sufficiency must needs come from [191] him. Accordingly, it is he who works in us to will and to complete [Phil. 2:13]; it is he who illumines us; it is he who forms new hearts in us, softening our hardness; it is he who moves us to pray; it is he who gives us the grace and strength to resist all Satan's temptations; it is he who makes us walk in his commandments [Ezek. 36:27]. But accordingly we must note that of nature we have in us election and will. Insofar as by sin one or the other [of us] is depraved, our Lord reforms and changes him from evil to good. Therefore the fact that we are ourselves capable of discerning, of willing, of doing this or that, is of a natural gift. The fact that we can elect, derive, or do any evil—that is of the corruption of sin. The fact that we desire to do good, and have the power to carry it out—this is of the supernatural grace of the Spirit, which regenerates us to a divine life. This, then, is how God acts in his children. It is that in wiping out their perversity, he conducts them by his Spirit into obedience to him. But these giddy ones in prattling that God does all, make him the author of all evil; and thereupon, as if the evil changes nature, being covered under the mantle of God's name, say that he is good. In this they blaspheme God very evilly, so as to transfer his power or his justice elsewhere. For inasmuch as God has nothing more proper to him than his goodness, he would have to renounce himself and turn himself into the devil, to do the evil that they attribute to him. And, in fact, the God they have is an idol, which we must hold in execration much greater than any idol of the pagans. But they think they have well washed their hands in replying: we say that all is good, since God has made it. As if they had it in them to change black into white! Well acquitted indeed are they, when after having called God a brigand, an adulterer, and a robber, they add that there is no evil in all that. Granted, but who has condemned murder, adultery, and theft, but God himself? It will therefore be necessary on this count for us to make him a liar in his word in order to excuse him in his works. But Scripture, say they, universally declares that God works all in all [1 Cor. 12:6]. I reply that they evilly and falsely apply Scripture to this point. For when St. Paul makes use of this sentence, he is speaking solely of the gifts of the Holy Spirit. So be it: the passage shows it; that he is exhorting the Corinthians to make good use thereof, since they are God's gifts: moreover, as he says, that no one can say a single word in praise of Jesus Christ, without speaking by the Holy Spirit from whom all good proceeds [1 Cor. 12:3]. But as for good, we willingly leave it to God. But when do they show that God pilfers like a thief? That he murders the innocent like a brigand? Accordingly, the shift they take is not to purge blasphemy but rather to redouble it.

Appendix **F** Notes on the *Duplex Cognitio*: A Patristic Source?[1]

Among the patristic sources usually cited for the origin of Calvin's well-known concept of the twofold knowledge of God and of humanity is Clement of Alexandria's *Paidagogos* 3.1, a reasonably close parallel. Yet Clement is never cited by name in the *Institutio* by Calvin.

If, however, one should combine the search for a patristic source of the *duplex cognitio* with that of the *theatrum mundi,* a source comes ready to hand. In *Institutio* 1.14.20, Calvin states:

> Meanwhile let us not be ashamed to take pious delight in the works of God open and manifest in this most beautiful theater. For as I have elsewhere said, although it is not the chief evidence of faith, yet it is the first evidence in the order of nature, to be mindful that wherever we cast our eyes, all things they meet are works of God, and at the same time to ponder with pious meditation to what end God created them. Therefore, that we may apprehend with true faith what it profits us to know of God, it is important for us to grasp first the history of the creation of the universe, as it has been set forth briefly by Moses (Genesis, chs. 1 and 2) and then has been more fully illustrated by saintly men, especially by Basil and Ambrose.

In his *Comm. in Gen.* 1:6, Calvin alludes to that same *theatrum mundi:*

> Whatsoever therefore he relates has to do with the adornment of that theater which he sets before our eyes.

The same verse of Genesis draws a similar comment from Basil of Caesarea (*Hexaemeron,* Hom. 6).[2] The quiet contemplation of the stars of the night sky, of the daily miracles of the visible world, will lead us to contemplate the invisible:

> You approach as a ready listener,
> one worthy to take your place
> in this venerable and blessed theater.

Despite our fallen state, we will recognize that though by nature earthly, we are the work of the divine hands.

1. *Inst.* 1.1.1; 2.1.1.
2. PG, 29:117–20.

If we learn these things
we will indeed know ourselves,
we will know God:
we will adore Him as Creator,
serve Him as Lord,
glorify Him as Father,
revere Him as Benefactor;
we will not cease to venerate Him
as Author both of our present life
and of the life to come. . . .

Like Calvin, Basil eschews all allegorical interpretation of Genesis 1, draw-ing forth from the literal sense (with reference to the scientific knowledge of his time) a religious commentary on the wisdom of God as it is seen in the the-ater of the created world.

Basil's words should be compared with the opening sentences of the *Institu-tio* of 1539 (ch. 1), together with the initial sentence of chapter 2 of that edition. The comparison should be made not with the ancient Latin translation of Eustathius[3] or that of Garnier-Maran,[4] but rather with the Latin version pub-lished by Erasmus at Basel in 1532, clearly the edition used by Calvin.

When did Calvin first come to know Basil of Caesarea? His *Hexaemeron* is explicitly referred to in Calvin's *Psychopannychia*.[5] At most, we might infer from this reference that Calvin had already read Basil in 1535; at least, that he picked up the reference secondhand; and that it may have been inserted in the *Psycho-pannychia* as late as 1542, the date of publication. The evidence of the *Institutio* of 1543 indicates Calvin was familiar with the *Hexaemeron* by that year. He used it in preparing the Genesis commentary in 1550 (revised 1554). By 1559, he had probably taken a fresh look at the *Hexaemeron*, when he revised the 1543 pas-sage at 1.14.20, inserting the word *theatrum*. My own guess would be that Basil was included among the authors he read in preparing for his exegetical work at Strasbourg around 1539. Yet the strong reference to *duplex cognitio* in *Institutio* 1536[6] leads to the conclusion that Basil was at hand when, in 1535, Calvin was framing the first edition of the *Institutio*.

Although the Greek Fathers are not widely used by Calvin, his otherwise preponderant use of Augustine is balanced at a few points by Eastern Fathers: John Chrysostom frequently, Gregory of Nyssa, and Basil of Caesarea. There is a strong Basilian ring to this crucial passage in Calvin.

---

3. For a modern edition of Eustathius, see *Eustathius: Ancienne Version Latine des Neuf Homélies sur L'Hexaéméron de Basile de Césarée. Édition Critique avec Prolégomènes et Tables par E. Amand de Mendieta et S. Y. Rudberg* (Berlin: Akademie-Verlag, 1958), 70f.

4. Published in Paris, 1721–30; repr. in PG, 29.

5. See Zimmerli, ed., *Psychopannychia*, 28, line 12.

6. *Inst. 1536a*, 20; *Inst. 1536b*, 15: "Nearly the whole of sacred doctrine consists in these two parts: the knowledge of God and of ourselves."

Part 2

Calvin's Poetry, Piety, and Morality

6

The Theologian as Poet: Some Remarks about the "Found" Poetry of John Calvin[1]

A translator and editor who dwells for a long time in intimate contact with the style of a great writer will develop an ear attuned to the moods of his language as well as to the substance of his thought. Translation, at best, is but an approximate rendering of the thought and style of an original: the translator must, in his work, become as skilled in compromise as he is in accuracy; in that act of compromise some of the most distinctive stylistic traits must perforce be sacrificed. The careful choice of words and their strategic placement, the refinements of syntax, the articulation of longer periods of discourse, the enjambment of parts, the interlacing of figures of speech—all these must often bow before the demands of clarity, brevity, and simplicity in rendering the thought from one language into another. Yet the translator knows that these marks of sometimes unpremeditated art often hold the key to the writer's passionate attestation of truth.

This is particularly true in the great theological texts of the Christian tradition. The most remarkable Christian poetry, in my view, has not been composed by hymnographers or by theologians writing consciously in poetic forms, great as the best of their work is. The finest poetry in the theological tradition is what is called today by literary critics "found poetry"—the poetic passages that the reader stumbles on embedded in prose contexts. These are passages whose elevated strophic style arises out of the spontaneous flow of thought and feeling, not cast in such forms by deliberate rhetorical intent.

This generalization is here made primarily with reference to theological works of the Greek and Latin tradition. It would have to be modified if one were to embrace, for example, the Syriac patristic tradition

1. From *Faith to Faith: Essays in Honor of Donald G. Miller on His Seventieth Birthday*, ed. by Dikran Y. Hadidian (Pittsburgh: Pickwick, 1978), 299–337. Used by permission.

249

of Aaphrates and Ephraem, whose homiletic proclamation of the faith
was cast in poetic forms, more suggestive of Semitic rather than classical models. And even in the realm of explicit poetry one must also recognize that there is a difference between the hymnody of the Greek and
Latin churches: the former is loosely strophic, the latter constrainedly
metrical, as John Mason Neale discovered when he recast first Latin,
then Greek, hymns into English meters.

But, these qualifications aside, our general rule can be usefully applied. The "poetry" with which we here have to deal would not be so
considered by those who wrote it. Steeped in the poetic structures of
the Bible, and especially in the parallelism of the Psalms, the Greek and
Latin Church Fathers were also well versed in classical rhetoric and poetic. It was therefore inevitable that at times of deepest feeling, of most
intense passion, of greatest desire to win adherents to the faith, poetry
flowed from their pens.

Two questions now arise: First, where do our theologians launch into
poetic speech? Second, what characteristics set off a poetic passage
from its prose context? Only a partial answer can be given to the first
question, for naught but the most preliminary investigations have as
yet been made by me into this vast field:[2] however, three broad interrelated categories can be discerned—the doxological, the christological,
and the soteriological. The greatest theologians soberly confess that
there are limits beyond which human language as the instrument of rational analysis and explication cannot pass when it has to do with God
and man. Then do those high theological flights, at this barrier, end not
in frustration but in doxology. At that juncture mind and heart break
forth into a hymn, a paean of praise to God. There theologizing, prayer,
song, converge and become one. And the content of that hymn is scriptural. The philosophically derived *termini technici* of Christian theology
return to their source, the words and images of Scripture. With Paul,
we exclaim, "O depth of wealth. . . ." This doxological response, then,
recognizes the utter ineffability of God's ways.

Before we give a detailed answer to the first question, let us turn to
the second question: What characteristics set off a poetic passage from
its prose context? Since Bishop Robert Lowth first analyzed Hebrew

2. As chair of the subcommittee for new hymns of the United Church of Christ Hymnal
Committee (1967–74), I made my first systematic search for "found poetry" in theological
writings. The results of this search were incorporated into the following publications:
Ford Lewis Battles, ed., *New Hymns for a New Day? An Anthology of New Hymnody to
Illustrate the Search for New Hymns* (Pittsburgh: Pittsburgh Theological Seminary, 1971);
Hymnal of the United Church of Christ (Philadelphia: United Church Press, 1974); and
Ford Lewis Battles, with N. Mikita and M. Ioset, *Adjutorium ad cultum divinum: A Supplement to the Worshipbook of the United Presbyterian Church in the United States of Amer-
ica for Use in the Chapel of Pittsburgh Theological Seminary* (Pittsburgh: Pittsburgh Theological Seminary, 1977).

poetry, much work has been done on the poetic forms of the Bible. Modern Bibles usually "line out" poetic passages, whether from the Psalms, the Prophets, wisdom literature, or occasional songs scattered throughout the historical books. Criteria for determining poetry have been elaborated by the form-critics, leading at least tentatively to the recovery of early Christian hymn fragments preserved in the New Testament.[3] Some of these criteria also applicable to postbiblical writings might include the following:

Criteria of Structure

(1) natural and easy division of text into lines of similar or equal length (= cola)
(2) parallelism of members (= anaphora)
(3) division into stanzas or strophes, consisting of two, three, or more cola, and an opening or concluding key word, or a summary statement
(4) ring-composition (or inclusio) or other chiastic constructions

The "poems" to which we will shortly refer exhibit all or some of these features. We shall examine first only one of the "hymns" imbedded in Paul's letters, the passage already alluded to, "O depth of wealth. . . ." (Rom. 11:33–36).

Table 45. Poetic structure of Romans 11:33–36
(Latin from Calvin's *Comm. Rom.* [Schipper, vii. 83])

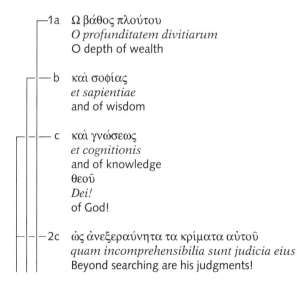

1a Ω βάθος πλούτου
    O profunditatem divitiarum
    O depth of wealth

b καὶ σοφίας
   et sapientiae
   and of wisdom

c καὶ γνώσεως
   et cognitionis
   and of knowledge
   θεοῦ
   Dei!
   of God!

2c ὡς ἀνεξεραύνητα τα κρίματα αὐτοῦ
    quam incomprehensibilia sunt judicia eius
    Beyond searching are his judgments!

3. See, e.g., Reinhard Deichgräber, *Gotteshymnus und Christushymnus in der frühen Christenheit* (Göttingen: Vandenhoeck & Ruprecht, 1967); and Gottfried Schille, *Frühchristliche Hymnen* (Berlin: Evangelische Verlagsanstalt, 1965), on hymns in the New Testament. The list of criteria that follows is from Markus Barth.

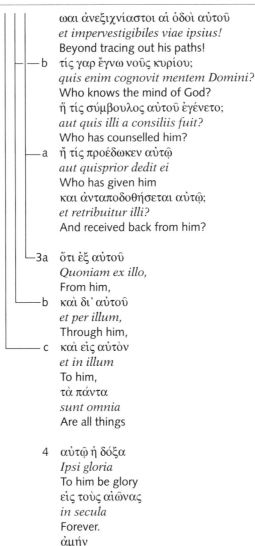

ωαι ἀνεξιχνίαστοι αἱ ὁδοὶ αὐτοῦ
et impervestigibiles viae ipsius!
Beyond tracing out his paths!

— b τίς γαρ ἔγνω νοῦς κυρίου;
quis enim cognovit mentem Domini?
Who knows the mind of God?
ἤ τίς σύμβουλος αὐτοῦ ἐγένετο;
aut quis illi a consiliis fuit?
Who has counselled him?

— a ἤ τίς προέδωκεν αὐτῷ
aut quisprior dedit ei
Who has given him
καὶ ἀνταποδοθήσεται αὐτῷ;
et retribuitur illi?
And received back from him?

—3a ὅτι ἐξ αὐτοῦ
Quoniam ex illo,
From him,

——b καὶ δι᾽ αὐτοῦ
et per illum,
Through him,

———c καὶ εἰς αὐτὸν
et in illum
To him,
τὰ πάντα
sunt omnia
Are all things

4 αὐτῷ ἡ δόξα
Ipsi gloria
To him be glory
εἰς τοὺς αἰῶνας
in secula
Forever.
ἀμήν
Amen.

This doxology at Romans 11:33–36 is announced in the first strophe by the word *bathos* (depth), followed by a series of three genitives: *ploutou, sophias, gnōseos* (ABC); these three are matched in the second strophe by three rhetorical questions, set in pairs, referring to the three genitives above in reverse order (CBA). In the third strophe there are three corresponding prepositional phrases (ABC). The final strophe is an ascription of glory and benediction. This passage provided in later times a prolific trinitarian liturgical pattern, as we shall note in a "hymn" from Augustine's *De Doctrina Christiana,* to be discussed presently.

The tricola of Paul's "hymn" are set in chiastic relation as noted: ABC-CBA-ABC.

This passage, and the other "hymns" in Paul's letters, are for the most part inspired centos of Old Testament texts.[4] The language and rhythms of the Psalter especially pervade his epistles, and other New Testament books as well. The canticles of the Gospel of Luke, and the hymns of the Book of Revelation come immediately to mind. The impact of the Psalter on all subsequent Christian thought and worship has been incalculable. Not only has the Psalter inspired paraphrases of itself and hymns imitating itself in the New Testament and in later Christian literature, but it also has led to the unconscious outbreaking into strophic utterance of the Church Fathers and their successors, to which we shall now turn.

Earlier we noted the most common themes of hymnic utterance—the doxological, the christological, and the soteriological. Doxological utterance is especially evoked when the Trinity is under consideration. No philosophical formulation can express, as poetry can, the dynamic tension between unity and trinity in the mind of the believer as he thinks on God. This is succinctly set forth in a quatrain of Gregory of Nyssa, found in his Fortieth Oration *On Holy Baptism* (cf. Calvin, *Inst.* 1.13.17):

οὐ φθάνω τὸ ἕν νοῆσαι	I cannot think on the One
καὶ τοῖς τριαὶ περιλάμπομαι	without being encircled by the Three.
οὐ φθάνω τα τρία διελεῖν	Nor can I think on the Three
καὶ εἰς τὸ ἕν ἀναφέρομαι	without being carried back to the One.

Note the repetition of the initial phrase, in alternate lines (1, 3):

οὐ φθάνω . . .

Also the repetition of the initial conjunction, in succeeding alternate lines (2, 4):

καὶ . . .

This gives a structure of ABAB to the quatrain. The alternation of

One . . . Three:
τὸ ἕν . . .
τοῖς τρισὶ . . .
τὸ ἕν . . .
τὰ τρία.

with identical repetition (1, 3) and modified repetition (2, 4) gives for

---

4. I have provided poetic translations of the generally agreed "hymnic" passages of the New Testament in *Adjutorium ad Cultum Divinum*, nos. 302–38.

this feature of the quatrain a structure of **ABBA**. Still another pattern is discerned in the use of the final verb:

> a) without homeoteleuton (1, 3):
> νοῆσαι
> διελεῖν
> b) with homeoteleuton (2, 4):
> περιλάμπομαι
> ἀναφέρομαι

This yields a structure of **ABCB**. Thus in these four brief lines the dynamic tension of One/Three is heightened by three structural features, superimposed on one another:

$$A : A : A$$
$$B : B : B$$
$$A : B : C$$
$$B : A : B$$

Quite a contrasting poetic statement of the Trinity is offered by Tertullian in his *Adversus Praxean,* in answer to the question, "If One, how Three?"[5]

I	Quasi non sic quoque	All of the One they are
	unus sit omnia	by unity of substance,
	dum ex uno omnia	While nonetheless is guarded
	per substantiae scilicet unitate	that mysterious economy
5	et nihilominus custodiatur	disposing unity in Trinity,
	oikonomiae sacramentum,	
	quae unitatem in trinitatem disponit,	
II	tres dirigens Patrem et Filium et	Setting forth Father and Son and
	Spiritum,	Spirit, as three:
	tres autem non statu	three not in quality
10	sed gradu,	but in sequence;
	nec substantia	not in substance
	sed forma,	but in aspect;
	nec potestate	not in power
	sed specie,	but in manifestation.
III	unius autem substantiae,	Yet of one substance,
16	et unius status	and one quality
	et unius potestatis:	and one power:
	quia unus Deus	For it is one God
	ex quo et gradus isti	from whom these sequences
	et formae	and aspects
	et species	and manifestations
	in nomine Patris	are reckoned out

5. From Tertullian, *Adversus Praxean* 2:4 in *Corpus Christianorum,* 2:1161; ET based on Ernest E. Evans, *Q. Septimii Florentis Tertulliani Adversus Praxean Liber* [Tertullian's Treatise against Praxeas] (London: SPCK, 1948). Cf. Calvin, *Inst.* 1.13.28.

	et Filii	in the name of the Father
25	et Spiritus Sancti	and of the Son
	deputantur.	and of the Holy Spirit.
IV	Qui quomodo numerum	How they keep intact the number
	sine divisione patiuntur,	without division,
	procedentes tractatus demonstrabunt.	the following discussion will demonstrate.

The heart of this hymnic fragment is contained in the second and third strophes, in which six nouns—*status, gradus, substantia, forma, potestas, species*—intertwined with *Pater, Filius,* and *Spiritus Sanctus* carry the tension between One and Three. Diagramatically the structure might be laid out as follows:

Table 46. Poetic structure of Tertullian's *Adversus Praxean* 2.4

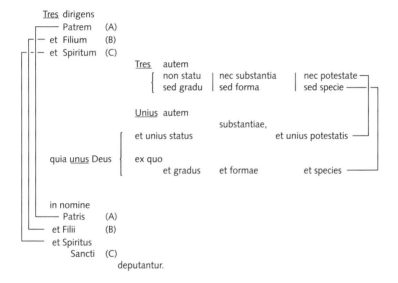

The trinitarian pattern that "frames" the piece is of the structure ABC *(Patrem/Patris; Filium/Filii; Spiritus/Spiritus Sancti).* The alternation of One and Three *(Tres dirigens. . . . Tres Autem. . . . Unius autem. . . . unus Deus)* is of the structure AABB. The series of six descriptive nouns (intertwined with the just mentioned One/Three structure) is twice announced, first in three *non . . . sed* pairs[6] in the ablative case (AB/CD/EF); then with chiasmus, in two triplets, *autem . . . et . . . et / et . . . et . . . et* (CAE/BDF). The answer to the question—"If One, how Three?"—then is at least introduced in this brief but highly articulated hymnic fragment, to be elaborated in the discussion that follows in Tertullian's treatise.

6. Note the homeoteleuton: -ū, -ā, -ē, in the first announcement in three pairs.

Yet another poetic effort to communicate the One/Three tension is a slightly longer piece of Augustine, *De Doctrina Christiana*.[7]

I	Unus Deus	One God
	ex quo omnia	from whom are all things,
	per quem omnia	through whom are all things,
	in quo omniain	whom are all things.*
II	Ita Pater et Filius et Spiritus Sanctus	So are Father, Son and Holy Spirit
6	et singulus quisque horum Deus,	each one of them is God,
	et simul omnes unus Deus;	all together they are one God;
	et singulus quisque horum plena substantia,	
	et simul omnes unus Deus;	
III	Pater nec Filius est nec Spiritus	The Father is neither Son nor Holy
11	Sanctus,	Spirit,
	Filius nec Pater est nec Spiritus Sanctus,	the Son is neither Father nor Holy Spirit,
	Spiritus Sanctus nec Pater est nec Filius.	the Holy Spirit is neither Father nor Son.
IV	Sed Pater tantum Pater,	But the Father alone is Father,
	et Filius tantum Filius,	the Son alone is Son,
15	et Spiritus Sanctus tantum Spiritus Sanctus	the Holy Spirit alone is Holy Spirit.
V	Eadem tribus aeternitas,	To the three belongs the same eternity,
	eadem incommutabilitas,	the same changelessness,
	eadem maiestas,	the same majesty,
	eadem potestas.	the same power.
VI	In Patre unitas,	In the Father is unity,
21	in Filio aequalitas,	in the Son equality,
	in Spiritu Sancto unitatis aequalitatisque concordia.	in the Holy Spirit the harmony of unity and equality.
VII	Et tria haec unum omnia propter Patrem,	And all these three are one because of the Father,
	aequalia omnia propter Filium,	are equal because of the Son,

7. 1.5.5. This short poem is but a small instance of the varied approaches to the explication of the Trinity, offered by Augustine in the *De Doctrina Christiana* and elsewhere. For a tabular resumé of these, see Ford Lewis Battles, *Itinerarium Fidei II* (Pittsburgh: Pittsburgh Theological Seminary, 1978), V.A.2. Space here precludes all but a cursory mention of the treasure of poetry in Augustine: occasionally in his sermons one finds passages even replete with end rhyme. Then there is *The Alphabetic Psalm against the Party of Donatus*, which I have translated into English in my Study Outline No. B 13 c: see Ford Lewis Battles, with Robert Benedetto, *Semita ad perspicendam mentem sancti Augustini: A Student's Guide to the Formative Controversies in the Life and Thought of Aurelius Augustinus, Bishop of Hippo Regius* (Pittsburgh: Pittsburgh Theological Seminary, 1977). The editors of the Bibliothèque Augustinienne edition of the *Confessions* (BA 13–14) have, in their French translation printed as poetry some thirty-five passages of varying length at the beginnings (and sometimes, ends) of the several books of that work. The impress of the Psalms is deep. For details on the roots of medieval Christian-Latin poetry in Augustine, see F. J. E. Raby, *A History of Christian-Latin Poetry from the Beginnings to the Close of the Middle Ages* (Oxford: Clarendon, 1927), 20ff.

| 25 | connexa omnia propter Spiritum Sanctum.[a] | are linked together because of the Holy Spirit. |

a. Augustine, *De Doctrina Christiana* 1.5.5, from Ford Lewis Battles and Eugen Rosenstock-Huessy, *Magna Charta Latina: The Privilege of Singing, Articulating, and Reading a Language and of Keeping It Alive*, rev. ed. (Pittsburgh: Pickwick, 1975), 30. *Rom. 11:36.

Quite clearly the inspiration for Augustine's "hymn" is in the prepositional sequence of Romans 11:33ff.: ἐξ . . . διά . . . εἰς . . . *(ex . . . per . . . in)*, out of which the first strophe is developed and which is recapitulated in the sixth strophe as *Pater, Filius, Spiritus Sanctus*. The One/Three tension is expressed in strophe II by anaphora:

> et singulus quisque . . .
> et simul omnes unus Deus

twice repeated. The same tension is recapitulated as bracketed between strophes III/IV and strophe V:

Table 47. Poetic structure of Augustine's *De Doctrina Christiana* 1.5.5

Again, strophes V, VI, VII contrast the common attributes of the Three *(aeternitas, incommutabilitas, maiestas, potestas)* and the distinctive attributes of each of the Three *(unitas, aequalitas, concordia unitatis aequalitatisque)*, finally expressing the oneness of the attributes in restating the nouns as adjectives:

> unitas . . . unum
> aequalitas . . . aequalia
> concordia . . . connexa

Among the other poetic features should be mentioned the homeoteleuton that marks strophe V: *-itas/-itas* : *-estas/-estas*.

Thus, with great variety, the three Fathers just examined approach the difficult topic of the Trinity in these brief fragments. Each in his own way is driven to a poetic formation of the paradox of One/Three. Equilibrium is struck, but there is no final resolution of the tension.

We turn now to a famous and oft-quoted "hymn" of Cyprian on the church, from chapter 5 of *De Unitate Ecclesiae*.[8] Just as Gregory of Nyssa, Tertullian, and Augustine reflected on the One and the Three, so Cyprian in this passage is reflecting on the One and the Many, with reference to the church:

I	Ecclesia quoque una est	
	quae in multitudinem latius	
	incremento foecunditatis extenditur.	
II	Quomodo solis multi radii,	[A–1]
5	*sed* lumen *unum:*	
	et rami arboris multi,	[B–1]
	sed robur *unum* tenaci radice fundatum;	
	et cum de fonte uno,	[C–1]
	rivi plurimi defluunt,	
10	numerositas licet diffusa videatur	
	exundantis copiae largitate,	
	unitas tamen servatur in origine.	
III	Avelle radium solis a corpore,	[A–2]
	divisionem lucis unitas non capit;	
15	ab arbore frange ramum,	[B–2]
	fractus germinare non potest;	
	a fonte praecide rivum,	[C–2]
	praecisus arescit.	
IV	Sic et Ecclesia Domini luce perfusa	[A–3]
20	per orbem totum	
	radios suos porrigat:	
	unum tamen lumen est,	
	quod ubique diffunditur,	
	nec unitas corporis separatur.	
25	Ramos suos in universam terram	[B–3]
	copia ubertatis extendit,	
	Profluentes largitur rivos latius expandit,	
	unum tamen caput est et origo una.	[C–3]
V	et una mater foecunditatis successibus	
	copiosa.	
30	Illius foetum nascimur,	
	Illius lacte nutrimur,	
	Spiritu ejus animamur.	

A tripartite threefold progression marks the "hymn": sun . . . tree . . . spring . . . / rays . . . branches . . . streams . . . / church: light . . . church: body . . . church: well-spring. The final strophe translates these metaphors into three aspects of the *mother* similitude:

> et una mater foecunditatis successibus copiosa:
> illius foetu nascimur,

8. For my adaptation of this as an English hymn, see *The Hymnal of the United Church of Christ*, no. 153: in this adaptation the chiasmus has been resolved to enhance stanzaic integrity.

illius lactu nutrimur,
spiritu ejus animamur.

This closes the circle by its return to the metaphor that in the first strophe introduced the passage:

ecclesia . . . in multitudinem latius
incremento foecunditatis extenditur.

The One/Many paradox is built up in threefold repetition in strophe II: *multi . . . sed . . . unum / et . . . multi . . . sed . . . unum / . . . uno . . . plurimi . . . unitas tamen.* It is further strengthened in strophe III by a triple use of imperatives: *avelle . . . frange . . . praecide.* Each of these is followed by a contradiction, all three instances being drawn from an observation of nature. The shift in strophe IV to application to the church is made the more dramatic in that what is said of the sun and its light affirms the oneness of the church's light, however widely diffused, while what is said of a tree or a spring is denied by the experience of the church.

Thus, at the heart of Cyprian's "hymn" are symmetrical elaborations of three scripturally common analogies, in the original Latin chiastically arranged:

Table 48. Poetic structure of Cyprian's *De Unitate Ecclesiae*

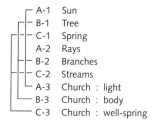

A-1	Sun	
B-1	Tree	
C-1	Spring	
A-2	Rays	
B-2	Branches	
C-2	Streams	
A-3	Church	: light
B-3	Church	: body
C-3	Church	: well-spring

But in these metaphors it is as much the difference as the likeness that is stressed. Like a tree, yes, but also unlike; like a stream issuing from a spring, yes, but also unlike. Such truth calls forth the poet in us to ponder, wonder, praise. Yet it was the very schism in the church at Carthage, fed by the Decian persecution of the Christians, which called forth this ringing assertion of the divinely given oneness of the church in the face of the internecine quarrels.

We have sketched, by way of introduction, a few examples of "found poetry" from Paul, Gregory of Nyssa, Tertullian, Augustine, and Cyprian. This treasury of unpremeditated song did not cease with the Church Fathers; among the Western Scholastics one need mention only Anselm, whose *Meditations* are of a high poetic order; it was still very much alive in the Reformation era. Of the Reformers, none had a deeper love of the Psalter or a better grounding in classical rhetoric than John Calvin. It is to the poetry of his prose writings, then, that this essay turns as the chief topic under discussion.

John Calvin as Poet

> By nature I was rather inclined to poetry, but bidding those things fare-well, for twenty-five years I have composed nothing, except that I was led by the example of Philip [Melanchthon] and Sturm at Worms to write a poem for fun. Therefore what I have given up, I do not possess. Viret also denies that the Muses are propitious enough toward him for him to sing anything poetic.[9]

Thus, with a fleeting mention of his one extant poem in a classical form, the *Epinicion*, Calvin dismisses a gift that he actually practiced throughout his life, but in implicit rather than explicit forms. True, the "poems" here identified in his *Institutio* and other writings can be ana-lyzed exclusively rhetorically, as Antoon Veerman has done, dissecting the stylistic features.[10] Yet when that is accomplished, one has tagged with the appropriate classical label this phrase or that sentence and given a verdict on Calvin's "classicism," but little else. The poetic pas-sages rise above such minute analysis and take on the character of hymns sung by one who was on fire with the love of Christ.

The substance of Calvin's "hymns" is Scripture; the rhetorical frame, too, is scriptural. As a Latin stylist, Calvin undoubtedly embellished his thought with the tropes and figures of classical rhetoric, as Veerman has shown. But there is probably more of David or Paul than of Cicero or the classical poets in what Calvin would never himself call poetry, but which we can readily line out in strophes.

Yet we must not underestimate the classical element in this. We need only look at the classical poets quoted or cited by John Calvin in his *Commentary on Seneca's De Clementia* (1532) or note the important place of classical poetry in his *Order of the Geneva Schools* (1559) to as-sess the function of poetry in his own formation and in that which he commended to the boys of the Académie. In the Seneca commentary he shows special familiarity with Horace, Ovid, and Virgil, though many other poets are cited.[11] In the *Order of the Geneva Schools*[12] bilingual in-

---

9. Calvin to Conrad Hubert, minister of Strasbourg, 19 May 1557: Epist. 2632, *CR*, 16:488.

10. A. Veerman, *De Stijl van Calvijn in de Institutio Christianae Religionis* (Utrecht: University of Amsterdam, 1943). Veerman confines his study almost entirely to the dedi-catory epistle to Francis I and Book I of the 1559 *Institutes*.

11. See Ford Lewis Battles, "The Sources of Calvin's Seneca Commentary," in *Studies in John Calvin*, ed. by G. Duffield (Appleford, Abingdon, Berkshire: Sutton Courtenay, 1966), 52f.; reprinted herein as ch. 2.

12. See *OS*, 2:368–70.

struction (French and Latin) begins in the seventh class (first grade); Greek is added in the fourth class (fourth grade). Beginning in the fifth class (the third grade), Virgil's *Bucolics* is used in teaching the rudiments of syntax; in the fourth class, quantity of syllables is taught through the study of Ovid's *Elegies, Tristia,* and *De Ponto.* By the third class (fifth grade) the students are reading Virgil's *Aeneid,* and the following year the reading of Homer is undertaken. Rhetoric is gradually introduced through the study of the Latin and Greek orators, beginning in the third class, with increasing concentration on it in the second and first classes (sixth and seventh grades). Hence, by the time they finished their seven years of study in the Académie, the students possessed the basic tools of rhetoric and poetic.

Alongside the thorough classical studies, there is of course biblical instruction. On Saturday afternoons, the Gospel of Luke is read in Greek in the second class; in the first class, the Letters of the Apostles. For all the students there is attendance at services on Sunday and on Wednesday morning. On Monday, Tuesday, Thursday, and Friday there is psalm singing immediately after lunch, and in the afternoon at assembly in the common room, the Lord's Prayer, Confession, Ten Commandments (in French). On Saturday afternoon, after recess, there is catechetical preparation for classes seven through three, and New Testament Greek for the two top classes.

Beyond the seven years of the *schola privata,* are the lectures of the public professors in the *schola publica,* the professors of Hebrew, Greek, and arts. Under the first is the study of Hebrew grammar and the Old Testament books; under the second, the study of Greek poets and orators and moral philosophy; under the third, the study of physics (natural science), Aristotle's *Rhetoric,* and Cicero's oratorical works and orations. The professors of theology lecture on the Scriptures.

Thus, throughout the scheme of education laid down for Geneva by Calvin, classical and biblical studies go hand in hand. We can see that for Calvin, rhetoric and poetic (and all the liberal arts) are but steps to a clearer understanding and advocacy of God's ways with his creation and of the key to that understanding, Scripture. As a young humanist and student of the law, Calvin had said: "It is the mark of rhetorical skill to turn those things that work against us to our own benefit and to the advantage of our use."[13] After his conversion Calvin was to press his rhetorical skill unreservedly into God's service.[14]

Even before coming to Geneva in 1536, Calvin recognized the crucial place of music and poetry in deepening and strengthening Christian pi-

---

13. *Comm. Sen. De Clem.,* 145.
14. On Calvin's use of rhetoric as an exegetical and theological tool, see "God Was Accommodating Himself to Human Capacity," 117–20, especially 119f.; reprinted herein as ch. 4.

ety.[15] The Psalms of David were, with Paul's Letter to the Romans, crucial in his own conversion. Like Paul's, his own prose is steeped in their rhythms.[16] For him the Psalter provides an "anatomy of all the states of the soul." Over two centuries before Bishop Lowth first analyzed in detail the parallelism that marks Hebrew poetry in general, and the Psalms in particular, Calvin had, like many Christian writers before him, taken them and their poetic structures into his very marrow.[17] His *Commentary on the Psalms* does not identify the several forms of parallelism—synonymous, antithetical, synthetic—but the principle of parallelism is understood. And these Hebraic patterns provide the vehicle for his deepest thoughts in the *Institutes* and other theological works.

Two theological writings precede the first edition of the *Institutes*, published in 1536. Probably the first of these was the twin preface (actually two quite different prefaces, Latin and French) to the French translation of the New Testament by his cousin Pierre Robert, written in either late 1534 or very early 1535. Elsewhere [*Inst. 1536*, Introduction, xxxv] I have called this French preface "the first draft of his theological restatement of his conversion experience." There are several passages of high poetry in this impassioned plea for the gospel; more correctly, the whole French preface may be seen as an extended Psalm that sums up salvation history. As such, it is in the tradition of Theophilus of Antioch or of Irenaeus' *anakephalaiosis*, Augustine's *City of God* (or shorter statements elsewhere in his works),[18] or—to speak of the New Testament—in the tradition of the speeches of Stephen or Peter or the longer chronicle of faith in the Epistle to the Hebrews. Consequently, the whole preface can be "lined out" in a strophic form.

It may be analyzed into seven sections, covering the history of salvation: (1) humanity made in the image of God; (2) humanity's fall, through pride; (3) the continuing love of fallen humanity by the God of mercy who reveals himself that humanity may find him, (a) through the whole of nature, (b) especially through a chosen people, Israel; (4) humanity, despite these gifts of mercy, continues to be false to God, making a new covenant necessary for the restoration of human beings; (5) the coming of the Savior; (6) the call of the gospel; (7) final appeal to those who can see to the right preaching of the gospel and the health of the church.

We shall turn in a moment to two passages from it that may illustrate the poetic idiom of which we speak.

15. See *Piety 1978*, 137ff.; and Charles Garside, *The Origins of Calvin's Theology of Music, 1536–1543* (Philadelphia: The American Philosophical Society, 1979).

16. Cf. Rom. 11:33–36, as analyzed above.

17. Cf. Calvin, *Inst.* 1.15.3 (on image/likeness).

18. See Ford Lewis Battles, *Itinerarium Fidei*, II, V.A.3.

The second theological writing that antedates the first edition of the *Institutes* is the *Psychopannychia*, an essay on the continued life of the soul after death, directed against the French Anabaptists, who apparently espoused a doctrine of soul-death or soul-sleep, occurring at the time of physical death. The treatise is in two parts, the first of which sets out Calvin's teaching on the continued existence of the soul after bodily death, while the second details and refutes the Anabaptist arguments favoring the sleep of the soul. Although the earliest theological writing of Calvin, it was not actually published until 1542. One "hymn" has been identified in this work.

Before we examine hymnic passages, it may be useful to recapitulate some of the features that set these lines apart from their immediate prose context, as preeminently "hymnic" in character. The most apparent one is anaphora, the repetition of the same word sequence, but usually not the very same words, in successive sentences. With this is often coupled chiasmus,[19] the reversal of the position of the verb or noun or other repeated elements in successive sentences. The text may easily be divided into lines of similar or equal length, technically called cola, usually exhibiting parallelism of members. These lines often fall naturally into stanzas or strophes, marked by anaphora or some other feature. At this point we are confining our attention to structural features, by which hymnic passages may be externally identified and analyzed, within the categories of rhetoric and form criticism. We shall also look briefly at the content of such passages: here, too, certain common features will emerge.

Let us first look at the passage from the preface of the French New Testament, which begins, "Sans l'évangile."[20] It comes from the sixth section, "On the Call of the Gospel."

I	Sans l'evangile	Without the gospel
5	tous sommes inutiles et vain,	All of us are useless and empty;
	sans l'evangile	Without the gospel
	nous ne sommes Chretiens,	We are not Christians;
	sans l'evangile	Without the gospel
	toute richesse est paovrete,	All wealth is poverty,
	sagesse est folye devant Dieu,	Wisdom is foolishness before God,
	force est faiblesse,	Strength is weakness,

19. Chiasmus, or at least the chiastic principle, is used by Calvin not only in the smaller elements, phrases, and sentences, but even in the larger structures: for example, in the *Institutes*, Books I–II illustrate a chiastic relationship in the unfolding of the two knowledges, of God and of man: knowledge of God as Creator: knowledge of man as created (Book I): knowledge of God as Redeemer: knowledge of man as fallen, the object of redemption (Book II).

20. Text from the preface to Pierre Robert's French translation of the New Testament (1534?), *OC*, 9:807; ET, "A Hymn to the Gospel," *Piety 1978,* 168.

	toute justice humaine est damnee de Dieu.	All human justice is condemned of God.	
II	Mais par la cognoissance de	But by the knowledge of the gospel,	
11	l'evangile		
	nous sommes faictz enfans de Dieu,	We are made children of God,	
	freres de Iesus Christ,	Brothers of Jesus Christ,	
	combourgeoys des saintz,	Fellow citizens of the saints,	
	citoyens du royaume des cieulx,	Citizens of the kingdom of heaven,	
15	heritiers de Dieu avec Jesus Christ	Heirs of God with Jesus Christ,	
III	par lequel les paouvres sont faitz riches,	By whom the poor become rich,	
	les foibles puissans,	the weak powerful,	
	les folz sages,	the fools wise,	
	les pecheurs iustifiez,	the sinners justified,	
20	les desolez consolez,	the desolate comforted,	
	les doubteux certains,	the doubting certain,	
	les serfz affranchies.	the slaves[a] set free.	
IV	C'est la puissance de Dieu	It is the power of God	
	au salut de tous croyans	For the salvation of all believers	
25	et la clef de la science de Dieu	And the key to the knowledge of God	
	que ouvre la porte du royaume des cieulx	Which opens the door of the kingdom of heaven	
	aux incredules les lyant en leurs pechez.	To unbelievers lying in their sins.	
V	Bienheureux sont tous ceux	Happy are all those	
	qui l'oyent et la gardent.	Who hear and keep it.	
30	Car par cela ilz monstrent	For by that they show	
	qu'ilz sont enfans de Dieu.	That they are children of God.	
	Malheureux sont ceulx	Miserable are those	
	qui ne la veulent ne ouyr ne ensuyvre:	Who wish neither to hear nor follow it:	
	car ilz sont enfans du diable.	For they are the children of the devil.	

a. Or "serfs."

Overall, the poem is marked by a general antithesis:

I) without the gospel. . . . II) with the knowledge of the gospel

This is sketched in the first two stanzas and announced in the first line of each. The antithesis is then worked out in a series of specific antitheses or contrasting phrases in stanza III:

III	poor/rich	(line 16)
	weak/powerful	(line 17)
	fools/wise	(line 18)
	sinners/justified	(line 19)
	desolate/consoled	(line 20)
	doubtful/certain	(line 21)
	serfs/freed	(line 22)

The first element of each member represents the "sans évangile" condition; the second, the transformation effected by the knowledge of the gospel.

The fourth stanza (c'est la puissance . . .) is marked by parallelism between the first member (first two lines, 23–24) and the second member (last three lines, 25–27):

IVa power of God . . . /   IVb key to knowledge of God . . .
      believers   unbelievers

It also is an amplification of the original antithesis.

The fifth stanza (Bienheureux sont tous ceux . . .) sets forth a clear example of antithetical parallelism, recapitulating the original general antithesis:

Va happy . . . /   Vb miserable . . .
    children of God (lines 28–31)   children of the devil (lines 32–34)

However, besides these general features and specific ones confined within the several stanzas, there is an interesting chiastic relationship between I and III (+ II). When one assigns a letter to each line of stanza I (a–g), the lines corresponding in thought in stanza III (+ II) bear the following relationship:

Table 49. Poetic structure of Calvin's preface to Pierre Robert's French New Testament

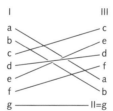

By means of these rhetorical devices, the scattered scriptural references and echoes are bound together in a literary unity. But there is nothing contrived or artificial in the structure; it is totally subordinated to the intended message and flows naturally from it.

To sum up:

(1) Repetition: no word or phrase is consistently repeated throughout: but *gospel* is either mentioned or pronominally referred to in nearly every line.
(2) The initial antithesis is elaborated in the following stanzas.
(3) In the unfolding of these antitheses there is cumulative movement.
(4) The overall structure is that of a ring:

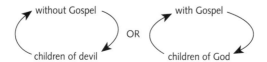

The second passage comes from the third section of the preface to the French New Testament. On the continuing self-revelation of the God of mercy to fallen man, through the whole of nature.

I	Car il a eslevé par tout,	For God has everywhere raised up,
5	en tous lieux,	in all places,
10	et en toutes choses,	and in all things,
	ses enseignes et armoiries,	His banners and blazons,
	voire soubz blasons de si claire intelligence	for under so clearly marked coats of arms
	quil n'y avoit celuy	none there is
	qui peult pretendre ignorance	who can pretend ignorance
	de ne congnoistre ung si souverain seigneur:	of knowing such a sovereign Lord
	qui avoit si amplement	Who has so fully
	exalté sa magnificance.	exalted His greatness.
II	C'est quand en toutes les parties du monde,	Since it is in all parts of the universe,
15	au ciel,	in heaven,
	et en la terre,	and in earth,
	il a escrit et quasi engravé	He has written and as it were engraved
	la gloire de sa puissance,	the glory of His power,
	bonté	goodness,
	sapience,	wisdom,
	et eternité	and eternity.
III	Sainct Paul donc a dit bein vray,	Saint Paul, then, has right truly said
20	que le seigneur ne se estoit iamais laissé	that the Lord has never left Himself without a witness:
	sans tesmoingage:	
	mesme evers ceulx ausquelz il n'a envoyé	even toward those to whom He has never sent
	aucune congnoissance	any knowledge
	de sa parole.	of His Word.
IV	Veu que toutes les creatures	Seeing that all creatures
30	despuis le firmament	from the firmament
35	iusque au centre de la terre,	even to the center of the earth,
	pouvoient estre tesmoings	can be witnesses
	et messagiers de sa gloire	and messengers of His glory
	à tous hommes:	to all men:
	pour les attirer à le cercher,	to draw them to seek Him,
	et apres l'avoir trouvé,	and after they have found Him,
	luy faire recueil et hommaige,	to render Him remembrance and homage,
	selon la dignité d'ung seigneur	as befits the dignity of a Lord
	si bon,	so good,
	si puissant,	so powerful,
	si sage,	so wise,
	et eternel,	and eternal,
	et mesmes aydoient chascune	and even help each one
40	en son endroict à ceste queste.	in his own place in this quest.
V	Car les oyseletz chantans	For the little song birds
45	chantoient Dieu,	sing God;

VI	les bestes le reclamoient,	the beasts call upon Him;
50	les elemens le redoubtoient,	the elements fear Him;
	les montagnes le resonnoient,	the mountains resound Him;
	les fleuves et fontaines luy iettoient oeillades,	the rivers and springs wink their eyes at Him;
	les herbes et fleurs luy rioyent.	the plants and flowers sport before Him.
55	Combien que veritablement	How truly indeed
	il ne feust pas mestier	is there no need
	de le cercher fort loing:	to seek Him far afield,
	veu que chascun le pouvoit	since each can
	trouver en soymesme,	find Him in himself
	en tant que nous sommes	seeing that we are
	tous sustentez et conservez	all sustained and preserved
	de sa vertu habitante en nous.[a]	by His power indwelling us.

a. From Calvin, *A Tous Amateurs de Iesus Christ et de Son Evangile, Salut* (preface to the French translation of the New Testament by his cousin, Pierre Robert). Text from *OC*, 9:793.39–41; 795.1–15.

This passage is actually a meditation on Paul's assertion (in Acts 14:17) that the Lord has never left himself without a witness. The clarity of God's self-disclosure in nature, our inexcusable blindness to those evidences, leading first to the giving of the law and finally to the incarnation of Jesus Christ: these are oft-repeated themes in Calvin's writings, notably in the early chapters of the *Institutes of the Christian Religion*. In this early writing (1534?) some of the elements are already visible. The poetic character of the passage is to be noted not so much in external features of style as in the inner patterning of themes.

Note the following parallelism, amplifying the ubiquity of the divine witness:

Stanza I	en tous *lieux*	(line 2)	A
	et en tous *choses*	(line 3)	B
Stanza II	. . . en toutes les parties du mode,	(line 11)	
	au ciel,	(line 12)	A <
	et en la terre . . .	(line 13)	
Stanza IV	toutes les creatures	(line 25)	
	despuis le firmament	(line 26)	B <
	iusque au centre de la terre	(line 27)	
Stanza V	les oyseletz. . . .	(lines 41–48)	A/B <
	les herbes et fleurs luy rioyent		

In stanza I there is synonymous parallelism: *lieux/choses* (A:B). In stanza II *lieux* is amplified into *toutes les parties du monde*, etc. (A <). In stanza IV *choses* is amplified into *toutes les creatures*, etc. (B <). In stanza V *choses* and *lieux* are intertwined in further parallel amplification (B/A <).

What has just been traced is but a facet of the larger theme of God's self-disclosure:

St. I	. . . a esleué par tout
St. II	. . . a escrit et quasi engravé
St. III	. . . ne se estoit iamais laissé sans tesmoingage
St. IV	. . . pouvoit estre tesmoings et messagiers . . .

What is the content of that self-disclosure?

St. I	. . . sa magnificence	
St. II	la gloire de sa puissance	a
	bonté	b
	sapience	c
	et eternité	d
St. IV	la dignité d'ung seigneur	
	si bon	b
	si puissant	a
	si sage	c
	et eternel	d

Note the amplification of *magnificence* (st. I) in stanza II. Then between stanzas II and IV there is a marked chiasmus, abcd—bacd. Stanza V[21] is perhaps the most poetically sustained strophe in the poem, with a six-fold synonymous parallelism:

les oyseletz	. . . chant*oient* Dieu
les bestes	le reclam*oient*
les elemens	le redoubt*oient*
les montagnes	le resonn*oient*
les *f*leuves	
et *f*ontaines	luy iett*oient*
	oeillades
les herbes	
et fleurs	luy ri*oyent*.

The verbs in their ending *-oient (-oyent)* display homeoteleuton.
Note the pattern of definite article . . . object:

(1)	les . . . Dieu
(2–4)	les . . . le
(5–6)	les . . .
	et . . . luy

---

21. Cf. *Inst.* 1.5.15: "We cannot pretend ignorance as an excuse for our failure to follow these evidences to a knowledge of God, when even mute and irrational creatures speak forth God's glory."

All these are small, some even insignificant touches, but together they give an impassioned tone to the passage. The final stanza draws the inference from the ubiquity of God's witness, that he is not to be sought afar off, but in us, whom he indwells, sustaining and preserving us. Thus, the ring is closed.

The next hymnic fragment comes from the beginning of the second part of the *Psychopannychia:*[22]

I	Vultis scire quae sit animae mors?	You wish to know what is soul's death?
	Deo carere,	To lack God,
	a Deo desertum esse,	To be forsaken by God,
	sibi relictam esse.	To be left alone.
II 5	Si enim Deus eius vita est,	For if God is its life,
	perdit vitam suam,	It loses its life
	cum perdit Dei praesentiam.	When it loses God's presence.
III	Atque ut quod dictum est	And to show in the parts
	in universum partibus ostendatur,	What has been said of the whole;
10	si extra Deum lux non est,	If outside God there is no light
	quae nocti nostrae luceat,	to light our night,
	ubi lux illa se subduxerit,	When that light has departed,
	anima certe in tenebris suis	The soul buried in its own darkness
	sepulta caeca est.	Is surely blind.
IV 15	Tunc muta est,	Then is that soul mute
	quae confiteri non potest ad salutem,	Which cannot confess unto salvation
	quod crediderit ad justitiam.	What it has believed unto righteousness.
	Surda est,	Then is that soul deaf
	quae vivam illam vocem non audit.	Which does not hear that living voice.
20	Clauda est,	Then is that soul lame,
	imo se sustinere non potest,	Nay, cannot bear up,
	ubi non habet cui dicat:	When it has no one to whom to say:
	Tenuisti manum dexteram meam	Thou hast held my right hand,
	et in voluntate tua deduxisti me,*	And in thy will thou hast led me.
25	nullo denique vitae officio fungitur.	In short it performs no office of life.

Of all the passages proposed for examination, this is perhaps the most diffuse. Its rhythms are more of thought than of rhetorical structure. Its most obvious feature is the series:

caeca . . . muta . . . surda . . . clauda

These in turn call our attention to the context. The piece begins with a question: "You wish to know what is the soul's death?" The answer is given in two strophes: first, in general terms, as alienation from God; then, after a transitional couplet—

22. From Calvin, *Psychopannychia* (1535?, pub. 1542), ed. by W. Zimmerli (1932), 68, lines 4–15. Literally translated here. For paraphrase, see *Piety 1978*, 169. *Cf. Ps. 73:23f.

> And to show in the parts
> What has been said of the whole—

that alienation is elaborated in terms of four physical functions: sight, speech, hearing, walking—metaphorically applied to the soul. One single scriptural base of these lines cannot be cited, but the theme that Calvin has here enlarged upon is the familiar passage of Jeremiah 5:21, and parallels, recalled by Jesus in Matthew 13:13, 15: "seeing, see not . . . hearing, hear not, neither do they understand." One is also reminded of Aeschylus (*Prometheus Bound* 456):

> Seeing, they saw in vain,
> And hearing, they did not hear.

The four references to physical functions echo some of Jesus' miracles, the healing of blindness, deafness, dumbness, and lameness. The quotation of Psalm 73:23f. (72:24) is from the Vulgate. In his later (1555–57) commentary on Psalm 73:23f., verse 24a reads "consilio tuo diriges me," rather than "in voluntate tua deduxisti me" [Schipper 3, 275f.]. Verse 23a, which is not quoted here in the *Psychopannychia* passage, asserts "et ego semper tecum"; what is alienation from God but to be unable to say, "I was continually with thee"?

The message of these lines is in Calvin's later thought greatly enlarged and deepened, as in *Institutes* 3.25.12 (1559), where the physical torments of hell are interpreted as figurative representations of the utter wretchedness of being cut off from all fellowship with God.

Again, the structure is that of the ring worked out in a loose chiasmus and with anaphora and parallelism suggested but not developed to the full. Running through the piece there is also the contrast between life in God's presence and death in his absence.

One of the substantial additions to the *Institutes* made by Calvin in 1539, an addition particularly rich in hymnic passages, was the "Little Treatise on the Christian Life," the firstfruits of his "closer look" at St. Paul's Epistles. The next two pieces are drawn from this. They have been strophically translated in my *Piety of Calvin*,[23] but from the French of 1541. Here we shall examine the original Latin form (table 50).

As one reads the first of these two passages, just quoted, from *Institutes* 3.7.1, one is struck by the thrice-repeated *Nostri non sumus*, with its also thrice-repeated counterpart, *Dei sumus*. Technically, these are two instances of tricola. At once the limits of a tightly constructed hymn are apparent. Note also the further anaphoric element:

> Nostri non sumus . . .
> ergo . . .

23. Text from *Inst.* 3.7.1 (1539); ET from *Piety 1978*, 56, 69.

Table 50. Poetic structure of Calvin's *Institutio* 3.7.1,
"On the Christian Life" (1539)

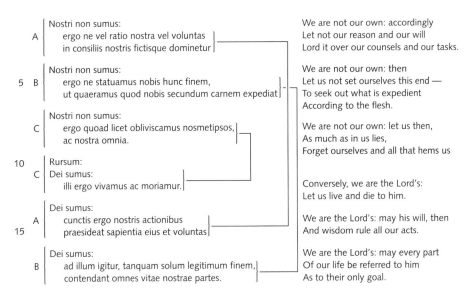

repeated three times. This is paralleled in the second strophe by:

> Dei sumus . . .
> ergo . . .

twice repeated. The third time it is slightly modified:

> Dei sumus . . .
> . . . igitur . . .

The overall structure is marked by the antithesis:

> We are not our own . . . / We are the Lord's . . .

This is, quintessentially, the double theme of *abnegatio* and *tolerantia crucis* of the "Little Treatise on the Christian Life," echoing Matthew 16:24: "If anyone will come after me, let him deny himself and take up his cross and follow me." The cumulative movement of the poem, by this interweaving of the two strands, heightens this. The antithesis is heightened by anaphora (as we have seen) and also by chiasmus. The content of the subsequent member of each colon of the two strophes is chiastically enjambed: A B C ~ C A B. This may be shown graphically in two ways:

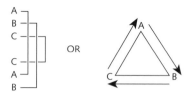

This short passage, then, poetically encapsulates the teaching of *Institutes* 3.6–10: the following of Christ as seen under its inner aspect (self-denial) and its outer aspect (bearing of the cross).

The second hymnic passage from the "Little Treatise on the Christian Life" (also 1539) is at *Institutes* 3.8.7:[24]

	Si innocentes ac nobis bene conscii	If, being innocent and of good conscience,
	impiorum scelere exuimur facultatibus,	We are stripped of our possessions
	ad inopiam quidem redigimur apud homines:	By the wickedness of impious folk,
	se verae apud Deum in caelis	We are indeed reduced to penury among men,
5	divitiae ita nobis accrescunt.	But in God's presence in heaven
	Si penatibus nostris extrudimur	If we are cast out of our own house,
	eo interius recipimur	Then we will be the more intimately received
	in Dei familiam.	Into God's family.
	Si vexamur et contemnimur,	If we are vexed and despised,
10	eo firmiores agimus	We but take all the firmer root
	in Christi radices.	In Christ.
	Si probris ac ignominia notamur,	If we are branded with disgrace and ignominy,
	eo ampliore loco sumus	We have but a fuller place
	in regno Dei.	In the kingdom of God.
15	Si trucidamur,	If we are slain,
	ita nobis ingressus patefit	Entrance into the blessed life
	ad beatam vitam.	Will then be open to us.

As one reads, the anaphora marks off this portion from its context. We observe the five-membered polycola, each colon introduced by *si* . . . and clinched by *ita* or *eo,* in the following pattern:

> (1)   si . . .   A
>   . . . ita . . .
> (2)   si . . .   B
>   eo . . .

24. From *Inst.* 3.8.7 (1539). Literally translated here. For translation from the French of 1541, see *Piety 1978,* 69.

(3)	si . . .	B
	eo . . .	
(4)	si . . .	B
	eo . . .	
(5)	si . . .	A
	ita . . .	

The first colon sets the overarching contrast of the whole:

ad inopiam . . . redigimur : *reduced to poverty*
divitiae . . . accrescunt : *wealth increases*

This contrast is amplified in each successive colon:

(2)	penatibus nostris	/	Dei familiam
(3)	vexamur . . . etc.	/	Christi radices
(4)	probris ac ignominiis	/	regno Dei
(5)	trucidamur . . .	/	beatam istam

The contrasts in strophes 2–4 are partly achieved through use of a comparative adverb or adjective *(interius, firmiores, ampliore loco)*. The cumulative movement ("ring-composition") is achieved in the successive cola (2–5), coming full circle from heaven (1) to the blessed life (5).

In these lines we see the joining of *Scriptura* and *experientia*.[25] Calvin, writing this in Strasbourg, has suffered a double exile, first from his native France, then from Geneva, city of his adoption. Thus have the events of his own life brought home to him the reality of the Christian's pilgrimage. The relation of the present life and the life to come, here sketched proleptically, is elaborated in the following chapters 9 and 10.

The next passage, on the ineffable mystery of the Lord's Supper, derives from the 1539 edition.[26]

	Si tamen ullis verbis complecti	If one may reduce to words
	tantum mysterium liceat:	so great a mystery,
	quod, ne animo quidem	which I see I do not even sufficiently comprehend
	satis me comprehendere video:	with my mind:
5	et libenter ideo fateor,	I therefore freely admit
	ne quis eius sublimitatem	that no man should measure its sublimity
	infantiae meae modulo metiatur.	by my little child's-measure.
	Quin potius lectores hortor,	Rather, I urge my readers not to confine
	ne intra istos nimium angustos fines,	within these too narrow limits
10	mentis sensum contineant:	their mind's

25. The bracketing of *Scripture* and *experience*, a recurrent theme in Calvin's thought, may be noted, e.g., at *Inst.* 1.7.5; 1.13.14, etc.
26. Calvin, *Inst.* (1539), c. 12, De coena Domini, 331 bis; ET *Inst.* 4.17.7.

sed multo altius assurgere   inquiry, but to strive to rise much
   contendant,   higher
quam meo ductu possint.   than I can lead them.
Nam ego ipse,   For, whenever this matter is
                                       discussed,

    quoties hac de re sermo est,   when I have tried to say all,
15 ubi omnia dicere conatus sum   I feel that I have as yet said little
    parum adhuc mihi   in proportion to its worth.
    pro eius dignitate dixisse videor. And although my mind can think
    Quanquam autem cogitando   beyond what my tongue can utter,
    animus plus valet,   yet even my mind is conquered and
                                       overwhelmed
20 quam lingua exprimendo: by the greatness of the thing.
    rei tamen magnitudine,   Therefore nothing remains
    ille quoque vincitur et obruitur   but to break forth in wonder at the
                                       mystery,
    Itaque nihil demum restat   which plainly neither the mind is
                                       able to conceive
    nisi ut in eius mysterii admirationem   nor the tongue to express.
       prorumpam,
25 cui nec mens plane cogitando,   Nevertheless, in one way or another
    nec lingua explicand   I shall sum up my views;
    par esse potest.   for, as I do not doubt them to be true,
    Sententiae tamen meae   I am confident they will be approved
    summam exponam utcunque: in godly hearts.
30 quam, ut nihilo dubito veram esse:
    ita piis pectoribus
    non improbatam iri confido.

Unlike most of the passages we are discussing, although it possesses a
number of rhetorical features, the structure is more internal than external, more a structure of intensity than of outward form. The arresting
feature is the twice-told paradox of ineffability at the heart of the passage:

                              (A)
ubi omnia dicere conatus sum   / parum adhuc mihi
                                      pro eius dignitate dixisse videor

                              (B)

quanquam autem cogitando ⎤
   animus plus valet   ⎥
        /   ⎥ / rei tamen magnitudine,
quam lingua exprimendo   ⎦   ille quoque vincitur et obruitur

The second form of the paradox embraces in its first member a further
subordinate paradox. Note the use of homeoteleuton, or end rhyme:
cogitando . . . exprimendo, then *cogitando . . . explicando* in the next sequence. This calls our attention to the following imperfect double dicola, with chiasmus, in the form of ABAB (see table 51):

Other, minor, features of the passage include the use of alliteration:

Table 51. Poetic structure of Calvin's *Institutio* 4.17.7,
"On the Lord's Supper" (1539)

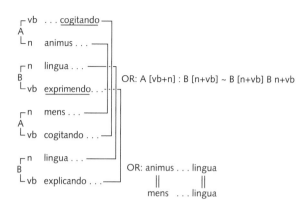

*M*eae *m*odulo *m*etiatur; and other examples of homeoteleuton: . . . contine*ant* . . . contend*ant;* vici*tur* et obrui*tur.*

The tone of the passage and its intent express the deepest humility before this ineffable mystery of God, and secondarily before any other human beings whose minds God may grant a higher flight than is given to Calvin; yet at the same time it expresses a sober confidence in the truth, however circumscribed and inadequately expressed, of our theologian's exposition of the sacrament of the Supper. It is this deep paradox of sinful human inadequacy yet quiet assurance that marks all that Calvin wrote of the faith. For these reasons this passage has been claimed as poetic.

The next poetic passage for examination is found in the midst of the long prayer of confession incorporated in the Wednesday Service of Penitence, a part of the 1543 *Form of Prayer and Songs of the Church*[27] that Calvin composed on the model of his earlier Strasbourg liturgy, upon his return to Geneva.

	Toutefois, Seigneur,	
1	Tu es nostre Pere,	Yet, O Lord, Thou art our Father,
	et nous ne sommes que terre et fange:	And we are but earth and mire;
2	Tu es nostre Createur,	Thou art our Creator,
	et nous sommes les oeuvres de tes mains:	And we are the work of Thy hands; Thou art our Shepherd,
3	Tu es nostre Pasteur,	We are Thy flock;
	nous sommes ton trouppeau:	Thou art our Redeemer,
4	Tu es nostre Redempteur,	We are the people Thou hast brought back;
	nous sommes le peuple que tu as rachepté:	Thou art our God,
5	Tu es nostre Dieu,	We are Thine inheritance.
	nous sommes ton heritage.	

27. *La Forme des Prieres et Chantz Ecclesiastiques* (1543), *OS*, 2:28; ET, *Piety 1978*, 126.

It is a cento of scriptural phrases, possibly traditional, and probably from Isaiah originally:

> Cola 1–2: Isaiah 64:8 (Colon 1: of Gen. 2:7)
> Colon 3: Isaiah 40:11
> Cola 4–5: Isaiah 44:22–24

The prayer of confession of which it forms a part expresses, in alternation, a note of abject human weakness and sin, over against one of ringing confidence in God's gracious mercy. The limits of the strophe are clearly indicated by anaphora: two alternating series of statements beginning with

> tu es . . .
>
> nous sommes . . .

The antithesis within each colon is introduced by these two phrases set in simple chiastic relation. The Scripture portions have been carefully selected for symmetry and also to sketch or at least suggest the history of salvation. Both cumulative movement and ring-composition are to be noted:

Table 52. Poetic structure of Calvin's *Form of Prayer and Songs of the Church*, "prayer of confession" (1543)

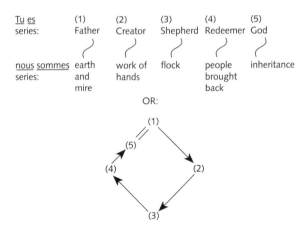

Before we leave Calvin's Strasbourg period, we should pause to look at one of the six Psalms attributed to Calvin in the first French language metrical Psalter with music, produced for the use of his Strasbourg congregation: *Alcuns pseaulmes et cantiques mys en chant.*[28] According to Hughes O. Old,[29] Psalm 113, together with Psalm 138 and the "Song of Simeon," was "intended for the Communion and Post-Communion

Thanksgiving." Unlike the other poetic passages with which this essay is concerned, this text was written in strict metrical form to be sung to a particular tune, by an unknown composer. Calvin has thus adapted here, as in the other Psalms in the book, tunes originally used for German paraphrases of the Psalms, to provide settings for French texts.[30] Unlike, however, the other metrical paraphrases in the collection, it is unrhymed. Hence the paraphrase of Psalm 113 lies between the "found poetry" scattered throughout Calvin's prose writings, and the normally rhymed paraphrases of other Psalms. Needless to say, this piece was quickly replaced with a rhymed version in subsequent editions.

Mention has already been made of Bishop Robert Lowth (1710–87). His analysis of Hebrew poetic parallelism is set forth in his *Praelectiones Academicae de Sacra Poesi Hebraeorum* (1741).[31] Before we look at Calvin's metrical paraphrase of Psalm 113, we shall use Lowth's threefold scheme of parallelism in examining the original Psalm. No two interpreters divide a psalm identically: the analysis here presented is however sufficiently typical to serve our purpose. We are employing, not Calvin's Latin, but the French taken from the French version of his commentary, as printed in *Opera Calvini*. The Psalm falls into three stanzas:

i. verses 1–3	parallelism
Louez l'Eternel, vous serviteurs du Seigneur	1 1–2 synonymous
louez . . . le nom du Seigneur.	2
Le nom du Seigneur soit benit	3 3–4 synthetic
dès ceste heure et à tout iamais.	4
Le nom du Seigneur est louable	5 5–6 synthetic
depuis soleil levant iusques à soleil couchant.	6

ii. verses 4–6	
Le Seigneur est haut eslevé par dessus toutes gens,	1 1–2 synonymous
sa gloire est par dessus les cieux.	2
Qui est semblable au Seigneur nostre Dieu,	3 3–4 to 6 synthetic
qui s'esleve pour habiter,	4 4–5 to 6 antithetical
Qui s'abbaisse pour veoir	5
au ciel et en la terre?	6

iii. verses 7–9	
Redressant le povre de la poudre,	1 1–2 synonymous
il esleve l'affligé de la fiente:	2
Afin qu'il le face seior avec les Princes,	3 3–4 synonymous
avec les Princes de son peuple:	4

28. Published 1539; for ET, with music edited by Stanley Tagg, see *Piety 1978*, 137ff. Psalm 113 appears at 161f.

29. *Patristic Roots of Reformed Worship* (Zürich: Theologischer Verlag Zürich, 1975), 89.

30. *Teutsch Kirchen ampt* (Strasbourg, 1524–25).

31. ET: George Gregory, *Lectures on the Sacred Poetry of the Hebrews* (1787; reprint, Boston: Joseph T. Buckingham, 1815).

Qui fait habiter la sterile avec famille,	5 5–6 synonymous
se resoiouissant mere d'enfans	6
Louez l'Eternel.	7

In his exposition of the Psalm (1555–57) Calvin makes the following chief points:

(1) The praises of God must be continued throughout the whole course of our life.

(2) The Psalmist extends the glory of God's name to all parts of the earth, thus rendering our apathy totally inexcusable.

(3) The loftiness of God's glory, as extolled by the Psalmist, leaves us no cause for indifference.

(4) The requirement that God's praises be celebrated is intensified by contrasting the height of his glory and power with his unbounded goodness.

(5) This contrast of God's majesty and condescension is made solely by way of accommodation to our weak capacity, and to amplify for us his fatherly mercy.

(6) The reference to God's condescension to the most lowly of mankind is to teach us that it is not by our proximity to him, but out of his own free choice that he chooses to care for us.

(7) This condescension toward the lowly points to God's providence: it is not in the theater of the world of nature, but in the theater of the state or kingdom of the church, where seemingly accidental or unexpected events occur, that God displays his wonderful power.

(8) The unexpected turning of a barren woman to fruitfulness further leaves us inexcusable if we do not attentively contemplate the works of God's hand.

Thus the very structure of the Psalm is intended to amplify the note of praise. This is undoubtedly why Calvin selected it for his Psalter. But he was faced with distributing the contents of the Psalm into a stanzaic structure amenable to a tune to which a German text had originally been set. Some expansion and amplification were therefore inevitable to fill out the five stanzas. Diagrammatically his paraphrase appears as set out in table 53).

Commentators on the Book of Psalms have often remarked that however far a translator may depart from the exact words of a psalm, the underlying structure, especially the parallelism, invariably shines through. Calvin has preserved the essential parallelism:

Stanza	Lines	Parallelism
1	1, 2, 3–4	synonymous
	5, 6–7	synonymous
	7a, 7b	antithetical
2	1–2, 3–4	synthetic

Table 53. Calvin's metrical paraphrase of Psalm 113 (1539)

Psalm 113, from *Opera Calvini*, 56.476f

Louez l'Eternel, vous serviteurs du Seigneur ———	*Sus louez Dieu ses Serviteurs,*
louez . . . le nom du Seigneur. ———————	*Louez l'il en est digne*
Le nom du Seigneur soit benit ———	*De la louange de son nom*
	* *Vestre bouche soit pleine.*
	* *Sa Sainct'et haulte maiesté,* 5
	* *Soit exalte'en sa grandeur,*
dès ceste heure et à tout iamais. ———	*Dez maintenant et sans cesse.*
5 *Le nom du Seigneur est louable* ———	*Tant qu'estend le soleil son cours*
depuis soleil levant iusques à soleil couchant. ⟨*	*Dessus toute la terre,*
	Le nom de dieu par tout reluit 10
	* *Plain de magnificence.*
Le Seigneur est haut eslevé ———	*Sus tous peuples et nations*
par dessus toutes gens; ———	*Le Seigneur Dieu est esleué*
sa gloire est par dessus les cieux. ———	*Mesmes tous les cieulx surmonté.*
Qui est semblable au Seigneur nostre Dieu, ———	*Ou a nostre Dieu son pareil* 15
	* *Qui luy ressembl'en gloire:*
10 *qui s'esleve* ———	*Lequel a si hault esleue*
pour habiter, ———	*Son trosne et habitacle?*
Qui s'abbaisse pour veior ———	*Dont il se baiss'a contempler*
ce qui se fait ———	*Les creatures qu'il maintient* 20
au ciel et en la terre? ———	*Tant au ciel comm'en la terre.*
Redressant ———	*Qui le pauur'en terr'abbatu,*
le povre de la poudre ———	*Faict sortir*
il esleve ———	*et esleue*
l'affligé ———	*Qui l'homme nud et aneanty* 25
de la fiente ———	*Suscite de la fiente,*
15 *Afin qu'il le face seoir avec les Princes,* ———	*Pour les haultement colloquer*
	* *Les ayant de miser'oste*
avec les Princes de son peuple:	*Entre les princes du peuple.*
Qui fait habiter ———	*Qui beneist en fecondité* 30
la sterile avec famille, ———	*Les femmes infertiles,*
se resiouissant . . . mere ———	*Celle qui ne pouvoit porter*
d'enfans. ———	*Multipli'en semence.*
Louez l'Eternel. ———	*Sous louez doncques le seigneur*
	* *Rendez la louang'a son nom* 35
	* *Telle que ses faictz meritent.*

	6, 7	synonymous
	5, 6–7	synthetic
3	1, 2	synonymous
	1–2, 3–4	synthetic
	3–4, 5–7	antithetical
	7a, 7b	antithetical
4	1, 2	antithetical/
	3, 4	synthetic
	1–2, 3–4	antithetical/
	5, 6–7	synthetic
	6, 7	synonymous
5	1, 2	synthetic
	3, 4	antithetical
	1–2, 3–4	antithetical
	5, 6–7	antithetical
		synonymous
		synonymous

From this evidence we can conclude that the models for Calvin's occasional poetic passages in his prose works come as much from the Hebraic as from the Greek. The rhetorical heightening that marks such passages is the work of a classical stylist, but one profoundly influenced by the Psalmist, the Prophets, and Paul.

One of the common themes in Calvin's writings is the "most beautiful theater" of the created universe, which, were we not so perverse in our fallenness, would offer ample proofs of God. Calvin expresses this theme in many and varied ways. One of the most striking instances is what may be called "The Hymn to the Sun and to Its Creator" (1543) in *Institutes* 1.16.2.

I	Nullius creaturae mirabilior vel illustrior est	No creature has a force more wondrous
	quam solis.	or glorious than that of the sun.
	Praeterquam enim quod totum orbem illuminat suo fulgore,	For besides lighting the whole earth with its brightness,
5	quantum istud est quod animalia omnia	how great a thing is it that by its heat
	suo calore fovet ac vegetat?	it nourishes and quickens all living things!
	terrae foecunditatem	That with its rays it breathes
	suis radiis inspirat?	fruitfulness into the earth!
	seminibus in eius gremio tepefactis,	That it warms the seeds in the bosom of the earth,
10	herbescentem inde viriditatem elicit,	draws them forth with budding greenness,
	quam novis alimentis	increases and strengthens them,
	suffultam auget ac confirmat,	nourishes them anew,
	donec in culmos assurgat?	until they rise up into stalks!
	quod perpetuo vapore pascit,	That it feeds the plant with continual warmth,
15	donec in florem,	until it grows into flower,
	et ex flore in frugem adolescat?	and from flower into fruit!
	quod tunc etiam excoquendo	That then, also, with baking heat
	ad maturitatem producit?	it brings the fruit to maturity!
	quod arbores similiter et vites ab eo tepefactae	That in like manner trees and vines warmed by the sun
20	gemmant primum ac frondescant,	first put forth buds and leaves,
	deinde florem emittunt,	then put forth a flower,
	et ex flore fructum generant?	and from the flower produce fruit!
II	At Dominus,	Yet the Lord,
	ut solidam horum omnium laudem	to claim the whole credit
25	sibi vendicaret,	for all these things,
	ante et lucem extare voluit,	willed that, before He created the sun,
	et terram omni herbarum et fructuum genere	light should come to be
	refertam esse quam solem crearet.	and earth be filled with all manner of herbs and fruits.
III	Non ergo solem faciet pius homo	Therefore a godly man will not make
30	vel principalem vel necessariam eorum causam	the sun either the principal or the necessary cause

quae ante solis creationem extiterunt,	of those things which existed before the creation of the sun,
sed instrumentum duntaxat quo utitur Deus,	but merely the instrument that God uses
quia ita vult:	because He so wills;
quum possit, eo praeterito,	for with no more difficulty He might abandon it,
35 per seipsum nihilo difficilius agere.	and act through Himself.

The first feature of this passage that strikes the reader as poetic is the carefully constructed sequence of the works of the sun as the agent of plant growth. A series of *quod* clauses is presented, with the verbs chiefly carrying the sense.

On closer inspection, the hymn turns out to be tripartite in structure:

(1)   Nullius creaturae . . . (line 1)
(2)   At Dominus . . . (line 23)
(3)   Non ergo . . . (line 29)

The first stanza is introduced by a general proposition, that the sun seems the highest creation of all. This is then amplified by a chiastically arranged anaphoric series (lines 3–22) that traces the work of the sun from seed to fruit:

lines	
3–4	totum orbem illuminat suo fulgore
5–6	animalia omnia suo calore fovet ac vegetat
7–8	foecunditatem suis radiis inspirat
9	seminibus in eius gremio tepefactis
10	herbescentem . . . viriditatem elicit
11–12	novis alimentis suffultam auget ac confirmat
13	in culmos assurgat
14	perpetuo vapore pascit
15	in florem
16	ex flore in frugem adolescat
17–18	excoquendo ad maturitatem producit
19	arbores . . . et vites ab eo tepefactae
20	gemmant . . . ac frondescant
21	florem emittunt
22	ex flore fructum generant

The chiasmus consists in alternation of word order or amplification (by added words) in the series of similar clauses (anaphora): object (o), verb (v), instrumental ablative (i). For example:

o.v.i.
o.i.vv.   * = expansion (added phrase)
o.i.v.
i*, *o.v. etc.

The strophic character is strengthened by homeoteuleton and assonance (rhyme and near-rhyme of verbs at end of lines), and also by the repetition of *quod,* together with the fuller connective sequence:

> quod . . . donec
> quod . . . donec
> quod . . . deinde.

The repetition of the word *flos* should also be noted:

> in florem . . .
> et ex flore . . . in frugem (also alliteration)
> florem . . .
> et ex flore . . . fructum (also alliteration)

The second stanza begins with *At Dominus.* . . . It consists of a single tightly constructed periodic sentence, expressing a stark contrast with the first stanza:

line		
23	1 Conj. Subj.	At Dominus
24	2 purpose clause	ut . . .
25	3	. . . vendicaret,
26	4a conj. for subordinate temporal clause:	ante . . .
26	4b obj. inf. compl. main verb	et lucem extare voluit
27	5 conj. 2nd subj. abl. phrase	et terram . . .
28	6a 2nd inf. compl.	refertam esse
28	6b conj. temporal clause	quam solem crearet

The third stanza swiftly resolves the antithesis set by the first two. We now realize the chain: nature . . . God . . . humanity . . . God. To summarize more fully: (1) the sun seems the highest creation of all, for all life and growth and fruitfulness depend on it; (2) yet in the order of creation, the sun is subordinated; (3) in consequence, the sun is not to be considered the principal cause of existence by godly man, for God could just as well abandon the structures of nature and act directly through himself.

Thus the four elements that we have noted in Calvin's poetic passages are exhibited also here:

(1) repetition: cola marked by *quod* and other features
(2) contrast: (A) the sun and its power (B) before the sun . . .
(3) cumulative movement:
    stages in the work of the sun: God accommodating his revelation
    man in the order of creation
(4) ring:
    Creator (creating creation to act intermediately)
    End (God acting directly through himself)

Our final poetic passage to be examined comes from Calvin's *Commentary on I Corinthians* (1546), 15:24: "Then shall be the end, when he shall deliver up the kingdom to God, even the Father, when he shall have put down all rule, and all authority and power." The scriptural verse itself exhibits parallelism:

Table 54. Poetic structure of Calvin's *Commentary on I Corinthians* 15:24 (1546)

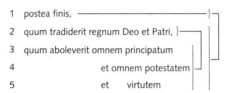

The overall parallelism of members is 1:2–5—synthetic or complementary. 2:3–5 is synonymous parallelism; the tricola of lines 3–5, also synonymous parallelism.

Sicuti finem accipiet mundus,	Even as the world will end
ita et politia,	so also will government
et magistratus,	and magistracy
et leges,	and laws
5 et distinctiones ordinum,	and distinctions of rank
et gradus dignitatum,	and levels of authority
et quicquid tale est.	and all such things.
Non differat amplius servus a domino,	No more will slave differ from master,
10 non rex a plebeio,	king from commoner,
neque a privato magistratus.	magistrate from private citizen.
Quia etiam tum in caelo	Then will cease in heaven
principatus Angelici,	The princedoms of angels;
tum in Ecclesia cessabunt	then will cease in the church
ministeria et praefecturae.	ministries and presidencies
15 Ut solus Deus per seipsum,	God alone may exercise
non per hominum vel Angelorum	His power.
manus potestatem suam	Why?
principatumque exerceat.	That not through the hands
	of men or angels,
	but through Himself
Manebunt quidem Angeli,	Indeed angels will remain,
20 manebit etiam illis sua excellentia;	to them too will remain their pre-eminence;
fulgebunt etiam justi,	the righteous too will shine,
quisquis pro gratiae suae mensura.	each according to the measure of his grace.
Sed Angelis abdicabitur principatus,	But the angels will resign their princedoms
25 quem nunc Dei nomine mandatoque	which in God's name and by His commandment
exercent;	they now exercise;

desinent Episcopi, Doctores, et	bishops, doctors, prophets
Prophetae,	
personam hanc sustinere,	will cease to play their role
et munus quo nunc funguntur,	and the office they now discharge
deponent.[a]	they will lay down.

a. Calvin, *Comm. I Cor.*, 15:24; *OO*, 7:206.

In translating this short five-line poem of Paul's into a larger strophe, Calvin uses both paraphrase and inference:

Scr. verse		Calvin
line		line
1	:	1 (paraphrase)
3–5	:	2–7 (paraphrase)
3–5	:	8–14 (inference)
2	:	15–18 (inference)
	:	19–22 (counter-inference)
3–5	:	23–29 (inference)

Let us now look at several particular features that prompt us, as we read, to deem this a poetic passage. First of all there is the emphasis on the future, driven home by the series of verbs in the future tense, where both sound (homeoteleuton) and sense express this: accipi*et* . . . differ*et* . . . cessa*bunt* . . . mane*bunt* . . . mane*bit* . . . fulge*bunt* . . . abdica*bitur* . . . exer*cent* (pres.) . . . desi*nent* . . . depo*nent* . . .

Lines 8–10 are an instance of tricola:

> servus a domino
> rex a plebeio
> a privato magistratus

The force of this anaphora is heightened by a double chiasmus—both in meaning ABBAAB[32] and in grammatical construction ABABBA:[33]

> lower . . . higher (abl.)
> higher . . . lower (abl.)
> lower (abl.) . . . higher

Or one can view this, from the Hebraic side, as a triple synonymous parallelism.

In lines 11–14 there is an instance of dicola in the form ABAB:

> in caelo principatus . . .
> in Ecclesia . . . ministeria et praefecturae

32. A = lower; B = higher.
33. A = nominative; B = ablative.

In lines 19–22 there is intertwined synonymous and synthetic parallelism:

19	Manebunt quidem Angeli,
	synon.
20	manebit etiam illis sua excellentis
	synon.
21	fulgebunt etiam justi,
	synthe.
22	quisquis pro gratiae suae mensura.

In lines 26–29 there is chiasmus, produced by setting the verb off against the remainder of the clause:

26–27 desinent . . . remainder of clause
28–29 remainder of clause . . . deponent

Beyond these smaller features of style, there are larger structures displaying a careful enjambment of the thought:

Table 55. Poetic structure of Calvin's *Commentary on I Corinthians* 15:24 (1546) (2)

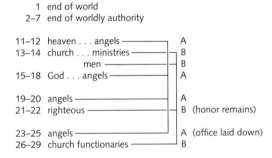

```
 1  end of world
2-7  end of worldly authority

11-12  heaven . . . angels ──────┐  A
13-14  church . . . ministries ──┤┐ B
         men ────────────────────┤┤ B
15-18  God . . . angels ─────────┤┘ A

19-20  angels ───────────────────┐  A
21-22  righteous ────────────────┤  B  (honor remains)

23-25  angels ───────────────────┘  A  (office laid down)
26-29  church functionaries ─────┘  B
```

This larger chiasmus takes the form of **ABBAABAB**.

Conclusion

Why should we examine John Calvin as a poet? Why should we claim as poetry passages that he would never recognize under that name? Can we not account for all the stylistic features of his writings without recourse to this additional category? Can we not with perfect clarity understand his ideas without confusing them with the poetic label?

Earlier, we remarked that the commentators on the Psalms have generally recognized the literary indestructibility of the Psalms against the most inadequate efforts to render the original Hebrew into other languages. There is a sense in which a similar statement can be made of

Calvin: his deep-set patterns of thought and style come through in even the most halting translation. This was the comment of a present-day biographer of Calvin with reference to my own translation of the *Institutes*.[34] If the reader is helped by "lining-out" the text, as I have done in my *Piety of Calvin*, he catches the inevitability of Calvin's spontaneous yet carefully framed structures. We must regard Calvin as a poet because his prose, compared with ours, is poetry. But there are of course degrees of the poetic in him. Some passages stand out above the rest as passionately intense: when the whole plan of God, when the whole long drama of God and man, are seen as in the twinkling of an eye, when all lines seem to converge in a few concentrated, compressed lines—then we must understand this with ear and heart as well as with eye and mind. Faith for Calvin is as much a matter of the heart as of the mind, as much affective as intellectual. These "faith-hymns" bespeak this twin emphasis. Yes, we must regard Calvin as a poet.

But he is a poet, like many of those Christian writers who preceded him, in both the classical and the Hebraic way. We said earlier that as poet he probably owes more to Paul and David than to Virgil or Horace or Ovid. Yet the rhythms of classical poetry were learned by him at a tender age, and are a not inconsiderable part of his style. Perhaps we can say that he is a living witness to the advice of Augustine, expressed in the *De Doctrina Christiana*, that classical rhetoric is to be pressed into the service of the church. There is therefore a true marriage of the Hebraic and the classical in him. In his commentaries on the Scriptures, Calvin recognizes that rhetoric bursts the bounds of particular languages: he makes natural, unforced use of Greek rhetorical categories in catching the drift of a prophet's or an apostle's speech. Yet he also understands what is distinctive about the Hebraic idiom.

This exegetical insight is carried over into the rhetoric of his theological discourse. He practices the rhetorical forms; he thinks and writes in those forms. And at the most intense moments of his discourse, the shackles of a prosaic style fall away in flights of poetry, of hymn, of song.

When Calvin is driving home those themes closest to his heart—the clear evidence of God in the theater of the universe and in the theater of human history and society and church, the consequent inexcusability of human blindness, the mystery of God's merciful condescension summed up in the incarnation of Christ, the great ring of the going forth from God and return to him of the physical creation, the ineffable mysteries of God before which we must stand in mute adoration: these themes demand a higher and deeper speech than mere prose can give.

In the over four hundred years since Calvin's death in 1564, Trent and Vatican I have been followed by Vatican II: those necessary scholastic

---

34. Duncan Norton-Taylor, "God's Man Calvin" (M.D. thesis, Oxford University, 1971), "author's note," 2.

responses on the part of Reformed Christianity to post-Tridentine Roman Catholic scholasticism, Dort and Westminster—necessary to preserve nascent Protestantism at a difficult juncture—await their successor. Today we hear the sweetly siren strains of cheap, trite grace, strummed and sung by our young Christian troubadours. They know not the virile Calvinian poetry of the faith: their song comes as a spontaneous reaction to the wilderness of dry prose wherein they discern the faith of their fathers-to-be. They are calling for the exodus to be resumed. But where is the Joshua who is to take over from Moses?

7   True Piety According to Calvin[1]

Piety Defined in Word and Act

Piety Defined by Calvin

In his first *Catechism* (published in French in 1537 and in Latin in 1538), John Calvin defined the untranslatable word *pietas,* which for him was the shorthand symbol for his whole understanding and practice of Christian faith and life:

> True piety does not consist in a fear which willingly indeed flees God's judgment, but since it cannot escape is terrified. True piety consists rather in a sincere feeling which loves God as Father as much as it fears and reverences Him as Lord, embraces His righteousness, and dreads offending Him worse than death. And whoever have been endowed with this piety dare not fashion out of their own rashness any God for themselves. Rather, they seek from Him the knowledge of the true God, and conceive Him just as He shows and declares Himself to be.[2]

Calvin more succinctly defined *pietas* in the *Institutes* as "that reverence joined with love of God which the knowledge of his benefits induces."[3] Besides *pietas* he set *religio*—"faith so joined with an earnest fear of God that this fear also embraces willing reverence, and carries with it such legitimate worship as is prescribed in the law."[4] Note that in these definitions of *pietas* and *religio,* a number of other basic terms are interlaced: *faith, fear, reverence, love, knowledge.* One might diagram their interrelationship as in table 56.

To grasp the full amplitude of *pietas,* let us examine a few of the many references to the word scattered throughout Calvin's commentaries and other writings. In the *Commentary on the Psalms* (119:78f.) he taught

---

1. From *Piety 1978,* 13–26. Used by permission.
2. *Catechism 1538,* 2.
3. *Inst.* 1.2.1.
4. Ibid., 1.2.2.

Table 56. Interrelationships of piety and religion

that the true nature of *pietas* is seen in the two marks of believers: (1) honor, the obedience rendered to God as Father; (2) fear, the service done God as Lord.[5] Distinct from this is the unbeliever's fear, which rests not on faith *(fides)* but on unfaith *(diffidentia)*.[6] Knowledge also enters largely into the concept of *pietas*. In the *Commentary on Jeremiah* (10:25) Calvin spoke of knowledge of God *(cognitio Dei)* as the beginning of *pietas*. Calling on God's name *(invocatio)* is the fruit of the knowledge of God and is evidence of *pietas*.[7] In the *Institutes* Calvin spoke of the first step toward *pietas* as "to know that God is a father to us."[8] Elsewhere he asserted that there is no *pietas* without true instruction, as the name *disciples* indicates.[9] "True religion and worship of God," he said, "arise out of faith, so that no one duly serves God save him who has been educated in His school."[10]

Calvin also related piety and love *(caritas)*. In *Praelectiones in Ezekiel* (18:5) he spoke of *pietas* as the root of *caritas*.[11] *Pietas* means the fear or reverence of God; but we also fear God when we live justly among our brethren.[12] This relationship between our reverential attitude toward God and our attitude toward neighbor is further developed in a sermon on Deuteronomy 5:16:

> And this is why the heathen have applied this word *pietas* to the honor we render to father, mother, and all those in authority over us. *Pietas*, properly speaking, is the reverence we owe to God: but the pagans, although they were poor blind folk, recognized that God not only wills to be served

5. *Commentary on the Psalms* (Ps. 119:78f.), *OC*, 32:249; cf. *Inst.* 3.2.26.
6. *Inst.* 3.2.27.
7. *Commentary on Jeremiah* (Jer. 10:25), *OC*, 38:96.
8. *Inst.* 2.6.4.
9. *Commentary on Acts* (Acts 18:22), *OC*, 48:435.
10. *Commentary on the Psalms* (Ps. 119:78f.), *OC*, 32:249.
11. *Lectures on Ezekiel* (Ezek. 18:5), *OC*, 40:426.
12. See renderings of *hāsîd, mansuetus,* etc., where piety is related to the kindness of man (Ps. 16:10, etc.).

in His majesty, but when we obey the persons who rule over us, in sum, He wills to prove our obedience at this point. And thus, inasmuch as fathers and mothers, magistrates, and all those who have authority, are lieutenants of God and represent His person, it is certain that if one show them contempt and reject them, that it is like declaring that one does not want to obey God at all.[13]

Yet Calvin places *pietas* higher than *caritas*, for God towers over man; still, "believers seriously testify, by honoring mutual righteousness among themselves, that they honor God."[14]

The connection between the pagan and Christian notions of *pietas* is pursued further in the *Commentary on John*. Here Calvin admitted "that some grains of *pietas* were ever scattered throughout the world" but "that by God, through the hand of philosophers and profane writers, were sowed the excellent sentiments to be found in their writings."[15] Aratus' couplet quoted by Paul (who spoke to infidels and those ignorant of true *pietas*) is "the testimony of a poet who confessed a knowledge engraved by nature upon men's minds."[16]

That Calvin's youthful classical studies had laid the groundwork for this classical as well as Christian understanding of the word *pietas* is clear from his *Commentary on Seneca's De Clementia*, published in 1532 when Calvin was twenty-two years of age. In explaining the Senecan phrase "nor the piety of his children," Calvin drew together what we may assume were the chief classical texts that were mingled, after his conversion, with scriptural and patristic uses to shape the word in his thought. Note that among the pagan classical writers is to be found a quotation from Augustine's *City of God*. Here are Calvin's words:

> Cicero, *Pro Plancio* (33.80): *What is piety, if not a benevolent gratitude to one's parents?* Quintilian (5.10.12): *Just as those things that are admitted by the general consent of mankind, such as that there are gods, and that piety is to be shown to parents.* Yet in order that my readers may understand what piety really is, I shall append Cicero's words from the *Topics* (23.90): *Equity is also said to have three parts: one pertains to the gods in heaven, the second to the spirits of the departed, the third to men. The first is called "piety," the second "sanctity," the third "justice" or "equity."* Thus far Cicero. But since parents are for us so speak in the place of the gods, to them is diverted what Augustine hints at (*De civitate Dei*, 10.1.3): *Piety, properly speaking, is commonly understood as worship of God, which the Greeks call eusebeia. Yet this eusebeia is said to be exercised by way of obligation toward parents also.* But we also use the term when we wish to express a

13. *Sermons on Deuteronomy* (Deut. 5:16), *OC*, 26:312.
14. Ibid. This is the habitual twofold division (God and man) that Calvin applied to the Decalogue (*Inst.* 2.8.11) and the Lord's Prayer (3.20.35).
15. *Commentary on John* (John 4:36), *OC*, 47:96.
16. *Commentary on Acts* (Acts 17:28), *OC*, 48:417.

particularly forceful love. Cicero (*Ep. Fam.*, 1.9.1): *I was very much pleased with your letter, which made me realize that you fully appreciate my piety toward you; for why should I say "my good will" whenever the term "piety" itself, most solemn and sacred as it is, does not seem to me impressive enough to describe my obligation to you?*[17]

As this collection of classical passages indicates, the words *pius* and *pietas* in classical Latin referred first to the relationship of children to their parents.[18] In the Roman family of the *paterfamilias* and the *materfamilias*, children were expected to fear, honor, obey, and love their parents. *Pietas* bespoke the mutual love and care between parents and their offspring.

The state was, after all (as Aristotle described it in his *Politics*),[19] but the extension of the family. The king or emperor was the *pater patriae*, the father of his country.[20] Parricide, in Roman eyes the most horrendous crime of which human beings are capable, and subject to the cruelest and most unusual punishment of all, was extended to assassination of the ruler, as the parent of all.[21] *Pietas*, then, in the larger sense, summarized all the feelings of loyalty, love of country, and self-sacrifice for the common good that marked Roman citizenship.

The early Christians, whose supreme Ruler and Father was God, without divesting the word *pietas* of its familial and national meaning, carried the word to a higher use. For them the whole complex of relationships between God the Father and his earthly children was summed up in this one word. For Calvin, then, there is in the word the classical overshine of filial obedience. *Pietas* bespeaks the walk of us adopted children of God the Father, adopted brothers and sisters of Christ the Son.

So far we have dealt mainly with the "inner" meaning of *pietas*. It also had an external meaning for Calvin. In *On the Harmony of the Gospels* (Matt. 12:7 and parallels) he argued, with our Lord, that certain types of manual labor were permitted on the Sabbath—those connected with the worship of God—and spoke of the *officia pietatis*, which we might render "religious duties." In the same passage Calvin suggested the modern hypocritical connotation of *piety*, speaking of the "hypocrites who pretend *pietas* by outward signs and grievously pervert it by sticking in carnal worship alone."[22]

---

17. *Comm. Sen. De Clem.*, 226–29.
18. Compare Justinian's comment: "For the power of the father ought to consist in piety, not cruelty" (*Digest* 48.9.5.); cited by Calvin in *Comm. Sen. De Clem.*, 254–57.
19. 1.3–13 (1253 bl–1260 b25); cf. *Nicomachean Ethics* 8.11 (1160 cl). Note is from Calvin, *Comm. Sen. De Clem.*, 170f.
20. Calvin, *Comm. Sen. De Clem.*, 263–39.
21. Ibid., 252–55; cf. 308f.
22. *OC*, 45:324f.; cf. *Inst.* 1.4.4, where Calvin contrasts true and false *pietas*.

Calvin's meaning will emerge more clearly as we seek out the scriptural basis of his concept of *pietas*. The New Testament word uniformly rendered by the Latin *pietas* is ευσέβεια. It is found almost exclusively in the pastoral and general Epistles, appearing elsewhere in the New Testament only at Acts 3:12. Of the fifteen references in the former, the Revised Standard Version translates all but three as "godliness." The word is used in the Septuagint to denote "the duty which man owes to God—piety, godliness, religion."[23] In the Septuagint the word is chiefly found in the Apocrypha.

Piety Mirrored in Calvin's Life

If this, then, is what piety meant for Calvin, we will certainly find in the accounts of his conversion, however meager, help in understanding how this concept was shaped in his own life.

Much ink has been spilled in discussion and speculation on the date, circumstances, and character of Calvin's decision to accept the Reformation faith. I have dealt with the shape of his conversion in my translation of the *Institution* of 1536.[24] Classic accounts of conversion usually cite some verse of Scripture as triggering the change. Augustine's experience of *"Tolle, Lege!"* ("Take up and read!") in the garden near Milan led him through Romans 13:13f. to Bishop Ambrose and Christian baptism. Luther was captivated by Romans 1:17. We have no such definite information on the specific Scripture that brought about Calvin's change of heart. A close study of the evidence has, however, led me to suggest that it very probably was Romans 1:18–25. More specifically the text may well have been Romans 1:21 ("for although they knew God they did not honor him as God or give thanks to him, but they became futile in their thinking and their senseless minds were darkened" RSV).[25]

The central themes of Calvin's piety are the honoring of God and being thankful to him; they are interwoven in the recital of his conversion in the preface to the *Commentary on the Psalms*[26] and in the account of the Reformed Christian's confession before God's judgment seat in Calvin's *Reply to Cardinal Sadolet*.[27]

Calvin's newfound faith is early expressed in his preface to the French translation of the New Testament made by his cousin Pierre

---

23. Walter Bauer, *A Greek-English Lexicon of the New Testament*, ed. and trans. by William F. Arndt and F. Wilbur Gingrich, 2nd ed. (Chicago: University of Chicago Press, 1979), 326.

24. See my introduction in *Inst. 1536a*, xviff.; *Inst. 1536b*, xxviff.

25. *Inst. 1536a*, xviif.; *Inst. 1536b*, xxvi–xxvii.

26. See *Piety 1978*, ch. 1.

27. See my introduction to *Inst. 1536a*, xxiiiff.; *Inst. 1536b*, xxxiiff. T. H. L. Parker rejected this passage from Calvin's *Reply to Cardinal Sadolet* as a "source." See *John Calvin: A Biography* (Philadelphia: Westminster, 1975), 162.

Robert (Olivétan).[28] Almost contemporaneous with this are the early pages of chapter 1, "On the Law," of the 1536 *Institution*. I call this in chapter 2 "The Kernel of Calvin's Faith."

It is the intolerable contrast between God's absolute perfection and man's fallenness that initiated Calvin's religious quest. Like Augustine, he saw no instant perfection succeeding the event of conversion—however *"subita"*[29] it seemed; there is rather a growth into the Christian life to a perfection beyond death—all the gracious gift of God in Christ. So he begins this "kernel" account of faith with the two knowledges: of God's glory, justice, mercy, and gentleness; and of fallen man's ignorance, iniquity, impotence, death, and judgment. In the third place, we are shown the law—the written law of the Old Testament and the inwardly written law of conscience—as God's first effort to bridge the gulf between Creator and created. The law is for us a mirror in which to discern and contemplate our sin and curse. It leads us to the impasse of being called to glorify, honor, and love our Lord and Father, but unable to perform these duties. Therefore we deserve the curse, judgment— eternal death. This was indeed the sequence of Calvin's experience, or more accurately, it was the shape which in retrospect he gave his experience in the light of the Pauline-Augustinian tradition and which he generalized in his teaching.

But the impasse, through God's mercy, is breached; another way is opened to us. It is forgiveness of sins through Christ. Calvin's "kernel," in its fourth and final section, comes back once more to the knowledge of ourselves, of our poverty and ruin. The lesson of this knowledge is that we learn to humble ourselves, cast ourselves before God, seek his mercy. Thus will Christ, our leader, the only Way to reach the Father, bring us into eternal blessedness. Our piety, then, is our pathway, in grace, from estrangement to reunion with our Creator. It is the way of suffering but also of joy.

Thus Calvin's conversion took a lifetime to be worked out. We cannot here summarize that brief but crowded life. But we can look at several episodes in it that will explain why he believed in the third use of the law—its pedagogical use as tutor to converted Christians—and denominated it the law's chief use.[30] His life will also exemplify his teaching on calling, that the Christian must, like a sentry, stand guard at his post while he lives.[31]

First, look at how Calvin was called to his initial ministry in Geneva. His initial vision of the Christian life (like Augustine's) was that of a re-

---

28. Introduction, *Inst. 1536a*, xxivf.; *Inst. 1536b*, xxxivff.

29. The word *subita* ("sudden, unexpected") has spawned a considerable literature. For discussion, see *Piety 1978*, ch. 1, line 257 (note).

30. Calvin called the law the perfect guide to all duties of piety and love (*Inst.* 2.8.51).

31. Cf. *Inst.* 3.9.4; 3.10.6.

tired, contemplative, intellectual study of the faith. William Farel, that hotheaded pioneer of the French-language Reformation who was spurned in his invitation to Calvin to work with him in Geneva, a city that had just chosen the Reformed faith, had recourse to imprecation and threat: "You are following," he thundered at Calvin, "your own wishes and I declare, in the name of God Almighty, that if you do not assist us in this work of the Lord, the Lord will punish you for seeking your own interest rather than his."[32]

And so, against his will, Calvin took up the task at Geneva as at the invitation of God himself. After Calvin's banishment in 1538 from Geneva, Bucer used the same threat to persuade him to assume pastoral and teaching duties at Strasbourg.[33]

Calvin was subsequently importuned from his happy pastoral relationship with a tiny French congregation in Strasbourg to return to Geneva.[34] It must be said that the Strasbourg sojourn was crucial in working out pastorally, practically, and liturgically the full meaning of *pietas*. In his study of the sufferings of the patriarchs, Calvin mirrored his own *tolerantia crucis:* Abraham, Isaac, Jacob, and the rest, David included, withstood terrible hardships, pain, suffering, because they were on pilgrimage. The hope that was to come fed them on their journey.[35] This, too, was the secret of Calvin's triumphant struggle against the overwhelming odds that faced him and his world. This, too, kept alive his feeble body, taxed as it constantly was beyond its strength. This, too, enabled him to maintain a ceaseless literary output of the highest order and one so decisive for posterity.

Piety in Calvin's View of the Christian Life

We have endeavored to define *pietas* in Calvin's own words and his own acts. Let us now turn to the principles of *pietas* as he worked them out in his *Institutes of the Christian Religion*. In doing this, it will be necessary to examine more fully the transition years (1538–41) of the Strasbourg exile, which we have just now lightly sketched.

The portion of Calvin's *Institutes* on which we would like to concentrate our attention at this time comprises, in the final Latin edition of that book printed in the author's lifetime (1559), chapters 6–10 of Book III.[36] One may search in vain the pages of the first edition of that work (1536) for any section corresponding to this one on the Christian life.[37]

32. Beza, *Vita Calvini*, in *OC*, 21:125.41ff.; ET by Henry Beveridge in John Calvin, *Tracts and Treatises*, 1:xxix.
33. See *Piety 1978*, ch. 1, line 445 (note).
34. See *Piety 1978*, ch. 1, line 469 (note).
35. *Inst.* 2.10f.
36. Translated in *Piety 1978*, ch. 3.
37. Section at 3.8.1ff. of the 1559 edition of the *Institutes* is hinted at in the 1536 edition. See *Inst. 1536a*, 55; *Inst. 1536b*, 40–41.

Actually (with some subsequent additions) it dates from 1539, the year of the second Latin edition, and remained in all editions from 1539 to 1554 the final chapter of the *Institutes*. Why was such an important subject so belatedly treated by Calvin?

The clue to the answer lies, I believe, in a comparison of what Calvin wrote before he went to Strasbourg in 1538 and what he wrote after that date. On the one hand, examine the *Institution* of 1536, the *Articles Concerning the Organization of the Church and Worship* of January 1537,[38] and the *Confession and Catechism of the Church of Geneva* of 1537–38.[39] On the other hand, examine the *Institutes* of 1539 (in which he placed the treatise "On the Christian Life"); his *Several Psalms and Songs Set for Singing*, also of 1539;[40] and his 1540 *Commentary on Romans*. Add to these the literary output immediately following his return to Geneva from Strasbourg in 1541—that is, the *Draft Ecclesiastical Ordinances* of 1541, *The Form of Prayers* of 1542, and the third Latin edition of the *Institutes* (1543). What does a comparison show?[41] We see a real growth in Calvin the churchman, in his grasp of the practical problems both of individual Christians and of the church as the society of Christians. All of these works are directed to the perfecting either of the Christian life or of the liturgical and disciplinary functioning of the church. Together they mark the significant changes that were later to be incorporated into Books III and IV of the 1559 *Institutes*. Both the *Institution* of 1536 and the *Catechism* of 1537–38 were cast in the traditional catechetical mold: Decalogue, Apostles' Creed, Lord's Prayer, sacraments. In Geneva the efforts to enforce acceptance of the *Confession* and *Catechism* of 1537–38, household by household, and oversight of morals, district by district, ended in failure and banishment from the city for both Farel and Calvin, as we have seen, in April 1538. What had gone wrong? Let us quickly review the facts.

On Sunday, 21 May 1536, the General Council of Geneva had unanimously voted by a show of hands to abolish the Mass and other papal ceremonies and abuses, images, and idols, and had sworn with God's help to live in the holy gospel law and Word of God. The duly appointed Reforming pastors, William Farel and John Calvin, had taken their city fathers at their word and had planned literally to transform the city into a gospel community that had its true center in the Lord's Table. This was not to be, however. The public documents of 1536–37, as a consequence, underwent (after Calvin's Strasbourg sojourn) a clarification of

38. See John Calvin, *Theological Treatises*, ed. and trans. by J. K. S. Reid, Library of Christian Classics, 22 (Philadelphia: Westminster, 1954), 47–55.

39. See "Letter" in *Catechism 1538*, viiff.

40. See *Piety 1978*, ch. 6.

41. Cf. Ford Lewis Battles, "Against Luxury and License in Geneva," 186ff.; see ch. 9 herein.

disciplinary procedures and a development of church polity in those of 1541–43. The *Institutes* of 1539 shows a greater maturity and fullness in its understanding of the formation of the individual Christian than does the *Institution* of 1536. Similarly, the next edition, that of 1543, quite surpasses both the first and the second editions in its grasp of ecclesiology. Calvin indeed learned from experience, both in the first two years in Geneva and in the three-year interim in Strasbourg under Martin Bucer's tutelage.

We may infer that the short treatise "On the Christian Life"[42] is in a sense the firstfruits of Calvin's reflection on his 1536–38 failure. He realized, it would seem, that catechetical statements on such topics as faith, repentance, justification, regeneration, election, and related heads of doctrine—however clearly stated—would not suffice to transform men's hearts, even though their minds might give intellectual assent to the new faith. A deeper reflection on the christological foundations of the Christian life, particularly as they had been set forth by the apostle Paul, was called for. This short treatise supplied the lack we have noted in the 1536 *Institution* and the *Catechism* of 1537–38.

We must, however, slightly qualify this judgment. The 1536 *Institution* contains certain short blank spaces in the text as printed, called *alinea*, at which points—in later editions—expansions of materials were made. This fact seems to bear out what Calvin himself says of his progress through the various editions of the *Institutes*, as he speaks to the reader in 1559: "I was never satisfied until the work had been arranged in the order now set forth."[43] Also, the *Catechism* of 1537–38, while largely an epitome of the prior edition of the *Institution*, does presage important changes to come in the *Institutes* of 1539.[44]

What, then, does the short treatise "On the Christian Life" tell us about Calvin's continuing pilgrimage of faith?

First, we see further reflection on the contrast between the philosophers and Scripture.[45] Calvin had, in his conversion, already rejected the Greek and Latin authors as moral guides. Here the contrast between them becomes sharper and more detailed. But some vestiges of their influence still remain. This can be illustrated by his attitude here expressed toward Stoicism. Rejected are Stoic notions of fate and of the passionless "wise man" and Stoic strictures against pity. We might here note in passing that even before his conversion Calvin had begun to

42. See *Piety 1978*, ch. 3.
43. *Inst.*, 3.
44. See my preface to *Catechism 1538* (p. x) and the comparative table at the end of that volume.
45. Cf. *Inst.* 1.15.8. The crucial place of man's Fall, not understood by the philosophers, was recognized by Calvin in his understanding of the soul in its present state (1.15.6–8; this is apparent mainly in the 1559 edition but to some extent in the 1539 edition), a reflection of Calvin's conversion insight.

show such an attitude, as his *Commentary on Seneca's De Clementia*, which we previously quoted, reveals. But the Stoics' call to follow God, their insistence that we are born to help one another, and their preaching of moderation and frugality[46] are sufficiently close to Calvin's Christian piety to remain a part of his moral teaching.

Second, since penning his first great theological essay of 1536, Calvin had come to know the early Church Fathers, both Greek and Latin, far better. The homilies of a Basil or of a Chrysostom or the writings of a Cyprian or an Ambrose filled in gaps in his pastoral knowledge. Most important of all, Augustine brought him to a deeper understanding of Paul.[47] He was therefore in a position in the spring of 1539, after five months as pastor of the French congregation in Strasbourg and a brief visit with Bucer to Frankfurt, to write this portion of his forthcoming second Latin edition of the *Institutes*. On 12 May Calvin began to lecture on the Epistles of Paul to the Corinthians.[48] On 16 October he dedicated his shortly-to-be-published *Commentary on Romans* to the Basil savant Simon Grynaeus. This concentration on Pauline studies is reflected in the treatise "On the Christian Life." Not only is it steeped in Paul's thought; Calvin's very purpose smacks of Paul's way of working in the churches: "to show some order whereby the Christian man may be led and directed to order his life aright." This is Calvin's announced intention.

The treatise "On the Christian Life" is a marvel of brevity. After a call to the holiness that God demands of his children, a holiness deep within the heart, Calvin began to describe the lifelong process of growth into Christian perfection in and through Christ.[49] Here Calvin was consciously standing on a middle ground between the two-tiered Roman Catholic notion of the Christian life[50] and the instant perfection he rightly or wrongly inferred from the teaching of the Anabaptists.[51]

He then moved on to describe the christological pattern as it unfolds inwardly in the heart—"Denial of Self."[52] The same following of Christ is then traced in the outward life as the "Bearing of the Cross."[53]

---

46. On Calvin's teaching on frugality and its relation to the "blue laws" of Geneva, see Battles, "Against Luxury and License in Geneva," 182ff.; see ch. 9 herein.

47. Referring to the Tenth Commandment, Calvin said, "It was Augustine who first opened the way for me to understand this commandment" (*Inst.* 2.8.50).

48. Cf. *Piety 1978*, ch. 3, line 558 (note).

49. See *Piety 1978*, ch. 3, lines 1–280.

50. In his *Reply to Cardinal Sadolet* (1539) Calvin confessed that his own Christian nurture (under the Romanism into which he had been born) was quite inadequate for right worship, hope of salvation, or duties of the Christian life. See *Inst. 1536a*, xixf. But cf. note 26, above.

51. See *Inst. 1536a*, 375f. (note on line 34, p. 152); *Inst. 1536b*, 286.

52. See *Piety 1978*, ch. 3, lines 281–905.

53. Ibid., lines 906–1505.

He next turned to an examination first of the present,[54] then of the future life.[55] I have sometimes asked my students reading Book III in the *Institutes* to stop after reading chapter 9 and write down their impressions, then go on to chapter 10 and do the same once more. At the end of chapter 9 Calvin sounds like a medieval monk, reflecting on the vanities of the world; at the end of chapter 10, he is clearly free of medievalism! The secret? *It is the hope of the life to come that gives meaning and purpose to the life in which we presently are.*[56]

As one reads these pages, one feels in a field of magnetic force, set between poles. Calvin's deep religious insight was born in controversy. Constantly he strove to find a middle, scripturally informed ground between extremes: here it lies between Roman Catholic and Anabaptist. When we study Calvin, we can never flatten out his thought, excerpt it, generalize from it. We must read it in its totality, and within the historical, biblical, and theological context out of which it came. Our own view and practice of the Christian life, in like manner, must issue from pondering on the deep antinomies of the faith in our own time. Yet there is a great deal that Calvin can say to us about the conduct of the Christian life in this last quarter of the twentieth century. Right in this section, for example, he enunciated a principle of Christian stewardship of nature and of style of living that speaks to our present ecological crisis.[57] Before the great technological advances of recent centuries, before the present age of extraterrestrial exploration, Calvin knew the planet Earth was what we today call a "closed ecosystem." Here and elsewhere in his writings he tells us how the creation is to be used by man.

> Moses now adds, that the earth was given to man, with this condition, that he should occupy himself in its cultivation. Whence it follows, that men were created to employ themselves in some work, and not to lie down in inactivity and idleness. This labor, truly, was pleasant, and full of delight, entirely exempt from all trouble and weariness; since, however, God ordained that man should be exercised in the culture of the ground, he condemned, in his person, all indolent repose. Wherefore, nothing is more contrary to the order of nature, than to consume life in eating, drinking, and sleeping, while in the meantime we propose nothing to ourselves to do. Moses adds, that the custody of the garden was given in charge to Adam, to show that we possess the things which God has committed to our hands, on the condition, that being content with a frugal and moderate use of them, we should take care of what shall remain. Let him who possesses a field, so partake of its yearly fruits, that he may not

54. Ibid., lines 1506–1952.
55. Ibid., lines 1953–2255.
56. See ibid., line 1662 (note).
57. See ibid., lines 2133ff. (note).

suffer the ground to be injured by his negligence; but let him endeavor to hand it down to posterity as he received it, or even better cultivated. Let him so feed on its fruits, that he neither dissipates it by luxury, nor permits [it] to be marred or ruined by neglect. Moreover, that this economy, and this diligence, with respect to those good things which God has given us to enjoy, may flourish among us; let every one regard himself as the steward of God in all things which he possesses. Then he will neither conduct himself dissolutely, nor corrupt by abuse those things which God requires to be preserved.[58]

Calvin believed, too, as we have said, in gradual growth in the Christian life.[59] Does not the very writing of this section illustrate his own growth, not to be complete until his death in 1564?

How may we sum up, for our own use, Calvin's teaching on *pietas*, on Christian discipleship? From Calvin's experience, as we have just reviewed it, and from our own experience of trying to live the Christian life in these times, we may infer a few general principles that may assist us in our search of a style of living commensurate with the gospel.

1. One cannot really understand a particular Christian's view of discipleship apart from his times and apart from his own distinctive experience of Christ.

2. Also, certain tacit assumptions that we make in our daily living must be identified, and at least momentarily set aside, if we are to understand a classic theologian's teaching: for example, (1) the myth of human self-sufficiency and of scientific-technological supremacy; (2) the treatment of God as a shadowy concept, not very important for daily life; (3) the notion of the Scriptures as a human book, rather like other books; (4) the rejection of an afterlife and the concentration of all human attention and effort on the present life; (5) the emphasis on the production of goods and the notion of human beings as consuming animals; and (6) the view of humans as creatures whose wants are to be satisfied.

3. Conversely, to understand Calvin's view of Christian discipleship, we must for the moment open our minds to certain basic assumptions that he makes: (1) humanity's total dependence on God; (2) nature being ours to use and enjoy, but with moderation and accountability; (3) God's providential care; (4) the contrast between philosophers and Scripture; (5) the afterlife being not only the goal of the present life, but its nourishment in hope; (6) all goods as the gifts of God's kindness to us; and (7) the account we will at the end render to God of their use.

---

58. *Commentary on Genesis* [on Gen. 2:15], trans. by John King, 2 vols. (Edinburgh: Calvin Translation Society, 1847–1850), 1:125.

59. See notes 49 and 50, above.

Obstacles to Piety According to the Polemical Tracts

One thing that has marked all great theologians, from the apostle Paul on, is that their finest theology has been called forth by specific requests for help. At bottom, then, true theology and true exegesis are an exercise of the pastoral office. Calvin claimed a double pastoral intent for the *Institutes:* (1) to introduce neophytes to the study of the Scriptures; (2) to justify the French evangelicals before a hostile government and (if we may add its corollary) to hearten these evangelicals in their effort to lead a Christian life under harsh circumstances.

Also for the heartening of beleaguered Christians, but even more pointed than Calvin's theological and exegetical works, are selected polemical works from his pen, most of them undertaken in response to anguished cries for help from evangelical Christians. This class of writings is virtually unknown except to specialists, yet they carry the teaching of *pietas* that necessary further step: to overcome the obstacles that commonly stand in the way of leading the Christian life for members of churches in the Reformed tradition. From this rich store of pastoral instruction, we have selected three tracts for a brief perusal: *On Scandals* (1550),[60] *Excuse to the Nicodemites* (1544),[61] and *What a Faithful Man . . . Ought to Do Dwelling amongst the Papists* (1543).[62]

On Scandals (1550)

Reformed Christians, especially the French, underwent great vexations on account of the faith. Calvin for a long time pondered writing a tract to amplify the spiritual advice he had already given in the *Institutes.* Many persecuted evangelicals sought refuge in Geneva; extensive correspondence also kept Calvin informed of the plight of the French Reformed who remained at home. In September 1546 Calvin wrote to Farel that he was suspending work on such a tract because of labors on the *Commentary on Galatians;* the tract was completed in August 1550. The occasion for it was the misfortune of his friend, Laurence de Normandie, who after accepting the Reformed faith gave up his country and social position in favor of the gospel, and in the space of a year lost his father, wife, and little daughter. It is understandable that Laurence was tempted to read in these events the curse of God attendant upon his change of religion. Calvin took up his pen both to console Laurence in his great loss and to strengthen him in the faith.

The gospel teaches that Christ himself is a scandal, and we cannot follow the gospel apart from scandal. The danger of this rock of offense

---

60. *OC,* 8:1–64; *OS,* 2:162–340. For a recent English translation, see Calvin, *Concerning Scandals,* trans. by John W. Fraser (Grand Rapids: Eerdmans, 1978).

61. *OC,* 6:589–614. For critical text, see Francis M. Higman, ed., *Three French Treatises* (London: Athlone, 1970).

62. *OC,* 6:537–88. Translated into English by "R. G." (Ippyswiche: J. Oswen, 1548).

has turned four classes of people away from the gospel: those who are so naturally modest as to be horror-struck at the scandal, and dare not even taste the gospel; those who are too lazy or sluggish or unteachable to bother with the gospel; those who reject the gospel because they are arrogant and perversely convinced of their own wisdom; and finally those who maliciously and deliberately collect all sorts of scandal and even invent many to deform the gospel out of hatred for it.

Calvin saw three sorts of scandals on which people stumble: those intrinsic to gospel teaching itself; those "annexed" scandals that arise out of the preaching of the gospel; those "adventitious" scandals that spring from moral depravity, hypocrisy, the ingratitude and vanity of worldly professors of the faith.

"Intrinsic" scandals characterize those who take offense at the gospel because of the simplicity of its language. The Christian doctrines, in Calvin's view, that commonly stir disgust in men's minds include the two natures of Christ, salvation obtained from Christ's sufferings alone, his becoming a curse for us and thus blessing us, our righteousness being in God only and not in ourselves, Christ's cross, our self-denial, and constancy in time of persecution. Here Calvin eloquently summarized the long chronicle of the church's sufferings.[63] Finally he noted the scandals of those who ascribe their sins to God or stumble at the doctrine of predestination.

The "annexed" scandals that arise when the gospel is preached lead to sects and controversies among Christian teachers. Some are offended because the gospel often gives rise to strife and war. Calvin replied that war is justified if it is for the souls; Christ foretold wars. The "cultured despisers" of the gospel (such as the circle of Rabelais) raise a scandal by converting Christian freedom into licentiousness.

Wicked ministers of the gospel living among the good are the cause of scandal; the gospel is not chargeable with their guilt; throughout its history offenses appear; the commingling of the wicked with the good is intended to prove the faith of the latter. Another source of offense is the easy enticement of some people from the profession of the truth. Over against this, Calvin set the courage of the women of Artois and the Netherlands.

"Adventitious" scandals spring from moral depravity, hypocrisy, and the ingratitude and vanity of worldly professors of the faith. Among the calumnies hurled at Reformed Christians by opposing preachers were the charges that the Reformed had abrogated auricular confession, condemned fasting, abandoned celibacy, and opened marriage to all.

Calvin closed the treatise with an eloquent admonition to unity under Christ, the sole foundation. He warns Christians

---

63. See "The Church as Pilgrim," in *Piety 1978*, epilogue.

that, having been provided with the remedies I have shown, they retain Christ as a foundation rather than, by a rash and improper attack, make him "a stone of stumbling and a rock of offence" for themselves. It is inevitable that many scandals are inflicted upon the faithful time and again in this world, since not even Christ was immune from them. Indeed, one can scarcely expect them to take a single step without Satan putting some scandal in their way. So they must walk through innumerable stumbling blocks. But however numerous, varied, and thickly piled they may be, yet nobody will be a Christian unless he emerges victorious.[64]

Excuse to the Nicodemites (1544)[65]

Laodicean lukewarmness, ever a problem in the Christian church, seems today one of the chief plagues of the old-line denominations in affluent America. Calvin had a name for the general class of such persons, "Messrs. the Nicodemites." They received their sobriquet from the well-known inquirer in John's Gospel. Calvin first encountered such people at the court of Marguerite at Ferrara, which he visited in 1536 on the eve of his detention by Farel in Geneva. Calvin directed several tracts against these siren prophets of religious compromise and sweet reasonableness. We shall look only at the *Excuse*.

Calvin's basic argument was that God is the Lord of the body no less than of the soul of the elect. Therefore the believer must honor God by public worship, upright life, and abstention from idolatrous conformity to the papal church. He directed his critique of religious lukewarmness against four kinds of "Nicodemites." There are evangelical priests and bishops who preach from Catholic pulpits the evangelical message but give their congregations the impression that they have thereby made acceptable the whole superstition-encrusted ecclesiastical shell in which the unreformed church hobbles. The second Nicodemite sect he found in the "delicate prothonotaries" who play religion with the ladies of the court and beguile them with sweet theological niceties, all of them condemning with one voice the too-great austerity of Geneva. This is the religion of the theological salon. A third group is comprised of the men of letters, given to philosophy and tolerance of the foolish superstitions of the papacy. For them it is enough to know God by books and contemplation in their ivory towers, without becoming strained or sullied by involvement in the organization of the community of faith, worship, and Christian action. These men half-convert Christianity into philosophy. In a rather extremely worded condemnation of them, Calvin said: "I would prefer that all human sciences were exterminated from the earth, than for them to be the cause of freezing the zeal of Christians and turning

64. Calvin, *Concerning Scandals*, 116.
65. See *Piety 1978*, ch. 3, lines 171ff. (note).

them from God."[66] The last group will raise a respondent chord in American hearts. This includes the merchants and common people, who would prefer that their pastors or priests not become so much involved in the fine points of doctrine and thereby disturb commerce and the workaday tasks and satisfactions.

What a Faithful Man . . . Ought to Do Dwelling amongst the Papists (1543)

A basic issue in the two works already examined is what a Reformed Christian is to do when pressed to conform to the religious practices and beliefs of the unreformed church that dominates his native place. Calvin was indeed aware of the bitter prospect of losing body and goods, of stirring the world to opprobrium against oneself, and of forsaking the ease of life in one's own country for harsh exile in a foreign land. (Here one is reminded of the impassioned lines at the close of the dedicatory letter to Francis I of France that introduces the *Institutes of the Christian Religion*.)[67] This is the very route Calvin himself had taken. Many had been asking him how they should live and worship in accord with their own conscience when law and custom work against this. The tract was a detailed answer to them; it is also an extended application of *pietas*.

What shall people do? Calvin replied: We must not measure our duty to God according to our own advantage or physical convenience. We are not to rely on our own brain but rather to trust God's own providence, that he will keep us even in the midst of a thousand deaths.

What should be the general principles of Christian behavior? If God declares his will to us through his Word, we should follow it and not debate with God. The first lesson in Christ's school is that if we are ashamed of him or his Word, he will be ashamed of us when he comes in judgment. God is not satisfied that we acknowledge him secretly in our hearts; we are to profess outwardly that we are his. Or, to put it in the language of the treatise "On the Christian Life," with which we have already dealt, "we belong to God."[68] Should everyone declare himself openly, whether or not anybody ask him about his faith? Only those called thereto should preach openly, but everyone should witness according to his gifts, inviting his neighbor to join in true worship and Christian instruction. Since we have no definite rule for all, let every person ask our Lord to be directed in true wisdom as to their duty, and then to do it with all their power.

The chief question to which Calvin addressed himself in this tract is this: "Should a true Christian go to Mass while among the papists?

---

66. *OC*, 6:600; cf. George H. Williams, *The Radical Reformation* (Philadelphia: Westminster, 1962), 603f.

67. Cf. *Inst. 1536a*, 17f.; *Inst. 1536b*, 13f.

68. See *Piety 1978*, ch. 3, lines 281ff.

Should a Christian worship images, relics (and such like ceremonies)? A prior question which must be answered is: What is idolatry? Idolatry is of two sorts: first, when a person through a false fantasy conceived in the heart or spirit corrupts and perverts the spiritual balm of the one only God; second, when a person gives or transfers the honor which belongs to God only, to any creature." (Parenthetically, this would confirm our earlier postulation that the Romans passage underlying this view of idolatry is in fact the key verse that triggered Calvin's conversion.)

What duty do we owe God? Is it not enough to hold God in secret within our hearts? Calvin answered with a resounding no! God must be glorified in *both* our hearts and our bodies, for the latter, too, are redeemed by Jesus' blood. Therefore, we must not prostitute our bodies, which are the very temple of the Holy Spirit, before an idol. When we kneel before an idol we derogate God's majesty. All this is, once more, the familiar call to holiness before the all-holy God.

But can we really label the Mass as pagan idolatry? Surely, though it may be corrupt, it is still men's intention by it to worship God and not a humanly devised idol; consequently, such calling on God's name, though perhaps idolatrous, is not perilous, is it? This argument did not impress Calvin. He responded: If you go about worshiping God in a perverse and unlawful manner, you are worshiping an idol.

What, then, about the practice of the Mass in Calvin's own day? One does not condemn all papal rites, but only those that are completely bad. No evangelical Christian can submit to daily Mass, for this is manifest idolatry. What, then, about high Mass? Is this not better since it is a memorial of the Lord's Supper? No, this is a corruption of the Lord's Supper and as such is idolatrous; also the priestly absolution that follows is a violation of God's authority.

Calvin then sketched the cultic acts that mark the daily life of an unreformed Christian, from birth to death, labeling them abominations to be avoided by faithful believers. But still a crowd of excuses for conformity to such practices must be dealt with. Of course it is wrong to participate in these rites, but if one does them out of fear of men, is this not a light fault? Surely far worse crimes than this are committed. Calvin replied that such hypocrisy is no light fault, for it runs clean counter to God's requirement that human beings sanctify and consecrate themselves to God—both in body and in spirit, but the spirit as chief takes the principal place.

Another excuse: What good would come of it if everyone declared that he would serve God purely? To this Calvin rejoined: If it pleases God, the faithful Christian will undergo persecution, flight, prison, banishment, and even death itself.

Still another excuse: Suppose everyone wished to leave idolatry; then all the countries under Antichrist's reign would be deprived of the faithful. Having thus departed, where could they settle, since the regions where God is purely called on cannot absorb any more population? To this Calvin replied: If this happened, our Lord would provide for his faithful in some way—either convert the hearts of the princes and magistrates, moving them to put down idolatry and establish the true worship of God, or at least soften them so they would not force the faithful to defile themselves against their consciences or would not act cruelly against them.

The supply of excuses is not yet exhausted. If those capable of following the gospel take themselves away, how, if the seed is removed, can the doctrine of the gospel be multiplied? Calvin's answer is sharp: If all who have been given knowledge of the truth did but half their duty, there would not be one corner of the world not filled with it. Lack of courage is the fault. Have faith that if one person moves away, God will raise up four in place of the one.

The final excuse is a taunt thrown at Calvin: It is very well for you to talk from your safe place! If you were in our place, you would do as we do! Calvin answered: I speak as my conscience prompts, without boasting. If I were in a place where I thought I could not avoid idolatry without danger, I would pray the Lord to strengthen me and give me constancy to prefer his glory over my own life.

After a call to martyrdom, Calvin gave his final advice to evangelical Christians. If you live in a land where you cannot worship purely, go into exile if you can. If you cannot flee, abstain from idolatry while purely worshiping God in private. But suppose one has not the strength or constancy or is held back by parents, family, or the like? As far as your infirmity permits, follow the surest and soundest counsel. Insofar as you depart from the right way out of fear of men, confess your sin to God. Try daily to be sorry in order that you may obtain God's mercy. Then ask your Father to draw you out of bondage or to establish a right form of the church throughout the world so you can duly honor him.

Thus do these tracts pastorally apply *pietas* to the troubled, perplexed lives of those who longed to work out the renewal that had already touched their hearts. It has been said that Calvin is a theologian for hard times. Though too often curtained over by affluence, the church is living in a hard time. All the forces contrary to a truly Reformed faith that stood in the way in the sixteenth century have their late-twentieth-century counterpart. Lukewarm Nicodemites and learned scoffers are in the very bosom of the church, and—I may say—the seminaries. It will not take much imagination to find the category of obstacle-makers to which each of us in our failure to follow Christ belongs. Deny self! Follow God! Bear your cross! Let the hope of the life to come give meaning for your present life! What excuses do we give for not following this way of *pietas?*

Notes on John Calvin, *Justitia,* and the Old Testament Law[1]

Notanda etiam est justitiae definitio:
Ut faciant quod in oculis Dei rectum est;
quod carnis rationi et judicio opponitur.[2]

Roman law is a vast field, one in which many great writers in jurisprudence have dealt far better than I can do with the concept of *justitia.* Furthermore, the harmonization of Roman and Mosaic legislation was the work of centuries, both in actual codification and in commentary as well. Roman law itself in its final and classic form is a marriage of the two streams, perhaps unequal partners, but nevertheless (beginning with the Theodosian Code of A.D. 438 and culminating in the Code of Justinian of A.D. 530ff.) a new creation. After its inauguration the perception of neither Hebraic nor Graeco-Roman institutions could ever be the same again.

In our own Reformed tradition—as distinct from the Roman Catholic, the Lutheran, and the Anabaptist traditions—the Mosaic legislation has been viewed from the vantage point of sixteenth-century humanistic legal scholarship as understood by John Calvin and as applied to Mosaic exegesis by him. Central to his exposition of law is the passion for justice—social, political, and religious. It seemed therefore good to me to examine the Mosaic and Graeco-Roman elements in Calvin's view of justice.

Calvin's Study of Roman Law
and Its Bearing upon His Understanding of Jewish Law

In an essay entitled "Calvin's Humanistic Education,"[3] I dealt summarily with the fortunes of Western European legal education in the

---

1. From *Intergerini Parietis Septum (Eph. 2:14): Essays Presented to Markus Barth on His 65th Birthday,* ed. by Dikran Y. Hadidian (Pittsburgh: Pickwick Press, 1981), 23–37. Used by permission.
2. Deut. 6:1; *OO* (1671), 1:344.
3. See F. L. Battles, "Calvin's Humanistic Education," 1972, esp. 54ff., ch. 1, above.

Middle Ages and Renaissance, and contrasted the traditional narrow glossator handling of the Code of Justinian with the new humanist effort to understand Roman law within its broad cultural context. Calvin's teachers represented the best of both traditions: Pierre de l'Etoile for the older school, Andrea Alciati and Guillaume Budé for the new humanist school of legal exegesis.

Calvin's first steps in exegesis were taken not in the Scriptures but in the law. His earliest exegesis is reflected in his youthful *Commentary on Seneca's De Clementia*. At the heart of his interpretation of Roman law and institutions is the classic concept of *epieikeia*, to which we shall turn shortly. When his conversion occurred, Calvin undertook an intensive study of Scriptures, giving particular attention to the relation of law and grace. That his view of the law contrasts with that of Luther may be attributed at once to his different temperament and also to the contrasting way he was introduced to Roman law.

Without further elaboration, we can confidently state that what Calvin wrote about the Mosaic law in general, and on justice and equity in particular, was profoundly affected by his early studies in Roman law at the Universities of Orléans and Bourges.

Contrasting Sixteenth-Century Attitudes toward Law

What was the milieu into which Calvin launched his first theological essay, *The Institution of the Christian Religion*, in 1536? Elsewhere I have pointed out that Calvin found himself at a midpoint between the theological extremes of papalism and Anabaptism.[4] More narrowly, in the Eucharist, he found himself midway between Luther and Zwingli. In respect to the legal institutions of his own day he found himself at yet another midpoint. At the one end of the continuum was the repudiation of law courts, and all they stood for, by the Anabaptists; at the other was a small group of Lutheran theologians (with whom Melanchthon was at least sympathetic) who desired to supplant the inherited legal structures by the Mosaic code, a sort of sixteenth-century counterpart to the biblical theocratic dreams of Zionists or Koranic dreams of the modern state of Pakistan at its inception.

For Calvin both of these extreme views were wrong. Both rejected juridical institutions and processes, but for opposite reasons and with opposite intent. Calvin's conception of justice and his handling of the law, both Mosaic and Roman, is shaped, by 1536, in response to these extremes. The Anabaptists took literally Paul's advice to quarrelling Christians not to have recourse to the law court and Jesus' strictures against the swearing of oaths. The Mosaic restitutionists apparently took literally Jesus' assertion that he came not to set aside the law but to fulfill it;

4. *Inst. 1536a*, introduction, xliiff.; *Inst. 1536b*, 48ff.

they read Paul's praise of the Jewish law without his distinctive teaching on its primary function for Christians. Thus both advocated radical dismemberment of the existing system of justice.

Some other way of approaching the law must be found, a way that asserted the God-given character of the contrasting legal systems of the nations, and at the same time the binding character of the essence of the Mosaic law for Christians. This task was central to Calvin's whole career. Its outworking may be seen not only in his theological and exegetical writings, but also in his framing of constitutions and regulations for the city of Geneva, and in the day-to-day moral discipline of the citizens. The chief literary sources for this to which one must turn in this brief essay are the following: (1) the Seneca commentary for the earliest evidence of his assimilation of legal concepts; (2) the *Institutes*, particularly the first and last Latin editions (1536 and 1559) for the analysis of Jewish and extra-Jewish law; (3) the *Harmony of the Four Last Books of Moses* (1563) for the exposition of the Mosaic codes. We shall deal with these in reverse order.

Calvin's Analysis of the Law

The Tripartite Character and Purpose of the Law

When, in the first century of our era, Christianity began to disassociate itself from its parent Judaism, and the flood of Gentile converts (excused from much of Jewish ceremonial and ritual) raised questions about the continuing force of the Mosaic legislation, some groups took the radical line of repudiating the whole Old Testament—the Gnostics; others clung in varying degrees to the Mosaic regulations. Stimulated by the pagan critique of Christianity, and following in the footsteps of Paul and the Epistle to the Hebrews, the second-century apologists inaugurated an analysis of the Mosaic code calculated to sort out the elements still in force from those that had been set aside. The distinction between moral and ceremonial law, with a typological or allegorical interpretation of the latter, was gradually worked out by the Fathers. In its completed form, this Christian analysis of Moses became tripartite: the heart of it was the moral law, centering in the Decalogue, with its Gentile analogue of the natural law residing in the conscience (see Rom. 1); the ceremonial law was abrogated as far as literal observance was concerned but still valid as a typology of the new dispensation to come in Christ; finally, the judicial law (in the civil and criminal sphere) was merely the Jewish counterpart of comparable laws in other societies. So thought Thomas Aquinas, Melanchthon, and Calvin. By thus sorting out the Mosaic legislation, Christians could read the Old Testament within the civil and ecclesiastical structures of their own time. This analysis, however, made a split between secular and religious in the Christian understanding of the Mosaic code that was most certainly not characteristic of Mosaism in its pristine form.

Calvin's Fourfold Grouping of the Mosaic Codes

Modern liberal biblical criticism handles the Pentateuch as incorporating layers of tradition from various periods, the work of human compilation. Earlier exegetes took more seriously the claim of Mosaic authorship and sought in other ways to concord or at least explain the discordant canons of Torah. There is a certain analogy between the critical problems of the Pentateuch and of the Gospels. Calvin grappled with both through the constructing of a *Harmony*.

He brought to the Torah the same capacity for grouping the scattered and often confusing legal traditions of a culture under coherent categories. Concerning Torah, Calvin makes the following assumptions:

(1) Exodus, Leviticus, Numbers, and Deuteronomy contain two principal parts—the historical narrative and the doctrine.

(2) The purpose is to instruct the church (seen as taking its origin in the Old Testament) in true piety (including faith and prayer), as well as in the fear and worship of God.

(3) The intent is to provide a rule for a just and holy life, with exhortation of individuals in the performance of their assigned duties.

(4) Moses related all this in an unconnected form, as opportunity occurred.

(5) The clue to the whole is the Decalogue, but for those unable to discern the teaching of the other laws or to classify them under their appropriate categories, the exegete here sets before them the plan of Moses so they may profit by his writings.

Calvin harmonizes the doctrinal content of Exodus–Deuteronomy under four heads: (1) preface, (2) Decalogue, (3) supplements to the two tables of the Decalogue, (4) the end and use of the law. (An outline of his *Harmony* is appended [table 58].) Let us briefly examine these.

The preface is intended to prepare the minds for the reception of the law. Statements concerning the dignity of the law are to conduce to the due reverencing of God. Therefore they are set before the precepts of the law. The second and prime head is, of course, the Decalogue itself. Both in *Institutio* 2.7–8 and in the *Harmony*, Calvin divides the two tables 1–4 (to God), 5–10 (to God through neighbor), and groups all else under the commandments. The commandments are a divinely given, brief, but comprehensively summarized rule of a just and holy life. To these must be affixed other precepts not physically connected with the commandments in the text, but bearing the same sense. In his arrangement Calvin affixes them to their respective commandments. The third head comprises the supplements or appendixes. The supplements to the commandments of the first table have to do with the outward exercises of worship; those to the commandments of the second table are the political laws. The purpose of these supplements is to aid in the observance of the moral law; they do not add or take away from what is laid down in the Ten Commandments, but are helps to the worship owed to God and *to the promotion of justice toward men*. The supplements, while they constitute in Calvin's analysis of the law a third category of material, are distributed in the *Harmony* under their respective commandments.

The fourth category concerns itself with the end and use of the law. With Paul, Calvin accepts Christ as the end of the law. The motivating force of threats and promises prepares us for instruction in *justitia* by showing us our guilt and inducing us to seek after the remedy. Only when we recognize ourselves inexcusable before God and void of all confidence in our own *justitia* can we reach our goal. The law, recalling to us our fallen condition but also God's fatherly adoption, is our tutor unto Christ.

The Uses of the Law

Already in his *Commentary on Seneca's De Clementia* (1532) Calvin worked through Plato's, Aulus Gellius', and Seneca's teaching on the uses of punishment. These are reset within a Christian context in the *Institution* of 1536. According to the classical scheme, punishment serves (1) to reform the one who is punished; (2) by punishing the person, to make the rest better; (3) by removing bad individuals, to let the rest live in greater security and at the same time to protect the dignity and authority of the one against whom the sin has been committed.[5] While not taking these "uses" of punishment over directly into either his scheme of the uses of the law or of the uses of church discipline,[6] one can see how Calvin read the Mosaic law through a classical Christian gloss. Your attention is called to table 57, "Uses of Punishment, Law, and Church Discipline."

A detailed study of these parallels in table 57 (which is not the purpose of this essay) would reveal that Calvin's view of *justitia*, as it is manifested in the discipline of society, is a composite of classical and biblical elements.

The Common Ends of Hebrew and Gentile Law

Earlier it was pointed out that Calvin sought a position on law and legal institutions between Anabaptist rejection and Mosaic restoration, two prominent tendencies of his time. In refuting these two views and

5. *Comm. Sen. De Clem.*, 300f. (1.22.1).
6. *Inst. 1536a*, 88–90; *Inst. 1536b*, 65–67; *Inst.* 2.2.7ff.; 4.12.5ff.

in formulating his own, Calvin assumes amid all the diversity of laws in the nations of the world that there is an underlying unity. All laws, he asserts, may be analyzed under two aspects: (1) the actual constitution of the law, (2) the equity on which the constitution is founded and rests. The constitution, or (as we might call it) the form of the law, varies somewhat according to the particular circumstances under which it was originally framed and to which it initially referred. However, the important thing is not so much these culturally induced differences among the corresponding common laws of nations; rather they are to be adjudged according to the degree to which they press toward the goal of equity. Equity, the goal and rule and limit of all laws, is prescribed in the moral law—the testimony of natural law and of the conscience that God has engraved upon the minds of mankind. In *Institutio* 4.20.16 Calvin examines the varied punishments meted out by different legal systems for common offenses forbidden in Commandments 8, 9, 6 and 7:

> God's law forbids stealing. The penalties meted out to thieves in the Jewish state are to be seen in Exodus (Ex. 22:1–4). The very ancient laws of other nations punished theft with double restitution; the laws which followed these distinguished between theft, manifest and not manifest. Some proceeded to banishment, others to flogging, others finally to capital punishment. False testimony was punished by damages similar and equal to injury among the Jews (Deut. 19:18–21); elsewhere, only by deep disgrace; in some nations, by hanging; in others, by the cross. All codes equally avenge murder with blood, but with different kinds of death. Against adulterers some nations levy severer, others, lighter punishments. Yet we see how, with such diversity, all laws tend to the same end. For, together with one voice, they pronounce punishment against those crimes which God's eternal law has condemned, namely, murder, theft, adultery and false witness. But they do not agree on the manner of punishment. Nor is this either necessary or expedient. There are countries, which, unless they deal cruelly with murderers by way of horrible examples, must immediately perish from slaughters and robberies. There are ages that demand increasingly harsh penalties. If any disturbance occurs in a commonwealth, the evils that usually arise from it must be corrected by new ordinances. In time of war, in the clatter of arms, all humaneness would disappear unless some uncommon fear of punishment were introduced. In drought, in pestilence, unless greater severity is used, everything will go to ruin. There are nations inclined to a particular vice, unless it be most sharply repressed. How malicious and hateful toward public welfare would a man be who is offended by such diversity, which is perfectly adapted to maintain the observance of God's law?[7]

While in this passage Calvin is specifically concerned to refute the Mosaic restorationists, he is also providing a principle for the harmoni-

7. *Inst.* 4.21.16.

zation of the judicial laws of all nations (including the Jews) and for the Christian determination of what constitutes a just or an unjust law.

Epieikeia: Clue to the Concept of Justice

In the *Nicomachean Ethics* (5.10) Aristotle distinguishes between *epieikeia* and *kata ton nomon dikaion,* or, to use the Latin terms, *aequitas* and *summum jus.* In law and in the interpretation and judicial application of law, we may describe these as clemency and the letter of the law. But all laws, however imperfect, are to be judged by the intention of the lawgiver. Equity endeavors to penetrate beneath the surface, the literal language of the law, the time-bound form in which the law was originally cast, to the spirit and intent of the original. This principle is used by Calvin very effectively in examining Jesus' interiorization of the Decalogue in the Sermon on the Mount, to which we shall shortly turn.

But Calvin's first use of the distinction is at various points in the *Commentary on Seneca's De Clementia.* He became acquainted with it in Budé's *Annotationes in Pandectas,* a partial commentary on the *Digest* of Justinian. Calvin adverts to the principle in commenting on Seneca's statement, "to use authority over slaves with moderation," with copious reference to classical authors.[8] Again, when Seneca speaks of guiltless persons who fall under punishment not through their own fault but through misfortune: if such persons ". . . are subjected to strict severity they can legitimately be punished, if to equity, legitimately condoned."[9] Equity is also appealed to by Calvin in interpreting Seneca's closing words, "Clemency may therefore assess the damages at any value it pleases." Such a principle gives flexibility to the judge in applying the law: the most just way to administer the law is not to be governed by its letter, but to show compassion in pronouncing sentences.[10]

This classical principle is carried over, after Calvin's conversion, to his Christian understanding of all law and becomes a prime rule of scriptural exegesis. In *Institutio* 2.2.21f. he teaches that in his fallen state man still retains enough of reason to distinguish him from brute beasts. One area in which this is seen is in man's retention of "some seed of political order." Here is set forth the theological rationale for the unity of human law to which we referred above:

> since man is by nature a social animal, he tends through natural instinct to foster and preserve society. Consequently, we observe that there exist in all men's minds universal impressions of a certain civic fair dealing and order. Hence no man is to be found who does not understand that

8. See *Comm. Sen. De Clem.,* 269ff.
9. Ibid., 69ff.
10. Ibid., 379ff.

every sort of human organization must be regulated by laws, and who does not comprehend the principles of those laws. Hence arises that unvarying consent of all nations and of individual mortals with regard to laws. For their seeds have, without teacher or lawgiver, been implanted in all men.

I do not dwell upon the dissension and conflicts that immediately spring up. Some, like thieves and robbers, desire to overturn all law and right, to break all legal restraints, to let their lust alone masquerade as law. Others think unjust what some have sanctioned as just (an even commoner fault), and contend that what some have forbidden is praiseworthy. Such persons hate laws not because they do not know them to be good and holy; but raging with headlong lust, they fight against manifest reason. What they approve of in their understanding they hate on account of their lust. Quarrels of this latter sort do not nullify the original conception of equity.[11]

Again, in his "Treatise on the Christian Life"[12] wherein he sets forth the twin principles of self-renunciation and the bearing of the cross, Calvin shows the place of equity in a well-ordered life. Basing his discussion on Titus 2:11–14, he states:

Thus, with reference to both Tables of the Law, he commands us to put off our own nature and to deny whatever our reason and will dictate. Now he limits all actions of life to three parts: soberness, righteousness, and godliness. Of these, soberness doubtless denotes chastity and temperance as well as a pure and frugal use of temporal goods, and patience in poverty. Now righteousness embraces all the duties of equity in order that to each one be rendered what is his own (cf. Rom. 13:7). There follows godliness, which joins us in true holiness with God when we are separated from the iniquities of the world. When these things are joined together by an inseparable bond, they bring about complete perfection.[13]

Yet nothing is more difficult than to attain such perfection. In *Institutio* 3.5.7 Calvin is faced with denying the reference of Matthew 5:25f. to purgatory, as made by the Roman Catholics. In this passage, he asserts, "Christ, in order to urge his followers more cogently to equity and concord, meant to show the many dangers and evils to which men expose themselves who obstinately prefer the letter of the law rather than to act out of equity and goodness."

Equity, then, is the prime principle for Calvin in understanding true justice. The social justice sought, for example, by the civil rights movement, in direct conflict with unjust laws, if examined under the rule of equity, would demonstrate the superiority of *aequitas* over *summon jus*.

11. *Inst.* 2.2.13.
12. Ibid., 3.6–10.
13. Ibid., 3.7.3.

It is this principle that should animate the framers of laws as well as the judges whose verdicts stand upon laws. It is upon this foundation that all human laws and their just application must rest. In this sense all human law is a great unity.

But these remarks do not exhaust Calvin's use of *equity*. The most sublime task to which it is put in his system is the harmonization of Decalogue and Sermon on the Mount. Through *epieikeia*, Calvin penetrates to the intent of the lawgiver of the Decalogue, an intent implicit in the Old Testament law but made explicit in Jesus' reading of the Commandments. Murder is more than a physical act: murder is committed in the heart before the hand does the deed, or even when the outward deed is never done. Working through the second table of the Decalogue, Calvin shows how Jesus "interiorizes" the Decalogue, transforming it from a moral code to an ethic of intention. The divine pedagogy exhibited in the Mosaic code operates by synecdoche: the part stands for the whole. The lawgiver has selected the most heinous instance in every class of offense to shock his hearers into a grasp of the class as a whole. Murder stands for all the feelings of enmity, envy, and rage that boil within and poison our relations with our fellows: inwardly we commit murder against the objects of our hatred. The very shock of "Thou shalt not kill" moves us to a broader and deeper examination of our moral state. So it goes with the other precepts as well. Through the classical principle of *epieikeia*, Calvin has plumbed the depths of the Decalogue and delineated at the same time the true Christian concept of *justitia*. For example, in the Sixth Commandment he sees this positive purpose: the Lord having bound humanity together in a certain unity, each one ought to concern themselves with the safety of all.[14] We must reverence God's image humanity, embracing our flesh in him. Thus unthinkable is murder, of which we are guilty not only in the act but in the plan, and even in the wish to kill.[15]

---

14. Ibid., 2.8.39.
15. Ibid., 2.8.40.

Table 57. Uses of punishment, law, and church discipline

The 3 Uses of the Law Inst. 1536.88–90	The 3 Uses of the Law Inst. 2:7.6ff.; cf. 4:20:14–21	The 3 Uses of Punishment Comm. Sen De Clem. 1:22:1	The 3 Uses of Church Discipline Inst. 4:12:5ff.
III It warns the believers, too, in whose hearts the Spirit of God already lives & reigns, what is right & pleasing in God's sight.	III The Pedagogical: admonishes believers & urges them on in well-doing (pars. 12–13)	I To reform the man that is punished[2] (125.7–26)	III To overcome men with shame for their baseness, that they may begin to repent

II It serves at least by fear of punishment to restrain certain men who, unless compelled, are untouched by any concern for what is right and just: this necessary for the public community of men for whose tranquility the Lord so provided in guarding against complete and violent confusion.	II The Restraining: restrains malefactors and those who are not yet believers (10f.)
	(a) protects community from unjust men[1]
	(b) deters those not yet regenerate
	  (i) brings those confident of their own self-righteousness to humility before God
	  (ii) restrains those uncontrolled in their own lust
		II By punishing him to make the rest live better[3] (125.26–37)
		
		IIIa By removing bad men, to let the rest live in greater security (Seneca, De Clem., 1:22:1/Calv. Comm. 125.37–126.1)
			II To keep the good from being corrupted by the company of the wicked
			
			I To banish the wicked from the fellowship

I While showing God's righteousness, i.e., what God requires of us, it admonishes each one of his unrighteousness and convicts him of his sin.	I The Punitive: mirrors our sin before God & leaves us inexcusable (pars. 6–9) (a) those to be redeemed thus realize their empty-handedness before God (b) the wicked are terrified, but because of their obstinacy of heart	IIIb To protect the dignity & authority of him against whom the sin has been committed[4] (Aulus Gellius, Noctes Atticae 7[6].14)	

1. cf. Inst. 4:20:19.
2. Greek: nouthesia, kolasis parainesis; Latin: monitio, animadversio.
3. Greek: paradeigma; Latin: exemplum
4. Latin: timoria

Table 58. Outline of Calvin's *Commentary on a Harmony
of the Last Four Books of Moses*

	The history (CTS 1.19–335)[a]
329[b]	The law (CTS 1.417–3.289)
	The First Commandment (CTS 1.417–2.106)
351	Passages relating to the exposition of this commandment 1.420
359	Ceremonial supplements of the First Commandment 1.454
	The institution of the Passover
365	Another supplement concerning the consecration of the firstborn 1.477
366	Another supplement concerning the payment of tribute 1.481
	Ditto on the shutting up of the leprous 2.7
	On the purification of the lepers 2.19
	On the pollutions that arise from issues 2.28
	On the defects that exclude people from the tabernacle 2.33
	Another supplement as to the general purification of the people 2.35
	Another supplement as to keeping themselves clean by the concealment of their impurities 2.44
	Another supplement 2.47
	Another supplement regarding clean and unclean beasts 2.53
	Another supplement regarding things accidentally unclean 2.68 *(per accidens)*
390	Judicial supplements 2.72
398	*The Second Commandment* (CTS 2.106–407)
400	Exposition of the Second Commandment 2.115
	The priesthood 2.187
431	On the high priest 2.235
	Rights of the priests 2.265
	Rights to tithes 2.275
	The sacred oblations 2.291
	Sacrifice 2.292
	The great yearly atonement 2.310
472	Political Supplements of the Second Commandment 2.386
478	*The Third Commandment* (CTS 2.408–432)
478	Exposition of the Third Commandment 2.410
484	Political supplements of the Third Commandment 2.431
484	*The Fourth Commandment* (CTS 2.432–472)
486	Passages relating to the exposition of the Fourth Commandment 2.440
487	Supplements to the Fourth Commandment 2.445
	The Year of Jubilee 2.450
495	The second table (CTS 3.5–189)
	First Commandment, the Fifth of the Law 3.5–19
	Supplements of the Fifth Commandment 3.13
498	*The Sixth Commandment* (CTS 3.20–68)
499	Exposition of the Sixth Commandment 3.22
500	Ceremonial supplements of the Sixth Commandment 3.25
502	Political supplements of the Sixth Commandment 3.33
511	*Seventh Commandment* (CTS 3.68–110)
	Supplements of the Seventh Commandment 3.71
	Political supplements 3.72
521	These supplements are judicial (political) 3.106
522	*Eighth Commandment* (CTS 3.110–179)
523	Exposition of the Eighth Commandment 3.111 (3g, 3s)
530	Political supplements 3.140

540   *Ninth Commandment* (CTS 3.179–186)
541   Exposition of the Ninth Commandment 3.181
542   Supplement 3.185
542   *Tenth Commandment* (CTS 3.186–189)
543   Sum of the law (CTS 3.190–196)
545   The use of the law (CTS 3.196–201)
546   Sanctions from promises and threats (CTS 3.201–289)
568   Return to the history (CTS 3.289–4–409)

a. First number in parentheses after each division refers to Calvin, *Commentary on the Four Last Books of Moses Arranged in His Form of a Harmony,* 4 vols. (Edinburgh: Calvin Translation Society, 1852–55).

b. Initial numbers refer to pages in *OO.*

Against Luxury and License
in Geneva

A Forgotten Fragment of Calvin [1546–47][1]

In the Genevan Library (Cod. 145, fol. 125) is a sheet in Calvin's hand, entitled by him *De Luxu*. The editors of the *Corpus Reformatorum* have published a transcription of the text (*CR*, 10a:203–206), with the comment: "It seems to be an unfinished study of the young Calvin, lacking any final editing. Here and there occur unfinished phrases and author's marginal notes."

My attention was drawn to this interesting piece as I was finishing the annotations to a forthcoming critical edition and translation of Calvin's commentary on Seneca's *De Clementia* (1532), while I ranged through the whole corpus of Calvin's writings for evidences of continuing classical influences—beyond this youthful humanist period—on his thought. The first and most obvious point that struck me was that Calvin referred in several places to actual pages of Erasmus' 1529 edition of Seneca, which, with Erasmus' earlier edition of 1516, he had exhaustively studied in the preparation of his *De Clementia* commentary. I communicated my discovery to A. M. Hugo, lecturer in classics at Stellenbosch University, South Africa, with whom I am collaborating on the *De Clementia*. He immediately pointed out several additional passages from Seneca. In a short period of work since then I have identified many additional citations. Over thirty references to, or quotations from, Seneca's *Epistulae Morales* and at least seven additional ones to his other philosophical writings—not to mention other classical, biblical, and patristic references—have now been noted.

My first thought was that these were additional notes, unused for the Seneca commentary, which through some miracle had been preserved.

1. From *Interpretation* 19 (1965): 182–202. Used by permission.

But I soon came to see that here was more than a leaf from a student's commonplace book. Two short and tantalizing references suggested that these notes were called forth by a definite historical situation:

> Examples [of the highest luxury] can be found close at hand. We've recently seen some in Geneva (205.35–36).

And

> After you have seen our dances you might say these gay fellows are going mad with laughter (206.38–39).

As I studied the piece further, the conviction came that Calvin is here speaking of his arduous campaign in Geneva for the improvement of public and private morality. He is concerned with all forms of luxurious living and conspicuous consumption not only as economically bad and deleterious to the poor but as a threat to the very life of an independent Geneva, through the sapping of the moral fiber of her citizenry. What is more, we see here the inner thoughts of Calvin as he laments the misunderstanding of his motives that his crusade has brought.

Calvin's most intimate thoughts, his soliloquies, are often cast in the form of references to others—biblical or classical. In the *Institutes,* David customarily performs this function; in the *De Luxu,* Calvin finds in certain ancient Romans sympathetic supporters of his Geneva task. Seneca is, of course, his prime mentor, but the elder Cato's fight against the repeal of the Oppian Law (195 B.C.) and against feminine luxury is not forgotten. There is at least a hint that Calvin thinks of himself as a sort of Cicero fighting through his eloquence the Catilines of his day. These points will be examined in this essay. The piece is a *cento,* then, of classical quotations whereby Calvin in a sort of shorthand form communicates through other men's thoughts his innermost feelings to paper.

My next task was to attempt to date the piece. This I have not done in any definitive way, as yet, for many of the necessary documents are not presently at hand. Still, at first sight the writing seems to fit best the events of 1546–47 when the struggles with the family of Amy Perrin and their faction over moral lapses culminated in the threat to Calvin's and his colleagues' lives, affixed to the church pulpit in June 1547, and in the mob scene at the Hôtel de Ville described in Calvin's letter of 17 December 1547, which ends with this pathetic phrase: "My influence is gone, believe me, unless God stretch forth His hand."[2] The conflicts over dancing, the right of the Consistory to treat matters of private morality as criminal cases, the debauchery of the youth and especially of trucu-

2. *Ep.* 977 (*CR*, 12:632f.; ET, 211).

lent women of the patrician class—all these seem to fit best the context and tone of the *De Luxu*.

It is quite possible that a comparable situation during Calvin's first Geneva sojourn, or an earlier point in his second Geneva period (1541), might fit the document. The latter date is suggested by the several parallels with the 1543 portions of the *Institutes of the Christian Religion*.[3] However, the *De Luxu* suggests a longer period of moral reform behind it than the rather inchoate efforts of 1536–38;[4] and it seems to reflect the aftermath of the new and far more efficient campaign inaugurated by Calvin upon his return from Strasbourg in 1541. While struggles of this sort did not cease after 1547, the program of moral reform moved thereafter with greater success and strictness. The *De Luxu* looks like a report at midpassage. The evidence for the date 1546–47 will be given below.

There is, however, beyond the problem of dating the document, a far more important aspect of it. It reminds us in a specific, historical way that at the heart of Calvin's moral teaching is a remarkable marriage of the scriptural and the classical. It demonstrates a continuity of Stoic—that is, primarily Senecan—influences on Calvin, extending beyond his early intimacy with that Roman's teaching. Particularly in the doctrine of *frugalitas*,[5] of a temperate mean between sensual indulgence and grim austerity (204.6f.), Calvin is supplementing the teaching of Jesus and Paul with the rich and sometimes almost Christian insights of Seneca.[6]

In the present document we have an interesting confluence of the historical and the theological. Calvin, upon coming to Geneva, found a congenial "blue law" tradition long antedating the Reformation;[7] he found economic and political and religious conditions that suggested the need for a continuation and intensification of moral and sumptuary

3. It is possible that the *De Luxu* might be looked upon as containing material assembled for the *Institutes* of 1543.

4. Paul Emile Henry, The *Life and Times of John Calvin, the Great Reformer,* trans. by H. Stebbing, 2 vols. (New York: R. Carter & Brothers, 1851–52), 1:125, cites the entries of the *Registre* for 4 September 1536 and 20 May 1537, for early instances of punishment for excessive luxury and worldly amusements. At the former date, "Some of the citizens and many others protested before the Council, not being able to endure the ministers who reproved their vices, *vouloir vivre en liberté.*"

5. See Georgia Harkness, *John Calvin: The Man and His Ethics* (New York: Henry Holt & Company, 1931), 162–68; Ronald S. Wallace, *Calvin's Doctrine of the Christian Life* (Edinburgh: Oliver & Boyd, 1959), "Christian Moderation," 170–92.

6. For a careful comparison of the ethics of Paul and Seneca, see J. N. Sevenster, *Paul and Seneca* (Leiden: E. J. Brill, 1961), esp. ch. 4, "The Life of the Individual," and ch. 5, "Social Relations."

7. See H. D. Foster, "Geneva before Calvin (1387–1536): The Antecedents of a Puritan State," *American Historical Review* 8 (1902–3): 217–40. Henry, *Life of Calvin,* 1:362, cites as evidence of the luxury of pre-Calvinian Geneva a colloquy by Matthew Cordier, which describes a "sumptuous feast at which the four syndics were present."

restraint;[8] he found in the classical heritage striking parallels to the Genevan situation. Just as his Old Testament preaching in a sense re-enacts the history of the Old Israel for the sixteenth-century Zion at Geneva, so his reflection on the struggles of the ancient moralists of Rome, faced with a comparable deterioration of public and private life in both Republic and Empire,[9] gives shape and direction to his Christian ethical teaching.

The plan is (1) to summarize the document, (2) to examine Calvin's search for a strategy of moral reform and the influence of Seneca on it, (3) to offer a translation of the *De Luxu* with annotations.[10]

The Document in Brief

The document can be quickly summarized. Calvin has earned odium from some for his moral crusade; yet he has had success in turning some to a better way of life. Moral discipline is especially to be applied to persons lightly corrupted and impressionable. Luxury, gluttony included, is childish. There is no need to frame specious scriptural "proofs" for luxury. A moderation closer to abstinence than to luxury is to be sought.[11] Sensual pleasures in this degenerate and unchaste time vitiate even otherwise kindly persons. Lavish, expensive, and effeminate dress makes us worse than dumb animals. We should not concentrate on the body at the soul's expense. Conspicuous spending is wicked. Luxury is a sort of "fifth column" within the city. It presses on people as yet uncorrupted and makes it well nigh impossible for men and women to lead a chaste life. The early Anchorites protested against excessive extravagance, but their witness has been drowned in the luxury of their successors. Luxury of the rich is a sin against the poor; public and private vices breed each other. In its lust and extravagance the present age is shameless: dancing, eating, drinking, dressing lavishly, using the mirror, hating offspring. Actors flourish while the poor starve.

Moral Discipline: The Search for a Public Strategy

"The unity of the city and the uniting of the citizens in the faith in Christ": these were the twin purposes adopted by the Council of Geneva

8. See André Biéler, *La Pensée Economique et Sociale de Calvin* (Genève: Librairie de l'Université, 1959), esp. pt. I, ch. 2, "La vie économique et les réformes sociales," 138–79.

9. In preparing his *Commentary on Seneca's De Clementia* Calvin had, in 1532, reviewed the frightful extravagance of first-century A.D. Roman life from G. Budé, *De Asse,* a learned treatise on ancient coinage.

10. For the purposes of this essay, the text as printed in *CR, OC,* 10a:203–6 will, with slight alteration, suffice as a basis for translation; from a microfilm kindly furnished by Geneva through the good offices of Professor René Rapin of the University of Lausanne.

11. See note 5, above.

on 21 May 1536, to be embodied in the regulations drafted in November of that year and voted by the Council in January 1537.[12] For the Geneva Reformers, the Lord's Supper was the center of that unity, and its protection from defilement by unholy hands their passion (*LCC* 22.50). Already in the 1536 Confession of Faith (art. 19) provision was made for excommunication. The Pauline principle—"evil communications corrupt good morals"—and Paul's catalogues of vices (as well as the excommunication procedure outlined in Matt. 18:15ff.) are reflected in these lines:

> we believe that it is expedient according to the ordinances of God that all manifest idolaters, blasphemers, murderers, thieves, lewd persons, false witnesses, sedition-mongers, quarrellers, those guilty of defamation or assault, drunkards, dissolute livers, when they have been duly admonished and if they do not make amendment, be separated from the communion of the faithful until their repentance is known (*LCC* 22.31f.).

On 16 January 1537, Calvin submitted to the Council *Articles Concerning the Organization of the Church and Worship* wherein considerable space is given to excommunication and to the procedure for dealing with vices (*LCC* 22.52f.). Provision is made for guardians of morals; there are to be chosen

> certain persons of good life and witness from among the faithful, persevering and not easily corrupted, who should be dispersed and distributed in all the quarters of the city, having oversight of the life and government of each of these, and if they see any vice worthy of note to find fault with in any person, that they communicate about it with some of the ministers, to admonish whoever it is that is at fault and to exhort him.

While the basis of moral discipline was therefore laid down before the exile of Calvin to Strasbourg (1538–41), Bucer's influence and the organization of the Strasbourg church are to be seen in the far more definite and workable regulations adopted immediately on Calvin's return to Geneva. Calvin presented in September–October 1541 the *Draft Ecclesiastical Ordinances*. The "certain persons of good life" vaguely responsible for moral oversight in the 1537 regulations have been transformed into the third order of the fourfold church organization—the elders, charged with the "oversight of the life of everyone"; also, from the three councils Calvin asked that twelve "men of good and honest life,

---

12. Hand in hand with this went the *Catechism* of 1537. For ET of this, see Paul T. Fuhrmann, *Instruction in Faith, 1537* (Louisville: Westminster/John Knox, 1977, 1992). Biéler, *La Pensée Economique*, 269ff., fully analyzes the centrality of the sacraments in Calvin's plan for the renewal and unification of society. This topic is also well developed, but purely theologically, in Wallace, *Calvin's Doctrine of the Christian Life.*

without reproach and beyond suspicion, and above all fearing God and possessing spiritual prudence" be chosen and distributed "in every quarter of the city, to keep an eye on everybody" (*LCC* 22.63f.). Among the duties of these overseers is that of bidding the people attend sermons, a theme earlier mentioned and frequently repeated in later proclamations and in the minutes of both Consistory and Council. In these documents we find lists of vices frequently rehearsed and legal procedures and fines spelled out.

The clarification of disciplinary procedures seen between the public documents[13] of 1536–37 and those of 1541 is paralleled in the successive editions of the *Institutes*. The basic presuppositions for excommunication and discipline are to be found in the editions of 1536–39; much fuller, however, is the edition of 1543, which shows the effect of the Strasbourg sojourn in its rich ecclesiological additions to Calvin's thought (especially *Inst.* 4.11–12).[14] While the effort to apply these principles remained a burden on Calvin and his co-workers, perhaps the period of greatest crisis was the years 1546–47, when open rebellion on the part of the Perrinist faction, and particularly of certain truculent women, led to the threat against the Reformers' lives of June 1547 and to the Hôtel de Ville incident of December 1547, to which reference has already been made.

The scriptural basis for the protection of communion through moral discipline is obvious. Not so apparent are the classical sources for this plan of urban uplift. The chief documents for this side are the *Commentary on Seneca's De Clementia* (1532),[15] the *De Luxu* itself, and certain letters containing classical allusions. The evidence demonstrates a continuing influence of Seneca and the Stoic tradition in Calvin's ethical teaching and moral discipline of the city. To analyze these classical elements in detail would far exceed the scope of this essay; three points will serve to illustrate our thesis: (1) the Senecan analysis of the uses of punishment, (2) Seneca's picture of the moral advocate and of his task of transforming the state, (3) the portrait of Cato the Censor as the classic embodiment of the warrior for virtue (in Seneca and Cicero).

In his *Commentary on Seneca's De Clementia* (1.22.1; p. 125), Calvin had in 1532 analyzed Seneca's three uses of punishment. In the *Insti-*

---

13. With these should be included the Laws of 1543, revised in 1568.

14. In *Ep.* 201 to Farel, 31 December 1539 (*CR*, 10b.441; ET, 43), Calvin remarks on the transgressions of Strasbourg University regulations by French students who had come there to lead a free life, that "the Church must therefore get more authority to bridle their wicked passions. Yet some allowance is to be made for men's folly. One ought not to make discipline so strict as to prevent people from playing the fool at times."

15. Calvin, in his *Comm. Sen. De Clem.*, 212 (87:lines 7ff.), using the analogy of the body politic, comments on Seneca's thought: "If then not every society is a city, but only that one which lives by upright morals and fair laws, those who do not obey the laws are not citizens, but 'cut off from the body' of a lawful city."

tutes of 1536–39 (with finishing touches of 1543), Calvin utilized these categories for his three uses of the law (2.7.6ff.) and three uses of church discipline (4.12.5ff.). The relation of these three documents can be best shown in table 59.

Table 59. Uses of punishment, law, and church discipline (2)

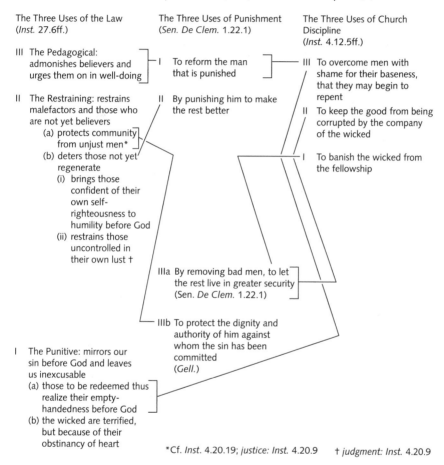

The Three Uses of the Law (*Inst.* 27.6ff.)

III The Pedagogical: admonishes believers and urges them on in well-doing

II The Restraining: restrains malefactors and those who are not yet believers
  (a) protects community from unjust men*
  (b) deters those not yet regenerate
    (i) brings those confident of their own self-righteousness to humility before God
    (ii) restrains those uncontrolled in their own lust †

I The Punitive: mirrors our sin before God and leaves us inexcusable
  (a) those to be redeemed thus realize their empty-handedness before God
  (b) the wicked are terrified, but because of their obstinacy of heart

The Three Uses of Punishment (*Sen. De Clem.* 1.22.1)

I To reform the man that is punished

II By punishing him to make the rest better

IIIa By removing bad men, to let the rest live in greater security (*Sen. De Clem.* 1.22.1)

IIIb To protect the dignity and authority of him against whom the sin has been committed (*Gell.*)

The Three Uses of Church Discipline (*Inst.* 4.12.5ff.)

III To overcome men with shame for their baseness, that they may begin to repent

II To keep the good from being corrupted by the company of the wicked

I To banish the wicked from the fellowship

*Cf. *Inst.* 4.20.19; justice: *Inst.* 4.20.9   † judgment: *Inst.* 4.20.9

To this should be added the classical distinction between those who are reformable and those who are unreformable (*Sen. De Clem.* 1.2.2; p. 24), which corresponds to the Pauline predestined (regenerate)/fore-ordained (unregenerate), each having appropriate punishment. The first or punitive function of the law is the Christian addition to the two Christianized pagan uses coming, of course, after Calvin's conversion (compare *Inst.* 2.7.6, n. 10, for Melanchthon's contribution to this threefold distinction). In the *De Luxu,* Calvin sets out to win by exhortation the "lightly corrupted" (203.4ff.). The value of rebuke and example is recognized. This tripartite strategy is to be noted in Calvin's use of preaching, private admonition, citation to Consistory and Council to effect his ends.

Second, in his *Moral Epistles* Seneca gives thought to the moral transformation of the state. In the context of a phrase alluded to by Calvin (203.19), Seneca says, *inter alia:*

> Preach against greed, preach against high living; and when you notice that you have made progress and impressed the minds of your hearers, lay on still harder. You cannot imagine how much progress can be brought about by an address of that nature, when you are bent on curing your hearers and are absolutely devoted to their best interests. For when the mind is young, it may most easily be won over to desire what is honorable and upright; truth, if she can obtain a suitable advocate, will lay strong hands upon those who can still be taught, those who have been but lightly corrupted (Sen. *Ep. Mor.* 108.12/*LCL* 3.236ff.).

Seneca develops at great length the strategy of moral admonition—against enervating luxury and on behalf of a healthy frugality:

> It is therefore indispensable that we be admonished, that we have some advocate with upright mind, and, amid all the uproar and jangle of falsehood, hear one voice only (*Ep. Mor.* 94.59/*LCL* 3.48f.).

> We should, therefore, have a guardian, as it were, to pluck us continually by the ear and dispel rumors and protest against popular enthusiasm (*Ep. Mor.* 94.55/*LCL* 3.46f.).

Calvin as drafter of Geneva's moral code is attempting to forestall the disaster envisaged in Seneca's dictum: "A state with defective laws will have defective morals" (*Ep. Mor.* 94.38/*LCL* 3.36f.). Seneca suggests a means of controlling morals: "the licentiousness of cities will sometimes abate through discipline and fear, never of itself" (*Ep. Mor.* 97.8/ *LCL* 3.112f.). In all this teaching Seneca assumes the mission of a high-minded *advocatus morum*.[16] So common is Seneca's preaching against luxury that there is no need to pile up references;[17] one will suffice. He asserts that luxurious banquets and elaborate dress are indicative of disease in the state (*Ep. Mor.* 114.11). In the *Commentary on Seneca's De Clementia*, Calvin had first handled in a general way some of Seneca's

16. Apparently Calvin had forgotten, in his assumption of the task of *advocatus morum*, at least a part of his own interpretation of Seneca, *Comm. Sen. De Clem.*, 124 (47:lines 8–10), 1.6.2: "There is one kind of men that ought to be cleansed of all vice, that is, those who are in charge of morals, and correct the vices of others." But how many judges live up to this standard?

17. On *Luxuria*, see, e.g., *Sen. Ep. Mor.* 78.22ff.; 89.20f.; 90.16ff.; 94.71; 95:24ff., 42; 97.1; 114.2, 9ff.; 119.14; 122.6, etc.

ideas about the state and its orderly rule. In the *De Luxu* is to be seen a direct application of Seneca's call for a higher morality to the cleansing of Geneva.

Third, one figure from history clearly emerges on the pages of the *De Luxu:* Marcus Porcius Cato the Censor (234–149 B.C.). That Calvin and his colleagues were accustomed to think of their work in terms of Cato's is suggested in Calvin's words to Viret, in which he assesses Farel's sometimes excessive zeal:

> I may therefore say of Farel what Cicero said of Cato, "That he acts indeed with good judgment, but in counsel does not always show the best" (*Ep.* 715/*CR*, 12:194).

Cato is Seneca's chief model of frugality and guardian of public morals. Calvin quotes approvingly a number of passages whose Senecan contexts contain references to Cato. Besides the allusion to Cato's "single horse" (205.29f.), Calvin suggests, perhaps, a parallel between Cato's fight to prevent the repeal of the Oppian Law against feminine luxury (206.47) and his own efforts against "Penthesilea"[18] Perrin, the Widows N—and Balthasar, the wife of Councillor Ameaux, Froment's wife, and others who by their luxurious or lecherous living and unruly behavior drew Calvin's admonition and anger especially in 1546–47.[19] Calvin found in Cato a person with a background and a mission not unlike his own: both could have lived in peace and comfort but chose the arena of public life instead; Cato was at first a new and unknown man, while Calvin was an outsider to the old families of Geneva. In Cicero's labors against Catiline, too, there was a parallel to be drawn with Calvin's campaign against Perrin and his henchmen (206.36).

Calvin himself, interpreting Matthew 19:20f., sums up the task of the reformer of morals:

> Therefore, when Christ commands the covetous rich man to give up all that he has, it is like commanding an ambitious man to give up all his honors, a voluptuary all his pleasures, or a shameless man all means of lust. Thus consciences untouched by any awareness of the general admonition must be called back to a specific awareness of their own evil (*Inst.* 4.13.13, 1543).

This "calling back" was the task Calvin and his colleagues set themselves. In these labors of moral discipline they repeatedly asserted the church's independence of the state, but their appeal to the secular arm

---

18. Penthesilea, Calvin's nickname for Francesca Favre, Amy Perrin's wife. The name was of a queen of the Amazons who fought before Troy against the Greeks, and was slain by Achilles [Virgil, *Aeneid* 1.491]. Calvin called Perrin "Caesar comicus."

19. See, e.g., *Ep.* 824 (*CR*, 12:377f.; ET, 173) to Farel, September 1546.

(compare *Inst.* 4.20.3) and the peculiar relationship between Consistory and Council left the separation of the two spheres less than clearcut. And the state, especially in the earlier years of reform, reciprocated by dictating on matters of purely ecclesiastical concern. Between 1536 and 1559, Calvin developed his six purposes of civil government (*Inst.* 4.20.2): (1) to cherish and protect the outward worship of God, (2) to defend sound doctrine of piety and the position of the church, (3) to adjust our life to the society of men, (4) to form our social behavior to civil righteousness, (5) to reconcile us with one another, (6) to promote general peace and tranquility. Calvin's opponents resented the curbing of their personal liberty[20] by the ministers and also the usurpation by the Consistory of certain functions normally associated with civil law. In the complex struggle a "mystical nationalism," sheer libertinism, and outright crime were pitted against the Calvinian party, until the latter grew in strength by removals of its opponents from the city and by the flocking to Geneva of refugees eager to take up the movement of reform. Thus, at the moment with which we are dealing here—1546–47— two fundamentally different views of the state stood in unresolvable opposition.[21]

Calvin: "Concerning Luxury"

When I undertake war not against some individual, but against this age, I know how much ill-will I bring upon myself among those in whom, &c. But some might possibly thank me and acknowledge how I have benefitted

[Page 203]
   5 them when, after my warning, they begin to repent; others will
       despise me disdainfully, as those indolent Maecenases are like to do,
       or will guffaw and crack their usual jokes. Indeed, no persons bear
  10 rebuke more unworthily or are more annoyed thereby than those
       who are unable to look upon themselves rationally. It seems enough
       for me to have gotten some to turn to a worthier life, and to have
       transformed the wickedness of men among whom neither truth nor
       honesty prevails. I am surely convinced I can accomplish something

20. Obviously, two conceptions of freedom are in opposition here. Calvin's view is of a "freedom . . . regulated with becoming moderation and . . . properly established on a durable basis" (*Inst.* 4.20.8), in contrast to the anarchistic tendencies of religious perfectionists, atheistic libertines, and old-line aristocrats.

21. Biéler's magistral study of Calvin's economic and social thought, mentioned above, is of prime importance for the understanding of the social history of sixteenth-century Geneva and of the theological norms that Calvin endeavored to apply to it. But Biéler, perhaps blinded by the fact of Calvin's conversion and overlooking the *De Luxu*, fails to do justice to the continuing influence of Seneca on Calvin's ethic. See Biéler, *La Pensée Economique*, 72.

15 among certain ones who sin more because the times, not they themselves, are lacking. For people are influenced by judgment and think
a man honest whose example they can see and even latch onto. Truth
will lay strong hands on those who are still teachable and only lightly
corrupted, when she gets a spokesman.

Take these delightful foods which force already glutted men to
20 eat—to label such prodigies of luxury we must search outside nature
for suitable terms. We look up to and adore absurdities in the same
way children in the dark are afraid of ghosts. And to be doubly
25 children—we have turned everything into shadows. Part of the remedy is to recognize the evil that is in them, as it often happens that
not even vices so please their authors that they dare praise them.

Now it is a dangerous disease when men flatter themselves and
30 seek to defend their wicked ways. Chrysostom, Hom. 17 on Genesis,
near the beginning.

[Page 204]

They rest their case on Joseph's many-colored cloak and Rebecca's
earrings and bracelets. How true is Cicero's statement: "Many imitate
the sumptuousness of L. Lucullus' villas, but who emulate his
5 uprightness?" In the many-colored cloak they demonstrate all their
pomp to be but childish absurdities. We do not condemn care be-
stowed on something; we wish men would follow a moderation
closer to abstinence than to luxury. On the first clothing, see Gen. 3.

So far has the world degenerated from those former customs that at
10 present a chaste man or a chaste woman is considered a prodigy of
nature. The talk of a dissolute man is broken and uncontrolled. Do
not think a mind temperate when speech gushes forth. These effeminate and dissolute fellows are men nevertheless in one sense: they
15 are ashamed to speak, and jolly well ought to be ashamed! How
Maecenas would have been praised for his kindness if he had not corrupted it with his lusts and sensual pleasures! At the peak of his licentiousness he restrained himself from shedding blood, from going
20 about injuring others, from oppressing anyone with his power. "Tis
said he was soft, not gentle."

Things arising from custom are loathsome and all normal activities are despicable. Why are persons so very wicked and shameless
as to bear rebuke when their conduct is examined? They fancy such
25 diaphanous garb as no passerby can overlook. Do you think it's one
body for which so much clothing is made ready? You are mistaken:
it belongs rather to months and days. Seneca Epist.: "Elegant dress
is not a manly adornment." We are worse than children delighted
with cheap necklaces; we go in for expensive absurdities.

30 Vice is never without some defense. "While we live by example, we
are not now controlled by reason, but led astray by custom." Be
ashamed—when you lavish great care on your comeliness—of being
35 surpassed by dumbanimals, lest your dress be marked by a mere
show of thrift. See Sen. C. 1, *Ep*. 5. Truer than I should like is that
saying of the ancients that those who labor so much in

[Page 205]

developing the body are little concerned with the cultivation of the soul. Such persons are not effeminate but castrated. It is absurd for them to dazzle the common folk with great outlays for clothes,
5 buildings, and banquets, when their filth, decked in such objects, still sticks out. They treat all men stingily to keep something to be liberal with—or rather, prodigal—toward themselves. Some dine frugally in order to build lavishly; others dispense with household furnishings
10 to concentrate on bodily adornment. We push one another into vices and though we are the cause of one another's wicked ways, we put forward as an excuse custom and the example of the crowd. A good part use the present age as their excuse; others, the place.

Such is life. What should I do? I should conspire against public
15 morals. I should proclaim a war against both fatherland and present age. I hear; but I reply: Does anyone who dies in a city plague on that account die the less? Campania broke Hannibal unconquered in war.

We must speak concerning funerals. Such pomp as we bring forth after death for our own pleasure yet cannot give to ourselves, we give
20 rather to an insensible corpse, as if we were going to get back some delight from such a show. How many persons are there who—if one should deprive them of clothing or of hair—would not think their very limbs torn off, so that now they no longer seem the same to
25 themselves? This is the slave dealer's art: to hide defects under some sort of finery.

The vices of individuals breed public error; in turn, public error breeds the vices of individuals. A man ashamed of mean attire will boast of costly clothing. Luxury is measured by the number of horses
30 a man drives. Yet Cato was content with one. See Seneca Ep. 88.

Nevertheless, I'll spare their ears. But individuals will not listen because they don't care to. On the contrary, just let me get them to listen in public. They would rather mix things human and divine, and
35 break all laws, than stop being enslaved to the highest luxury. Examples can be found close at hand. We've recently seen some in Geneva. Oh, if poverty were sometime hallowed in churches and in public, people would not be ashamed thereafter to admit it in private. See Sen. fol. 21.

40 Seneca, *On Shortness of Life*, page 374, against cowls, &c. In taking such a position against custom, I'll be charging God with crime. If things went well with men, they should have sought their customary way of life from good men. Now when public agreement on vices
45 is thrown up to me, what else are they boasting about than that we have landed in a time when one is no longer permitted to lead a holy and honorable life among corrupt men.

Against men's tonsures. [You say,] "It is the glory of Christ." You dare practice such deception? Is it not a sacrilege? This perversity
50 of extravagance led the ancient Anchorites to prescribe for themselves a humbler sort of garb, in order to dissociate themselves from the common yearning of all men. Then, as good arrangements usually go bad, monks came eventually to seek holiness or at least the

55 reputation for sanctity from cowls, hoods, tonsures, and like trifles.
These Anchorites, I say,

[Page 206]

if they were living today—what would they do, or with what remedy
would they fortify themselves, when they could no longer bear the
extravagance creeping in upon an age as yet only partially corrupted?
For they did not even sufficiently apprise their descendants of that
5 remedy. We see how many sleek monks come to the point of deliberately calling a white garment a tool of luxury.

Let no one say: I dress harmlessly, &c. All men bear the blood of
the poor. How can these sainted chaps make their way back, save
10 through the poor? Especially lawyers, &c. The prophet has said:
"Your hands are full of blood," but I will say your whole body has become infected because it is decked in such clothing. They will say,
"This is no new example." Granted. Human affairs have really never
15 gone well enough that more people wouldn't be pleased if they went
better. Still, the ancients' luxury could be called niggardliness in comparison with this trash.

Let us recall that dire denunciation hurled at Noah's times.
20 You might say some persons bear about with them the scent of the
perfumer's shop. "It's no sweet smell always to have a sweet smell."
Not only all parts of the body, but even clothes are counterfeit. Our
25 feasts serve not our stomachs but our ambition. That statement of
Valerius on Tubero's banquet must be disputed; our ancestors wished
to be magnificent in public but thrifty in private. Now, if they had
learned private thrift, they would not have affected public luxury; as
30 it is, they parade in public the vices they have conceived at home.

Many many are to be seen who like Bias lug everything about with
them; others, even more than they really possess. People used to be
concerned about even using adornment; now with luxury on the
35 increase, they are quite unconcerned. How long this talk of voluptuaries? "Money for clothes: no one calls this a benefit." Senec. fol. 354.

After you have seen our dances you might say these gay fellows are
40 going mad with laughter. Seneca uses the proverbial expression,
"with head uncovered," in the sense of "without shame." They must
be admonished to be fairer toward us. For they are given to vices
which cannot bear easy remedies. Such persons are chiefly
45 concerned with what they eat, drink, wear.

A few things should be said about the honest use of the mirror.
Whatever was once called "women's world" is now a man's baggage,
nay a soldier's pack! Our native land's hatred of offspring is to be
50 censured. Augustine says: "Out of your abundance actors are steeped
in luxury, while the poor lack even necessities."

Endnotes: *De Luxu*
[Page 203]

1) war. C. Bellum . . . suscipio. The phrase *bellum suscipere* is common
with Cicero. Perhaps Calvin here has in mind two passages in Cic.
Off. The first of these, at 1.11.35, is a phrase lying between two quoted

in *Sen. De Clem.* (1.22.1, p. 125, and 1.18.1, p. 111): "Wars, therefore, are to be undertaken for this end, that we may live in peace without being injured." The other, at 1.23.80, is prefaced by the phrase (1.22.78): "The examples of civil courage are therefore no less meritorious than those of military; and they require a greater share of zeal and labor than the latter." Again (1.23.79): "the civilians who preside over public affairs are equally serviceable to their country as they who wage wars." The passage (quoted at *Inst.* 4.20.12, n. 32 [1539]) referred to is: "Now in engaging in war we ought to make it appear that we have no other view than peace. But the character of a brave and resolute man is not to be ruffled with adversity, and not to be in such confusion as to quit his post, as we say, but to preserve a presence of mind, and the exercise of reason, without departing from his purpose." The metaphor of waging war is continued at 205.15, where literary echoes suggest Calvin's association of his moral campaign with that of Cato, and that of Cicero against Catiline.

3f.) in whom, &c. In these lines Calvin reveals his inner feelings about his campaign of moral reform in Geneva and the response of others thereto. Among the letters that express his purpose and his steadfast courage at this time, one should read *Ep.* 792 (*CR*, 12:338f.; ET, 144), to his former friend and now enemy, Amy Perrin. Calvin's intention is to impress upon Perrin "the necessity of earnestly seeking to acquire the primary virtue of obedience to God, and respect for the common order and polity of the church."

6) Maecenases. C. supini illi Maecenates. Cf. Juv. *Sat.* 1.66: Et multum referens de Maecenate supino.

9) annoyed. C. aegre audiunt. Cf. *Comm. Sen. De Clem.* 2.5.2.

11) life. C. ad meliorem frugem redeant. Cf. Cic. *Cael.* 12.28, cited by Calvin, *Sen. De Clem.* 1.2.1 (p. 22.38).

13–14) lacking. C. qui temporis vitio magis quam suo peccant. Cf. Sen. *Ep. Mor.* 114.8: Quod vitium hominis esse interdum, interdum temporis solet.

17–19) spokesman. C. Istis, inquam, adhuc docilibus et leviter corruptis forte iniiciet manum veritas, ubi advocatum nancta erit. Cf. Sen. *Ep. Mor.* 108.12: . . . adhuc docilibus leviterque corruptis inicit manum veritas, si advocatum idoneum nancta est. Cf. C. *Sen. De Clem.* 1.5.4.

19–20) to eat. Reminiscent of Sen. *Ep. Mor.* 119.14: ". . . a luxury which seeks how it may prolong hunger even after repletion, how to stuff the stomach, not to fill it, and how to rouse a thirst that has been satisfied with the first drink." Cf. Calvin, *Inst.* 4.12.21 (1543), against the eating of delicacies under the pretense of fasting.

25–26) them. C. Pars remedii est malum suum nosse. Cf. Sen. *Ep. Mor.* 6.1; 28.9f.

30) Genesis. This reference should probably be to 204.8 ("Genes. 3"). Chrysostom Hom. Gen. 18 (on Gen. 3.21; *PG*, 53:150): "Let the rich hear, and let those who luxuriate in woven cloth and are clad in silks learn how from the beginning the kindly Lord, teaching human nature, because the first man was condemned to the death penalty on account of transgression, and needed clothing to cover his shame, made for

man garments of skins, in order to teach us to shun a soft and dissolute life, not to follow an idle and languid one, but to embrace a more austere life." Chrysostom now raises questions about woman's preference of silk over wool, and about luxurious attire. He then quotes 1 Tim. 6.8 as his scriptural norm. Seneca, too, recommends simple clothing—as that made from the skins of wild beasts and other animals. But his reason for eschewing luxurious attire is to keep out the cold in the most natural way, not to cover human shame (*Ep. Mor.* 90.16).

[Page 204]

1) cloak. C. Ioseph polymitam. Cf. C. *Comm. Gen.* 37.3 (*CR*, 23:335f.): tunicam multicolorem, tunica versicolor. Cf. Sen. *Ep. Mor.* 114.21: qui lacernas coloris improbi sumunt.

1–2) bracelets. C. inaures armillasque Rebeccae. See Gen. 24.22, 30. Cf. C. *Comm. Gen.* 24.22 (*CR*, 23:335f.; ET, CTS 2.20f.). To summarize C's main points: (1) any kind of luxury—including pomp and ambition in adorning the body—is highly displeasing to God; (2) not for us to forbid every kind of ornament—but moderation and even abstinence is to be cultivated (cf. 204–7) to avoid women's insatiable cupidity; also to avoid outbreak of ambition; (3) women who desire to shine in gold, seek in Rebecca a pretext for their corruption—but why don't they live her austere and rustic life as well, &c.

2–4) uprightness. C. L. Luculli villarum magnificentiam imitantur multi, probitatem vero quis? Cf. Cic. *Off.* 1.39.140: ut L. Luculli, summi viri, virtutem, quis? at quam multi villarum magnificentiam imitati sunt?

6) care. C. Epimelian. ejpimeleiåa. Possibly Calvin has in mind such a passage as Acts 27.3.

6–7) luxury. C. modum adhiberi volumus, qui sit abstinentia proprior quam luxuriae. Cf. C. *Comm. Gen.* 24.30 (*CR*, 23:336): non tantum mediocritas colenda est, sed etiam abstinentia, quoad fieri potest. On moderation, see the references to Harkness and Wallace, mentioned above; also *Inst.* 3.10.1–4; 3.19.7ff., &c. Biéler, *La Pensée Economique;* 213ff., expounds Calvin's view of *sobrietas*, summing it up as "neither excess nor asceticism."

8) Gen. 3. Cf. C. *Comm. Gen.* 3.21 (*CR*, 23:78; ET, CTS 1.182): "example, by which he would accustom us to a frugal and inexpensive mode of dress. And I wish those delicate persons would reflect on this, who deem no ornament sufficiently attractive unless it exceed in magnificence. Not that every kind of ornament is to be expressly condemned, but because when immoderate elegance and splendor is carefully sought after, not only is that Master despised, who intended clothing to be a sign of shame, but war is, in a certain sense, carried on against nature." On modesty in dress, see the references to Calvin's commentaries and sermons given by Wallace, *Calvin's Doctrine of the Christian Life,* 179f. The Bernese fashion of "Les hauts de chausses chaplés aux genoux" was forbidden by the Council (RC 25 May 1547; *CR*, 21:405), and in the *Laws of Geneva,* ET (1643), 34.

10–11) uncontrolled. C. Vox infracta et soluta discincti est hominis. Cf. Sen. *Ep. Mor.* 114.4: Quid ergo? Non oratio eius aeque soluta est, quam ipse discinctus?

11–12) forth. C. Ne putes animum continentem ubi oratio diffluit. Cf. Sen. *Ep. Mor.* 114.4: Magni vir ingenii fuerat, si illud egisset via rectiore, si non vitasset intellegi, si non etiam in oratione diffueret. On loose talk, see Wallace, *Calvin's Doctrine of the Christian Life*, 173, citing *Serm. Dt.* 5.18 (*CR*, 26:341).

13) effeminate and dissolute. Cf. *Inst.* 2.8.44 (1539): "There is a good point in Archelaus' statement to a youth wearing excessively wanton and dainty clothing that it does not matter in what member he is unchaste. . . ." (Gellius, *NA* 3.5.2; cf. Plut. *Moralia* 126A.) See Sen. *Ep. Mor.* 122.7, on men's use of women's garments (cf. *CR*, 28:20) and *Ben.* 6.38.3 on dealers in luxuries who exploit the effeminacy of youth.

15–20) How Maecenas . . . gentle. C. Maecenas quantum laudem mansuetudinis ferre potuerat, nisi eam ipsam lascivia delitiisque suis corrupisset. In summa rerum omnium licentia sibi temperavit ne sanguinem funderet, ne per iniuria grassaretur, ne quem potestate sua premeret. Dictum est mollem fuisse, non mitem. Cf. Sen. *Ep. Mor.* 114.7–8: Maxima laus illi tribuitur mansuetudinis, pepercit gladio, sanguine abstinuit, nec ulla alia re, quid posset, quam licentia ostendit. Hanc ipsam laudem suam corrupit. . . . Apparet enim mollem fuisse, non mitem.

20–21) despicable. C. Fastidiuntur quae ex more sunt et sordida sunt omnia solita. Cf. Sen. *Ep. Mor.* 114.10: cum adsuevit animum fastidire, quae ex more sunt, et illi pro sordidis solita sunt. . . .

23–25) overlook. C. Volunt omnia adeo esse pellucida ut oculis etiam transeuntium nihil transsilire liceat. Cf. Sen. *Ep. Mor.* 114.21: . . . qui perlucentem togam sumunt, qui nolunt facere quicquam, quod hominum oculis transire liceat. Cf. also Sen. *Ben.* 7.9.4, echoing the same thought, on women's transparent silk dresses. The whole passage is on extremes of luxury.

25–26) days. While an exact Senecan parallel has not been found, two other contexts provide similar reasoning. *Ep. Mor.* 89.21 asks if the possession of many bed chambers can be for one person; 114.26, of many cooks, kitchens, food, wine, &c. for one belly.

27–28) adornment. C. and Sen. *Ep. Mor.* 115.2: Non est ornamentum virile concinnitas.

28–29) necklaces. C. Nos pueris peiores sumus quod illos parvo aere empta monilia delectant. . . . Cf. Sen. *Ep. Mor.* 115.8: . . . parentibus quippe nec minus fratribus praeferunt parvo aere empta monilia. Lit.: "bought for a mere penny."

30) defense. C. Nunquam vitium sine patricinio. Cf. Sen. *Ep. Mor.* 116.2: Nullum est vitium sine patricinio.

30–32) custom. C. Dum ad exempla vivimus, iam non ratione componimur, sed abducimur consuetudine. Cf. Sen. *Ep. Mor.* 123.6: Inter causas malorum nostrorum est, quod vivimus ad exempla, nec ratione componimur sed consuetudine abducimur.

32–33) animals. C. Pudeat quum formam exacta cura excolueris a multis (better: mutis) animalibus vinci. . . . Cf. Sen. *Ep. Mor.* 124.22: Quid excolis formam? Cum omnia feceris, a mutis animalibus decore vinceris.

[Page 205]
1–2) soul. Cf., e.g., Sen. *Ep. Mor.* 92.33: Nemo liber est, qui corpori servit.

2–3) castrated. C. Hi non enervati mollitia sed castrati. Cf. Sen. *Ep. Mor.* 19.9: . . . nisi illum (Maecenatem) enervasset felicitas, immo castrasset.

6–8) They treat . . . lavishly. C. Sunt enim in omnes sordidi ut aliquid supersit unde sint erga se liberales, aut potius profusi. Alii coenant frugaliter ut luxuriose aedificent. Cf. Sen. *Ep. Mor.* 20.3: Observa te itaque, numquid vestis tua domusque dissentiant numquid in te liberalis sis, in tuos sordidus, numquid cenes frugaliter, aedifices luxuriose.

8–9) adornment. Cf. Sen. *Ep. Mor.* 114.9.

10–11) vices. C. and Sen. *Ep. Mor.* 41.9: . . . in vitia alter alterum trudimus.

13–14) place. C. Bona pars saeculum excusat, alii locum. Cf. Sen. *Ep. Mor.* 50.1: Quaedam enim locis et temporibus adscribimus.

14–15) morals. C. Coniurarem adversus publicos mores. Cf. Sen. *Ep. Mor.* 87.9: alter (Scipio) enim cum hostibus nostris bellum, alter (Cato) cum moribus gessit. See note on *bellum suscipere* at 203.1, above.

15–16) war. C. Bellum indicerem et patriae et saeculo. On *bellum indicere,* cf. Sen. *Ir.* 3.2.4: Ad arma protinus ignesque discursum est, et indicta finitimis bella, aut gesta cum civibus.

17–18) in war. C. Hannibalem bello invictum fregit Campania. Cf. Sen. *Ep. Mor.* 51.5: Una Hannibalem hiberna solverunt et indomitum illum nivibus atque Alpibus virum enervaverunt fomenta Campaniae. Armis vicit, vitiis victus est.

18ff.) funerals. Seneca has much to say about death, grief, mourning, and funerals; see, for example: *Ep. Mor.* 63.13 and *Brev. Vit.* 20.4. In Calvin's works, see *Inst.* 3.5.10; *Project d'Ordonnances Ecclesiastiques* (1541), on burial (*CR,* 10a:27). Note especially his *Response à cinq Questions, 2°* (*CR,* 10a:256) on mourning customs, wherein Calvin advises avoidance of too great rigor and austerity, but also all superfluous pomp, &c.

24–26) finery. C. Haec mangonum ars est aliquo lenocinio vitia abscondere. Cf. Sen. *Ep. Mor.* 80.9: Mangones quicquid est, quod displiceat, aliquo lenocinio abscondunt. . . .

26–27) individuals. C. Singulorum vitia publicum errorem faciunt: tum publicus error singulorum vitia. Cf. Sen. *Ep. Mor.* 94.54: Et ideo in singulis vitia populorum sunt, quia illa populus dedit.

27–28) clothing. C. Qui sordida veste erubescit, pretiosa gloriabitur. Cf. Sen. *Ep. Mor.* 87.4: Qui sordido vehiculo erubescit, pretioso gloriabitur.

28–30) *Ep.* 88. C. Nunc ad luxuriam pertinent quot quisque ducat equos. At Cato uno contentus fuit. Cf. Sen. *Ep. Mor.* 87.10: . . . Catonem uno caballo esse contentum.

30–31) ears. C. Parcam tamen eorum auribus. Cf. Sen. *Ben.* 2.11.6: . . . ejus auribus pepercisse.

31–33) public. C. Verum singuli non audient quia nolunt. Modo hoc rursum obtineam ut publice audiant. Cf. Sen. *Ep. Mor.* 89.19: . . . et quia verum singuli audire non vultis, publice audite.

33–34) divine. C. Potius humana omnia ac divina permisceant. . . . Cf. Caesar *B.C.* 1.6, fin.: omnia divina humanaque jura permiscentur. This proverbial expression is a favorite of Calvin.

35–36) Geneva. C. Vidimus nuper in Genuens. If the ascription of date here
given is correct, "nuper" would suggest a point at the end of the period 1546–1547.

36–38) public. C. O si aliquando in templis et in publico consecretur pauper-
tas. . . . Cf. Sen. *Ep. Mor.* 95–72 (on Tubero): Quid aliud paupertatem
in Capitolio consecrare? With this should be compared C. *Inst.* 4.5.17–
18 (1543), where the early frugality and the present opulence of
churches are contrasted, and the neglect of the poor emphasized. Also
see *Inst.* PA 4 (1536; *OS,* 3:18.23–25) and 4.4.8 (1543). On Seneca's
treatment of poverty and wealth, see the summary in Sevenster, op.
cit., 200ff. Calvin, *Ep.* 700 (*CR,* 12:169f.; ET, 145), writing to M. de Fal-
ais in September 1545, clearly elucidates his conception of Christian
poverty, quoting 1 Cor. 7.31 as his norm. His view must be clearly distinguished from the medieval monastic ideal. See also *Inst.* 3.7.8: poverty with piety happier than riches with forgetfulness of God. Wallace,
Calvin's Doctrine of the Christian Life, deals with poverty in his chapter
on "Christian Moderation," esp. at p. 177. See also note on 204.6–7,
above. At 4.20.13, Calvin allows the use of tax revenues for the magnificence of the princely household in keeping with the dignity exercised, but not to the point of waste and expensive luxury. And private
persons should not rashly "decry any expenses of princes, even if these
exceed the common expenditures of the citizens."

40) cowls. Calvin here refers, in Erasmus' 1529 edition of Seneca's works,
to *Brev. Vit.* 16.3 (fol. 374). Seneca asserts that mortals make the gods
an excuse for their sins, and that the poets help them in this. Calvin
applies this thought to monks and their cowls: monks and priests say
it is godly to wear the habit and tonsure; therefore, they are not to be
blamed for being careful about such externals. Thus, God becomes
an excuse for their sinful emphasis on religious externals.

41) crime. C. Inscripsero Deum sceleri. Cf. Sen. *Brev. Vit.* 16.3: auctores
illi inscribere deos. This is doubtless an echo of Ovid, *Metam.* 15.128:
Inscripsero Deum sceleri.

47–48) tonsures. C. caesariem. The word is here rendered "tonsure" to fit the
monastic content. Its primary meaning is a dark (= beautiful) head
of hair, usually that of a man. In this place, Calvin is referring to any
kind of fussy care of the head, whether of monk or dandy. In *Inst.*
4.19.25ff. (1543), Calvin deals with the tonsure in detail, offering in
section 27 a short historical sketch of men's hair styles; this is echoed
in his comments on Absalom's hair, *Serm.* 46 on 2 Sam. 14:26 (11
September 1562; *Suppl. Calv.* 1.404.9ff.). Among the Senecan passages dealing with excessive luxury, e.g., care of the hair, &c., see
Brev. Vit. 12.

48) Christ. C. Est gloria Christi. Cf. C. *Inst.* 1536, 4.19.25: . . . gloriam Dei
contemplari. . . . (*OS,* 1:207.22).

49ff.) Anchorites. This contrast between ancient and contemporary monasticism is more fully developed from Aug. *De Opere Monachorum*
23.27 at *Inst.* 4.13.10ff. (1543).

54) cowls. C. *Inst.* 4.13 (1543), with an almost Erasmian spirit, ridicules
cowls: "these hooded Sophists" (sec. 14), "our hooded friends" (sec.

16), "who wrap themselves in a cowl and a thousand impious superstitions. . . ." (sec. 17).

[Page 206]

6f.) remedy. Calvin here alludes to the idleness of monks, a familiar theme in the *Institutes*. *Inst.* PA 4 (*OS*, 3:18.29–19.1, 1536): "a monk who does not labor with his hands must be considered equal to a thug, or (if you prefer) a brigand . . ." &c. Ibid. 4.12.10: "our present-day monks find in idleness the chief part of their sanctity." Biéler, *La Pensée Economique*, 408, cites C. *Comm. Mat.* 19.21 on this.

8) poor. Cf. *Inst.* 4.20.13, n. 33, where Calvin calls the tax revenues "almost the very blood of the people, which it would be the harshest inhumanity not to spare." C. Pauperum sanguinem omnes ferunt. Cf. Jer. 2.34. See also C. *Prael. in Jer.*, in loc., *CR*, 37:539. Geneva. at war or in political tension with her neighbors, suffered from extremes of poverty and wealth. Church schemes for poor relief and sumptuary laws to restrain the rich sought to meet the problem. The fourth order of the church, that of the diaconate, was framed to serve the poor and the sick, &c. See Biéler, *La Pensée Economique*, 158f.

9) sainted chaps. C. beautulis. This may be an echo of Persius, *Sat.* 3.103f.: . . . tandemque beatulus alto/compositus lecto. . . .

10–11) blood. Isa. 1:15.

14–15) better. C. Nunquam enim tam bene habuerunt res humanae ut pluribus meliora placerent. Cf. Sen. *Ep. Mor.* 115.17: Nemo enim est, cui felicitas sua, etiam si cursu venit, satis faciat.

18–19) Noah's times. Gen. 6:5–8. See C. *Comm. Gen.*, ad loc., *CR*, 23:116–19.

20–21) shop. C. Dicas quosdam secum ferre unguentarias tabernas. Cf. Sen. *Ep. Mor.* 108.4: . . . qui in unguentaria taberna resederunt et paullo diutius commorati sunt, odorem secum loci ferunt.

21) smell. C. Non bene olet, qui bene semper olet. This proverb comes from Martial, 2.12.

24–25) ambition. C. Non gulae serviunt coenae nostrae, sed ambitione. Cf. Sen. *Ep. Mor.* 60.3: Non fames nobis ventris nostri magno constat, sed ambitio. Also, *Ben.* 3.28.3: libidinis et gulae servus. *Ep. Mor.* 124.3: gulae ac libidini addictos.

26–28) private. Seneca's references to Tubero, one of which is cited by C. at 205.36–38, above, suggest a passage from Valerius Maximus, *Facta et Dicta Memorabilia*, 7.5.1, here paraphrased. Other references by Valerius to Tubero may be seen at 4.3.7 and 4.4.9. Tubero's well-known austerity is also brought out in the words Cicero ascribes to him in Rep. 1.9ff.

31–32) with them. C. Plerosque videre est qui instar Biantis omnia sua secum portant, alios etiam plus quam habeant. See Valerius Maximus, 7.2., ext. 3, where Bias' saying reads: Ego vero . . . bona mea mecum porto. Cic. *Par. St.* 1.1.2: Ego vero . . . facio. nam omnia mea porto mecum.

36) How long . . . voluptuaries? C. Hoc verbum delicatorum quousque tandem? A reminiscence of Cic. *Cat.* 1.1.1: Quousque tandem abutere, Catilina, patientia nostra? Henry, *Life of Calvin*, ii, 62, draws a historical parallel that suggests the drift of this rhetorical question:

"Calvin saw in Perrin only the libertine Genevese citizen, who, rash, active and frivolous, was on the way to become a Catiline." The analogy then is: Calvin: Cicero :: Perrin : Cataline.

37) benefit. *CR* has: Vestiarium neutro quem apud Senec. fol. 354. The Senecan passage referred to (*Ben.* 3.21.1) reads: Est aliquid, quod dominus praestare servo debeat, ut cibaria, ut vestiarium: nemo hoc dixit beneficium. Our translation reflects the latter. See also *Tranq. Anim.* 8.5.

38–39) dances. It may be instructive to review the anti-dancing campaign of the Geneva Reformers. Their opposition to dancing is laid down in the catalogue of vices in the Confession of Faith (1536), Art. 19, and in the Articles (1537). The Draft Ordinances of 1541 include among the vices from which the ministers must be free, "dances and similar dissoluteness" (LCC 22.61). Among the later proclamations, one (*Laws of Geneva*, ET, 1643, 29) enjoins the citizens "to haunt and come diligently to the Sermons of the Word of God" and "to live holily and peaceably, to be obedient according to their duties to Magistrates, Fathers, Mothers, Lords and Masters, defending and inhibiting all blasphemy, despising of God and his Ministers, dishonest words, vain songs, drunkenness, dissolutions, excess, arrogancy, and insolency, plays or games, idle running from house to house, cut or embroidered hose, chiding, dissensions, fighting or brawling, injuring of others, and all other things not lawful and contrary to the holy word of God and his Commandments and the Acts and Proclamations heretofore made." In the schedule of fines (ibid., p. 36), among other items, is the following: "that no manner person do sing any vain, dishonest, or ribald songs, neither to dance, nor make masques or mummeries, or any disguisings in no manner or sort whatsoever it be, upon pain to be put three days in prison with bread and water and 40s. for every time so offending."

So much, then, for the legal basis. The Registers of Council and Consistory abound in references to such offenses. In 1546–47, for example, the problem of dancing is mentioned, especially in April (1546) and June (1547). Calvin's letters of the same period (e.g., *Ep.* 791, 832, 921, 924, 930, 940, 977) deal with loose living, including dancing. In *Ep.* 791 (April 1546; *CR*, 12:333–37; ET 163), Calvin writes to Farel: "After your departure the dances caused us more trouble than I had supposed," and goes on to describe the conflict of the Consistory with the Perrins. A report had come that there had been dances at Belle Rive and at the house of Anthony Lect., but the ministers were unable, even with threats, to obtain through questioning the names of the dancers. Mme. Perrin denied the right of the ministers to inquire into the affairs of her family. On 12 April the Syndic Corne and others were imprisoned for dancing.

On 20–22 April Jacques Gruet and others were questioned by the Consistory about the dances and were imprisoned for dancing and lying. Calvin was reported to have criticized the dancers as "ruffians." In the next year, at a meeting of the Consistory on 23 June, some women (including Perrin's wife) were again charged with dancing.

The women boldly told that their chastisement was not the ministers' task, but that of their husbands: "with proud and rebellious words and great blasphemies they insulted the ministers." Calvin writing to Viret (*Ep.* 921; ET, 199) describes how Francesca Perrin insulted the minister Abel, calling him a "coarse swineherd" and "a malicious liar," and subsequently insulted him afresh at the city gate as she was escaping from prison. The following day this unruly faction put a threat to the ministers' lives in a church pulpit: "the people did not wish to have so many masters; the ministers had gone far enough in their course of censure; the renegade monks like them had done nothing more than afflict all the world in this way; if they persisted in their course, people would be reduced curse the hour in which they emerged from the rule of monachism." The Libertine, Jacques Gruet, accused of a part in the plot, was later executed as a dangerous heretic. The crisis in the opposition was reached in December, when, warned of a sedition, Calvin bravely entered the mob at the Hôtel de Ville, and quieted the crowd.

Finally, Calvin's discussion of dancing in his sermons is to be examined. Wallace derives Calvin's opposition chiefly from 1 Cor 15.33, dancing being considered a form of evil communication. Is dancing—provided there be no illicit intercourse—so bad? Calvin stubbornly answers that it is in fact the prelude to such adultery, and both opens the door to, and announces the entrance of Satan (*Serm. Dt.* 5.18, *CR*, 26:340f.; Wallace, *Calvin's Doctrine of the Christian Life*, 175, n. 4). In keeping with his "interiorization" of the Decalogue through the Sermon on the Mount, Calvin's exposition of the Seventh Commandment (*Inst.* 2.8.41–44), while it does not expressly mention dancing, broadly treats fornication as including, besides the act itself, "the seduction of another's modesty with wanton dress and obscene gestures and foul speech." That dancing remained a topic for preaching to the end of Calvin's life is demonstrated by Serm. 41 on 2 Sam 13.11–14 (1562, *Suppl. Calv.*, 1.363.14f.): "Why do the men wish their wives and daughters to dance? In order that they may be adulteresses and go to perdition and acquire everlasting ignominy." Again in Serm. 80 on 2 Sam. 23.2 (1563, *Suppl. Calv.* 1.699.45ff.), Calvin contrasts the effect of David's "holy song" and that of the drum and flute, which causes the crowd in their dancing and dissipation to lose control, honor, shame—like "unbridled calves."

44–45) wear. Cf. Matt. 6.31.

46) mirror. A reference to Seneca's discussion of the use of mirrors at *Q. N.* 1.17.

47) woman's world. See Livy *AUC* 34.7–9; cf. *RC* 6 April 1545 (*CR*, 21:350). It is instructive to summarize this entire context for the parallel it affords with Geneva in 1546–47. In 215 B.C., when during the Second Punic War Hannibal was ravaging Italy (cf. 205.17–18) a law was introduced at Rome by the plebeian tribune, Caius Oppius, to limit the luxury of women. This law, called the Lex Oppia, provided that "No woman should possess more than half an ounce of gold, or wear a garment of various colors (cf. 204.1, 4f.), or ride in a carriage

drawn by horses, in a city, or any town, or any place nearer thereto than one mile; except on occasion of some public religious solemnity" (Livy, 34.1, ET, C. Edmonds, Cambridge, Mass.: Harvard University Press, 1939). Subsequently, after the end of the Second Punic War at Zama in 202 B.C., economic conditions began to improve. In 195 B.C., public pressure, amounting almost to sedition, broke out in Rome for the repeal of this law. Prominent in the disorders were the women of Rome themselves, as they thronged the forum and the streets, demanding the restoration of their right to finery.

The speeches that the historian Livy puts into the mouths of Cato the Elder (234–149 B.C., Censor 184) opposing the law's repeal, and Lucius Valerius (plebeian tribune) favoring the relaxation of sumptuary controls, are a treatise on the two ways to handle luxury in the state. Cato, having just threaded his way through a milling crowd to the forum, is scandalized by the seditious attitude of the women; if husbands and fathers exercised their prerogatives, the unruliness of the women would be solved. He contrasts the ancestral emphasis on "women in the home" with the changed situation: "We, it seems, suffer them, now to interfere in the management of state affairs, and to introduce themselves into the forum, into general assemblies, and into assemblies of election. To admit equality between the sexes will be to bring about the superiority of women over men. If their revolt against severity is successful they will, by abrogating one law, undermine the rest. Laws are made for the general welfare, not to suit individuals; they should not be repealed just because they offend individuals. "Often have you heard me complain of the profuse expenses of the women—often of those of the men; and that not only of men in private stations, but of the magistrates: and that the state was endangered by two opposite views, luxury and avarice; those pests, which have been the ruin of all great empires."

Cato points out that the law usefully removes the possibility of being ashamed of frugality or of poverty, the worst shame of all (cf. 205.27f.). Yet rich matrons hate, above all, "equalization." The rich, unrestrained, can indulge in luxuries that the poor, in trying to emulate, spend beyond their means. If the Oppian Law be repealed, Cato concludes, women will cease to feel shame toward the things they should be ashamed of, and turn their shame toward those that ought not to rouse it.

To this plea against the law's repeal, Lucius Valerius, tribune of the people, speaks in support of his move to set it aside. Cato has, he avers, spent more time in rebuking the women than in defending the law. Against Cato's charges of female sedition, the tribune cites examples from earlier times of the public intervention, of the women in times of crisis, of their contribution of their gold to the public treasury, &c. (34.5).

As to the law itself, Valerius asserts that the state makes two kinds of laws: some are permanent in character and should not be repealed: others are temporary: "Those made in peace are generally repealed by war; those made in war, by peace" (34.6). The Oppian Law was passed when the victorious Hannibal was about to storm Rome itself. Drastic measures were necessary that time: "Who does not clearly see that the poverty and distress of the state, requiring that every private person's money should be converted to the use of the public, enacted this law, with intent that it should remain in force so long only as the cause of enacting the law should remain" (34.6). Cf. *Inst.* 4.20.16: different circumstances demand differently framed laws; but they must have a common basis in equity.

Valerius now makes an impassioned plea that the women should not remain the "forgotten class" in the new affluence that has come to Rome. While men, children, even horses are splendidly clad, should women alone be kept in drab attire? While the wives of the allies travel in splendor, should the wives of the Romans walk the city streets on foot? "Elegance of appearance, and ornaments, and dress, these are the women's badges of distinction; in these they delight and glory; these our ancestors called 'the women's world.' What else do they lay aside when in mourning, except their gold and purple? And what else do they resume when the mourning is over?" (34.7).

Furthermore, allowing gold ornaments to the womenfolk provides a kind of reserve fund for public and private emergencies. To Cato's argument that, if the law be repealed, it will be impossible to reenact any of its former restrictions, Valerius counters that the women really wish to have their dress and adornment regulated not by a law, but by their own husbands and fathers.

Needless to say, on the following day, even greater crowds of women made public demonstration for repeal, and kept up their pressure until the tribes voted to set the law aside.

48) offspring. μισοτεκνία. See Plut. *Mor.* 4F (*De Liberis Educandis* 7). Cf. C. *Sen. De Clem.* 1.13.5 (p. 94).

50–52) necessities. See Aug. *Ep.* 138.2.14 (*PL*, 33:531). The next section of this epistle is quoted by Calvin, *Inst.* 4.20.12, 1543.

The Chief Lineaments
of Calvin's Religious Experience[1]

I. The Preparation

1. Brought up a Christian from childhood: my father intended me as a young boy for theology;
2. But God's Word was suppressed;
3. There was a notion current that a few persons had a monopoly on religious thought—and all the rest of us should go to them as to oracles;
4. My Christian nurture was quite inadequate for right worship, hope of salvation, or duties of the Christian life;
5. Belief in Christ's saving work I had, but not a work available to me;
6. *Fear* of the day of resurrection—dominated me in private and also taught to me by my Christian teachers;
7. They preached God's clemency but that it comes only to those who deserve it, that is, deserve it by their own works;
8. They rightly thought we are miserable sinners, needing God's clemency for salvation;
9. But how was I to obtain that clemency, that mercy?
   a. by CONFESSION to a priest
   b. by SATISFACTION through good deeds
   c. by SACRIFICES & SOLEMN EXPIATIONS
10. Then they dwelt on the dreadfulness of God's presence—
    a. we must flee to the saints to intercede for us before God;
    [b. when my father saw that the science of law made those who cultivate it wealthy—he changed his mind, hoping for my material gain;
    c. thus I was called back from the study of 'philosophy' to learn law; I followed my father's wish and attempted to do faithful work in law; but God, by the secret leading of his providence, turned my course another way.]

1. Calvin's religious experience is suggested by the Confession of the Evangelical Layman before God's Judgment-Seat (*Reply to Cardinal Sadolet,* in J. K. S. Reid, *Calvin's Treatises,* 250–53) and by the preface to Calvin's Commentary on the Psalms (1555–57). Bracketed passages have been taken from the preface to Calvin's Commentary on the Psalms, and harmonized with the passages from the *Reply to Cardinal Sadolet.* For a strophic translation of the preface, see *Piety 1978,* 27–42.

II. The Travail of Conscience

1. I dutifully performed all these satisfactions & sacrifices;
2. These gave me some intervals of quiet;
3. But I was still far from true peace of conscience;
4. Whenever I descended into myself or raised my mind to God—extreme terror seized me which no satisfaction or expiation could cure;
5. The closer the self-examination, the greater the pricks to my conscience;
6. My only solace—to delude myself by trying to forget God & conscience;
7. Thus the "Christianity' which I followed actually led me away from Christian profession.

III. The Call of the Gospel

1. Now certain preachers were heard calling Christians back to the source of their faith, and clearing away the dregs;
2. My first reaction: strenuous & passionate resistance [for I was very firmly addicted to the papal superstitions];
3. Like all men, I tried to keep in the course once undertaken and could not come to confess that I had been in ignorance & error all my life;
4. I resisted these new teachers especially because of my great reverence for the church—and fear of schism from her.
5. But these preachers clearly distinguished between schism from the church, and the effort to correct the faults of the church;
6. they showed how the church had been presided over by Antichrists repeatedly in times past;
7. All this pointed out that these new teachers were sincerely trying to up-build the church, not tear it down, and were actually doing the same thing as had been done in the past by men whom I considered among the saints;
8. They also justified their attack on the pope whom I had reverenced as Christ's vicegerent: the pope, holder of an empty title, got his power when the world was plunged into ignorance and deep sleep—his office does not rest on the Word of God, or on a legitimate act of the church—but is self-appointed;
9. Also only by throwing off the papal tyranny can we truly have the kingdom of Christ among us;
10. Now they confirmed their attack on the papacy by powerful arguments and 'tumbled him down' by the Word of God;
11. They proved the true order of the church had perished, the power of the keys had been perverted, Christian liberty had collapsed, the kingdom of Christ had been prostrated when this primacy was erected;
12. These new teachers told me I couldn't safely wink at these things as if they were of no concern of mine—for even to err out of ignorance gives no impunity.

IV. The Conversion

1. My mind [more rigid than suited my age] was now prepared for serious attention;
2. Light broke upon me; I realized in what a dunghill of error I had wallowed and how much pollution and impurity I had thereby contracted

[this was a sudden conversion which brought me out of the deep mire of superstition];

3. Now greatly alarmed at the misery into which I had fallen, and much more at that which threatened me in eternal death;

4. I condemned my own past life, not without groans and tears, and accepted thy life, O Lord;

5. My mind now submitted to God, and I was so inspired with such a desire to carry my study further that, although I did not drop other subjects, I had no zeal for them;

[6. I experienced as nothing but pure mockeries, those ceremonies, under which the Romanist masters held great mysteries to exist.]

V. First Steps in the Christian Life

[1. I was fired with enthusiasm to study the faith, although without forsaking other studies entirely;

2. Within a year, many who yearned for pure doctrine came to me to learn it;

3. I, being of a retiring disposition, tried to hide, but in vain, for people treated wherever I dwelt as a sort of public school;

4. Thus God never left me alone in any place, but thrust me into the limelight;

5. Still seeking peace, I left my native France for Germany (i.e., German Switzerland).]

Appendix 2 — The Antithetical Structure of Calvin's *Institutes*[1]

Book I

A. Knowledge of God the Creator
    i. chs. 1–3/4)   True (scriptural) vs. false (philosophical)
    ii. ch. 5a/5b)   knowledge of God
B. Revelation
    chs. 6–8/9   Scriptural (true) vs. Extrascriptural (false: Schwärmer) revelation
C. God as Object of Worship
    chs. 10–11/12 Idols (false) vs. God (true)
D. The Godhead
    ch. 13a/13b   True vs. false (chiefly Servetus) views of the Trinity
E. Creation: Hexaemeron; Angels; Demons
    ch. 14a/14b   True vs. false views
F. Knowledge of Man (as created): Soul; Body
    ch. 15a/15b   True (scriptural) vs. false (philosophical) views of man
G. Providence
    i. ch. 16a/16b   True (scriptural) vs. false (philosophical) views
    ii. ch. 17a/17b   True vs. false attitudes toward providence
    iii. ch. 18a/18b   True vs. false views of how God's providence works toward the ungodly

Book II

A. The Fall and Degeneration of the Human Race: Condition of the Human Will (Knowledge of Man as Fallen), chiefly against the Roman Catholic view;
    i. ch. 1a/1b   True vs. false understanding of man's fallen condition (original sin)
    ii. ch. 2a/2b   True vs. false views concerning the human will (bound vs. free)
    iii. ch. 3a/3b   Total (true) vs. partial (false) corruption of man's nature
    iv. ch. 4a/4b   God's dominion (true) vs. human freedom (false)
    v. chs. 1–4/5   Will: free (false) vs. unfree (true) (Summarizing antithesis)

1. Note: 'a' and 'b' herein refer not to separate sections of the chapters, but to two voices heard antiphonally through a chapter.

B. Law and Gospel
  i. Why the Law was given
      ch. 7a/7b   True vs. false views
  ii. The Decalogue expounded
      ch. 8a/8b   True vs. false views: in reference to the Law in general and
      the individual commandments in particular
  iii. Christ revealed in Law and Gospel
      ch. 9a/9b   True vs. false views
  iv. Relation of Law (OT) and Gospel (NT)
      chs. 10–11a/10–11b   True vs. false views (e.g., those of Servetus)
C. Christ
  i. Necessity of the God-man as Mediator
      ch. 12a/12b   True vs. false views (chiefly Osiander)
  ii. Incarnation
      ch. 13a/13b   True vs. false views (chiefly Menno Simons)
  iii. Unity of the Two Natures in One Person
      ch. 14a/14b   True vs. false views (chiefly Servetus)
  iv. The Offices and Work of Christ on our Behalf
      chs. 15–17a/15–17b   True vs. false views

Book III

A. The Working of the Spirit in Men's Hearts (ch. 1): Foundation of Book III
B. Faith
  ch. 2a/2b   Scholastic (false) vs. true notion of faith
C. Repentance
  i. ch. 3a/3b   Antitheses between true repentance and false views of re-
      pentance (especially the Radical Reformers' insistence on perfection-
      ism)
  ii. chs. 3/4–5   True repentance vs. scholastic views of repentance (in-
      cluding confession, satisfaction plus indulgences and purgatory)
D. The Christian Life
  i. ch. 6a/6b   True vs. false view of Christian life in general
  ii. chs. 7–8a/8b   True denial of ourselves vs. false patience of the Stoics
  iii. chs. 9/10   Balance between the anticipation of the life to come and
      the true enjoyment of the present life, fed by it; subsidiary antitheses:
  iv. ch. 10a/10b   The right attitude toward the present life: poised be-
      tween the false extremes of strictness and laxity
E. Justification by Faith
  i. Justification by faith vs. justification by works and its derived doc-
      trines (merits, supererogation, etc.), the scholastic position: Set forth
      in ch. 11:13–20, but also the chief substance of chs. 12–18
  ii. Justification by faith in the whole Christ vs. Justification by faith in
      Christ's divine nature alone (the Lutheran Osiander) (ch. 11:5–12)
F. Christian Freedom
  ch. 19a/19b   True vs. false views of freedom
G. Prayer (ch. 20)
  In the midst of an affirmative interpretation of prayer in general, and the
  Lord's Prayer in particular, together with related topics, Calvin stresses a

course between rejection of prayer as useless and prayer bound to set forms.

H. Predestination

Fundamental antithesis: God's freedom vs. man's freedom, expressed in a series of subordinate antitheses:

    i. ch. 22   Unconditioned election by a totally free God vs. election dependent on God's foreknowledge of our merits (traditional non-Augustinian Roman Catholic position)

    ii. ch. 23   Incomprehensible nature of predestination vs. efforts of human reason, going beyond scriptural boundaries, to fathom it

    iii. ch. 24   Secret degrees of predestination and reprobation vs. various theories which allow some place to the human will

I. Final Resurrection

ch. 25a/25b   Immortality of the soul plus resurrection of the body at last day vs. various opposing views

Book IV

A. Nature and Organization of the Church

    i. chs. 1/2   True vs. false church

    ii. chs. 3–4/5–7   True vs. false officers and government of the church

B. Ecclesiastical Power

    i. Burdens laid on men and women by the church

    ch. 8a/8b   Power of church in articles of faith vs. papal practice

    ch. 9a/9b   True vs. false councils

    ch. 10a/10b   True church constitutions (in accord with God's Law and human conscience) vs. papal constitutions

    ch. 11a/11b   Right relationship between spiritual and temporal jurisdiction vs. papal usurpation of both

    ch. 12a/12b   True church discipline (informed by love) vs. false church discipline (excessive laxity or excessive severity)

    ii. Burdens laid on men and women by themselves

    ch. 13a/13b   Simple obedience to God's will vs. human vows (including monasticism) which counterfeit and make impossible true obedience

C. Sacraments

    i. The general antithesis:

    True Sacraments (chs. 14–18, summarized at end of ch. 18) vs. False Sacraments (ch. 19)

    ii. Baptism

    ch. 15a/15b & 16   True Baptism vs. False Baptism and False Baptismal Practices

    iii. Lord's Supper

    ch. 17a/17b   A series of antitheses between the "true" doctrine and various false ones (transubstantiation, ubiquity); also between the "true" administration and various false ways of administering the Lord's Supper

    ch. 17/18   True Lord's Supper vs. False Papal Mass

D. Civil Government (ch. 20)

    i. sects. 1–2:   True view vs. false view of spiritual/civil government

       a. overthrow civil in favor of spiritual
       b. set aside spiritual in favor of civil
    ii. sects. 3ff. contain a series of subsidiary antitheses against various aspects of false view (1); view (b) is not elaborated (but cf. sect. 9)
  iii. sects. 10–12: true vs. false view of use of force and war
  iv. sect. 13: true vs. false view of taxation
   v. sects. 14–16: true vs. false view of Mosaic Law in relation to civil government
  vi. sects. 17–21: true vs. false view of Christian use of law courts
 vii. sects. 22–32: true vs. false attitudes toward unjust rulers
       a. rights of revolution
       b. obedience even when God's will is contravened

Appendix 3

Chief Motifs in Calvin's *Institutes*[1]

    a. figures from plant life
    b. figures from rivers and springs
    c. figures from the contrast of fire and light / darkness
    d. comparisons of life to a way or a journey; nautical figures
    e. figures of sight and taste
    e'. mirror
    f. figures of military life
    f'. initial military service of the recruit (tyrocinium)
    g. figures of the life of a child and family
    g'. school, teaching
    h. figures from hunting; animal life
    i. figures from the law; government, business
        (richest and most original; contract with Pauline figures)
    j. figures from various arts and professions
    k. medical analogies, health and illness; the body
    l. figures from building
    m. figures taken from various solids, liquids
    n. the labyrinth
    o. the theater
    p. miscellaneous

a. Figures from Plant Life

2.1.7	rotten branches from a rotten root, etc.: original sin
2.1.8	a burning furnace gives forth flame and sparks
2.3.9(1)	branch, fruit
2.3.9(2)	a branch plucked from the earth and deprived of moisture ceases to bud: apart from God we can do nothing
3.5.9	Paul's metaphor of wood, hay, stubble
3.2.12	seed of life sown in hearts of the elect
3.2.17	sprouting palm tree: faith sustaining godly hearts

1. From Antoon Veerman, *De stijl van Calvijn in de Institutio Christianae religionis* (Utrecht: Kemink, 1943), but expanded.

3.2.21(1)	root of faith
3.2.21(3)	Word an incorruptible seed
3.2.31	fruit needs living root of a tree: faith needs the Word
3.21.5	dry tree trunk / choice of Abraham and his descendants
3.23.1	planted as sacred trees in God's field: predestinate
3.24.17	remnant / a flower picked by God
3.25.4	seed sown, and from its death in the soil comes forth wheat: resurrection (1 Cor. 15:36)

b. Figures from Water, Rivers, and Springs

1.17.1	thunderstorm below; serenity above (cf. Cowper's hymn)
2.1.8	water ceaselessly bubbles up from a spring
2.3.3	river in flood: the soul unrestrained by God
2.10.17	ocean tides: instability of the world
2.10.18	whirlpool of death
2.15.5	fountain: Christ from whom flows abundant grace
2.17.2	God, the fountainhead of all righteousness
3.11.9	fountain: Christ
3.20.1	overflowing spring: God's bounty in Jesus Christ
3.21.1	wellspring: God's free mercy
3.24.3	water/pipe/fountain: grace/means/God
3.24.4	bottomless whirlpool: trying to find out God's judgment about oneself

c. Figures from the Contrast of Fire and Light/Darkness

1.1.2(1)	eye: relative whiteness (our sense of sight relative)
1.1.2(2)	eye: ground/sun
1.11.11	try to spread darkness over the eyes of the simple folk
2.2.12	sparks still gleaming in man's now fallen nature
2.2.25	light of the sun/eyes: grace of illumination/mind (Aug.)
2.7.16	shadow: ceremonial law
3.2.6	sun:rays::Word:faith
3.2.21(2)	light of faith still lurks beneath the ashes
3.2.34(2)	sun: Word of God (those with sight/blind)
3.9.2	smoke, shadow: human life
3.12.2	eyes—nearby objects vs. sun (cf. 1.1.2)
3.12.4	stars at night/in daytime: man's innocence vs. God's purity
3.14.18	rays of the divine countenance: gifts bestowed by God
3.24.4	abyss of sightless darkness: trying to find out God's judgment about oneself
4.11.7	darkness:light::Romanist jurisdiction: Christ's
4.14.9	splendor of sun shining upon blind eyes: sacraments without H/S
4.14.10(2)	bodily eyes illumined by sun: minds illumined by sacraments

d. Comparison of Life to a Way or a Journey; Nautical Figures

1.5.13–15	life as a way
1.6.3	ditto
2.2.12	man's mind in its dullness wanders through error and darkness

2.2.18(1)	traveler passing through a field at night—lightning flash (also *c*)
2.5.19	Christ's parable of the traveler (Luke 10:30)
2.7.13	race: life
2.10.20(1)	open up the way with a key
2.10.20(2)	blazing a trail through forest
3.4.17	a sea or land journey never completed: tormented person trying to confess all his sins
3.4.18	anchor on the high seas/wayside rest of traveler: brief respite afforded by Romanist confession
3.4.20	whole ship of their kingdom
3.14.4	runner off his course: zeal of the unjust (Aug.)
3.18.6	people who decide to migrate to another place of a lasting abode: our "treasures in heaven"
3.20.3	sacred anchor: God
3.21.2	walking in pathless waste outside the pathway: exceeding the bounds of Scripture
3.21.3	reef: predestination

e. Figures of Sight (see also c, above) and Taste; see also e' Mirror, below

1.6.1	spectacles for bleared eyes: Scripture
2.8.4(1)	eye of the mind
3.2.19	prisoner in a cell who sees the sun only obliquely through a narrow window; weak, but real, initial faith
3.2.34(1)	veil: human discernment
3.17.14	God's judgment far transcends men's bleared vision
3.21.2	to see in darkness
4.14.9	splendor of sun shining upon blind eyes (*c*, above)/voice sounding on deaf ears: sacraments without H/S
4.19.16 n42	blind in the sunshine

e'. Mirror (cf. Keesecker)

1.5.1	order of universe
1.5.3	human race
1.5.11	God's works
1.8.7	Moses' song
1.14.1	Moses' history
1.14.5	ministry of the angels
1.14.21	creatures a mirror of God's attributes
1.15.4	soul, of the Trinity (Aug., falso)
2.3.2	Rom., ch. 3, whole image of our nature
2.7.2	Christ, for the ancient Hebrews
2.7.7	law
2.11.1	earthly inheritance of the Hebrew people
2.12.4	Christ
2.12.6	man
3.2.6	Word
3.18.9	law: perfect mirror of righteousness
3.20.24	radiance of God's face a mirror for the saints (falso)

3.24.5	Christ
3.25.3	resurrection
4.1.5	God's teaching
4.14.1	sacraments
4.14.6	sacraments

f. Figures of Military Life

2.2.3	charioteer, chariot, horse
2.5.6	battle: conflict with theological opponents
2.16.10	grappling hand-to-hand with the armies of hell, etc.
3.2.21(4)	armed combat with unbelief
3.4.20	siege engine (a frequent figure: 1.8.10; 2.5.1; 2.5.19)
3.20.13	banners: passages in Scripture bidding us invoke God's help
3.21.5(1)	hurling the stones of their insults toward heaven
3.8.7	special badge of God's soldiery
3.9.4	sentry duty
3.10.6	ditto
3.23.1	battle trumpet
3.25.1(1)	sentry duty
3.25.1(2)	"hard military service"

f'. Initial Military Service of the Recruit (tyrocinium)

2.8.51
3.2.39
3.7.2
3.18.4

g. Figures of the Life of a Child and Family

1.13.1	nurses talk baby-talk to infants: God accommodates the knowledge of himself ("baby-talk")
2.8.16	wife/adulteress
2.8.18	marriage: church membership
2.11.13(2)	householder deals differently with his children at various ages: God's various dealings with men under the two covenants
3.11.7	vessel: faith
3.19.5	ditto
3.20.38	love the father of the family—love the whole family: love God—love his other children
3.21.4	mother stooping to child: Scripture accommodating its pace to our capacity
4.8.13	well-governed house: wife obeys the husband's authority: church under Christ
4.10.14	child/adult: Jew OT/Christian NT (Paul?)
4.12.1(1)	discipline needed in society, family, however small: discipline needed in church
4.12.1	father's rod: discipline
4.17.1	householder provides food, etc., for his family: God provides for our spiritual well-being through his sacraments

g'. School, Teaching (not including Pauline references to Law as tutor)

3.21.3	school of H/S: Scripture (cf. l'eschole de Dieu: *Sermons sur l'épitre aux Galates*, 12 (*CR*, 50:424); 26 (*CR*, 50:597)
4.17.36	ditto
3.11.9	schoolboy
2.15.2	teacher: Christ
3.1.4	inner teacher: H/S
3.2.4,6	teacher: Christ
3.20.48	ditto
4.8.13	well-ordered school where teaching of the schoolmaster alone is heard: church under Christ
1.9.1	inner teacher: H/S
3.2.34	ditto
4.14.9	ditto
4.17.36	schoolmaster: H/S

h. Figures from Hunting; Animal Life

2.2.26	like an animal, man follows the inclination of his nature
2.3.2	mad beast: soul unrestrained by God
2.4.1	horse and rider: man's will/God and devil
2.7.12(2)	whip/balky ass: law/flesh
3.17.9	spawn a viper's brood: justification by works righteousness
3.23.1	God makes sheep out of wolves
3.23.2	bridle (and often)
3.24.4	innumerable, inextricable snares: trying to find out God's judgment
4.1.8	"many sheep are without and many wolves within" (Aug.)
4.12.1	bridle, spur: discipline
4.19.7	apes: imitation
4.19.16	kill beasts in their own arena
	(also common: net, snare, fetter, halter)

i. Figures from Law, Government, Business
(richest and most original; contact with Pauline figures)

2.7.6	scales: Law
2.7.12(1)	servant/master: believer/Lord's will
2.7.13	policeman *not* // law
2.8.2	like impoverished debtors
2.8.4(2)	debt, payment of
2.8.37	if a son obedient to his parents is snatched from life before attaining maturity . . . the Lord unwaveringly perseveres in the fulfillment of his promise no less than if he furnished 100 acres of land to one to whom he promised only one
3.4.19	men dragged by neck to prison: reluctance to go to confession
3.4.31(1)	judge/father: God's judgment of chastisement and of vengeance
3.4.31(2)	flogging of son/slave: God's judgment of chastisement and of vengeance

3.15.3	holder of usufruct of field ungratefully claims ownership of it: ungratefulness
———	liberated slave hides his past and claims to be freeborn: ungratefulness
3.20.23	advocates before earthly judge must be admitted to the bar: intercession of saints (falso)
3.20.37	son his own best advocate before his earthly father: Jesus before God
4.5.11	system of stewards and tenant farmers: parish absenteeism
4.6.2	one district, one governor .:. whole world, one governor: one pope over whole church (falso)
4.13.20	in human contracts only those promises bind us in which he with whom we contract wishes to be considered bound: absurd to fulfill what God does not require of us
4.14.5(1,2)	seals attached to government documents: sacraments/promises
4.14.7	seals: sacraments
4.14.10	convincing a stubborn opponent by reasoned argument: Spirit as sole author of faith
4.15.16	letter's authenticity not affected by the letter bearer: sacrament/minister
4.18.5	death of testator confirms a testament: death of XP confirms NT

j. Figures from Various Arts and Professions

2.10.20	paint a portrait
2.11.13(1)	farmer sets different tasks for different seasons: God's various dealings with men under the two covenants
3.4.22	shoemaker tilling field: priest forgiving sins
3.18.8	a king is more capable of making a shoe than a shoemaker is because he is infinitely more eminent: Schoolmen's contention we are justified by the benefit of love because it exceeds faith
3.19.5	servants assigned certain tasks for each day by their masters: those bound by the yoke of the law/sons
4.5.11(1)	city-bound usurer claims to be a plowman or vinedresser / soldier in active service claims to be a lawyer: pastors of churches who wish to seem so but not to be so
4.11.2	the locksmith's art

k. Medical Analogies, Health and Illness, the Body

1.17.5	just because a corpse lying in the sun putrefies, this does not mean that the sun's rays stink: God not defiled by a man's wickedness
2.3.2(2)	health of body: health of soul
2.5.3	God's healing hand: election
2.10.11	amputation of a limb: Abraham's separation from his beloved nephew
2.11.14	physician uses various remedies on various patients and at various times for the same patient: God's accommodation of his dealings with men

2.14.1	soul/body: divinity/humanity of Jesus Christ
3.7.7	sick member of the body helped by other members: needy person helped by alms
3.8.5	medicine: cross
4.2.1	man's life ended when his throat is pierced or mortally wounded: falsehood breaks into the citadel of religion
4.17.5	bread imparts vigor to the body: true partaking in Christ causes his life to pass into us and become ours

l. Figures from Building

| 2.8.11 | shattered building: overthrown worship of God |
| 4.2.11 | foundations and ruins remain when buildings are pulled down: God kept some vestiges of his church alive at all times (also the usual edification motifs from Scripture) |

m. Figures taken from Various Solids, Liquids, etc.

2.2.18(2)	sprinkle their books with droplets of truth
2.3.6	stone: heart
2.5.15	wine: God's grace
2.10.13	more stupid than blocks of wood
3.8.10	stock: valiant and constant man
3.14.5	oil will sooner be pressed from a stone than any good work from us
3.15.7	oil from a stone: merits from free will
4.1.11	touchstone: standard by which the genuineness of each church is tested
4.14.17	when pouring out wine or oil, it disappears unless the mouth of the vessel is open to receive it: sacraments without faith
4.17.33	rain falling upon a hard rock flows off because no entrance opens into the stone: wicked by their hardness repel God's grace
4.17.34	pour wax upon melted wax and both mix together: receive the flesh and blood of the Lord, so XP is in him and he is in XP
4.18.20	water poured into wine dilutes it / yeast sprinkled over lump of dough makes it sour: man, in adding anything of his own, pollutes the cleanness of God's mysteries
4.20.8	as elements cohere only in unequal proportion, so countries are best held together according to their own particular inequality

n. The Labyrinth

1.5.12	man's mind (see n.36)
1.6.3	splendor of the divine countenance to which we are conducted by the thread of the Word
1.13.21	men's indulgence into curiosity
3.2.31	disgressions of the prophet Isaiah into God's governance of the universe
3.6.2	the world
3.8.1	Christ passed from a labyrinth of all evils to heaven's glory

3.19.7	the inextricable maze of conscience bound by unrequired religious obligations
3.20.14	frustration of men who pass up God's promises
3.21.1	human curiosity about divine predestination
3.25.11	human speculation about the afterlife
4.7.13	the office of bishop / a labyrinth (from Greg. I)
4.7.22	the present papacy

o. The Theater

1.5.8	heavens and earth
1.6.2	ditto
1.14.20	ditto
2.6.1	the beautifully ordered universe
3.9.2	our awareness of death when confronted therewith: moment's applause in the theater after some pleasing spectacle is over
3.20.23	church

p. Miscellaneous Figures

1.3.2	most startled at the rustle of a falling leaf: the despiser of God under divine vengeance
2.2.1	borne aloft on a reed stick: crediting too much to ourselves (Mark 11:7?)
——	smoke: men's babbling
2.5.14	God moves just as we throw a stone (an erroneous comparison of Cochlaeus) (*m*, above)
2.10.14	final boundary and goal: death (Horace)
2.15.4	prosperity in the world dependent upon abundance and peace: eternal life / Christ's benefits to us and His defense of us against outside attacks
3.4.16	pit of sins, faces of crime, heads and long tail of Hydra
3.8.8	poverty, diseases, disgrace, dread: cross
3.9.2	smoke: human life
3.11.12	weave his rope: Osiander's reasoning about "essential righteousness"
3.12.4(2)	riches heaped up in a dream: men's supposed righteousness before God
3.18.6	riches hidden from us: our duties
3.20.11	not to ask blessings from God, the bestower of all good things: like a man neglecting a treasure buried and hidden in the earth, after it has been pointed out to him
3.21.5	hurling stones of insults toward heaven
3.24.3	deep abyss: God's eternal ordination
3.25.1	prison
4.12.12	"the mousetraps of his treachery"

Appendix 4 Tabulation of Biblical Citations in the *Institutes*[1]

OLD TESTAMENT	2,424	Lamentations	3
		Ezekiel	98
Genesis	254	Daniel	38
Exodus	164	**Major Prophets**	625*
Leviticus	65		
Numbers	23	Hosea	32
Deuteronomy	155	Joel	21
Pentateuch	661*	Amos	11
		Obadiah	1
Joshua	10	Jonah	8
Judges	30	Micah	7
Ruth	1	Nahum	0
1 Samuel	52	Habbakuk	14
2 Samuel	34	Zephaniah	4
1 Kings	51	Haggai	2
2 Kings	42	Zechariah	19
1 Chronicles	3	Malachi	27
2 Chronicles	7	**Minor Prophets**	146*
Ezra	1		
Nehemiah	6	**APOCRYPHA**	19
Esther	1		
Historical Books	238*	Tobit	1
		Wisdom	1
Job	68	Ecclesiasticus	11
Psalms	580	Baruch	2
Proverbs	82	1 Maccabees	1
Ecclesiastes	21	2 Maccabees	3
Song of Songs	3		
Poetical Books	754*	**NEW TESTAMENT**	4,330
Isaiah	324	Matthew	542
Jeremiah	162	Mark	60

1. Based on the index to *Inst.*, and the citations in F. L. Battles, *New Light on Calvin's Institutes*.

359

Luke	235	Titus	49
John	466	Philemon	2
Gospels	1,303*	**Paul's Letters**	2,187*
Acts	276	**Hebrews**	244
Romans	598	James	57
1 Corinthians	428	1 Peter	116
2 Corinthians	205	2 Peter	24
Galatians	183	1 John	88
Ephesians	282	2 John	0
Philippians	84	3 John	0
Colossians	132	**Canonical Letters**	292*
1 Thessalonians	33		
2 Thessalonians	36	**Revelation**	28
1 Timothy	105		
2 Timothy	50	TOTAL	6,773**

Ford Lewis Battles Bibliography[1]

1949

"Hugo of Saint-Victor as a Moral Allegorist." *Church History* 18 (1949): 220–40.

1950

A Translation and Critical Study of the First Book of the Homilies of Gregory the Great: On the Prophet Ezekiel. Ph.D. dissertation, Hartford Seminary Foundation, 1950. 427 pp.

Review of *Ignace Goldziher Memorial Volume,* Part I, edited by David Sámuel Löwinger and József Somogyi. *The Muslim World* 40 (1950): 65–68.

1952

"A Hymn for Seminaries." *The Hartford Seminary Foundation Bulletin* 13, no. 2 (June 1952).

"A Hymn of Praise." *The Hartford Seminary Foundation Bulletin* 14, no. 2 (December 1952).

1953

Translator and editor, "On the Pastoral Office" by John Wyclif. In *Advocates of Reform: From Wyclif to Erasmus,* edited by Matthew Spinka, 32–60. Library of Christian Classics, 14. Philadelphia/London: Westminster/SCM Press, 1953.

Translator and editor, "On the Eucharist" by John Wyclif. In *Advocates of Reform: From Wyclif to Erasmus,* edited by Matthew Spinka, 61–88. Library of Christian Classics, 14. Philadelphia/London: Westminster/SCM Press, 1953.

Translator and editor, "The Enchiridion" by Desiderius Erasmus. In *Advocates of Reform: From Wyclif to Erasmus,* edited by Matthew Spinka, 295–379. Li-

1. From Peter De Klerk, "Bibliography of the Published Writings of Ford Lewis Battles," in *Reformatio Perennis: Essays on Calvin and the Reformation in Honor of Ford Lewis Battles,* ed. by B. A. Gerrish, with Robert Benedetto (Pittsburgh: Pickwick Press, 1981), 195–209. Used by permission; revised and expanded. In addition to the published works listed herein, a considerable body of unpublished material comprises the Ford Lewis Battles Papers housed at the H. Henry Meeter Center for Calvin Studies, Calvin College and Seminary, Grand Rapids, Michigan.

brary of Christian Classics, 14. Philadelphia/London: Westminster/SCM Press, 1953.

With Irving Lowens and Raymond W. Lindstrom. *Hartford Harmony: A Selection of American Hymns from the 18th and Early 19th Centuries.* Hartford, Conn.: Hartford Seminary Foundation Bookstore, 1953. Reprint, 1955.

Review of *A History of the Crusades,* vol. 2: *The Kingdom of Jerusalem and the Frankish East, 1100–1187,* by Steven Runciman. *The Muslim World* 43 (1953): 209–10.

1955

With Eugen Rosenstock-Huessy. *Magna Charta Latina. The Privilege of Singing, Articulating and Reading a Language and of Keeping It Alive.* Pittsburgh: Pittsburgh Theological Seminary, 1955. Revised edition, 1973. Reprint, Pittsburgh Reprint Series, 1. Pittsburgh: Pickwick Press, 1975.

"Stanzas for Communion." *The Hartford Seminary Foundation Bulletin* 21 (Winter 1955–56).

1957

Review of *The Theology of Calvin,* by Wilhelm Niesel, translated by Harold Knight. *Religion in Life* 26 (Summer 1957): 470–72.

Review of *Calvin's Doctrine of the Work of Christ,* by John F. Jansen. *Religion in Life* 26 (Summer 1957): 470–72.

1959

With Goodwin Batterson Beach. *Locutionum cotidianarum glossarium. A Guide to Latin Conversation.* Hartford, Conn.: Hartford Seminary Press, 1959. Second revised edition, 1961; third revised edition, 1967.

"Some Axioms of Church History." *The Bulletin of the Hartford Seminary Foundation* 26 (February 1959): 49–66.

1960

Translator, *The Institutes of the Christian Religion* by John Calvin. 2 vols. Edited by John T. McNeill. Library of Christian Classics, 20–21. Philadelphia/London: Westminster/SCM Press, 1960.

1961

Review of *Calvin's Doctrine of the Knowledge of God,* by Thomas Henry Louis Parker. *Interpretation* 15 (1961): 102–4.

"Two Dried Sausages" [Fragment of a Drama in Five Acts]. *Toledoth* 1 (May 1961): 5–22. Also in *The Hartford Quarterly* 2 (Summer 1962): 7–19.

"A Litany of the Beatitudes." *Toledoth* 3 (December 1961): 7–12.

1962

The Sources of Calvin's Commentary on Seneca's De Clementia. Hartford, Conn.: The Hartford Seminary Foundation, 1962.

"Is Christ Divided? Thoughts upon I Corinthians 11:17–22." *Toledoth* 4 (May 1962): 4–7. Also in *The Muslim World* 52 (1962): 259–61.

Review of *Lectures on Romans*, by Martin Luther, translated and edited by Wilhelm Pauck. *Interpretation* 16 (1962): 321–24.

1963

"Englishing the Institutes of John Calvin." *Babel* 9 (1963): 94–98. Reprint, Richard C. Gamble, ed., *Articles on Calvin and Calvinism*, vol. 4, 232–36. New York: Garland Publishing, 1992.

1964

Review of *Studies on the Reformation. Collected Papers in Church History:* Series two, by Roland Herbert Bainton. *The Westminster Bookman* 23 (March 1964): 25–26.

With John Jermain Bodine. "Some Thoughts on Church History." *The Hartford Quarterly* 4 (Spring 1964): 31–41.

Review of *Reformation Studies: Essays in Honor of Roland Herbert Bainton*, edited by Franklin Hamlin Littell. *The Hartford Quarterly* 4 (Spring 1964): 85–88.

"Art and Worship: Friends or Foes?" *The Reformed Journal* 14 (May–June 1964): 7–10.

Review of *Documents of the Christian Church*, edited by Henry Scowcroft Bettenson. *The Hartford Quarterly* 4 (Summer 1964): 80–82.

Review of *Medieval Political Philosophy: A Sourcebook*, edited by Ralph Lerner and Muhsin Mahdi. *The Muslim World* 54 (1964): 204–5.

"An Ancient Church Historian Looks at the Second Vatican Council." *The Hartford Quarterly* 5 (Fall 1964): 15–28.

1965

An Essay on the Catholicity of Protestantism as Seen in the United Church of Christ. Hartford: The Hartford Seminary Foundation, 1965.

Temple or Tomb? Reflections on Papal History, Sketched in Dramatic Form. Hartford, Conn.: The Hartford Seminary Foundation, 1965.

"Against Luxury and License in Geneva: A Forgotten Fragment of Calvin." *Interpretation* 19 (1965): 182–202. Reprint, Richard C. Gamble, ed., *Articles on Calvin and Calvinism*, vol. 3, 198–218. New York: Garland Publishing, 1992.

"Hildebrandine Histrionics." *Toledoth* 6 (May 1965): 2–3.

Translator, "Expostulation of Jesus with a man perishing through his very own fault," by Desiderius Erasmus. *The Hartford Quarterly* 5 (Summer 1965): 64–67.

Translator, "Enthusiasm for Erasmus," by Huldreich Zwingli. *The Hartford Quarterly* 5 (Summer 1965): 67–68.

With Dale Jay Cooper. Translator, "Academic Discourse," by John Calvin. *The Hartford Quarterly* 6 (Fall 1965): 76–85. Revised version in *Institution of the Christian Religion. Embracing almost the whole sum of piety, & whatever is necessary to know the doctrine of salvation: a work most worthy to be read by all persons zealous for piety, and recently published. Preface to the most Christian King of France, whereas [i.e., wherein] this book is offered to him as a Confession of Faith*, by John Calvin. At Basel, 1536. Translated and annotated by Ford Lewis Battles, 462–71. Atlanta: John Knox Press, 1975.

Review of *The Four Major Cults: Christian Science, Jehovah's Witnesses, Mormonism, Seventh-Day Adventism,* by Anthony Andrew Hoekema. *The Hartford Quarterly* 6 (Fall 1965): 99–100.

1966

An Analysis of the Institutes of the Christian Religion of John Calvin. Hartford, Conn.: The Hartford Seminary Press, 1966. Revised edition with the same title by Ford Lewis Battles assisted by John Robert Walchenbach. Pittsburgh: Pittsburgh Theological Seminary, 1970. Second revised edition, 1972; third revised edition, 1976. Reprint, Grand Rapids: Baker Book House, 1980.

New Light on Calvin's Institutes. A Supplement to the McNeill–Battles Translation. Hartford, Conn.: Hartford Seminary Press, 1966.

With Edward J. Furcha. *Stanzas on the Trinity.* Hartford, Conn.: The Hartford Seminary Foundation, 1966. Reprint, Pittsburgh: Pittsburgh Theological Seminary, 1968.

"The Sources of Calvin's Seneca Commentary." In *John Calvin. A Collection of Essays,* edited by Gervase E. Duffield, 38–66. Courtenay Studies in Reformation Theology, 1. Grand Rapids/Appleford, England: William B. Eerdmans Publishing Co./Sutton Courtenay Press, 1966.

"On the Poetry of History." *Toledoth* 7 (May 1966): 4–7.

"Milan. A.D. 390." *Toledoth* 7 (May 1966): 14.

"The Passion and Death of the Prophet Mani." *Toledoth* 7 (May 1966): 15–17.

Review of *Misunderstandings between East and West,* by George Every. *The Hartford Quarterly* 7 (Fall 1966): 68.

Review of *Preparatory Reports. Second Vatican Council,* translated by Aram J. Berard. *The Hartford Quarterly* 7 (Fall 1966): 68.

1967

A First Course in Church History and History of Doctrine. The Patristic Era and the Middle Ages. Pittsburgh: Pittsburgh Theological Seminary, 1967–68. 2 vols. Revised editions, 1968–69, 1969–70, 1971–72, 1972–73, and 1975–76. Seventh revised edition entitled *Itinerarium fidei: Outline for a First Course in Church History to A.D. 1500.* Pittsburgh: Pittsburgh Theological Seminary; Grand Rapids: Calvin Theological Seminary, 1977–78.

Seventy Decisive Years in American Hymnody (1799–1868). Hartford, Conn.: The Hartford Seminary Foundation, 1967.

Review of *John Hus' Concept of the Church,* by Matthew Spinka. *The Hartford Quarterly* 7 (Winter 1967): 76–77.

Editor, "Bellamy Papers." *The Hartford Quarterly* 7 (Spring 1967): 64–91.

1968

Abelard and Peter Lombard. Study Outline 11. Pittsburgh: Pittsburgh Theological Seminary, 1968.

Translator, *Arius: Thalia. A Hypothetical Reconstruction of the Text.* Reconstructed Documents, 2. Pittsburgh: Pittsburgh Theological Seminary, 1968.

Augustine: City of God. Study Outline 9. Pittsburgh: Pittsburgh Theological Seminary, 1968. Reprint, 1973.

Augustine: Confessions and Other Treatises. Study Outline 7a. Pittsburgh: Pittsburgh Theological Seminary, 1968.

Boethius: Theological Treatises. Study Outline 8 (10). Pittsburgh: Pittsburgh Theological Seminary, 1968. Reprint, 1972.

Church and State in the Early Centuries. Pittsburgh: Pittsburgh Theological Seminary, 1968.

From the Apostles to the Schoolmen. Foundations of Church History. Pittsburgh: Pittsburgh Theological Seminary, 1968.

Editor, *Henry and Hildebrand: Reflections on Papal Power, with a Concluding Glimpse at the Avignonese Papacy.* By A. Burfiend, P. Kamuyu, and F. Dole. Pittsburgh: Pittsburgh Theological Seminary, 1968.

Heresy in the Early Church. Pittsburgh: Pittsburgh Theological Seminary, 1968. Reprint, 1972.

Translator, *Hilarius: Filius Dei vivi verbum. Stanzas Drawn from Book II on the Trinity.* Reconstructed Documents, 3. Pittsburgh: Pittsburgh Theological Seminary, 1968. Reprint, 1972.

Editor and translator, *Monasticism and Monastic Life, with a translation of The Imitation of Christ,* Book I. Pittsburgh: Pittsburgh Theological Seminary, 1968.

Review of *Memory and Hope: An Inquiry Concerning the Presence of Christ,* by Dietrich Ritschl. *Perspective* 9 (1968): 80–82.

1969

The Apologists. Study Outline 1. Pittsburgh: Pittsburgh Theological Seminary, 1969. Reprint, 1972. Reprint, Allison Park, Pa.: Pickwick Publications, 1991.

Editor, *Athanasius,* by Paul Kokenda. Study Outline 6. Pittsburgh: Pittsburgh Theological Seminary, 1969. Reprints, 1971 and 1972.

Translator and editor, *Bonaventura to Luther. Late Medieval and Reformation Piety and Dissent: A Miscellany.* Spirituality of the Reformers, 1. Pittsburgh: Pittsburgh Theological Seminary, 1969.

With André Malan Hugo. Translator, *Calvin's Commentary on Seneca's De Clementia.* Renaissance Text Series, 3. Leiden: E. J. Brill for the Renaissance Society of America, 1969.

Translator, *Institution of the Christian Religion. Embracing almost the whole sum of piety, & whatever is necessary to know the doctrine of salvation: a work most worthy to be read by all persons zealous for piety, and recently published. Preface to the most Christian King of France, wherein this book is offered to him as a Confession of Faith,* by John Calvin. Pittsburgh: Pittsburgh Theological Seminary, 1969. Revised edition, 1972. Newly revised edition, Atlanta: John Knox Press, 1975. Revised edition, Grand Rapids: The H. H. Meeter Center for Calvin Studies/William B. Eerdmans Publishing Co., 1986. Reprint, "Introduction." In Richard C. Gamble, ed., *Articles on Calvin and Calvinism,* vol. 2, 245–87. New York: Garland Publishing, 1992.

Irenaeus. Study Outline 2. Pittsburgh: Pittsburgh Theological Seminary, 1969. Reprints, 1971 and 1972. Reprinted with *Clement of Alexandria,* Allison Park, Pa.: Pickwick Publications, 1993.

John Chrysostom: On the Priesthood. Study Outline 6b (7). Pittsburgh: Pittsburgh Theological Seminary, 1969. Reprint, 1972.

Editor, *John of Damascus: The Fount of Knowledge,* by Daniel Sahas. Study Outline 11. Pittsburgh: Pittsburgh Theological Seminary, 1969. Reprint, 1973.

Hugo of Saint Victor. Study Outline 14. Pittsburgh: Pittsburgh Theological Seminary, 1969. Reprint, 1973.

Origen: On First Principles. Study Outline 4. Pittsburgh: Pittsburgh Theological Seminary, 1969. Reprint, 1972.

Peter Lombard. Study Outline 15. Pittsburgh: Pittsburgh Theological Seminary, 1969. Reprints, 1971 and 1973.

Editor, *The Piety of Caspar Schwenckfeld.* Translated and compiled by Edward J. Furcha. Spirituality of the Reformers, 2. Pittsburgh: Pittsburgh Theological Seminary, 1969. Reprint, 1971.

Translator and editor, *The Piety of John Calvin. An Anthology Illustrative of the Spirituality of the Reformer of Geneva.* Pittsburgh: Pittsburgh Theological Seminary, 1969. Reprinted with corrections, 1970. Revised edition, 1973. Newly revised edition entitled *The Piety of John Calvin. An Anthology Illustrative of the Spirituality of the Reformer.* Music ed. by Stanley Tagg. Grand Rapids: Baker Book House, 1978. Reprint introduction, "True Piety According to Calvin" in Donald K. McKim, ed., *Readings in Calvin's Theology,* 192–211. Grand Rapids: Baker Book House, 1984.

Tertullian and Cyprian. Study Outline 5. Pittsburgh: Pittsburgh Theological Seminary, 1969. Reprints, 1971 and 1972.

"Calvin and the Computer." In *Summary of Proceedings. Twenty-third Annual Conference, American Theological Library Association, Pittsburgh Theological Seminary, Pittsburgh, Pennsylvania, June 16–19, 1969,* 87–112. Wilmore, Ky.: Asbury Theological Seminary, 1969.

Review of *Reformers in Profile,* edited by Brian Albert Gerrish. *Journal of Ecumenical Studies* 6 (1969): 103–6.

Review of *The Style of John Calvin in His French Polemical Treatises,* by Francis M. Higman. *Church History* 38 (1969): 534.

1970

The Documents of Vatican II in Historical Perspective. The Background, Drafting, and Implication for the Future of the Church. Pittsburgh: Pittsburgh Theological Seminary, 1970.

Editor, *Epiphanius panarion,* by Daniel Sahas. Study Outline 17. Pittsburgh: Pittsburgh Theological Seminary, 1970. Reprint, 1972.

Editor, *The Formation of the United Church of Christ (U.S.A.),* by Hanns Peter Keiling. Bibliographia Tripotamopolitana, 2. Pittsburgh: Clifford E. Barbour Library, Pittsburgh Theological Seminary, 1970.

With Donald E. Gowan. Translator, *Hymn Texts Drawn from the Old and New Testaments.* Pittsburgh: Pittsburgh Theological Seminary, 1970.

Review of *Geneva and the Consolidation of the French Protestant Movement, 1564–1572. A Contribution to the History of Congregationalism, Presbyterianism, and Calvinist Resistance Theory,* by Robert McCune Kingdon. *Perspective* 11 (1970): 344–46.

Review of *Calvin et Vatican II. L'église servante,* by Alexandre Ganoczy. *Journal of Ecumenical Studies* 7 (1970): 807–9.

Review of *Melanchthon and Bucer,* edited by Wilhelm Pauck. *Interpretation* 24 (1970): 527.

1971

Editor, *New Hymns for a New Day? An Anthology of New Hymnody to Illustrate the Search for New Hymns.* Pittsburgh: Pittsburgh Theological Seminary, 1971.

Editor, *Desiderius Erasmus: On Really Doing Theology,* by Donald Conroy. Study Outline 18. Pittsburgh: Pittsburgh Theological Seminary, 1971. Reprint, 1973.

Peter Abelard. Study Outline 13. Pittsburgh: Pittsburgh Theological Seminary, 1971. Reprint, 1973.

Representative Christian Thinkers. From Ignatius of Antioch to the End of the Middle Ages. Pittsburgh: Pittsburgh Theological Seminary, 1971.

With Daniel Sahas. Translator, *The Sermons of Nestorius.* From the texts of F. Loofs and F. Nau. Pittsburgh: Pittsburgh Theological Seminary, 1971. Reprint, 1971. Third printing with corrections, 1973.

"Anointed of God," No. 10; "Creator Spirit, Come to Us," No. 15 and 16; "The Carol of the Two Adams," No. 6; "Who Prays, But Hears Prayer?" No. 11; "How Long, Lord?" No. 8. In *A New Song 3.* St. Louis: Division of Publication, United Church Board for Homeland Ministries, for the Executive Council and the Commission on Worship, United Church of Christ, 1971.

"Bernard of Clairvaux and the Moral Allegorical Tradition." In *Innovation in Medieval Literature. Essays to the Memory of Alan Markman,* edited by Douglas Radcliff-Umstead, 1–19. Pittsburgh: Medieval Studies Committee, University of Pittsburgh, 1971.

"Christ, Our Peace Indeed," No. 4; "God So Rich in Mercy," No. 5; "Creator Spirit, Come to Us," No. 6; "The Carol of the Two Adams," No. 8 and 9; "Who Prays, But Hears Prayer?" No. 10; "A Christian Must by Faith Be Filled," No. 11; "All Speech Far Transcending," No. 16; "How Long, Lord?" No. 17; "In Boundless Mercy," No. 19. In *New Hymns for a New Day? An Anthology of New Hymnody to Illustrate the Search for New Hymns.* Pittsburgh: Pittsburgh Theological Seminary, 1971.

"Frederick Neumann and His Work." In *God's Fifth Columnist and Other Writings,* 5–10. Appleford: Marcham Manor Press, 1971.

Review of *The Early Christians after the Death of the Apostles,* edited by Eberhard Arnold. *Encounter* 32 (1971): 170–71.

Review of *Speech and Reality,* by Eugen Rosenstock-Huessy. *Perspective* 12 (1971): 279–80.

1972

With Charles Miller. *A Computerized Concordance to Institutio Christianae Religionis 1559 of Johannes Calvinus.* Based on the Critical Text of Petrus Barth and Guilelmus Niesel (Books 1–2: 1967 [i.e. 1957]; Book 3: 1959; Book 4: 1962) corrected from the original text of 1559. Pittsburgh: Clifford E. Barbour Library, Pittsburgh Theological Seminary, 1972. 7 microfilm reels. Printed introduction, lemmatic index and other aids. Bibliographia Tripotamopolitana, 8. Pittsburgh: Clifford E. Barbour Library, Pittsburgh Theological Seminary, 1972. See also Richard Wevers, *A Concordance to Calvin's Institutio 1559*, 6 vols. Grand Rapids: Digamma Publishers, 1992.

Translator and editor, *John Calvin: Catechism 1538*. Pittsburgh: Pittsburgh Theological Seminary, 1972. Revised edition, 1974. Reprinted with corrections, 1975 and 1976. See also John Hesselink, *Calvin's First Catechism (1538)* (Louisville: Westminster/John Knox Press, 1997).

Translator, *Pelagius: The Christian Life and Other Essays*. Reconstructed Documents, 7. Pittsburgh: Pittsburgh Theological Seminary, 1972. Reprint, 1973 and 1977.

Review of *The Constructive Revolutionary: John Calvin and His Socio-Economic Impact*, by William Fred Graham. *Interpretation* 26 (1972): 351–53.

Review of *John Bunyan*, by Richard Lee Greaves. *Perspective* 13 (1972): 247–48.

Review of *Early Christians Speak*, by Everett Ferguson. *Church History* 41 (1972): 401.

1973

Compiler, *Indices to the Four Books of Sentences of Peter Lombard*. Pittsburgh: Pittsburgh Theological Seminary, 1973.

With John W. Neely, Jr. *Three Rivers of the Spirit Hymnal*. Pittsburgh: Pittsburgh Theological Seminary, 1973.

Review of *The Life and Legal Writings of Hugo Grotius*, by Edward Dumbauld. *Perspective* 14 (1973): 59.

1974

"Two Adams Walked upon the Earth" [The Carol of the Two Adams], No. 71; "Anointed of God," No. 120; "Creator Spirit, Come to Us," No. 148; "The Church of Christ Is One," No. 153; "A Christian Must by Faith Be Filled," No. 168; "In Boundless Mercy," No. 251; "Glory to the Father," Nos. 316 and 324; "Praise to the Father [giving life]," Nos. 317 and 359; "As You Have Promised, Lord," Nos. 321 and 328; "Glory Be to Our God in Heaven," No. 323. In *The Hymnal of the United Church of Christ*. Philadelphia: United Church Press, 1974.

Review of *Arminius: A Study in the Dutch Reformation*, by Carl Oliver Bangs. *Journal of Presbyterian History* 52 (1974): 83–84.

1975

With Edward J. Furcha. Translator and editor, *Selected Writings of Hans Denck*. Edited and translated from the text as established by Walter Fellmann. Pittsburgh Original Texts and Translation Series, 1. Pittsburgh: Pickwick Press, 1975.

Editor, *St. Anselm: Monologium, Proslogium and Cur Deus Homo*, by LindaJo Booker and William V. Rowe. Study Outline 12. Pittsburgh: Pittsburgh Theological Seminary, 1975.

Translator, "The Placards of 1534." In *Institution of the Christian Religion. Embracing almost the whole sum of piety, & whatever is necessary to know the doctrine of salvation: a work most worthy to be read by all persons zealous for piety, and recently published. Preface to the most Christian King of France, whereas [i.e. wherein] this book is offered to him as a Confession of Faith,* by John Calvin, 437–40. Atlanta: John Knox Press, 1975.

Translator, "Martin Bucer on the Lord's Prayer." In *Institution of the Christian Religion. Embracing almost the whole sum of piety, & whatever is necessary to know the doctrine of salvation: a work most worthy to be read by all persons zealous for piety, and recently published. Preface to the most Christian King of France, whereas [i.e. wherein] this book is offered to him as a Confession of Faith,* by John Calvin, 441–61. Atlanta: John Knox Press, 1975.

With Donald Morrison Conroy. Review of *Erasmus and the Seamless Coat of Jesus. De Sarcienda Ecclesiae Concordia [On Restoring the Unity of the Church]. With Selections from the Letters and Ecclesiastes,* by Desiderius Erasmus and edited by Raymond Himelick. *Journal of Ecumenical Studies* 12 (1975): 272–73.

"Seminar on the Unity of the Church." 4th ed. Pittsburgh: Pittsburgh Theological Seminary, 1975.

1976

Translator, *Enchiridion. Of Commonplaces of John Eck against Martin Luther and His Followers,* by John Eck. Pittsburgh: Duquesne University, 1976. Revised edition, Grand Rapids: Calvin Theological Seminary, 1978. Reprint, Grand Rapids: Baker Book House, 1979.

"The Future of Calviniana." In *Renaissance, Reformation, Resurgence.* Papers Presented at the Colloqium on Calvin and Calvin Studies held at Calvin Theological Seminary on April 22 and 23, 1976, edited by Peter De Klerk, 133–73. Grand Rapids: Calvin Theological Seminary, 1976.

Review of *The Christian Tradition. A History of the Development of Doctrine,* vol. 2: *The Spirit of Eastern Christendom (600–1700),* by Jaroslav Pelikan. *Christian Scholar's Review* 5 (1975–76): 408–9.

Review of *The Spirituality of John Calvin,* by Lucien Joseph Richard. *Journal of Presbyterian History* 54 (1976): 281–82.

1977

With N. Mikita and M. Ioset. Compiler, *Adjutorium ad cultum divinum. A Supplement to the Worshipbook of the United Presbyterian Church in the United States of America for use in the chapel of Pittsburgh Theological Seminary.* Pittsburgh: Pittsburgh Theological Seminary, 1977.

With Robert Benedetto. Compiler, *Semita ad perspicendam mentem sancti Augustini. A Student's Guide to the Formative Controversies in the Life and Thought of Aurelius Augustinus, Bishop of Hippo Regius.* Pittsburgh: Pittsburgh Theological Seminary, 1977. 4 parts.

"God Was Accommodating Himself to Human Capacity." *Interpretation* 31 (1977): 19–38. Reprint, Donald K. McKim, ed., *Readings in Calvin's Theology,* 21–42. Grand Rapids: Baker Book House, 1984; Richard C. Gamble, ed., *Articles on Calvin and Calvinism,* vol. 6, 13–32. New York: Garland Publishing, 1992.

With Morgan Simmons. "The Consultation on Ecumenical Hymnody." *The Hymn* 28 (1977): 67–68, 87.

Review of *The Patristic Roots of Reformed Worship,* by Hughes Oliphant Old. *Church History* 46 (1977): 398–99.

1978

Calculus Fidei. Some Ruminations on the Structure of the Theology of John Calvin. Grand Rapids: Calvin Theological Seminary, 1978. Portions edited for publication in *Calvinus Ecclesiae Doctor. Die Referate des International Congress on Calvin Research, 25–28 September 1978 in Amsterdam,* edited by W. H. Neuser. Kampen: J. H. Kok, 1980. Reprint, Richard C. Gamble, ed., *Articles on Calvin and Calvinism,* vol. 7, 195–220. New York: Garland Publishing, 1992.

Translator, *Six Psalms of John Calvin.* Psalms 25, 36, 46, 91, 113 and 138. Harmonizations by Stanley Tagg. Grand Rapids: Baker Book House, 1978.

The Theologian as Poet. Some Remarks about the "Found" Poetry of John Calvin. Grand Rapids: Calvin Theological Seminary, 1978. Also in *From Faith to Faith. Essays in Honor of Donald G. Miller on His Seventieth Birthday,* edited by Dikran Y. Hadidian, 299–337. Pittsburgh Theological Monograph Series, 31. Pittsburgh: Pickwick Press, 1979.

"Introduction: Frederick Neumann (1899–1967)." In *Where Do We Stand? A Selective Homiletical Commentary on the Old Testament,* vol. 1: *Law and Revelation. The Torah,* by Frederick Neumann, ix–xi. Brooklyn, N.Y.: Theo. Gaus., 1978.

"Introduction." In *Where Do We Stand? A Selective Homiletical Commentary on the Old Testament,* vol. 2: *Faith and Reality in History,* by Frederick Neumann, 1–2. Brooklyn, N.Y.: Theo. Gaus., 1978.

Review of *An Introduction to the Reformed Tradition. A Way of Being the Christian Community,* by John Haddon Leith. *Interpretation* 32 (1978): 218, 220.

Review of *The Reformation. A Narrative History Related by Contemporary Observers and Participants,* edited by Hans Joachim Hillerbrand. *Calvin Theological Journal* 13 (1978): 257–58.

1979

"An Exchange." In *Bibliography Paul Leser. On the Occasion of His 80th Birthday on February 23, 1979,* edited by Absalom Vilakazi, 44–49. West Hartford, Conn.: University of Hartford, 1979.

"Foreword." In Jack B. Rogers and Donald K. McKim, *The Authority and Interpretation of the Bible: An Historical Approach,* xv–xvi. San Francisco: Harper & Row, 1979.

Review of *John Calvin. A Biography,* by Thomas Henry Parker. *The Journal of Religion* 59 (1979): 254–55.

1980

Translator, "John Calvin: The Form of Prayers and Songs of the Church, 1542: Letter to the Reader." *Calvin Theological Journal* 15 (1980): 160–65

1981

"Notes on John Calvin, Justitia and the Old Testament Law." In *Intergerini Parietis Septum (Eph. 2:14). Essays Presented to Markus Barth on His 65th Birthday,* edited by Dikran Y. Hadidian, 23–37. Pittsburgh Theological Monograph Series, 33. Pittsburgh: Pickwick Press, 1981.

Contributors

ROBERT BENEDETTO is associate librarian and associate professor of bibliography at Union Theological Seminary in Virginia. He has previously served as deputy director of the Presbyterian Church (U.S.A.) Department of History in Montreat, North Carolina. He collaborated on a festschrift, *Reformatio Perennis: Essays on Calvin and the Reformation in Honor of Ford Lewis Battles* (Pickwick, 1981), and has published numerous bibliographies and indexes, including *Guide to the Manuscript Collections of the Presbyterian Church, U.S.* (Greenwood Press, 1990) and *P. T. Forsyth Bibliography and Index* (Greenwood Press, 1993). Forthcoming works include *Presbyterian Reformers in Central Africa* (E. J. Brill, 1996) and, with Darrell L. Guder of Louisville Theological Seminary and Donald K. McKim of Memphis Theological Seminary, a *Historical Dictionary of the Reformed Churches* (Scarecrow Press, 1997).

I. JOHN HESSELINK is professor of systematic theology at Western Theological Seminary in Holland, Michigan. A minister of the Reformed Church in America, Dr. Hesselink was a missionary in Japan for twenty years. For twelve of those years he taught at Tokyo Union Seminary and also lectured at Meiji Gakuin University in Tokyo. Prior to becoming professor at Western Seminary, he served as its president for twelve years. He is the author of *On Being Reformed*, 2d ed. (Reformed Church Press, 1988) and *Calvin's Concept of Law* (Pickwick, 1992). Forthcoming works include *Introduction to Calvin's Theology Based Primarily on Ford Lewis Battles' Translation of Calvin's First Catechism (1538)* (Westminster/John Knox Press, 1997) and *Sovereign Grace and Human Freedom: How They Coalesce* (Eerdmans, 1996).

DONALD K. McKIM is academic dean and professor of theology at Memphis Theological Seminary. A minister of the Presbyterian Church (U.S.A.), Dr. McKim was interim pastor of the Central Presbyterian Church in Downingtown, Pennsylvania, and the Trinity Presbyterian

Church in Berwyn, Pennsylvania. Previously he taught at the University of Dubuque Theological Seminary where he was professor of theology. He has edited *Major Themes in the Reformed Tradition* (Eerdmans, 1992), *Encyclopedia of the Reformed Faith* (Westminster/John Knox, 1992), *A Guide to Contemporary Hermeneutics* (Eerdmans, 1986), *How Karl Barth Changed My Mind* (Eerdmans, 1986), and *Readings in Calvin's Theology* (Baker, 1984). He is the author of *The Bible in Theology and Preaching* (Abingdon, 1994), *Theological Turning Points* (John Knox, 1988), and co-author of *The Authority and Interpretation of the Bible: An Historical Approach* (Harper & Row, 1979). He is currently preparing, with Robert Benedetto of Union Theological Seminary and Darrell L. Guder of Louisville Theological Seminary, a *Historical Dictionary of the Reformed Churches* (Scarecrow Press, 1997).

Index

accommodation, 35, 35n43, 37, 117–37
  Christ's incarnation as, 135–37
  in the church fathers, 120–24
  in classical rhetoric, 119–20
  God's avenues of, 131–32
  and God's self-portraits, 126–31
  and scriptural inconsistencies, 124–26
  Scripture as, 132–35
Accursius, 54–55
Adagia, 69, 238
ad fontes, 24, 32, 139–40
Advocates of Reform: From Wyclif to Erasmus, 20
Against the Libertines (1545), text of, 241–46
"Against Luxury and License in Geneva." *See De Luxu*
Alciati, Andrea, 50, 56–57, 60, 70, 72–73, 83, 308
Alexander the Great, 229–30
Alexandria, School of, 121, 128
Ambrose, 228, 292
Anabaptists, 34, 95, 108, 112–14, 159, 160, 263
angels, 125, 163. *See also* table H
Annatationes in Pandectas, 59, 69–74, 313
Anselm, 259
Antapologia, 55, 57
Antioch, School of, 123
apologies, 100–101
approximation, 37
Apuleius, 74, 81
Aquinas, Thomas, 37, 309

Aristotle, 66n5, 292, 313
Arius, 123
Armstrong, Brian G., 38n56
Articles Concerning the Organization of the Church and Worship (1537), 323
Ashley, Clinton, 117n2
Augustine, 105, 108, 145n19, 181
  Calvin's use of, 246, 298
  conversion, 142, 293
  on God as teacher, 128
  and the metaphor of descent, 238
  on original righteousness, 144, 144n16
  use of accommodation, 35, 123–24, 133, 286
  use of poetry, 256n7

Barth, Markus, 251n3
Basil of Caesarea, 245–46
Basil the Great, 228, 230
Battles, Emily, 22
Battles, Ford Lewis, 19–41
  and Calvin's theology, 29–32
  concern for lucidity and precision, 25
  essays, overview of, 32–41
  faith, 27–29
  interest in the sources, 24, 24n12
  publications of, 20n2
  relationships, 19–23
  and study outlines, 20n2, 24n11
Battles, Marion Davis, 21–22, 22n6
Battles, Nancy, 22, 29n26
Béda, Noël, 48
Benedetto, Robert, 237n6

Berkhouwer, G. C., 123
Bernard of Clairvaux, 239–40
Beza, Theodore, 58, 60, 62
Biéler, André, 328n21
Bohatec, Josef, 59, 66n2, 69, 69n27
Briçonnet, Guillaume, 94
Bucer, Martin, 106, 135, 238–39, 295, 298, 323
Budaeus, Gulielmus, 33, 66n2, 68, 69–74, 80
    discussion of legal terms, 70–71
    and Greek philosophy, 72
    and literature, 72–73
    political philosophy, 71–72
    on Roman institutions, 71
Budé, Guillaume, 51, 56, 59–60, 95, 308, 322n9
Budé, Jean, 60
Budé, Jean-Louis, 60
Budé, Mathieu, 60

Calvin, Gérard, 49, 53
Calvin, John
    conversion, 21, 26–27, 26n17, 141–55, 292
    humanistic education, 33, 47–64, 66n3
    religious experience, 343–45, 343n1
    See also poetry, in Calvin's works
Calvin's theology
    key elements
        centrality of Jesus Christ, 31–32
        Holy Spirit, 31n31
        knowledge of God, 31
        revelation, 30–31
    structure of, 35–38, 139–78
    theses concerning, 155–72
    See also descent, metaphor of; dichotomy; limits, theory of; piety; poetry, in Calvin's works; true/false principle; *virtutes Dei*; web of meaning
Calvinus Juvenalis, 20–21
Capito, Wolfgang, 97–98
captus, 35, 37, 130–31, 133, 173–74
Carlstadt, Andreas, 115
Catechism of 1538, 21
    Battles' editions of, 25
Cato (the elder), 320, 327
Cercle de Meaux, 94

Chemin, Nicolas du, 55, 56–57
Chrysostom, John, 24, 35, 108, 123, 181, 230, 246
church order, in the 1536 *Institutes*, 112
Cicero, 65, 72, 74–75, 77–79, 120, 131, 144, 320
Clement of Alexandria, 35, 128, 230, 245
Code of Justinian, 54, 70, 307, 308
Cognatus, Gilbertus, 69, 84
Collège de la Marche, 48, 53
Collège de Montaigu, 48–49, 53
Cordier, Mathurin, 48, 52–54, 62
Cujas, Jacques, 50
Cyprian, 29

Danès, Pierre, 60–61
Dantzig, Tobias, 29n26
De Asse, 59, 70, 71, 72, 322n9
De Doctrina Christiana, 286
Deichgräber, Reinhard, 251n3
De Luxu, 40–41, 319–22
    dating of, 320–21
    and moral discipline, 322–28
    summary of, 322
    text of, 328–41
Denck, Hans, 128
descent, metaphor of, 237–40, 238n8
d'Étaples, Jacques Lefèvre, 94
dichotomy. *See* true/false principle
Documents of Vatican II in Historical Perspective, The, 29
Dowey, Edward A., Jr., 31, 35n43
Draft Ecclesiastical Ordinances (1541), 323–24
duplex cognitio, 31, 149–52, 159, 173, 245–46

Eck, John, 134, 153, 180n5
Education of a Christian Prince, 69, 71
epieikeia, 40, 116, 308, 313–15
Epinicion, 260
Erasmus, Desiderius, 33, 68–69, 74, 238
Eucharist, typology of, 162n58
Excuse to the Nicodemites (1544), 303–4

faith, in the 1536 *Institutes*, 105–6

fate, 125
Farel, Guillaume, 60, 92, 295, 296
Francis I, 34, 51, 94, 95
freedom, Christian, in the 1536 *Institutes*, 111–12

Ganoczy, Alexandre, 26n18, 48, 53, 92, 106
Geneva
  Calvin's educational plan for, 63–64, 260–61
    curriculum of the *schola privata*, 62–63
    curriculum of the *schola publica*, 63
  fortunes of education in, 61–62
God
  nature of, 124
  "repentance" of, 125
  scriptural portraits of
government, civil, in the 1536 *Institutes*, 112–16
Gregory of Nyssa, 246

Harmony of the Last Four Books of Moses (1563), 310–11. *See also* table 58
Henry, Paul Emile, 321nn4, 7
Hilary of Poitiers, 123
Holy Spirit, working of in providence, 168–72. *See also* table N
Homer, 67n12
Hugo, André Malan, 33, 51, 59–60, 61, 66n2, 68, 76, 319
hymnody, 25, 250n2

Ignatius of Antioch, 129
Institutes of the Christian Religion
  antithetical structure, 347–50
  Battles' revisions of, 29
  chief motifs, 351–58
  1536 edition, 34–35, 91–116
    as apology, 93–100
    catechetical chapters, 104–10
    chapter 6, 110–16
    dedicatory letter to Francis I, 100–104
    original catechetical intent, 91–93

"kernel of Calvin's faith" in, 39, 149–52, 293
Library of Christian Classics edition, 19
outworking of the *exemplar* in, 155–60
spiritualist/papist spectrum in, 160–62
tabulation of biblical citations, 359–60
Irenaeus, 121
Irnerius, 54

justice. *See* law
Justin Martyr, 101

knowledge, of God. *See duplex cognitio*
knowledge, of ourselves. *See duplex cognitio*
Krusche, Werner, 31n31

Lambert, Francis, 92
Large Catechism (1529), 104
law
  as accommodation, 133–34
  Calvin's analysis of, 309–13
  Calvin's study of Roman law, 307–8
  in the 1536 *Institutes*, 104–5, 115–16
  medieval teaching of, 49–50, 54–55
  sixteenth-century attitudes toward, 308–9
L'Estoile, Pierre de, 50, 55–56, 308
Lewis, C. S., 26
limits, theory of, 36–37, 172–78
Lombard, Peter, 24, 110
Lowth, Robert, 250–51, 262
Luther, Martin, 105
  catechisms of, 104, 159
  conversion, 142, 293
  and the metaphor of descent, 237
  on Psalms–Romans constellation, 144–45, 144–45n
  and the rise of the Reformation, 153, 153n40
  and Rome, 94, 110

McNeill, John T., 19
Major, John, 53

Manichees, 124
Marcionite/Manichaean pattern,
    180n6
Maximus the Confessor, 124
Melanchthon, Philipp, 28, 115, 308,
    309, 325
Miller, Donald G., 23
Münster, 95, 98, 112, 115

Nazianzus, Gregory, 230
Neale, John Mason, 250
Newton, Isaac, 36–37, 175–78
Nijenhuis, Wilhelm, 28n24
Normandie, Laurence de, 301
Number: The Language of Science,
    29n26

On Christian Doctrine, 123–24
"On the Christian Life," 297–300
On First Principles, 122–23
On Scandals (1550), 301–3
Order of the Geneva Schools (1559),
    260–61
Origen, 121–23, 128, 129, 177, 230

Parker, T. H. L., 31, 293n27
Perrin, Amy, 320, 327
Philippus Beroaldus the Elder, 33, 74–
    75
Philo Judaeus, 121
piety, 27, 39–40, 289–306
    in Calvin's view of the Christian life,
        295–300
    as defined by Calvin, 289–93
    mirrored in Calvin's life, 293–95
    obstacles to, 301–6
    See also table 56
Piety of John Calvin, The, 26, 27, 286
Placards affair, 95, 98
Plato, 66n4, 144
Plutarch, 78, 81, 80, 81, 131
poetry
    in Augustine's *De Doctrina Christi-
        ana*, 256–57. *See also* table 47
    in Calvin's works, 38–39, 249–87
    in the *Commentary on I Corin-
        thians*, 283–85. *See also* table 54
    in *Form of Prayer and Songs of the
        Church*, 275–76. *See also* table 52

in the *Institutes* (1543—1.16.2),
    280–82
in the metrical Psalter, 276–79. *See
    also* table 53
in "On the Christian Life," 270–73.
    See also table 50
in "On the Lord's Supper," 273–75.
    See also table 51
criteria of structure, 251–60
    anaphora, 251, 263
    chiasmus, 262, 263n19
    cola, 251, 262
    inclusio, 251
    stanza, 251
    strophe, 251
in Cyprian's *De Unitate Ecclesiae*,
    258–59. *See also* table 48
in Gregory of Nyssa's *On Holy Bap-
    tism*, 253–54
in Paul's letters, 251–53. *See also* ta-
    ble 45
in Scripture, 253
in Tertullian's *Adversus Praxean*,
    254–56. *See also* table 46
polemical tracts, 180n3
    and obstacles to piety, 301–6
    and the value of opposition, 161,
        161n57
prayer, in the 1536 *Institutes*, 106–7
preface to the French New Testament,
    133, 140, 147–49
    poetry of, 262, 263–69. *See also* ta-
        ble 49
Psalms commentary, of Calvin, 142,
    144–45
Psalms–Romans constellation, 144–
    45, 144–45n19, 262
Psychopannychia, 34, 95–98, 106, 112,
    140, 146, 238n8, 246
    poetry of, 262, 269–70
Puckett, David L., 38n56

Quintilian, 75, 77, 80, 120
Quintus Curtius Rufius, 229

Ramus, Peter, 179n1
Reply to Cardinal Sadolet (1539), 26,
    142, 143, 146–47
rhetoric, 117–19
    classical, 119–20

medieval divisions of, 54
Richard, Lucien Joseph, 27n23
Robert, Pierre. *See* preface to the
    French New Testament

sacraments
    as accommodation, 135
    in the 1536 *Institutes*, 107–10
sacraments, false, in the 1536 *Insti-
    tutes*, 110
Saunier, Antoine, 53, 61–62
Schille, Gottfried, 251n3
Schwenkfeld, Caspar, 128
Scripture
    bracketed with experience, 273n25
    superiority over pagan philoso-
        phers, 67n13, 144n16
"Seminar on the Unity of the Church,"
    28–29
Seneca, 68, 75–77, 319, 320, 326–27
Seneca commentary, 47, 114–15, 117,
    291–92, 308, 311, 319, 324–26
    Alciati's influence on, 57
    and the *Institutes*, 91n2
    sources, 33–34, 65–85. *See also* ta-
        bles A–B
        classical authors, 79–81
        classical intermediaries, 81–82
        humanist compilers, 82–84
        Latin poets, 67, 67n11
Servetus, 105, 135, 159, 160
Small Catechism (1522), 104, 159
Smits, Luchesius, 91n2, 106n18
Sommaire (1525), 92
Sorbonne, the, 51, 94, 153
speculum Institutionis. *See* dichot-
    omy
Spinka, Matthew, 20
Sprenger, Paul, 26n18
Standonck, John, 48
Stapulensis, Faber, 144–45n19
Strasbourg sojourn, 295, 296–97
Strauss, Jacob, 115

Suetonius, 67, 74, 80

Tagg, Stanley, 25
Tempete, Pierre de la, 48
Tertullian, 120, 216
Theodore of Mopsuestia, 123
theatrum mundi, 225–31, 237. *See also*
    table 41
true/false principle, 30, 36, 140–41,
    163n62, 179–81
    and "fractionings off," 172
    successive dichotomies of, 167–68
    underlying presuppositions/analyt-
        ical procedures, 162–67
    and the working of the Holy Spirit
        in providence, 168–72
    See also tables 1–37

University of Bourges, 50
University of Orléans, 49–50
University of Paris, 48–49, 51

Valla, Laurentius, 78n87, 83
Veerman, Antoon, 30, 260, 260n10
via media, 35n42, 36, 36n46, 140,
    153–55, 176
virtutes Dei, 142–43, 223–36. *See also*
    tables 42–44

Walchenbach, John, 22n6, 180n4
Warfield, B. B., 31n31
Watanabe, Nubuo, 21
web of meaning, 215–19. *See also* ta-
    bles 38–40
Wendel, François, 171
*What a Faithful Man . . . Ought to Do
    Dwelling amongst the Papists*
    (1543), 304–6
Williams, George H., 93
Wolmar, Melchior, 57–58, 108
Wright, David F., 35n44

Zwingli, Ulrich, 74, 82, 82n97, 94,
    104, 107, 136, 238